THE
SWORDSMEN
IN POWER

By the same author

Stewards, Lords and People: The Estate Steward and His World in Later Stuart England (1992)

(with Cherry Walker, eds) *The Correspondence of Lord Fitzwilliam of Milton and Francis Guybon his Steward 1697–1709* (1990)

(ed.) *The Correspondence of Sir John Lowther of Whitehaven 1693–1698* (1983)

(ed.) *Commercial Papers of Sir Christopher Lowther 1611–1644* (1977)

The Sydney Traders 1788–1821 (1972/1982)

Builders and Adventurers (1968)

THE SWORDSMEN IN POWER

WAR AND POLITICS UNDER THE ENGLISH REPUBLIC 1649–1660

Roger Hainsworth

SUTTON PUBLISHING

First published in 1997 by
Sutton Publishing Limited · Phoenix Mill
Thrupp · Stroud · Gloucestershire · GL5 2BU

British Library Cataloguing in Publication Data
A catalogue record for this book is available from the British Library

ISBN 0 7509 0571 9

Endpapers: *The Victory at Dunbar*. Ashmolean Museum, Oxford.

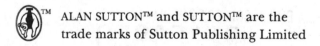

ALAN SUTTON™ and SUTTON™ are the
trade marks of Sutton Publishing Limited

Typeset in 10/13pt New Baskerville.
Typesetting and origination by
Sutton Publishing Limited.
Printed in Great Britain by
Hartnolls, Bodmin, Cornwall.

Absolutely the Soldier, or Sword, is rampant this year.

William Lilly, Astrologer, January 1649

Contents

List of Illustrations

List of Maps

Abbreviations

Abbott, *W. & S.O.C.*	Abbott (ed.) *Writings and Speeches of Oliver Cromwell* (Oxford, 1939/1988) 4 vols
Ashley, *Monck*	Maurice Ashley, *General Monck* (1977)
Baumber, *General-at-Sea*	Michael Baumber, *General-at-Sea: Robert Blake and the Seventeenth Century Revolution in Naval Warfare* (1989)
Buchan, *Cromwell*	John Buchan, *Oliver Cromwell* (1941)
Capp, *Cromwell's Navy*	Bernard Capp, *Cromwell's Navy: the Fleet and the Revolution 1648–1660* (Oxford, 1989)
Clarke Papers	*Clarke Papers*, ed. C.H. Firth (1901), 4 vols
Davies, *Restoration*	Godfrey Davies, *The Restoration of Charles II 1658–1660* (1955)
DNB	*Dictionary of National Biography from Earliest Times to 1900* (Oxford, 1903) 22 vols
Early Modern Ireland	*A New History of Ireland, iii Early Modern Ireland 1534–1691*, eds Moody, Martin & Byrne, (Oxford 1976)
Firth, *Last Years*	C.H. Firth, *The Last Years of the Protectorate* (1909)
Fraser, *Cromwell*	Antonia Fraser, *Cromwell: Our Chief of Men* (London, 1973)
Gardiner, *C. & P.*	S.R. Gardiner, *History of the Commonwealth and Protectorate 1649–1656* (1901)
Gentles, *New Model Army*	Ian Gentles, *The New Model Army* (Oxford, 1992)
Hutton, *Republic*	Ronald Hutton, *The British Republic 1649–1660* (1990)
Pepys, *Diary*	*The Diary of Samuel Pepys*, ed. Robert Latham & William Matthews (1970) 9 vols
Powell, *Blake*	Revd J.R. Powell, *Robert Blake: General-at-Sea* (1972)
Roots, *Rebellion*	Ivan Roots, *The Great Rebellion 1642–1660* (1966)
Sherwood, *Court*	Roy Sherwood, *The Court of Oliver Cromwell* (1977)

The First Dutch War	*Letters and Papers Relating to the First Dutch War 1652–1654*, (eds) S.R. Gardiner & C.T. Atkinson, Navy Record Society, 13, 17, 30, 37, 41, 66 (1899–1930)
Trevor-Roper, 'Cromwell's Parliaments'	H.R. Trevor-Roper, 'Oliver Cromwell and his Parliaments' in his *Religion, the Reformation and Social Change* (1956/1972)
Underdown, *Purge*	David Underdown, *Pride's Purge* (Oxford, 1971)
Woolrych, *Commonwealth*	Austin Woolrych, *Commonwealth to Protectorate* (Oxford, 1982)
Woolrych, *Milton*	Austin Woolrych, 'Historical Introduction 1659–1660' to *The Complete Prose Works of John Milton*, vii (New Haven, 1980)
Worden, *Rump*	Blair Worden, *The Rump Parliament* (Cambridge, 1974)

Preface

The turbulent English seventeenth century has always attracted historians but their attention has not been evenly spread. The heaviest concentration of books and shorter pieces has been devoted to the first forty years. The Civil War and the revolution which followed it seemed so astonishingly unexpected even to the participants, let alone to their posterity, that prodigious efforts of scholarly research and debate have been mobilized in trying to explain them. What happened after the death of the king has attracted less attention, although some scholars, frequently acknowledged in the following pages, have produced masterly analyses of particular aspects of the period. There is also a very considerable literature on Oliver Cromwell, the Republic's crucial figure.

The present volume seeks to provide a narrative which will introduce readers new to the period to one of the most dramatic decades in British history and to show how the drama continued for readers who have followed it through the Civil War and its immediate aftermath in the pages of such authors as Dame Veronica Wedgwood and more recently Christopher Hibbert. It is a decade of intense interest, and has provided valuable lessons about power and its misuse, and the danger of army officers imposing simplistic solutions to complex and confused political situations. Certainly Britons were left with a salutary hostility to standing armies which endured for at least two centuries, and they established a tradition of the dominance of civilian authority over the military which endures to this day. After the Americans gained their independence some feared that their military hero, Washington, might become a new Cromwell, while President Lincoln's Secretary of War feared the victorious generals Grant or Sherman might aspire to Cromwell's power. Such fears were groundless. The lessons of England's republican experiment had bitten as deep in North America as in England.

I have been assisted particularly at Adelaide University by the help and encouragement of Dr Christine Churches, who read the page proofs in their entirety, by Martin Holt who proof-read the manuscript, to Christine Crothers for drawing the maps and battle plans, and at Sutton Publishing by Jane Crompton, commissioning editor, whose forbearance of my delays has been heart-warming, and by Anne Bennett, my editor, who is a prodigy of tact and helpfulness. I must also thank my colleagues at the University of Adelaide, Frank McGregor and Wilfrid Prest, for much helpful discussion along the way. I wish particularly to thank my wife, Margaret, whose constant support has made all possible.

Britain during the Republic, 1649–1660

Prologue: The Regicide

I go from a corruptible to an incorruptible crown, where no disturbances can be, no disturbance in the world.

Charles I on the scaffold, 30 January 1649

The nation's capital was gripped by a hard frost. The wind was light but easterly and keener than an axe, soughing across the marshes of the Thames estuary, and harping among the thickets of masts and yards and ice-stiffened rigging of the colliers and merchantmen lying below London bridge. London lay largely silent beyond the wharves under its pall of sea-coal smoke save for the muffled tramp of soldiers, occasional barked orders, and the sounds of unusually large numbers of horses, coming from those cramped streets and alleys. Men standing silent on the wharves or on the ships' decks blew on their hands with foggy breath and peered furtively and uneasily at the city. There most shops were closed and many citizens remained shut within their houses. Others had thronged down the road which led from Charing Cross to Westminster though Whitehall Palace or had taken up positions in the parks which lay between St James's Palace and Whitehall. All knew it was the last morning of the king's life for some time between ten o'clock in the forenoon and four that afternoon he would be executed outside his own Palace of Whitehall.[1]

In his small bedroom in St James's Palace King Charles had woken early, between five and six o'clock. He roused his constant attendant, Thomas Herbert, who was in the midst of a confused dream about the king and Archbishop Laud, executed in 1646. Herbert was a Parliamentarian who had been appointed to this service by the king's captors. Although one of the king's enemies during the Civil War he seems to have served him sympathetically and unstintingly during the last months of his life and would one day be rewarded by the king's son with a baronetcy for his respectful compassion.[2] The king remarked: 'Herbert, this is my second marriage day. I would be as trim today as may be for before tonight I hope to be espoused to my blessed Jesus.' He asked for an extra shirt for he did not wish to shiver with cold and so appear afraid when he stood on the scaffold. After he had told Herbert how to distribute his few possessions Bishop Juxon arrived to pray with the king and administer the sacrament.

1

Between nine and ten Colonel Hacker, an ardent Puritan who had treated the king with harsh discourtesy, arrived to conduct him to Whitehall. Today Hacker was subdued and trembling, as if he had foreseen the hangman's noose which lay ahead of him. They were joined by Colonel Matthew Thomlinson, the king's other gaoler, a man who had refused to be a judge at the king's trial, and had allowed him to take leave of the two royal children who were Parliament's captives.[3] Surrounded by files of soldiers the king walked through the bare parks under lowering clouds, the spectators mute on either side. At Whitehall the party entered by an outside staircase near the Cockpit, and the king crossed the public road by the arch of the Holbein Gate. He was placed in a small bedchamber to await the summons to the scaffold. This had been built outside a window of the Banqueting Hall which looked on to a small area easy to guard and largely inaccessible to the public. There then ensued a delay of some hours because Parliament would not allow the execution to proceed until it had passed a law banning all proclamations of the succession of Charles II.

Finally at almost two o'clock Hacker returned and conducted the king between two lines of soldiers all the way through the corridors of the palace to the Banqueting Hall, a once splendid room built for the king by Inigo Jones, but which was now cold and sombre, most of its windows boarded up. Many spectators had invaded the palace and called out blessings and prayers, unhindered by the soldiers, as he strode by them. These stood gloomy and silent, their conduct very different from that at the king's trial when they had blown tobacco-smoke in his face as he passed. Taken to the scaffold the king found it surrounded by so many soldiers that there was no opportunity to speak directly to spectators crowded together beyond them. His final words were addressed to his immediate companions: Juxon, Hacker, his guards, the executioner and his assistant, both heavily disguised, and two or three short-hand writers with notebooks and inkhorns who took down his words. He admitted no wrong-doing but forgave those who had encompassed his death. Remembering the Earl of Strafford's fate, for which he had never forgiven himself, he remarked 'an unjust sentence that I suffered to take effect is punished now by an unjust sentence on me'. Finally he knelt at the block and at his sign the executioner struck off his head with a single blow. According to a seventeen-year-old spectator the crowd then uttered such a groan as he never heard before and desired he might never hear again.[4] It was the symbolic moment of the English Revolution.

CHAPTER ONE

The Swordsmen Emerge

No man goes further than he who knows not whither he is going.

Oliver Cromwell

If I would have given way to an arbitrary way, for to have all Laws chang'd according to the Power of the Sword, I needed not to have come here.

Charles I on the scaffold, 30 January 1649[1]

The English Revolution was accomplished if not completed, and the Republic was in place. By what road had these revolutionaries, both civilians and Swordsmen, travelled to this unexpected destination? Probably no revolutionary leader was more astonished at discovering where he had arrived than Oliver Cromwell. At his birth in 1599 the English had lived for decades under a fearsome shadow – the threat of civil war over a disputed succession. Four years after Cromwell's birth the shadow was dispelled by the peaceful succession of James Stuart of Scotland, a Protestant king with two sons and a daughter to succeed him. Despite this good fortune, less than forty years later the nightmare of civil war would become a reality. The causes and course of these disasters cannot be recounted in detail here.[2] Suffice to say that although the English 'political nation'[3] became increasingly alienated from the Stuart monarchy during those forty years the origins of the English Revolution lie during Charles I's reign, not that of his father.

Certainly James Stuart had been unloved and he in turn had shown little affection for institutions which the English believed vital to their liberties. James considered the institution of Parliament a disagreeable medieval anachronism in the age of 'enlightened absolutism' into which Europe was steering. He also detested the English Common Law, which his subjects impertinently believed bound him as it bound them. James at least appreciated the structure of the English church and considered the bishops a vital prop to the throne. Unfortunately, English Protestants tended to envy Scotland's religious Reformation which had gone further than had been permitted by the Elizabethan religious settlement, and hoped the king would advance the Reformation in his new realm. James, however, considered that the Reformation had gone too far in Scotland, where he had found the hectoring tutelage of Presbyterian divines detestable. Financial matters further strained relations between king and subject because although the obsolete medieval system by which the Crown was supposed to meet the expenses of peacetime government from the revenue of the royal estates had been rendered absurd by the diminution of the estates, inflation, and huge increases in the cost of government, the Crown's finances remained unreformed, not least because parliaments feared to make the king financially independent. As a result James exploited unconstitutional financial expedients which antagonized his propertied subjects. However, if there were tensions in James I's reign he managed to keep the ship of state on an even keel and had his son displayed equal statecraft all should have been well.

Charles I was arguably the man least fitted to ascend the English throne of those who have mounted it during the past four centuries, a disaster to his people and himself. Charles believed that he ruled by Divine Right and that ordinary considerations of ethical behaviour did not apply to him, particularly when he was defending his perception of kingship against (as he perceived them) subversive opponents. As self-righteous leaders will he equated disagreement with his views with disloyalty. He dangerously shared his father's exalted views on kingship without his father's recognition that kingship is the art of the possible. His incapacity for compromise and flexibility was dangerously combined with irresolution. He often deceived faithful advisers by agreeing to reverse a bad policy without revealing that he had no intention of abandoning it permanently. He began badly by allowing the much detested Duke of Buckingham to gain the emotional ascendancy over him that he had exercised over his father. Buckingham disastrously involved England in war with both Spain and France simultaneously, an attempt to play at being a great power without even the naval and military resources mobilized by Elizabeth, which achieved nothing but misery and a further depleted Treasury. Fortunately, Buckingham was murdered, although the king never forgave his subjects for their joy at the news. Charles's early parliaments were not as consistently opposed to the king as some have depicted them, nevertheless Charles learned to loathe parliaments between 1625 and 1629 and for the next eleven years dispensed with them altogether. However, it was his policies rather than his dispensing with Parliament which alienated the landed nobility and gentry who were normally the chief support of the Crown. His fiscal policies, which greatly extended the worst practices of his father, alarmed and antagonized the propertied because it suggested that they held their property at the king's pleasure rather than by legal right. Notwithstanding, by these and other constitutionally dubious expedients, and by avoiding war, he managed to rule without the need to call a parliament for eleven years.

His religious policy was to be of more serious significance for it alienated vast numbers of his subjects at all social levels. Moreover, although men were united to oppose that policy they would prove to be badly divided over what should replace it. This division made the civil war possible, for a civil war could only occur if the king's subjects were sufficiently divided for him to form a party large enough to provide him with an army. Religion was then as inextricably intertwined with politics as economics is now. Religious observance was a fundamental requirement of an orderly society. Religious beliefs were so fundamental to society's moral health and political stability that most believed that citizens could not be allowed to agree to differ about them. A tolerance of varied beliefs and practices would mean a tolerance of heresy which God would punish. It was generally accepted that the religion of the king was the religion of his people because subjects who chose a different variety of worship would have dangerously divided loyalties. Of course, in reality English society was divided by several forms of religious belief, no matter how much its values and institutions insisted that there should be only one. Apart from the Catholic minority the Protestant community contained two very different religious attitudes. The moderate majority were prepared to accept the Elizabethan settlement, with its Episcopalian church government and its traditional ceremonies, although most moderates would have preferred a more austere version of Calvinism. They hoped for further reform from the king and his bishops, most of whom under James had been moderate Calvinists like himself.

The substantial Anglican minority of more radical Protestants, called 'the godly' or 'the saints' by themselves and 'Puritans' by their opponents, longed for a more thorough reformation, with increasing desperation as its achievement seemed ever more unlikely. They believed that the English were a people chosen by God to achieve a proper reformation of religion, and since king, church and people were betraying God's design His vengeance would fall on guilty and innocent alike. The Puritans' prime target was the bishops, but, believing the Catholic Church to be Antichrist, they also wished to purge their church of such 'superstitious' Papistical relics as altars, images, elaborate vestments, organ music and singing. A few pious Separatists, known as the Pilgrim Fathers, escaped this superstition-ridden church by flight to New England. The Puritans, who saw themselves not as Separatists but as the true Anglicans, had remained within the church, increasingly resentful, increasingly hopeless, outnumbered by the conforming mass. Unlike the moderate majority they desperately feared Catholicism, seeing it as determined to return God's chosen kingdom to Antichrist. To a Puritan like the future parliamentary leader John Pym, to disbelieve in an ongoing 'Popish Plot' was to confess oneself a dupe or an accomplice. Moreover, Puritans believed that Papists were not confined to practising Catholics but included all Anglicans contented to conform within a church disfigured and corrupted by Popish practices and images. Such Anglicans were a Papist fifth column, and none more so than the bishops, even those who were Calvinists, for it was the nature of the office rather than the opinions of the holder which corrupted. When the Puritans found themselves ruled by a new king who not only allowed his queen to practise her Catholic religion openly but even chose Catholic noblemen to form part of his Court and Council the victory of Antichrist appeared to move closer.

In fact the Puritans' golden time was coming and paradoxically it would be provided by the two Englishmen they most feared: Charles I and his Archbishop of Canterbury (from 1633), William Laud. Charles turned his back on his father's moderate Calvinism, against predestination, against the extempore preaching which Puritans so valued, in favour of Arminianism. Laudian Arminianism involved a heavy emphasis on the prescribed prayers, services and rituals of Cranmer's Prayer Book. Enclosed altars must be placed hierarchically at the east of the chancel where they appeared to be more an object of idolatrous worship than a table for serving communion. Arminianism produced even more Papistical gilding of worship with music, vestments and ceremony. Puritans were outraged to find Arminian bishops teaching that the Roman Catholic church was not Antichrist but a 'true church' which had simply been led astray by its pontiffs. Vacant bishoprics were filled with Arminians, as were livings, royal chaplaincies and fellowships of university colleges. Through these pliant instruments Charles and Laud alienated the moderate Protestant mainstream and drove many into the arms of the Godly. If 'heresy' on this scale persisted, God's vengeance on his straying English would be terrible. Some 20,000 English folk, predominantly members of Puritan congregations, fled into the wilderness of Massachusetts between 1629 and 1640. The vastly more numerous Puritans who remained behind, their ranks expanded by outraged moderates, could only passively resist their bishops' domination or practise an agonized outward conformity. Nobody questioned the king's right to rule with or without parliament. Yet unless the king did summon a parliament they had nothing to hope for because only then would Puritans and moderates be able to organize petitions against Arminian heresies and 'evil councillors' like William Laud. Evil councillors loomed large in men's minds because Scripture condemned resistance to the lawful 'magistrate', here Charles I. Resistance to sinister crypto-Catholic advisers was another matter. Nevertheless, these deeply loathed religious innovations, and the much resented unconstitutional taxation, could not be actively resisted because the king was determined never again to summon parliament. Then with breathtaking political ineptness Charles resolved to extend his Arminian policy to Scotland.

The consequences were a revolution in Scotland and two invasions of

England by Scottish armies.[4] Scots of all social ranks signed the Covenant, which rejected Arminian innovations, including a new Scottish prayer book, summoned a revolutionary assembly and recruited an army to defend the Presbyterian Kirk. Charles sought to keep the Covenanters in check by making concessions which he intended to revoke once he had mustered his own army. Undeceived the Covenanters responded by abolishing episcopacy and marching south. The first Bishops' War of 1639 was a bloodless affair because Charles was bluffed into signing a treaty at Berwick. However, with characteristic bad faith, this was a treaty which he never intended to honour. The Irish Lord Deputy, Strafford, a much hated exponent of absolutist efficiency over parliamentary muddle, was summoned from Dublin in September 1639, but although he offered to furnish an Irish army to stamp out rebellion even he advised the king to summon Parliament. Armies have to be paid. Since his funds and credit were drying up Charles accepted the inevitable and Parliament met on 13 April 1640. Most MPs were in sympathy with the Scots and some, like the Puritan leader John Pym and his circle, were in treasonable communication with them. Moreover, the parliamentary leaders had learned from past disappointments to refuse supply until the king granted redress of grievances. The king dissolved the 'Short Parliament' in angry despair but it had lived long enough to show the Scots that the king's cause had fewer friends in England than their own. A second invasion would inevitably bring the recall of Parliament, so once more the Covenanting army advanced south under the command of Alexander Leslie, a former field marshal in the Swedish army. The capacity of the Scots to produce large field armies and the incapacity of the king to muster an army capable of dispersing them was as significant as it was remarkable. The Covenanting movement had let loose an extraordinary military phenomenon, for their 1640 armies contained 24,000 men or almost 10 per cent of their total adult male population. (These figures are comparable with Swedish enlistments during the Thirty Years War, and Sweden was the only country in Europe with a system of national conscription.[5]) This army, particularly formidable because many officers and men had served as mercenaries in foreign wars, was to transform English politics for a generation and, indirectly, make possible the Civil War. By launching what was known as the 'second Bishops' War' it had ensured the summoning of what would be called the 'Long Parliament'. Certainly it would seem very long to the king.

Parliament met on 3 November in an uncompromising mood. The country's expectations were dangerously high. Parliament was expected to solve the country's problems and the king was expected to allow it enough time to do so because his 'evil advisers', especially Laud and Strafford, would be removed. Subsidies must be raised to pay off the Scots and the half-starved English army which still confronted it. Charles must accept legislation forbidding his unconstitutional taxation; his illegal collection of customs duties must cease. Above all the Arminian policy must be reversed. Nobody expected a civil war. The king had no hope of one and his opponents had no need of one. The king's policies had been so detested that he had no party and few friends. The king's Puritan opponents seized the leadership of the Commons, a junta of advocates of a greatly extended religious reformation led by John Pym and including John Hampden, Sir Arthur Hesilrige, William Strode and Denzil Holles. Pym was MP for Tavistock. Beginning his parliamentary career as early as 1614 he had been a leading parliamentary opponent of the king in the 1620s. After the Short Parliament's dissolution he had petitioned for a new parliament and the indictment of the king's advisers. It was Parliament's misfortune that he was to die in 1643. Strode had been imprisoned for years for his opposition to the king in the 1629 Parliament. Holles had also been arrested but escaped abroad. Hampden, MP for Buckinghamshire, had fought unconstitutional taxation in the courts, unsuccessfully but to great acclaim. An obscure Huntingdonshire gentleman, Oliver Cromwell, was a junta-member of lesser note. Pym proved to be the skilled parliamentary manager the Long Parliament badly needed. It was a 550-man assembly of mainly country gentlemen looking for quick legislative solutions to the grievances of their neighbours but too unorganized to grapple with national problems. They were impatient to return home, correctly perceiving London to be dangerous to both health and purse. Since parliamentarians tended to be prolix, undisciplined debaters this hope was vain, but many would slip away during the long summer of 1641.

Pym hoped to persuade Parliament to modernize the Crown's financial position to obviate the need for unconstitutional fiscal expedients and make the government better able to react to foreign dangers, and yet to reduce customs duties and sweep away monopolies to the benefit of England's commerce. In return the king would appoint Puritan advisers who would ensure that the king accepted the constitutional reforms proposed and that the Arminian policy was never revived. It was a bold programme but difficult to guarantee once Parliament was dissolved, for it would have depended on the good faith of a king who regarded promises to opponents as temporary expedients. However, it was never to be achieved and in the reasons for this lie the causes of the Civil War. The junta correctly assumed that the king knew of their treasonable correspondence with the leaders of the Scottish revolution. This might have been forgiven, but the judicial murder of Strafford never would be. Strafford had offered the king an Irish army, 80 per cent of it Catholic, to suppress the Protestant Scots. (He had said 'this kingdom' and it was mendaciously claimed that he had meant England, not Scotland.) The focus of great hatred both in Parliament and in London, which was a forcing house of revolution during the opening months of the Long Parliament, Strafford had only reluctantly ventured to Westminster because the king promised to protect him. In fact Parliament, finding it could not convict him of treason in court, passed an act of attainder which simply declared him guilty and condemned him to death. Members who shrank from this outrage were terrified into voting for it by howling mobs of London apprentices. The mobs also besieged the defenceless Palace of Whitehall until the king agreed to sign a bill which was also a death-warrant. For this the king never forgave himself and would never forgive those who had made him their accomplice. Laud was imprisoned in the Tower where it was hoped that age and infirmity would soon finish him off. (Having clung obstinately to life until 1645 he was then summarily executed – one of Puritan bigotry's more unappetizing episodes.) Some Catholic Privy Councillors fled abroad. The execution of Strafford, however, ensured that the leaders of the Commons and their allies in the Lords could never trust their lives and estates to the generosity of their king. Certainly it made for a division between the revolutionary leaders and the back-benchers. The latter wished for a speedy settlement and a return to rural obscurity. The leaders knew that their lives hung on Parliament's continuation. The king, who in his youth had acquired valuable parliamentary experience as a member of the Lords, contemplated this situation with interest and decided that time was on his side. If he held on, yielding when he must, resisting when he could, his enemies might fall out and he might form a party with which to regain power and exact revenge. Should some controversial issue or issues divide both Parliament and the country he could hope to raise his standard and suppress these subversive subjects by force of arms. Meanwhile, the traumas of the Strafford affair had alienated many members of both houses from the junta – although they were not an 'opposition' and were wholly unorganized.

Although this developing situation ensured that Pym's vision would never be fulfilled, there were real legislative achievements during the first phase of the Long Parliament which lasted until the autumn of 1641. The subsidies were voted at last while an act of May 1641 ensured Parliament's short-term survival by forbidding its dissolution without its own consent. This prevented the king's suddenly dissolving the House to get at his enemies, and persuaded City merchants to lend against the slowly arriving taxes and so gradually pay off both the northern armies. Laws of constitutional significance were enacted, including several which clipped the king's prerogative. The Triennial Act guaranteed at least a fifty-day session of parliament every three years. The old quarrels over Customs and its Book of Rates were settled in Parliament's favour; the king was only voted Tonnage and Poundage for two months to keep him poor and therefore honest. The prerogative courts of Star Chamber and High Commission were abolished. Various extra-legal forms of taxation were outlawed in August. These defeats for the Crown in the first phase were succeeded by developments in the second phase (which lasted until the summer of 1642) which gave the king grounds for hope. The issues which still confronted the Parliament were as divisive as Strafford's attainder: the settlement of religion and the control of the king both for the leaders' own safety and to protect the constitutional reforms already achieved. The radicals wished to replace the bishops, blamed for Arminian innovations and hated for their persecution of Puritan resisters, with a church government run by a committee of laymen. However, a substantial minority of the Commons and a majority of the Lords would have been content to strip the bishops of their political and judicial powers – probably a majority of the Commons if many had not been terrified by the anti-episcopalian London mobs. The king had already abandoned Arminianism, the moderates argued, while the radical movement was putting out disquieting sectarian shoots and demands for religious toleration of nonconformity.

As for the king, he was determined not to surrender any more of his prerogative powers, and many members of both Houses saw no reason why he should. The pendulum of radicalism was beginning to swing back for many believed it had already swung too far. In October 1641 the Irish Rebellion broke out with the massacre of 5,000 Protestants and the deaths of a still larger number from exposure, hunger and harsh treatment, which seemed to confirm the radicals' warnings of Catholic conspiracies. Earlier such a catastrophe would have united men of disparate opinions. In 1641 it divided them still further because of the problem of who should control the relieving army. Command was the prerogative of the king, but give Charles an army to suppress rebellion in Ireland and he might prefer to employ it suppressing what he saw as rebellion in England. The king was then in Scotland, where by an unhappy coincidence it appeared that he had been involved in a failed conspiracy to murder the Duke of Hamilton and the Earl of Argyle as the first step in overthrowing the Covenanters. The radicals in London now made a demand the Scots had successfully put after the failed plot: the right to approve the king's choice of ministers. This was the equivalent of declaring that the king was unfit to rule and so others must rule for him. It was too much for the moderates in both Houses and helped to give the king his party. In an attempt to overawe opposition and rally waverers the radicals moved the 'Grand Remonstrance', a lengthy document which rehearsed all the people's grievances since 1625 and called for control of the ministry and the abolition of episcopacy. It was carried by a dangerously slim majority after a debate so fierce men feared blood would be shed in the chamber. At the same time Pym and the junta demanded that Parliament control both the militia which would defend England against a possible Irish invasion and the army to suppress rebellion in Ireland.

The divisions in Parliament were reflected in London, where the Lord Mayor and Aldermen were now firmly moderate Royalist, but the December elections had given the radicals control of the Common Council and thereby of the trained bands, the country's most efficient militia companies. It was just in time. Now back from Scotland, the king felt he could move against the junta and invaded the Commons with a file of soldiers to arrest Pym, Hampden, Strode, Holles and Hesilrige. Forewarned, the five members took refuge in the City where the king's writ no longer ran. Six days later Charles retired to Windsor and despatched his Catholic queen to safety in France with their younger children. It was now clear that the king could only regain control of his capital by force of arms, although it would take a further eight months for war to erupt, during which both the king and Parliament sought to rally support against the other. During this period about two-fifths of the Commons and all but thirty or so peers abandoned Parliament, although not all those capable of fighting joined the king.

The course of the English Civil War must not detain us. It was immensely destructive of life and property, although not to the degree the Thirty Years War was simultaneously inflicting on Europe.[6] The parliamentary forces were at first perceived as weaker and less military than the Royalists, and the latter had the aura supplied by the king's leadership. Moreover, although the king's camp contained a wide spectrum of political opinions, at least they all knew that they were fighting to overthrow the junta-led Parliament. Few Parliamentarians believed that they were fighting to overthrow the king. They simply wanted to persuade him to accept their constitutional and political programme. How one persuaded a king to do this by defeating him in battle was less clear. One thing seemed certain: they would forfeit their lives if they lost. The Parliamentarians had one great advantage: the king could not win unless he took London, and he was never to command an army capable of investing it, while its now formidable defences could not be penetrated by a sudden assault. They also had the financial and commercial wealth of the City of London behind them, and were strongest in the richest and most agriculturally advanced counties of the south-east. Moreover, the navy, which might have strangled London by blockade, joined Parliament. Finally the Scots intervened on Parliament's side. Gradually the Royalists grew weaker and the Parliamentarians grew stronger as the latter developed both new leaders and a new army. After the decisive defeat of the Royalists at Naseby and a successful campaign in the Royalist-dominated west the war became a matter of mopping up small formations and reducing castles and walled towns.

Three elements in the story of the Civil War must be considered further because they proved of crucial importance later. The first was the intervention of the Scots' Covenanting Army. In September 1643 by a treaty called 'The Solemn League and Covenant' Parliament promised to establish a Presbyterian government for the English church. In return Alexander Leslie, now Earl of Leven, crossed the Border the following January to reinforce Parliament's northern army. This military intervention was helpful rather than decisive, but the true significance of the 'Solemn League' is that it proved a Shirt of Nessus for both countries. Few Englishmen even among Parliament's leaders liked the Presbyterian system of government while the soldiers, who were increasingly under the influence of sectarian preachers, loathed it for its hostility to nonconformity. Nevertheless, a majority of civilian members of the Long Parliament and some army officers, including Sir Thomas Fairfax, believed that they must not seek to evade what they had undertaken. This was certain to lead to trouble between army and Parliament later. As for the Scots, they had bound themselves to a policy of making their Kirk secure by forcing Presbyterianism on their more powerful and deeply resentful neighbour. The Scots army, which by January 1644 had thrice crossed the Border on behalf of Parliament, would one day be compelled by that policy to cross it twice on behalf of monarchy with consequences appalling for the king, for Scotland and ultimately for Presbyterianism.

The second element was the emergence of Oliver Cromwell as one of the foremost soldiers in Europe.[7] Cromwell was forty-three when war broke out. He immediately abandoned Westminster for the battlefield, seized Cambridge and prevented its college plate disappearing into the king's war-chest. He raised a 'double' regiment (fourteen troops) of disciplined cavalry which would be nicknamed 'Ironsides' by Prince Rupert, the opponent best qualified to appreciate them. Cromwell had recognized that, as he told Hampden, there was no point in facing Rupert's cavalry, composed of gentlemen's sons, with 'decayed serving men and tapsters'. What were needed were 'men of a spirit . . . that is like to go as far as a gentleman will go'. He did not require his cavalry officers to be of gentle birth, declaring that if godly men were chosen captain then godly men would follow them. He was indifferent to what form their 'godliness' took. Reforming Anglicans, Presbyterians, Congregationalists, Baptists, all were welcome. This religious toleration displeased his Parliamentary masters, the first rumble of a coming storm. During 1644 the reputation of Cromwell, now a lieutenant-general, rapidly rose, while those of the moderate-minded Earls of Essex and Manchester gradually declined. Although Manchester, along with Sir Thomas Fairfax and the Scots Earl of Leven, was at Marston Moor in July it was Cromwell's cavalry which gave the army victory. This victory was not followed up, for which Cromwell blamed Manchester's sloth (or irresolution), and it was negated by Essex's defeat in the west. Here Cromwell's career is necessarily subsumed in the third and most important element of all: the formation of the New Model Army. This remarkable army, which decisively won the war, would become one of the most feared and effective in Europe. Most important of all, the emergence of the New Model Army saw its officers, the Swordsmen, become the most potent political force in England during the next fifteen years.

On 15 November Cromwell attacked Manchester in the Commons in a memorandum which dissected his vacillations. The memorandum revealed fundamental divisions over war-aims. (It also recorded Manchester's famous remark: 'If we beat the king ninety-nine times he would be king still, and his posterity, and we subjects still, but if he beat us but once we should be hanged and our posterity undone'. Cromwell had replied, 'My lord, if this be so, why did we take up arms at first?')[8] The Manchester camp, which was supported by some MPs and by several of the rump of the House of Lords, simply wanted to force the king to negotiate and impose on him the constitutional settlement of 1641, with the bishops deprived of all secular functions and church government settled on Presbyterian lines (to fulfil the Solemn League and Covenant). This ensured intolerance of sectarian nonconformity and so was unacceptable to much of the army, while the survival of the bishops was unacceptable to all radicals. The moderates believed the radicals meant to depose the king and embroil England in social disruption and religious fragmentation. However, Cromwell, for all his social conservatism, realized that in a civil war against the king there could be no negotiation before the Parliamentary army had achieved total victory. The radicals in Parliament who shared Cromwell's military perception moved to combine the various Parliamentary armies into a single body under a unified command, willing to fight beyond regional boundaries, and with reduced desertion and improved discipline secured by religious commitment and regular pay.[9] A complementary piece of legislation, 'the Self-Denying Ordinance', was manoeuvred through the Commons. This made military command incompatible with membership of the Parliament (although officer-MPs compelled to resign could be reappointed), and Essex and Manchester chose to resign. Cromwell was permitted to remain temporarily Lieutenant-General of Horse under Sir Thomas Fairfax as Army Commander, and permanently so after his success at Naseby.[10] Fairfax was an experienced soldier (he had served abroad in the 1620s), an able commander, an exacting disciplinarian and untainted by the political squabbling which had produced the New Model Army. The latter's disciplined effectiveness owed much to Fairfax and Cromwell, still more to regular pay and much to religious enthusiasm. A high proportion of officers and a substantial proportion of soldiers were Puritans, some acquiring religious commitment in its ranks. Officers and men gathered for prayers, held fast days, enjoyed extempore sermons and advanced into battle convinced they were God's chosen instruments. The Royalists called it the New Noddle Army. They could mock it but they could not match it, as was shown on 14 June 1645 when the king and Rupert attacked it at Naseby. While Rupert was at first successful against General Ireton on the left, Cromwell repeated his exploit of Marston Moor, achieving victory on the right before wheeling round to save the left. Fairfax held the infantry firm in the centre until he could rout the king's army with Cromwell's cavalry late in the afternoon. The Royalists suffered 5,000 casualties, the New Model Army only 150. The result was decisive strategically as well as tactically because this victory would not be wasted. Fairfax marched into the west, advancing from victory to victory. Soon Prince Rupert and the Prince of Wales fled abroad. King Charles sought refuge with the Scots. The Great Civil War was over.

Charles hoped the Scots' resentment at the growth of the sects within the New Model Army and the lack of enthusiasm for Presbyterianism out of it would rupture the alliance with Parliament. Lord Leven marched his army and his prisoner to Newcastle where the king played the game he knew best: duplicitous negotiation. However, his duplicity now duped no one. His correspondence, captured after Naseby, had shown how little he was to be trusted. Charles, not 'evil councillors', had planned to bring Irish Catholic soldiers to massacre English Protestants, had wooed Catholic support in Europe with promises of converting England into a Catholic vassal state. However, both Scots and English shrank from deposing him. The Covenanters demanded that he reorganize the Anglican church on Presbyterian lines. From France, the queen urged him to agree: better be a Presbyterian king than no king at all. Parliament presented equally unpalatable terms at Newcastle in July 1646: king and subjects must fulfil the Solemn League and Covenant, episcopacy must remain abolished, repressive penalties must be imposed on Catholics, Charles's most important supporters must be exempt from pardon; Parliament would control the armed forces for twenty years. However, the king still held to certain fundamental principles. Above all he would not undermine the monarchy which he must one day bequeath to his heir. The exasperated Scots finally sold him to Parliament in return for cash to pay their soldiers, who now trooped thankfully home. The king was taken to Holdenby House, Northamptonshire. Church bells rang as he passed, bonfires signalled his progress, garlands bedecked the streets and onlookers cheered. If this ephemeral popularity persuaded Charles that he had the country's support, and that therefore endless procrastination would win by stealth what he had lost by war, it would prove a terrible misjudgement.

The king's belief that his enemies would fall out was soundly based. His belief that this meant that he could save the monarchy unscathed for his sons proved illusory. The relations between the Swordsmen, their soldiers and their sectarian civilian allies in the House of Commons on the one hand and their far more numerous Presbyterian opponents in the House on the other, and the relationship of both to the dissembling, equivocating king provided the principal theme of the period from 1646 to the second Civil War of 1648. The New Model Army had been a remarkable, war-winning creation. Now the Parliamentarians discovered that it was a tiger they could no longer afford to ride but from which they found it difficult to dismount. Too expensive to keep, the Army would resist disbandment for three reasons. Many soldiers would not disband until nonconformity was secure. Most would not go home without legislative protection from civil and criminal suits brought by old enemies or disgruntled civilians for alleged damage committed during the war. None would disband before their pay arrears were settled. Yet something must be done. County Committees were complaining that their counties were being reduced to beggary by the cost of the institution created to defend them. Parliament hoped to disband half the regiments and send the remainder to Ireland, notoriously a military graveyard. The soldiers would have none of it, demanding amnesty and their arrears. The worst blunder of all was that the Presbyterians had alienated the Swordsmen, Cromwell included, by proposing to dismiss all officers above the rank of colonel apart from Fairfax, have all officers retained take the Covenant and make army service a bar to membership of the House. They had pulled the Swordsmen's nose. Could they successfully defy their anger? They were to discover they could not.

Parliament itself was polarized between the Presbyterians and Independents, the latter including long-serving officer MPs like Cromwell and others newly recruited since 1645. Among these was Cromwell's son-in-law, Henry Ireton, the son of a Puritan gentleman, who was the leading political ideologue of the Army Council from 1647 to 1649. The labels Independent and Presbyterian covered a complexity of religious and political convictions, the details of which are still controversial. The division had emerged during the war, when the issue had been whether to aim for total victory or simply compel the king to negotiate a settlement. The Presbyterians, increasingly aghast at the radical political and religious convictions brewing in the New Model Army, itself a creation of their political opponents, wanted a national church with no provision for individual conscience, and continued negotiation with the king. The Presbyterian party attracted both landowners who disliked Presbyterianism but believed the monarchy was necessary to the traditional social order, and the wealthy London merchants who had supported the war. The Independents (sometimes rather anachronistically described as Congregationalists) wanted liberty of worship for the independent congregations, favoured some radical reform and allied themselves with the Army, whose regiments began appointing representatives called 'agitators' to negotiate with Parliament about their grievances. (The label 'agitators' then lacked pejorative overtones, simply connoting elected spokesmen.) As conservative officers resigned, radical officers replaced them. Cromwell, despite being conservative politically and socially, favoured religious toleration because he believed that varied witness should be tolerated lest the truth be suppressed unwittingly. An Independent MP, he sought to prevent the establishment of a Presbyterian church and the disbandment of the Army which, like all Independents, he considered essential to prevent the fruits of victory being thrown away. Unable to reconcile the Parliamentary conservatives and the Army, he elected to make the Army's cause his own in June 1647. This was only two days after the junior officers of the Army had acted decisively by seizing the king and bringing him to the Army's current rendezvous at Newmarket. (The lowly instrument was Cornet George Joyce of Fairfax's regiment with a horse troop. His name later entered the pantheon of radical heroes and was invoked at least as late as the American Revolution.)

The Army now became thoroughly politicized. Cromwell set up a General Council composed of the generals, known as the Grandees, and two officers and two soldiers from each regiment to govern its affairs and to negotiate with the king. However, it was an unstable power centre because it was increasingly divided between the Grandees and some junior officers and soldiers influenced by the more radical doctrines of the Levellers, who tended to republicanism. The Levellers had become vocal in London before the end of the Civil War, drawing support from shopkeepers, artisans, apprentices and yeomen. They were inspired by the writings of John Lilburne, William Walwyn and John Wildman (who were minor gentry). Although they were republicans they were not as radical as their name 'Levellers' suggests, speaking for middling folk rather than the people as a whole. In general they opposed restrictions, whether political or religious, imposed by church or state, or economic, imposed by guilds and monopolists, and they opposed all customs and excise duties. They advocated annual, or at most biennial, parliaments elected by a wider franchise among the economically independent, a redistribution of parliamentary seats, freedom of speech and the press, no state church, Presbyterian or Anglican, and the abolition of tithes and advowsons, that is, the right to appoint ministers to livings, itself a form of property. They also advocated cheaper justice, court proceedings in English and abolishing imprisonment for debt. Their demands won a wide following among ordinary people and regimental officers and soldiers. The movement began to spread after the publication of Lilburne's pamphlet *England's Birthright Justified* in 1645. Parliament promptly imprisoned Lilburne and imprisoned him again from 1646 to 1648, but this did not stop him from pamphleteering. Cromwell and Ireton feared the Levellers' influence on the soldiers but grudgingly accepted Leveller support partly in the hope of limiting the damage they might do.

Discovering that some Presbyterian MPs were intriguing with the king and the Scots, even with Queen Henrietta Maria and the Prince of Wales, to restore Charles to power, and finding that there was no progress in their demands for amnesty and pay, the Army began to advance on London. They sent ahead a call for the arrest of eleven crypto-Royalist plotters, including Denzil Holles, which was ignored. Shortly afterwards a mob of London apprentices invaded the House and compelled the members to pass a resolution inviting the king's return to London without prior conditions. Many Independent MPs promptly took refuge with the advancing regiments. Cromwell had slowed the Army's advance because he wanted a negotiated settlement. He feared political anarchy and social disruption if the agitators obtained a settlement from Parliament at musket point. The senior officers had discovered that they also were riding a tiger. The regiments which were the source of their power might turn and rend them if they resisted the soldiers' demands too stubbornly. The soldiers completed their march on London. Denzil Holles and other leading Presbyterian plotters fled abroad. The trained bands sensibly would not confront the New Model veterans on the battlefield and the mobs fearfully melted away as the troops entered the city with laurel leaves in their hats. Fairfax maintained an iron discipline, permitting no plundering or harassing of the citizens, but the Swordsmen had arrived.

From the complex political situation emerged two competing proposals for post-war settlements. The first was the *Heads of Proposals* drawn up by Ireton with Cromwell's approval, which the Grandees had submitted to the king at the end of July 1647. The *Heads* provided for regular and more representative parliaments and wide religious toleration. Parliamentary control of the militia would last ten years. Pardons for the defeated were to be more comprehensive. These were arguably the best terms the defeated king ever received, not least because his successor would inherit a monarchy which was not hopelessly impaired. Nevertheless, blind to reality, always better able to deceive himself than others, Charles rejected them as part of his policy of divide and win. Division there was, highlighted by the appearance of the second and third sets of proposals shortly after the Army arrived in London as a radical reaction to the *Heads of Proposals*. The rank and file had been captivated by some of the Leveller demands and feared that the Grandees were sacrificing the interests of the soldiers to obtain a settlement which would keep political power in traditional hands. Furious at the slowness of reform and at the continuing negotiations with the king, radical spokesmen produced two documents of protest, *The Case of the Army truly Stated* and *An Agreement of the People*, the latter emerging from a collaboration between John Wildman and the agitators, which called for a republic in which the people were sovereign and their instrument of government a parliament elected by manhood suffrage. Fairfax responded by agreeing to have the issues debated at a general rendezvous on Putney Heath in October 1647. There the Grandees discussed the *Agreement of the People* with the agitators and others but found it too radical to accept, perceiving it as a threat to property and the social order. Not Cromwell, certainly not Fairfax, not even the more radical Ireton, could conceive of men with no 'interest' in the state 'other than breathing' (as Cromwell put it) sharing in political power. So far Cromwell had been carried along by events like a man in a swift-flowing current who can neither stem the flow nor swim against it. Now he demonstrated his political skills. Fairfax must order the regiments to disperse to meet later at a new rendezvous, and the agitators must rejoin their regiments. The regiments could then be kept disunited because they need not call a general rendezvous in the future. The return of the agitators meant that they vanished from the General Council so that the senior officers could more easily achieve a political solution without radical interference. When two regiments mutinied, mustering with copies of the *Agreement* in their hats, Cromwell rode furiously among them, cowing them into submission by sheer force of personality. The mutiny collapsed and a ringleader was shot. How much support the Leveller programme had among the soldiers remains controversial. Only a small minority of soldiers were declared Levellers, and an even smaller minority of the officers, but some Leveller ideas had a wider acceptance. However, other Leveller demands were against the soldiers' interests, particularly that for abolishing customs and taxes, for how else would they be paid? Certainly Leveller support in the Army declined once Parliament set about trying to satisfy the prime demands of payment of arrears and wartime indemnity.

Charles was by now a political whore, available to anyone but committed to nobody. It was the turn of the Scots. Hoping for a Scots–Royalist alliance to restore him, he escaped to the Isle of Wight where the governor of Carisbrooke Castle held him prisoner but did not prevent him negotiating what would be known as the 'Engagement' with Scots Commissioners who visited him there in December. Despairing of Parliament's fulfilling its promise to establish Presbyterianism, and alarmed at the proliferation of 'heretical' sects and the radical agitation of the Levellers, the Scots 'engaged' to invade England the following year in conjunction with Royalist uprisings. Charles agreed to accept Presbyterianism for a trial period of three years and to suppress the sects in return for his former civil and military powers. The generous terms of the Engagement, hammered out by the Duke of Hamilton and the Earl of Lauderdale, outraged the Kirk. The ministers could not prevent the attempt but hampered recruitment by hostile preaching while Argyle and the Campbells held aloof. Thus occurred that unnecessary tragedy, the second Civil War of 1648. The Scots army which invaded England in August was badly led, poorly organized, ill armed and worse provisioned. It was no match for the best cavalry in Europe with Cromwell in command, and the Scots were quickly routed at Preston. The ill-coordinated local eruptions in Wales, Kent, Essex and a Royalist-inspired mutiny in the navy were soon suppressed.[11]

The patience of the Army was now exhausted. At a prayer meeting at Windsor on 22 April it had already been decided to call 'that man of blood to an account for the blood that he had shed'. Parliament now divided on stricter lines, the radicals backing the Army, the moderates joining the Presbyterian majority, for a further attempt to negotiate with Charles. The king was happy to do so but his readiness only ensured his destruction. Cromwell had quite unnecessarily remained in the north with that competent commander John Lambert at the siege of Pontefract Castle, allowing the more radical Ireton to dominate events in London. Fairfax, who had recently succeeded to his father's Scottish peerage, preferred to occupy himself in raising money to pay his soldiers. Apparently he felt that if he could not control events he would divorce himself from responsibility for them. (Although he would be appointed one of the king's judges he declined even to attend the trial.) Meanwhile the Army Council fashioned a weapon which would finally kill the king. *The Remonstrance of the Army*, laid before Parliament in November, accused the king of being responsible for all the bloodshed of 1648 and declared that those who persisted in negotiation were traitors. Again the army occupied London, 7,000 troops surging into Westminster. Charles was imprisoned at Windsor. On 6 December Colonel Thomas Pride and his infantry 'purged' Parliament by arresting or turning away those members who still persisted in negotiating with the king, leaving only sixty radical Independents in the House. Oliver Cromwell returned that night and accepted the decision with ostensible reluctance as the only way to retain the unity of the Army. Reluctant to try the king but recognizing that the army would accept nothing less, Cromwell at first thought it would be unnecessary to kill him. Once again he was allowing himself to be carried along by the current. Cromwell was often slow and uncertain about political decisions, showing none of the swift decisiveness he displayed on the battlefield, but at some point he would make up his mind so abruptly as to astound his closest associates. During the trial Cromwell suddenly concluded the king must die and from that moment Charles was doomed. A majority of the Purged Parliament had appointed a High Court of about 150 members, including army officers of whom Fairfax was one, to try the king in Westminster Hall. Despite Colonel Algernon Sidney's acid comment that 'no court could try this man and this court could try no man', and the king's refusal to accept the illegal tribunal's standing, defiantly claiming that he represented 'the liberties of England', the court convicted him and sentenced him to death.

With the king dead, and the Purged Parliament moving to abolish the monarchy and the House of Lords, the radicals both in and out of the Army believed that their hour was come and there would follow an extensive programme of reform. They were the first left-wing socio-political movement in England who were to be disappointed by the failure of a parliament to enshrine their ideals and ideas in legislation. They would not be the last, but they probably had a right to be most disappointed because they were the beneficiaries not of some constitutional evolution, but of a dramatic revolution which had killed a king, proclaimed a republic and forcibly deprived the aristocracy of their own institution of government. Nevertheless they would not see their dreams fulfilled. Their dreams are best summarized by the Leveller-inspired *Agreement of the People* of the previous year. Although Cromwell's crushing of resistance after Putney Heath had set the *Agreement* aside, a new version appeared during winter 1648/9. Again this was the fruit of cooperation between the Levellers and the Army, especially the revolutionary-minded junior officers, although Fairfax and Ireton successively presided over a sixteen-man committee's deliberations on the new *Agreement,* held in Whitehall Palace. MPs were also invited but only the 'left-wing' republican Henry Marten regularly attended. The new *Agreement* was intended to be a blueprint for a constitutional settlement which included the dissolution of the Purged Parliament in spring 1649. It was difficult for the Levellers, both civilian and military, to bring Ireton, now Commissary General of Horse, to accept their more radical aims. Ireton may have seemed a dangerous radical to many MPs, but to the junior officers and to such Leveller ideologues as John Lilburne and William Walwyn he was a conservative brake on their revolutionary aspirations. On 14 December a draft was submitted to the Council of the Army, a body which amounted to about 160 men including co-opted civilians (thirty of them ministers), and was in fact much larger than the Purged Parliament.[12] The draft assumed the abolition of the monarchy and House of Lords even though they were to survive for more than a month, and stipulated the Long Parliament should dissolve on 30 April 1649. Future parliaments, to be called 'Representatives', would consist of only 300 members representing constituencies with radically redrawn boundaries which would more accurately reflect centres of population. Electors would be male householders assessed for poor relief who were not wage-earners or servants and who had signed the *Agreement* and, of course, who were not Royalists. The Representative would appoint as executive a Council of State, responsible to the Representative, which would govern between the biennial meetings of the Representative. This new form of parliament would be significantly shorn of powers the Long Parliament had asserted. It had no power of compulsion over religion, no power to conscript for military service abroad, and no power to call people to account for their wartime activities (except Royalists). Parliament had no power to punish where there was no law, thereby abolishing Attainder, and no power to violate the principle of equality under the law. The *Agreement* guaranteed freedom of commerce, guaranteed trial-by-jury, prescribed a maximum interest rate of 6 per cent, abolished imprisonment for debt, the excise and all tithes and even capital punishment save for homicide. Many of the clauses clearly suited the interests of the Levellers' prime constituency: tradesmen, small businessmen and other people of modest property. It also shows its preference for local government over centralized authority, local congregations over a state church.

In all of this it differed little from the original *Agreement of the People* of 1647. Despite Lilburne and Wildman's resistance the Council of Officers sought to modify it. The government, they argued, must have the power to preserve civil peace so an absolute liberty of religion could not be permitted. Moreover, well-affected people must support the *Agreement* or it would fail and so it should contain no clause which would deter them from signing it. Colonel Whalley pertinently argued that the religious question had divided even the Army so his hearers could judge how bitterly it would divide the country. Ireton also insisted that governments had always had a duty to restrain sin and no future government could be prevented from doing so. In the end, after a four-day debate (8–11 January) and reference to a committee, and a fierce denunciation of conservative objections by George Joyce speaking for the junior officers, a compromise was reached. Apart from Papists and Anglicans still using the Prayer Book, all who professed faith in Christ would be allowed to practise their religion freely. There would be no compulsory attendance at the state church whose ministry would be maintained out of the public treasury, not by tithes. A further modification saw the Representative have the power 'to call to account and punish public officers for failing in their trust' even though no law existed to fit the case. This may show the officers' anxiety to permit nothing which might be used to prevent the king's trial. Cromwell spoke against a clause which Ireton saw as fundamental: that which specified the date of Parliament's dissolution. Ireton felt that if the *Agreement* did not provide a complete settlement of government after the abolition of the monarchy, parliaments would continue to be elected in the old way and that meant that a Royalist parliament would be elected. Cromwell had an old-fashioned regard for Parliament, and felt it should decide its own dissolution.

The final *Agreement of the People* was brought to the Commons on 20 January where it was respectfully received with promises of consideration 'as soon as the present weighty and urgent affairs will permit'. This promise was not kept, and significantly the senior officers never reminded the House of its failure to do so. While this must have annoyed the activists they were never to be able to press for it. The Grandees' attention was focused on the trial and Regicide, and even many Levellers were less interested in a new constitution than in gaining their aims through legislation passed by the Purged Parliament. As for the sects, if the government let them alone, which largely it did, they had the substance without the document. Nevertheless the *Agreement* is significant in demonstrating what the more ardent revolutionaries wanted, or at least would settle for, and its total neglect by the Purged Parliament demonstrates the limitations of that body as a revolutionary institution after the Regicide. The Levellers and the junior officers would also be disappointed by the Purged Parliament's reform record.[13] Reform requires parliamentary bills and bills need a parliament uncluttered by routine business. The Purged Parliament, however, was perpetually entangled in a thicket of business because it had administrative responsibilities for the country as a whole unknown to previous parliaments.

The second reason was even more fundamental. After the Regicide the Purged Parliament desperately needed to broaden its base. It claimed to represent the people with no justification whatever, and needed more members to give it at least an appearance of respectability. It quickly found a formulaic 'test' which would permit some MPs to resume their seats. On 1 February Parliament determined that members who recorded their dissent from the motion of 5 December which had declared that the terms of the king's proffered 'treaty' were an acceptable basis for negotiation with him should be readmitted. Many MPs agreed to sit on that basis. Such members had been appalled by the Regicide but accepted that the country must be governed and that they had a responsibility to prevent a descent into anarchy. The more of these conservative country gentlemen were admitted to the House the less radical the Purged Parliament became and the less likely to embark on an extensive programme of religious and social novelties. Too many of the members strongly believed in a national church organized on Presbyterian lines with enforced conformity to it. Parliament had pursued this dream until Pride's Purge, although unable to suppress the radical independent congregations because the army protected them. (Of these independent congregations thirty-six, the majority, had been formed in London, but they also existed in provincial towns and in the army. The army planted them in garrison towns while some ex-soldiers founded others on their return to civilian life.) Nothing had changed after the Purge once the conservative-minded took their seats. They could not practise religious intolerance because the army would not allow it but the radicals' desire for legislated toleration would not be realized because the MPs would not act. The hard core of revolutionaries were now a minority. Over half of the House were people who before the war would have been among the rulers of their native counties, and in turn they looked for leadership based squarely on social rank. Only four MPs, apart from such army officers as Ireton himself, out of a total of 213 had shown enthusiasm for changes of the extent proposed in the *Agreement of the People*. Meanwhile the Regicides in the House were more anxious to persuade the conservatives to support the Commonwealth than to enact divisive reforms. The swing from revolutionary fervour to conservative pragmatism can be encapsulated in a single issue of minor importance. In 1649 men had dreamed of pulling down the cathedrals and selling their materials for the benefit of the poor. The Purged Parliament got around to discussing this a couple of years later – but now the beneficiary was to be the navy. In the end nothing happened.

The most immediate task in February 1649 was to set up an alternative government. This was all the simpler because Charles and his ministers had been the country's government in name only since before the Civil War. The Long Parliament and its overworked committees, the Council of Officers, such wartime bodies as the County Committees and the regional Associations, had run the country. The House of Lords was abolished on 6 February, the monarchy the following day. What was needed was an efficient executive to carry out Parliament's policies. The answer was the Council of State, which resembled the executive proposed by the *Agreement*, not least because Parliament would determine its membership. A committee of the more revolutionary members drew up a list of nominees, which included officers and peers as well as MPs. The number of officers aroused deep concern and was hotly debated, and Ireton and the religious radical Colonel Thomas Harrison were rejected in favour of two civilians. Of the remaining thirty-nine nominees only seven were serving officers – but they included Fairfax and Cromwell. Another six had been officers during the war, and some soon would be again.[14] The rejected Ireton had drafted an engagement which members would have to support, including a declaration of approval of the Regicide, and the abolition of monarchy and House of Lords. Many would not give retroactive consent to acts they believed illegal. Among them were Colonel Algernon Sidney, Fairfax and the five peers.[15] Cromwell suggested a compromise by which new members would only be expected to accept the republican form of government 'for the future'. A minimalist oath indeed, by which men promised to support the government of which they had just become members. Even this was too much for Fairfax, who wrote his own engagement in which he avoided the dread word 'republic' by undertaking to defend the government 'without king and House of Peers', that is, the government which he found to be ruling England without acknowledging any awareness of how it had come to be there.

The fact that he was allowed to do this suggests just how desperately the new rulers of England felt they needed the prestige of the head of the New

Model Army to bolster their government. However, it can have been of small comfort to the junior officers or for the Levellers to realize that barely half of those appointed to the Council had sat in either the Parliament or the tribunal which condemned the king, and that Parliament had gone out of its way to snub the Army by rejecting Ireton and Harrison. True, Cromwell was a member, but he had been in Yorkshire for the Purge – some said deliberately – had been a very late convert to executing the king, and was now busily persuading as many moderate to conservative MPs as he could to take their seats in the House. Nevertheless, however increasingly unrevolutionary the complexion of this revolutionary creation, England at least had a government. It even had a chief justice, a chancellor and a bench of judges, although they were serving with varying degrees of reluctance and anxiety. The question now was: could it survive the anger and resentment of its many enemies at home and abroad?

CHAPTER TWO

The Republic and Its Enemies

You have no other way to deal with these men but to break them or they will
break you.

Cromwell on the Levellers [1]

Although the revolutionary leaders were in power there would have been
anxious, even fearful, faces among those who thronged the draughty,
creaking corridors of the Palace of Whitehall in the dreary winter of 1649.
For all their determination to maintain a resolute demeanour many could
be seen whispering in corners, muffled in their cloaks, their broad-
brimmed hats low over their eyes, unconsciously fingering their sword hilts.
They were beleaguered by enemies at home and abroad. The old ally
Scotland stubbornly remained a kingdom, furious that a King of Scots
could be put to death without any consultation with the Scottish
government. This passive enmity might turn to active hostility and bring a
new Scottish invasion if ever the Presbyterian leaders succeeded in
persuading Charles II not only to accept Presbyterianism for Scotland but
also to agree to impose it on England. This northern threat seemed the
more likely because while the English had not consulted the Scots when
they put Charles to death, the Purged Parliament's ordinance abolishing
monarchy had carefully referred only to England and Ireland. The Scots
were left to proclaim their own republic. Instead they had proclaimed
Charles not only King of Scotland but of Britain, thereby denying the
ordinance by insisting that Charles was King of England and Ireland also.[2]
This remarkable provocation was pointless if they did not intend to help
Charles regain the English throne. Ireland also remained a kingdom, at
least beyond musket range of the garrisons in the few towns still held by
Parliament. The overwhelming majority of the Irish population was
Catholic, but it was far from unconditionally Royalist. The Irish in arms for
their religion would accept Charles II and even assist him to recover his
throne if he guaranteed their religion, but they were not so ill-advised as to
insist that Charles impose their religion on the English and Welsh as a
condition of their support. Only a military conquest of both kingdoms,
something never achieved by English armies in the past, would make these
countries safely republican.

There appeared to be more distant perils when the anxious Republicans peered abroad. Although New England was safely in support, Virginia and Maryland remained resolutely Royalist, as did the Barbados, and, nearer home, the Channel Islands and the Scillies remained nests of Royalist privateers. On the continent the news of the Regicide had sent courts into mourning, outraged by the act and alarmed by the precedent it had set. Charles and his mother Henrietta Maria hoped briefly, and the Republicans feared longer, that some continental power or coalition might assemble an invasion fleet to restore Charles to his throne. The Marquess of Montrose had pursued this chimera before setting out on his equally hopeless invasion of Scotland. The Czar of Russia, from a safe distance, did indeed call for such a coalition, but in vain. The Empire, France and Spain had endured too much during the Thirty Years War, only just concluded, lightly to embark on such an enterprise. Indeed France and Spain were technically still at war. England had not been a significant European power since 1642. Her Civil War had taken her out of the mainstream of European politics, which suited the courts of France and Spain very well. It was convenient to have England chaotically divided and for Charles, who might if restored re-establish order and potency, to remain in helpless exile. This complacent if cynical attitude would soon be rudely shocked when it was discovered that the army which had won the first and second Civil Wars was as potent as ever – and had been joined by a powerful navy well able to strike at foreign enemies.

Nevertheless in the aftermath of the Regicide the new government felt beset at home and abroad. Before we dismiss its anxieties as groundless it should be remembered that in 1688 a Prince of Orange with no real claim to the throne would launch a successful invasion of England using the Dutch fleet and take that throne from its rightful occupant. In 1649 Charles II had an undisputed claim in the eyes of most English people, and would have no monarch to displace but only a Rump Parliament with not the feeblest claim to legitimacy. Early events brought no comfort. No foreign state recognized the new Republic. There was one country in Europe from which the Republic might have expected a sympathetic reception: the United Provinces. The Dutch had rebelled against their Spanish monarch more than half a century earlier and after a desperate struggle had achieved their independence. Although the House of Orange had led the rebellion the Dutch had resisted its monarchical aspirations and established a republic. Surely the republican Dutch would extend the hand of friendship? On 18 April a special envoy was sent to The Hague to announce that the Commonwealth intended to maintain a substantial embassy there in order to promote a happy understanding between the two republics. The envoy was Dr Isaac Dorislaus, a Dutchman long resident in England, who had served Parliament faithfully as a lawyer on the prosecution team during the trial of the king. His arrival outraged the

English and Scottish Royalists who haunted The Hague in frustrated idleness. Strickland, the resident ambassador, got wind of their plots and warned Dorislaus so that he was not deceived by an attempt to lure him from his inn. Undeterred, on 2 May the conspirators broke in and slew him at his dinner table. While the Dutch government protested its innocence in the affair, it did nothing to prevent the murderers' flight to the Spanish Netherlands. Meanwhile Charles was an honoured guest of the Prince of Orange and the Dutch accepted Charles's claim to be King of England, making no demur as he and his court plotted an invasion of Ireland or Scotland, or both, or when he received the Scottish commissioners sent to obtain his consent to their offensive demands. If the Dutch were the only continental friends the Republic could hope for the outlook was bleak indeed.

In fact the Commonwealth faced a brighter future than it realized because of an age-old principle: if the feeble never lack enemies the strong never lack friends. The English Republic would have friends enough when it showed itself to be menacingly strong on land and sea, but first domestic enemies would have to be suppressed. These included the Royalists, shattered by their second defeat in 1648 and demoralized by the Regicide. The Royalists knew that large numbers of their fellow countrymen had been appalled by this blow at the traditional structure of government. The Regicide and the proclamation abolishing the monarchy destroyed an institution which had endured for almost a thousand years. It was still regarded with superstitious reverence, but a reverence tinged with practicality among the better informed. England had endured destructive times when the monarchy was weak and overmighty subjects were free to prey upon their weaker neighbours. However, if the popularity of the monarchy had survived the unpopularity of Charles I there was no obvious way for the Royalists to exploit it. The New Model Army could suppress any rising, and there was no hope of its disbanding, partly because the regime needed its protection, and partly because the army would not demobilize until it was paid in full and guaranteed security for the things for which it had fought.

However, if the army was a solution to the problem of the regime's enemies, it was also a problem in itself. The Republican government's unpopularity was chiefly due not to the Regicide but to the very existence of that army with its constant exactions, foraging, forced billeting, and the sectarian violence of some of its soldiers towards such institutions as the parish churches and their festivals and ceremonies. Nevertheless, so long as the army which made the regime so unpopular continued to protect it from its unpopularity it need not fear the Royalists. No matter how alarming the civilian MPs found their dependence on the New Model Army, they found anything which weakened its loyalty more alarming still. Some officers disapproved of the Regicide and felt alienated from the parliamentary cause. They might turn to Royalism in the future. However, civilian Royalists were powerless to overthrow the regime and the officer crypto-Royalists were helpless because so many of their soldiers were republicans. The Levellers presented the threat which most worried the Commonwealth government during the winter and spring of 1649, simply because many regiments were infected by their ideas and they were supported by some officers and many soldiers. Other threats appeared less immediately menacing. The Scots remained quiet if sullenly hostile, distracted briefly by Montrose's incursion and preoccupied by the long drawn-out attempt to coerce the young king to swallow Presbyterianism. The Irish had little hope of mounting a successful invasion unless the king came in person to lead it and unless Ormonde's army overwhelmed the Commonwealth's forces there (which in the spring of 1649 appeared disturbingly likely). If the Dutch, French or Spanish refused to recognize the new regime at least they had not declared war on it. The Army, however, was all about them and although it had brought on the revolution which had created the Commonwealth it was a doubtful friend and the Leveller infection had priority over all other dangers.

The Army was aggrieved, and with reason. Senior officers were resentful that Ireton and Harrison had not been appointed to the Council of State. Junior officers and other ranks resented the ignoring of the *Agreement of the People*, although Ireton and the other Grandees were less concerned. Much more on the minds of the soldiers, however, was the failure of the Purged Parliament to pay their arrears, although it sent a courteous reply to a petition from the officers. Fortunately the pay situation had eased a little during the revolutionary winter because Fairfax had occupied himself with the problem while Cromwell was engaged with the king's trial. The new Corporation of London struggled to get London's taxes paid, and Fairfax arranged that the money paid by specific counties was allocated to specific regiments, which speeded payment. Nevertheless, large arrears remained. Parliament tackled the problem by raising the land tax by a third, and by abolishing the church's deaneries and chapters and offering their land for sale to raise more funds.

It was almost too late. Serious trouble was brewing. The soldiers and junior officers were not only incensed against the politicians, they were incensed against their own generals, Fairfax perhaps apart. This was the more dangerous because the second Civil War had greatly enlarged the army and many recruits came from places where radical notions were widespread. Senior army officers should never allow themselves to be divorced from their men by the pleasures of political activity at the seat of government. This axiom applies with double force to the leaders of a revolutionary army. Yet during the cold hungry winter of 1648/9 the Grandees were engrossed in the trial of the king, in the setting up of the new government, in the new modelling of the navy and in the trial of the five surviving principals of the second Civil War (three of whom were beheaded: the Duke of Hamilton, the Earl of Holland and Lord Capel). The soldiers nursed their wrath to keep it warm and read with interest the subversive pamphlets of John Lilburne and his colleagues. One reflective and well-read soldier put forth a pamphlet of his own, urging that since Parliament claimed that the people were the source of all power, the same principle should apply within the New Model Army. The soldiers should sack the Grandees and their colonels and elect new commanders.

As is the way when armies become disaffected the senior officers tackled the problem by combining repression with redress of grievances. They met on 22 February, well aware that Lilburne had returned to London and that his pamphlets were subverting their regiments by encouraging the soldiers to meet, to plot, to petition and to write pamphlets of their own. This must cease. Soldiers were forbidden to meet in private, and regiments were forbidden to combine behind a petition, although individual soldiers could petition against a genuine grievance. Such individual petitions would be brought to the commanding officers of the regiments who would transmit them to Fairfax who would lay them before Parliament. Some officers even hoped Parliament would allow them to try civilian agitators among the soldiers by martial law. Colonel Hewson, in rejecting the alternative of civilian courts, bluntly argued that 'we can hang twenty before they will hang one'. This demand was never granted although Lilburne got wind of it and denounced it. Lilburne himself claimed that he only began to address his pamphlets to the soldiers in response to the army officers' repression. He presented a petition to the Commons on 26 February, ceremoniously ushered in by the sergeant-at-arms. Significantly entitled *England's New Chains*, it attacked the officers for many sins ranging from their watering-down of the *Agreement of the People* (why should Parliament meet only six months in two years while the Council of State governed during the other eighteen?) to the army's censorship of the press, which naturally outraged him, to the inclusion of military officers in the Council of State which he claimed violated the *Agreement*. He castigated the officers for their proposal to try civilians by martial law and called for a purge of the high command. The same day a petition arrived from the soldiers which not only complained about their material grievances, but also called for extensive reforms, including the abolition of tithes, liberty of conscience, freeing prisoners for debt, and the relaxing of the code of martial law. They also urged speedy provision for the poor whose miseries, they claimed, cried aloud for redress. Parliament declined to endorse this petition but neither did it condemn it.

The growing gulf between the senior officers and their former Leveller allies was widened still further in March when Fairfax produced a petition to the Council of Officers, allegedly written by eight troopers from different regiments. They asserted the soldiers' right of petition without their officers' consent, denounced the Council of State and the High Court of Justice and demanded the democratization of the army. 'Is it not the soldier that endureth the heat and burden of the day' they roundly demanded, 'and performeth that work whereof the officers beareth the glory and name?' They were promptly tried by court martial and sentenced to ride the wooden horse face to tail, have their swords broken over their heads and to be cashiered from the army. One repented and was forgiven, two went into hiding, but the others endured this humiliation cheerfully enough before being carried off in a coach by well-wishers to feast in a tavern. Two weeks later the five produced that eloquent pamphlet *The Hunting of the Foxes*, which is believed to have been authored by Richard Overton.[3] This again attacked the officers and all the institutions of the new republic with equal ferocity, declaring that while the 'old king's person and the old lords are removed' Cromwell, Ireton and Harrison ruled the Council of Officers and the Council ruled the state and since all were in the Commons in one house they were 'under a more absolute arbitrary monarchy than before'. The uncomfortable element of truth in this ensured that the breach between the senior officers and the Levellers was now unbridgeable.

Lilburne attacked again on 24 March with *A Second Part of England's New Chains*, which called on Parliament to reconstruct the General Council of the Army by furthering the election of agitators and implement more fully the *Agreement of the People*. Enough was enough. On 27 March Parliament declared the pamphlet a seditious book, calculated to promote mutiny in the army on the eve of the expedition to Ireland. Files of soldiers arrested Lilburne, Overton, Walwyn and Prince, who were alleged to be joint authors of the publication and who were to be proceeded against as traitors. They were carried before the Council of State where Lilburne, brought in first, refused to remove his hat until he saw that several councillors were also Members of Parliament. Assuming that he was about to be tried and condemned by this body he denied that the Council was a legal entity but even if it was it had no power to try him. To this John Bradshaw replied the Council claimed no such jurisdiction. Later Bradshaw enquired if he was the author of the pamphlet, to which Lilburne retorted that the Council was reviving the discredited Star Chamber practices by requiring that he incriminate himself. He then threatened to set fire to any place he was imprisoned in if it was guarded by the army even if that meant he must die in the flames he had kindled. Looking fixedly at Cromwell who watched him in sombre silence he declared that he had not found 'so much honour, justice or conscience' among the army Grandees that he would trust his life to them 'or think it safe under their immediate fingers'.[4] It was a decidedly

Lilburnian performance, but Cromwell was not amused. Once removed from the chamber and listening at the door Lilburne could hear Cromwell addressing the Council, pounding the table with his fist as he declared that they had no other way to deal with the Leveller leaders than to 'break them or they will break you' and then all their years of toil and blood and treasure would have been expended for nothing. The four Levellers were relegated to the Tower to await trial.

Before the final campaign against the Levellers began two other pockets of subversion were stamped on. The City of London, to the irritation of all republicans, had a Royalist Lord Mayor, Abraham Reynoldson. His stubborn resistance had left London the only urban centre in England which had not proclaimed the abolition of the monarchy. On 2 April the Lord Mayor acknowledged at the bar of the House that his conscience would not permit him to do so. He was deprived of his office, sent to the Tower and fined £2,000 and replaced by the more compliant Thomas Andrews, although even he could not muster enough courage to make the proclamation until 30 May. Even then when it was read at the Royal Exchange some prominent merchants openly protested and one was arrested. However, despite the hostility of several former aldermen, now barred from office, Common Councillors and merchants, the spark of resistance here had been crushed. London was now safe from Royalism.

The radicalism which had made the revolution possible could still produce strange prodigies among the civilian population which might discredit the more moderate revolutionaries who held the reins of power. While in the Tower awaiting trial Lilburne and his colleagues issued a manifesto which must have puzzled some of its readers. The founders of the Levellers were protesting against the term 'Leveller' being applied to them. They were not, they indignantly asserted, in favour of 'equalling of men's estates and taking away of the proper right and title that every man has to what is his own'. This unexpected appearance of John Lilburne, champion of property, had been inspired by the news that a new movement had appeared under the label of 'the True Levellers', although they are better known to posterity as the 'Diggers'. Unlike Lilburne, who had always confined his demands to political reform, this group, led by Gerrard Winstanley and William Everard, had an abhorrence of landlords and indeed all forms of individual landownership. In his writings Winstanley argued that only the abolition of private property could bring an end to tyranny and the horrors of war. In a manifesto published on 26 April Everard, who had been a soldier until he was cashiered for his radical opinions, declared that all landlords were thieves and murderers and beneficiaries of the Norman yoke, and it was time for free-born Englishmen to throw off their hegemony. Labourers were exhorted to work no more for hire but rather to join with their fellow victims and take over all common lands and cultivate them communally, to dig for victory, so to speak, or at least for independence and Utopia. About three dozen True Levellers on 16 April had seized waste land near Oatlands, Surrey, and began to dig it and sow crops. The Council of State, alarmed by this manifestation of primitive communism which might encourage wider rural disturbances, ordered Fairfax to send a couple of Ironside companies to disperse them. The officer who commanded the companies was reluctant to interfere with the Diggers, finding them peaceable folk too strongly imbued with a notion of universal love to be a menace to the state.

The day following, Winstanley and Everard found their way to military headquarters at Whitehall and into Fairfax's presence, although they refused to remove their hats before him because, as they pointed out, 'he was but their fellow creature'. Everard claimed that a vision had directed him to cultivate the earth but that he and his followers only intended for the present to work on waste lands. In time landowners, seeing the evil of their ways, would voluntarily surrender their estates and live communally, happy to receive food and clothing in common, with no need for corrupting money. Fairfax had no experience of 'flower-power' to guide him although he and his family had considerable experience of landowning, but he dismissed this odd couple courteously enough. The Diggers had little impact on English society. They appear an amiably dotty by-water amid the seventeenth-century radical movements, but are more interesting than their inconsiderable numbers might suggest. This is chiefly because of the attractive personality of Winstanley, the son of a Wigan mercer, and his remarkable writings, which provided the first detailed blueprint of a communist society. However, if they were no danger either to landowners or the state, they could be a nuisance to poor husbandmen, who gained part of their livelihood from waste and jealously guarded their rights in it. Such folk indignantly dug up the seed sown at Oatlands and abused the invaders, although the little community struggled on until in November Fairfax was finally prevailed upon to disperse the commune.[5]

The struggle against the Lilburnian Levellers now entered its final phase. Since Cromwell believed that they must be broken or they would break the Commonwealth it was reasonable to expect that broken they would be. The leaders at least were incarcerated. The problem lay with the army and the degree to which it was infected with Lilburnian radicalism to the point of political unreliability, an infection dangerously combined with the grievance about pay arrears. When Parliament had sent a deputation to the Guildhall on 12 April seeking loans from the merchant community to finance the conquest of Ireland the merchants had been assured that there was no danger that the army, once the money was in its hands, would refuse to go. Cromwell himself assured the merchants that he had complete confidence in the discipline of the army; there were no 'divisions and distractions', although he admitted 'it had been attempted'. Cromwell's confidence was premature. Throughout April Lilburne and Overton, who had such freedom of movement that they were only technically imprisoned, had striven to persuade soldiers to depose their officers, overthrow the Purged Parliament and implement the Leveller programme of political reform. Lilburne probably realized that such a revolution was improbable, yet still they despatched agents into the rural areas of southern counties and into Wales and Lancashire to encourage the rural poor to unite with the soldiers. The combination failed because civilians saw no identity of interest with soldiers, rather perceiving them as authors of their misery after the third hungry winter in succession. Nevertheless, the soldiers were repeatedly urged to demand a new General Council of the Army elected by themselves which could guarantee the rights and liberties of Englishmen by enforcing the *Agreement of the People*. This propaganda had some impact and the senior officers were alarmed by reports of disaffection among widely scattered regiments. One captain in Lancashire had refused to disband his troop but rather tripled its size, his soldiers vociferously declaring their support for the Levellers. In Somerset soldiers were crying for a new parliament which would free the Leveller leaders and uphold the principles of the *Agreement*. There were reports of disaffected garrisons in various centres, Lancaster and Oxford among them. The only comfort was that the infection was so widely scattered geographically and among different companies that it was difficult for the ringleaders to concentrate the disaffected into a formidable force.

As he had in January Fairfax ordered all officers to leave London and rejoin their commands, and forbade any officer to quit his post for more than twenty-four hours, unless he had specific business at Whitehall. In London the Leveller leaders continued to work on the civilian population as well as the soldiers, with a petition demanding a jury trial for themselves and the implementation of the *Agreement of the People*. Several hundred women bearing a petition with 10,000 female signatures arrived before Parliament making the same demands but also seeking relief for London's poor. One member, uninhibited by the constraints of more recent times, told them to go home and wash their dishes, and Speaker Lenthall, protected by soldiers brandishing pistols, ordered them to 'meddle with their housewifery'. A gentlewoman had the temerity to assure Cromwell himself that if the Leveller leaders lost their lives the women would ensure that their slayers suffered the same fate, roundly declaring, 'we shall have your life if you take away theirs'. The women besieged the House for four days, the members more infuriated that their tormentors were women than by their demands.

The senior officers were made even more aware of the unsuitability of London as a place to billet their companies, or even allow individual soldiers to visit, when broadsheets were scattered in the streets calling on the soldiers to rise against their officers, and by the appearance of a very radical newsbook, *Mercurius Militaris*. Aimed at the soldiers, it accused the Grandees of manipulating the choice of regiments for the Irish expedition. They responded by ordering troops of horse to move to new quarters outside London to protect them from such noxious influences. However, when Colonel Edward Whalley's cavalry regiment was ordered to new quarters in Essex, Captain Savage's troop mutinied, seized their colours and gathered with their horses at the Bull Inn near Bishopsgate. When Savage, formerly a Berkshire yeoman or minor gentleman, tried to seize the colours from them, one of them, Robert Lockyer, snatched them from his hand declaring that 'the colours belonged to them as well as to him, and that they had as well fought for them as he', to which his companions cried 'All!, all!' Even when Whalley himself rode up with several of his officers and a force of loyal troopers, the men still refused to mount-up for the ride to Essex unless they received pay to settle what they owed for their quarters. When Whalley promised this they widened their claim to arrears, which he had no power to grant. He again ordered them to mount, calling on Lockyer by name to do so. Lockyer sought the advice of his fellows who clamoured for him to refuse, as did a swelling crowd of sympathetic civilians.

The worst nightmare of the Purged Parliament appeared to be coming true: a combination of soldiers and a civilian mob mounting a rising against the government in London. However, Whalley drove off the mob and suppressed the mutiny by *force majeure*. About sixty mutineers slipped away but Whalley arrested fifteen, including Lockyer. At this point a clattering of hooves on the cobbles announced the arrival of Fairfax and Cromwell, whose awareness of the danger had only fed their fury for, as a contemporary put it, they were 'furiously breathing forth nothing but death to them all'. The fifteen were marched to Whitehall under guard and tried by court martial the following day: one was acquitted, three were left to Whalley to punish or forgive, while of the remainder five were sent to ride the wooden horse while six alleged ringleaders were sentenced to death. The condemned apologetically sought mercy which Cromwell was inclined to grant, but Fairfax insisted that one must be executed so Lockyer, the most conspicuous ringleader, was marched to St Paul's Churchyard to die by firing squad. A hastily published Leveller letter calling Fairfax a murderer hardly helped Lockyer's cause. The young man told the sympathetic crowd that he regretted he was dying over a dispute about pay rather than for the liberties of his countrymen for which he had fought since 1642. Disdaining a blindfold he gazed fixedly at the six troopers in the firing squad and entreated them to spare his life. This call for further disobedience met with stony silence, so after a prayer Lockyer raised his arms and was shot dead.

He fell a victim of Leveller agitation as much as of his commander-in-chief. Fairfax was determined to recall the soldiers to their duty by an exemplary punishment because he feared that Leveller agitation was undermining his army. Cromwell was no more soft-hearted. It was a difference of judgement. Cromwell had feared that the execution of a Londoner, a popular hero once he had been condemned, might ignite the explosion in the city which the government feared. However, Fairfax knew that regiments must soon sail for Ireland. Disunity and disaffection in an army about to fight a campaign against superior numbers could only be hazardous, perhaps fatal. The event confirmed Fairfax's judgement in the long run, although this was not immediately obvious. Lockyer's funeral was exploited as a major political protest, with a long procession of several thousand mourners led by six trumpeters marching solemnly from Smithfield through the City and back to Moorfields. The political significance of the event was marked by many in the procession wearing black and sea-green ribbons – sea-green being a colour associated with the Leveller Colonel Rainborow who had been murdered by Royalists the previous year. Many soldiers joined the procession, which only confirmed that London was no place to billet soldiers. Meanwhile the Leveller agitation continued unabated across several counties but was particularly vigorous in the west and around Oxfordshire.

The issue of the Irish expedition had helped to bring the army's divisions to the surface, but it also helped to resolve them. It revealed malcontents and distinguished the reliable. In April units for an expeditionary force had been chosen by lot at Fairfax's headquarters without reference to the views of their members. The lots fell on four regiments of horse commanded by Ireton, Scrope, Horton and Lambert, and on the foot regiments of Eure, Cook, Deane and Hewson, together with five regiments of dragoons. The soldiers were informed that they would not be compelled to sail for Ireland but if they insisted on remaining in England they must return to civilian life. Some soldiers had vowed never to leave England until the Leveller demands were met and 300 or more of these in Hewson's infantry regiment threw down their arms. They were promptly cashiered and given only a small sum to carry them home while sufficient volunteers from other regiments came forward to replace them. The trouble, however, had only just begun. The great majority of soldiers were uninfected by Leveller views but all were concerned about their arrears of pay and many of these hungry creditors of the state felt vulnerable when those who refused Irish service were sacked without their arrears being paid.

It was an opportunity for the unscrupulous to exploit. William Thompson was a sociopathic villain who exploited Leveller ideology for purposes which would have appalled the Leveller ideologues. Cashiered from the army for his violence in 1647 he had been imprisoned early in 1649 for his activities. He was bailed out by Lilburne and went off into Essex where he raised an irregular force combining trouble-makers and genuine Levellers. His force having been dispersed and himself briefly arrested he then removed to the neighbourhood of Oxford, a seriously infected area. There he assembled a band of about 300 and if he had succeeded in joining up with the mutinous force commanded by the Leveller Lieutenant Rowley, roaming just to the north, could have been dangerous because the Oxford garrison was much under the influence of Leveller propaganda. However, the Levellers were painfully to discover that poachers do make the best gamekeepers, for an officer formerly noted for his Leveller sympathies, Colonel John Reynolds, was to play several decisive parts in ending all Leveller hopes of a successful army mutiny. His first intervention was near Banbury where with 160 men he confronted and dispersed Thompson's much larger force, taking many scores of prisoners before Rowley could combine with it. This was a major success but the danger was not over. Four troops of Scrope's cavalry regiment at Salisbury were told by their commander that they were to go to Ireland and promptly declined. Startled to be told that this was mutiny and that Fairfax and Cromwell were going to march west to suppress such mutinies they decided to mutiny indeed, seized the colours and began a march for Bristol. Scrope, left with only eighty men, discovered that two other of his troops at Malmesbury had also mutinied and marched off to join their colleagues. Reinforced by about ninety mutineers from Ireton's regiment they all came together at Old Sarum.

Meanwhile in London the government acted swiftly. The Leveller leaders were separated and closely confined. Five regiments of horse and foot were mustered in Hyde Park under Fairfax and Cromwell for the march west. The infantry were completely reliable, for it was noticeable that it was the horse regiments everywhere which were most influenced by Leveller propaganda. There was a material reason. The cavalrymen had to pay for food and lodging for both themselves and their horses, and the recent inflation had sometimes meant they were serving the state at a loss. Despite some muttering even among Cromwell's own troopers the force of about 2,500 men listened to addresses by both generals and then marched out. They soon began to close on the recalcitrant band of Scrope and Ireton men who had abandoned their march towards Bristol and instead had advanced north-east through Wantage towards Abingdon, probably aiming for Oxford and its sympathetic garrison. Before the two forces could meet its leaders began exchanging negotiators, Fairfax despatching the former Leveller Colonel White to treat on his behalf. However, although the 900 mutineers were ready to treat they still demanded the implementation of the *Agreement of the People* as well as their pay arrears. Moreover, despite Fairfax's mingled threats and promises, the rebellious band refused to halt their march. However, when it tried to cross the Thames at Newbridge it was foiled by the ex-Leveller Colonel Reynolds who had placed a strong bridgehead there. Continuing west they successfully forded the Thames and wound their way wearily into the cloth-making town of Burford. They were so sure that Fairfax would leave them in peace until the negotiations were concluded that they posted few pickets and scattered among the houses and inns to sleep.

Fairfax and Cromwell considered that the rebels had forfeited all such consideration by refusing to halt as ordered and, although their men had marched thirty-five miles that day, struck in the night with their cavalry, Colonel Reynolds in the van. Most mutineers, who had been awakened by the pistol shots of a few resisters as the troops swept into the town, melted away in the night while about 340 were imprisoned in the church. The latter at first insouciantly held to their demands, but when they were curtly informed that they would all be shot as mutineers they at once demonstrated the force of Dr Johnson's dictum that the imminence of execution wonderfully concentrates the mind. They unconditionally promised to resume their obedience, and begged for mercy. This was Fairfax's object all along, and his council of war sentenced just four of the ringleaders to death, Cornets Thomson and Denne and two corporals, Perkins and Church, who proved more staunchly obdurate than their officers. The four were brought to the churchyard while many of their followers watched from the roof and tower of the church. Cornet Thomson died first, 'contrite and in great terror', Perkins and Church courageously. Denne, a former Baptist minister, had repented with such enthusiasm that he claimed he no longer wished to live, had bought himself a winding sheet to be interred in, and even began a tract pointing out his errors to other malcontents so Fairfax pardoned him at the last moment. Filled with joy at his reprieve he was half carried up into the pulpit where he preached on the sin of mutiny to his astonished comrades, 'howling and weeping like a crocodile'. Before this remarkable spectacle Cromwell had himself mounted the pulpit to assure the soldiers that Providence had spared their lives rather than their commanders, but he conceded that many of their grievances were real and would be remedied as early as possible.

A few days later Thompson and Lieutenant Rowley and a mixed band of ruffians and genuine Levellers were dispersed near Wellingborough by Colonel Reynolds, playing his final part in the drama. Thompson himself, declaring they should not take him alive, wounded several of his opponents before being shot dead from his horse in a final charge. The Leveller-Army rebellion now spluttered out. At Oxford the garrison had waited too long, for although there was trouble in September it was quickly suppressed. Lilburne and his colleagues could be brought to trial without serious risk to public order. Many Englishmen felt relieved and grateful to the Grandees. Ironically it was at Oxford, with its Royalist tradition in the university and its Leveller-infected garrison, that the exertions of Fairfax, Cromwell and their colonels first received formal recognition. Four days after Burford the university summoned a special convocation at which Fairfax and Cromwell, suitably gowned, were inducted as doctors of the university, while Harrison and Hewson, among others, received honorary MAs. It may be the home of lost causes but Oxford has always responded to the glamour of power. In the capital the reception was even more rapturous, not only in the deeply relieved Purged Parliament but in the previously hostile City. The merchants welcomed the prospect of a stable government, safe from radical or Royalist insurrection.

While Fairfax and Cromwell were suppressing mutiny in the field the members of the Purged Parliament were undermining the causes of disaffection by tackling the soldiers' material grievances. They voted increases of pay which helped to relieve the injustices imposed by inflation, particularly on the cavalry. In June they voted to tackle the apparently insoluble problem of pay arrears by selling Crown lands, a short-term solution which in the long term involved squandering the state's greatest asset. These efforts tended to sever the dangerous connection between soldiers and Levellers. The Levellers had even spoken up on behalf of Ireland, even for Irish Catholics, and begged the soldiers not to impose on that unhappy country the tyranny under which England groaned. However, many soldiers were willing to serve on the Irish expedition if their arrears were settled and their pay was increased. Parliament's readiness to tackle these grievances ensured that the army would fight unitedly in the Irish and Scottish campaigns which lay ahead. The Levellers, deprived of army support, were helpless, and during the summer the Council of State released Walwyn and Overton and permitted Lilburne a trial by jury which promptly acquitted him. The Commonwealth, once seeming so vulnerable before its many enemies, was now in a position to strike directly at them, for not only had the government restored the New Model Army to disciplined obedience but there had also been a remarkable transformation afloat: the emergence of a New Model Navy.

CHAPTER THREE

The Navy New Modelled

The sea's our own; and now all nations greet,
With bending sails, each vessel of our fleet;
Your power resounds as far as winds can blow
Or swelling sails upon the globe may go.

William Waller

A man-of-war is the best ambassador.

Oliver Cromwell

When Cromwell took over the government of the three kingdoms in 1653 he was possessed of two of the most remarkable weapons any government has ever had under its control. He had played a large part in the creation of the first, the New Model Army, and in a very real sense it had created him. The second was the Commonwealth Navy, a more recent phenomenon but a giant which no state in Europe could match, and which the chancelleries of Europe had been compelled to take seriously. For a decade it was almost continuously and usually successfully in action against a variety of enemies: Royalists, privateers, the French, the Portuguese, the North African corsairs, the Dutch Republic and the Spanish Empire.

The navy's rise in so short a time is one of the more remarkable occurrences of this remarkable period. The core of the Commonwealth navy was the old 'ship-money fleet' of Charles I. Although this force was a pigmy when compared with the fleets Admirals Blake and Deane, Monck and Montague would command, it possessed some powerful ships. The English were already building warships designed as large artillery-platforms able to mount heavy iron guns capable of delivering an awesome broadside. Ships designed on the contrary principle, lightly built and armed for speed, crammed with men, so that a battle could be won by charging, boarding and capturing the enemy, would find such broadsides devastating. The largest was the 1,500-ton *Sovereign of the Seas* (or *Royal Sovereign*), her three gundecks mounting more than 100 guns. The other ships of the fleet were more moderate in size and more useful in battle, for they could open their gunports in a heavy swell which the severely rolling *Sovereign* decidedly could not. Charles I's fleet was ill-adapted to its prime function, which was to clear the Channel of the Barbary corsairs and other pirates who had long infested it. The *Sovereign* cost ten times as much as one two-decked 'frigate' of the kind England so badly needed to protect her commerce in the 1630s. ('Frigate' then meant a medium-sized capital ship with two gundecks, swifter and more manoeuvrable than a first or second rate but not the fast scout with one main gundeck of Nelson's day.) Charles paid dearly for his error. His expensive fleet was left with its pay long in arrears and poorly provisioned, and his sailors repaid his neglect by joining the Parliamentary side during the Civil War. Like all civil wars this war was decided by campaigns on land, but the navy's contribution was important. In royal hands the navy would have blockaded London and could have brought the Parliamentary government to its knees. Instead, by helping to protect commerce from Royalist depredations it helped to sustain customs revenues which partly financed the war. The navy helped to frustrate the important royalist campaigns of 1643 by supplying and supporting Plymouth and Hull in the rear of Charles I's armies. It sent gunners and guns ashore to assist in such sieges as Newcastle and Bristol and transported stores and ammunition. The presence of the fleet's major men-of-war in the Channel probably discouraged Charles's brother-in-law, Louis XIII of France, from sending an expeditionary force to his assistance. During the war the navy had an effective lord high admiral in the Earl of Warwick and a number of resolute and skilled officers, of whom the most important was Warwick's vice-admiral, William Batten. The latter was a professional seaman who had been Surveyor of the Navy before the war. Like Warwick he was of the Presbyterian faction and the two commanders had tried to ensure that their officers shared their religious and political alignment. The Self-Denying Ordinance of 1645 compelled Warwick to surrender his command but Batten stayed on as vice-admiral and was left temporarily in command of the fleet.

The salutary relationship between Parliament and navy was not to survive the Royalist defeat in the Second Civil War as the New Model Army's increasing radicalism and thirst for vengeance on the king became more apparent. At least as early as 1646 Batten, like many moderates, had become fearful that the Independents in the Commons and in the New Model Army would bring down the old constitutional order. Towards the end of that year he had met the Scots Commissioners at Tynemouth, who had expressed similar anxieties to him. In 1647 when the army mutinied rather than disband and the Grandees took the side of their regiments, Batten was warned that the Independents might attempt to subvert the navy. In August the army occupied London and Independent MPs began treason proceedings against their leading opponents. Six of the accused fled abroad. Their ship was captured and carried into the Downs where Batten simply let them continue their flight. The outraged Independents decided the navy must be placed in more reliable hands. Having had no success in subverting the navy from below, they would subvert it from the top. In September Parliament nominated new admiralty commissioners, including Henry Marten and Colonel Thomas Rainborow. Batten was compelled to resign, to the deep displeasure of most of his officers, a hundred of whom had supported in writing his action over the six fugitives. This effectively demonstrated how far apart the fleet and the Independent-dominated government had drifted. Rainborow, who came of a naval family and had himself commanded a man-of-war as recently as 1643, now became vice-admiral and commander of the Winter Guard. Not only was he the obvious choice but the Independents were aware that he was a supporter of the Levellers and preferred to have him at a safe distance offshore. The House of Lords, however, even more fearful of his Leveller views than the Commons, blocked his appointment, and this left a dangerous vacuum. After the king's flight to the Isle of Wight in November the Commons, fearing the navy might help Charles to escape to France or Scotland, appointed Rainborow vice-admiral over the Lords' veto.

Rainborow moved quickly to send ships to suppress Irish privateers and to block any attempt by the Dutch admiral, Tromp, to rescue the king from Carisbrooke Castle. He kept a watchful eye on his captains ready to dismiss any political deviants. Meanwhile the Commons and the Navy Commissioners grappled with the difficult task of appointing new captains, a task made dangerously prolonged by their own divisions. By the spring of 1648 the situation throughout England and Wales appeared perilous. Oppressive county committees, the much resented garrisons of soldiers in every town of any significance, the resentment of heavy taxes which were needed to maintain that detested army, when combined with a political deadlock rendered civilians disaffected, indeed rebellious. There were several disturbances in February, fighting broke out in South Wales in March, while in May, as the Commissioners were at last achieving a list of appointments to the navy, including trustworthy military officers, Kent rose in rebellion. While Royalists naturally sought to exploit these outbreaks they were not their originators. A strong nostalgia for old ways, old rulers, old forms, was combined with a lively hatred of certain Independent leaders, both locally and in London. A rebellion in Kent was much more serious than one in South Wales, for the county included London's south bank and the Thames lifeline could be cut downstream by hostile forces on its banks. Moreover, Kent's Channel coast and control of the Thames estuary made it an obvious target for a continental invasion force. However, if rebellion there was potentially more dangerous it was also easier to suppress with so many regiments in or close to London. Fairfax soon defeated the rebels, storming Maidstone on 1 June, driving them from Rochester and Dover and compelling their surrender at Canterbury on 9 June. By then, however, as Commissioner Peter Pett had warned from Chatham, the poison had spread to the navy, and particularly to those ships lying in the Downs safe from Fairfax's regiments.

The government had directed Rainborow to station ships off the Medway to prevent movements in or out of Chatham and ordered the *Fellowship* and the *Hector* to put to sea to avoid capture by the rebels. Stronger guards must be posted to protect the giant *Sovereign* and the *Prince*, both laid up in Chatham docks. Trinity House, the association of shipmasters, was urged to keep its members loyal. These sensible decisions came far too late. Pett at Chatham soon found his communications with London cut while the rebels seized Upnor Castle, which guards the Medway. Captain Jervoise of the *Fellowship* allowed the rebels to take over his ship. Senior dockyard officials revealed themselves to be disaffected, and the rebels were soon in full control of the *Sovereign* and the *Prince*, even removing some of their guns and stores. A week before Fairfax stormed Maidstone Vice-Admiral Batten's former chaplain, Samuel Kem, succeeded in boarding the flagship *Constant Reformation* while Rainborow was absent. He had promised to bring over the navy, and mutiny soon broke out and spread to other ships. Officers who remained loyal to Parliament were imprisoned by their men. Rainborow and his family were seized, bundled into a boat and sent to London. Meanwhile the mutineers called for Warwick to resume command. The Derby House Committee sent urgently to Rear-Admiral Bethel at Portsmouth to take precautions against the mutiny spreading there, reinstated Warwick as lord high admiral on 29 May and he sailed for the Downs with an offer of indemnity if the mutineers submitted. Finding he could not persuade them to submit and powerless to compel their obedience, he returned to London, his mission a failure.

On land it was another matter. Fairfax's victorious advance soon ended the mutiny at Chatham and Pett recovered control of the *Fellowship* and the two battleships. On shore the mood swung against the rebellion but Fairfax could not persuade the seamen to submit. The mutinous fleet left the Downs and sailed for Yarmouth but failed to draw in the northern squadron at Harwich, then considered blockading the Thames (much their best strategy), but in the end resolved to place themselves under the command of the Prince of Wales and sailed to Helvoetsluys. The original six mutinous ships had been joined by three others. While two of Admiral Bethel's ships at Portsmouth remained loyal they would not fight against ships which were disloyal, nor put to sea until they were paid. In the end they were paid off at Deptford lest they sail to join the rebels. In effect half the Summer Guard of thirty-nine ships were either in rebel hands, or so out of control they had to be paid off, or so potentially mutinous no reliance could be placed on them. Fortunately Sir George Ayscue still commanded two loyal men-of-war in the west while the rumour that Rear-Admiral Penn, commanding in the Irish Sea, had defected proved to be false. This brought some comfort to the beleaguered government, but things were bad enough and grew worse. The mutiny of important elements of the fleet and the unreliability of crews which nominally remained loyal had been an enormous shock. Unlike Charles I in 1642, the government could not blame the mutiny on long arrears of pay and starving times at sea and ashore. The demands of the seamen were political, echoing the rebels of Kent. Down with tyrannical county committees; down with the New Model Army; down with heavy taxes; down with the sectaries who wished to destroy the king; down with the extremist Independents. It is possible that Batten may have played a part in producing the situation which the combination of Rainborow's appointment and the Kent rebellion had exploded. He had secretly negotiated with the Scottish Commissioners and offered to take some ships to rescue the king. He was alarmed when he was summoned to London (correctly assuming it was to answer for his misdeeds), and sailed off in the *Warwick*, a ship he jointly owned with his old commander, intending to join the mutinous ships at Helvoetsluys.

The mutineers had already left Helvoetsluys and, carrying the Prince of Wales and Prince Rupert with them, had appeared off Yarmouth, and then spent several weeks in the Downs. There Batten eventually found them, was knighted by the prince and restored to his old command. However, apart from picking up a few London-bound merchantmen, which were ransomed (to the disgust of the seamen who saw them as prizes to plunder), Batten and the princes achieved nothing. A command brought from the king to rescue him from Carisbrooke was ignored by the sailors and the Royalist officers were beginning to wonder whether they were the fleet's commanders or the sailors' prisoners. They were learning a bitter lesson: a mutinous fleet appears powerful but is of no more military significance than a mob, and the longer the mutiny continues the feebler it becomes. Warwick was desperately trying to put a fleet together to attack them, despite the problem of assembling trustworthy crews, and despite the hostility of the majority of Trinity House pilots who were petitioning for direct negotiations with the king. After an abortive descent on the Thames at the insistence of the mutineers, who hoped to detach the ships which Warwick was assembling, the fleet returned to Helvoetsluys. There in the autumn Warwick pursued them, anchoring not far away although a flotilla commanded by Tromp soon arrived to interpose and prevent any assault on them. After weeks of negotiation Warwick contrived to get several ships to come over to him while Prince Rupert saved the rest by moving them into the safety of the inner harbour. Their top-masts and yards were sent down, some of their guns unshipped, and their crews were lodged ashore for the winter. The crews' morale had been lowered by desertion and disorder and by their experience of the harsh and dictatorial Rupert. The flotilla, now shrunk to about a dozen ships, seemed only a feeble shadow of the fleet Batten had commanded in 1647. Warwick decided they were no danger to his government's interests and sailed for home on 21 November. He foolishly left no ships on watch as a precaution and Rupert promptly celebrated his departure by preparing his ships for a change of base. On 21 January the flotilla weighed for Kinsale in Ireland. However, if Rupert believed that the mutinies, the resistance of Trinity House masters and the hostility of the English civilian population were going to make his sortie rewarding and with little hazard he would be disillusioned. He had the melancholy distinction of being the opponent on whom the New Modelled Navy cut its teeth.

The new modelling of the navy began shortly after the death of the king. After Warwick's return to the Downs with the fleet he was left in command there but not trusted. When he named Admiral Bethel to command the Winter Guard he was sternly told that the appointment was quashed, and he found he could do nothing without Parliament's express permission. No doubt the government wished to be rid of him, for not only was Warwick's loyalty dubious, he was ageing and unfit. However, they would have hesitated to put any strain on the navy's allegiance at this delicate time when they were accomplishing the judicial destruction of the king. Warwick himself kept a discreetly low profile, doing nothing openly to discourage the Regicide. Meanwhile the government moved first to strengthen its administrative hand by expanding the role of the parliamentary Naval Committee from merely financial matters to the full range of naval affairs and strengthening its Radical membership by the addition, among others, of Cromwell and Ireton. In February 1649 they finally sacked Warwick. Rainborow had been assassinated by cavaliers late in 1648 but the government was still determined to have their navy commanded by trusted soldiers, particularly since they knew it must be expanded rather than laid up. Since the navy would be compelled to operate in several theatres at a time, they divided the command, appointing three respected soldiers, Colonels Robert Blake, Richard Deane and Edward Popham. Popham had commanded men-of-war in the 1630s. Deane, who had been one of Charles I's judges, had been a merchant shipmaster, and had been considered as a possible replacement for Batten as vice-admiral as early as 1647. Blake, who was already aged fifty, was the son of a wealthy Somerset merchant who had abandoned his dream of becoming an Oxford don on inheriting his father's business in 1625. As a civilian he could only have been to sea, if at all, as a supercargo. Yet this unlikely appointee was destined to be ranked second only to Nelson in the roll of British admirals. Moreover, Blake established the navy as a formidable force in Europe and the Mediterranean almost from scratch, whereas Nelson rose in a navy which was already dominant. Blake was not one of Cromwell's circle but would have earned that soldier's respect by his extraordinary defence of Lyme Regis against heavy odds, and then for his initiative in surprising and seizing Taunton and holding it against Lord Hopton for a year until he could be relieved. Earlier he had persisted in defending a fort at Bristol after the town had been surrendered, and Rupert had ordered him hanged under the rules of war. However, he was finally allowed to march out with the rest, a clemency uncharacteristic of Rupert which he must later have regretted. Blake, who was member for Bridgwater, was a Presbyterian in religion (his soldier's sense of discipline prejudicing him against the sects) but a republican in politics, and so had survived Pride's Purge.[1]

Trusted though they were, these generals-at-sea did not retain all the powers Warwick had wielded during the Civil War. The Council of State kept authority in its own hands, although it soon delegated its duties to the Admiralty Committee, which not only supervised naval finances and fitting out and allocating ships but also the vital function of choosing naval officers. The committee's principal member was the experienced Sir Henry Vane, Treasurer of the Navy since 1642 and an admiralty commissioner since 1645. Another was Valentine Walton, Cromwell's brother-in-law, and four Regicides joined later: Bond, Challenor, Purefoy and Stapley. The navy was firmly in Radical hands. The system has been criticized as slow and cumbersome, and indeed Vane himself called in 1651 for a new body of full-time, permanent, professional administrators, although unsuccessfully. Nevertheless the Commonwealth's system of naval administration served it well.[2] On 16 January the Purged Parliament appointed sixteen 'Regulators' who would investigate all branches of the navy, including the dockyards and the corps of officers, and who would hopefully rid it of the 'manifest distempers' which had proved so dangerous during the mutinies of the previous year and of officers and officials who were unreliable and inefficient. The Regulators axed Batten as Navy Commissioner in absentia, and the Master of Trinity House, Richard Crandley, who had proved too committed to the monarchy the previous autumn. The resolute Peter Pett at Chatham, scion of a famous shipbuilding dynasty, naturally survived, and the other appointments proved loyal and hard-working. Trinity House was reformed, its new committee including two regulators, a navy commissioner and General-at-Sea Deane himself. The Customs was placed in the hands of a new syndicate. Naturally it would have been utterly destructive to purge the docks of all formerly mutinous master-craftsmen, carpenters, sailmakers, gunsmiths, etc., and the ships' crews of all warrant officers, boatswains and gunners. The regulators kept on contrite dockside craftsmen, and left it to the generals-at-sea to pardon those of their crews they considered once more reliable. Moreover, retaining the loyalty of the crews, both officers and men, was assisted by policies designed to make naval service more attractive by making pay higher and more regular, and redressing the grievances about prize money. This policy was to reach its full flower during the Dutch War.

Retaining or dismissing captains was a delicate, much-debated problem. Of the forty-three commanders named for the Summer Guard of 1647 twenty-seven vanished into permanent retirement and fully a quarter of the survivors of the purges of 1648 now found themselves on shore, Warwick's friend Bethel among them. Some captains may not have wished to serve the Republic, others were not invited to do so. Loyal men replaced them, although the process was slow and difficult. By January 1649 Robert Moulton commanded the fleet in the Downs. He had served in the parliamentary navy since 1643, and possessed considerable shipping interests now managed by his son. Edward Hall, whose Radical views on the monarchy had brought about his dismissal in 1646, now found himself a flag-captain in 1649, a rear-admiral in 1650 and commanding the Mediterranean squadron in 1651. In 1649 Sir George Ayscue, who had commanded parliamentary warships in the Civil War, was appointed to the vital command of the Irish Sea squadron. Nehemiah Bourne, who had settled in Massachusetts in 1637 where he became a considerable ship-owner, had returned to fight as a major in Rainborow's regiment. He declined a naval post in 1649 because of his heavy commercial commitments, but in 1650 Vane persuaded him to take a commission and he was to play a strong supporting role to Blake, Deane and Monck during the Dutch War. Even more important was John Lawson, also recruited by Vane in 1650. Trained in that harsh nursery of seamen, the East Coast collier fleet, he had commanded a hired vessel in the Civil War which he partly owned before serving for five years as a captain of foot. He too would rise to senior command in the coming naval wars. In the new navy the tendency to employ the title 'general-at-sea' rather than 'admiral' for the highest ranks only emphasized the army's control.[3]

Once purged of the disaffected and administratively reorganized, the navy could safely be strengthened. The Commonwealth faced an array of enemies. Scotland and Ireland had proclaimed Charles II. A descent on England by an Irish army, probably led by Charles himself, appeared a real possibility. The Scots had changed from doubtful friends to enemies. Moreover, the authority of the Commonwealth must be asserted in the North American colonies, especially Royalist Maryland, Virginia and Barbados. The kings of France and Spain would probably shrink from any armed intervention on behalf of Charles, but they would cheerfully license privateers to plunder English commerce unless such overt hostility was made unbearably expensive. Both the Channel Islands and the Scilly Isles were nests of Royalist privateers, as to a lesser degree was the Isle of Man.

Finally there was Rupert's substantial flotilla at Kinsale, which was already preying on commerce bound for London or the western outports. Only a fleet which was both loyal and efficient and also larger than any England had possessed since the Armada campaign could tackle these widely spread problems. As early as March 1649 the Commonwealth began ordering new warships. During the next three years twenty were built, and twenty-five were purchased or taken as prizes, almost doubling the navy's size. Ideology demanded the existing great ships be renamed: the *Charles* became the *Liberty*, the *Henrietta Maria* the *Paragon*, the *Royal Prince* the *Resolution*, while the giant *Royal Sovereign* became simply the *Sovereign*, a reference to England's sovereignty of the seas which the Commonwealth was determined to establish. Three new frigates built in 1650 were named *Fairfax*, *Speaker* and *President*, and after the Dutch War a 1,000-ton first rate would rumble down the slipways christened *Naseby*. This followed a trend to name new naval vessels after Ironside victories which the *Worcester* (1651) continued. Meanwhile on new and existing ships gangs of craftsmen carved the Commonwealth's coat-of-arms on their high elaborate sterns. The shipbuilding and refitting and purchasing took time, however. In the spring of 1649 the Commonwealth government had no time to spare because its problems were immediate.

Blake, Popham and Deane had already received a formidable set of instructions. Rupert's flotilla and all royalist privateers must be sunk or captured; the navy must prevent any invasion from continental Europe; all supplies for Ormonde's Royalist army in Ireland must be intercepted; the fisheries and English trade routes must be protected. Meanwhile, to emphasize the fearsome power the new government controlled two more of the Navy's 'great ships', the *George* and the *Unicorn*, would be brought from reserve, fitted out, and sent to show the flag off the Flemish coast. Rupert had sailed on 21 January and had reached Kinsale without hindrance. Moulton's flotilla in the Downs had endured the humiliation of seeing him sail past unscathed, but they had been too few to tackle him. Parliament, panicked by the mutiny, had dispersed the fleet so that any future disaffection would not infect the whole. Rupert's sortie proved traumatic for English merchant ships entering the Western Approaches during the ensuing weeks. It would have been even worse if Rupert had succeeded in combining into one squadron his own flotilla and all other Irish privateers which could have given him a force of more than thirty ships. Nor could he simply expand his fleet by adding prizes to it because he suffered from the weakness common to privateering commodores: while he could turn some prizes into privateers he could never find sufficient mariners and gunners to man them. Meanwhile Dunkirkers and other Royalist privateersmen threatened the Straits of Dover and the North Sea and found rich pickings. In July Thomas Plunket, a former Parliamentarian now turned Royalist, who commanded a flotilla of privateers, attacked a convoy off Newcastle, scattering the out-gunned escort and capturing thirty prizes. Eight merchantmen were seized off Flamborough Head in August, while in September the Council learned that sixteen ships were fitting out at Dunkirk and Ostend to attack shipping within the Thames itself. Constant complaints of privateering reached the ears of the Council from London merchants, who were currently their warm supporters but liable to become their virulent critics unless matters improved.

It was clear that Rupert must be the first priority but Moulton's ships in the Downs were too few to mount an attack on Kinsale, so the Council sent his squadron westward to guard the approaches to Plymouth until reinforcements arrived.[4] The Council was struggling to mobilize all of the English fleet save the two first-rates, *Sovereign* and *Resolution*, for the Commonwealth had resolved to set out a strong Summer Guard of forty-nine warships and eight armed merchantmen, which would keep the sea for eight months rather than the usual six. The dockyards were severely strained by these demands so the Council sent ships westward as they became available rather than waiting until all were ready. Having taken steps to protect the North Sea and Iceland fisheries, to convoy merchantmen to Holland and to dispatch the *Nonsuch* to stop up Ostend's privateers, Popham sailed in April in the *Liberty*, a second-rate, with the *Constant Warwick*, *Assurance* and *Increase*. He successfully rendezvoused with Moulton off Lundy on 20 April. There in thick weather the two commanders scored the Republic's first naval success: the capture of the *Thomas*, a member of Rupert's squadron, and a Guinea Company frigate lost to the Royalists the previous year. Ayscue sailed from Chatham in the *St George* to take up command of the Irish Sea squadron. His vice-admiral William Penn also posted off to Portsmouth to take command of the *Lion*. He was soon sailing westward in consort with a powerfully armed merchantman, *Hercules*, and the *Victory* soon followed. Finally in May Blake sortied in the *Triumph* with four other ships.

Having united with Moulton and Popham Blake arrived off Kinsale on 21 May. Telescopes from the *Triumph*'s foretop soon identified Rupert's three largest ships, the *Constant Reformation*, *Swallow* and *Convertine*, together with other former naval vessels, two prizes and three smaller vessels.[5] It was a very strong force for a privateering commodore but no match for the heavily armed men-of-war which now besieged it. Rupert was bottled up. Deane went off to serve on land and Popham sailed for home to report. It is symptomatic of how serious the maritime situation had been that Parliament promptly called for a day of thanksgiving at his news. This was somewhat premature because Blake could not reach Rupert behind Kinsale's strong fortifications. Meanwhile Rupert's sailors, deprived of prizes, grew mutinous, while those he had pressed into service from prizes would happily have killed him and threatened to do so. Cromwell's army arrived in Ireland in August. However, it came by Dublin and its first lunge was north to Drogheda. Robert Blake, the only general-at-sea left off Kinsale, continued his long blockade in frustrated isolation. Relief was at hand, although not in the form Blake sought. The English garrison at Cork declared for the Commonwealth on 16 October and surrendered the town. This exposed Kinsale, only seventeen miles away, but just when Blake was planning to take advantage of the port's vulnerability dirty weather drove him to shelter at Milford Haven. As soon as the weather moderated Rupert, who had been negotiating with the King of Portugal for a base at Lisbon, seized his opportunity and headed south with the seven ships for which he could muster crews.

Rupert in Lisbon was a worse thorn in the Commonwealth's flesh than bottled up in Kinsale. In Kinsale he would be captured as soon as the army and navy could mount a combined operation. In Lisbon he would be under the protection of the King of Portugal. Moreover, the estuary of the Tagus was a splendid base from which to prey on English shipping coasting up from the Straits, while cruises further west might find rich pickings among the West Indies, North American and Canary Island trades. In the spring of 1650 watchers at the mouth of the Tagus saw the sails of a considerable English fleet steering for the entrance. Blake had arrived at last and quickly sent a polite message to King John expressing the hope that there would be no objection to his mounting an attack on the privateer flotilla. Remembering how Warwick had been criticized for not attacking the Royalist fleet at Helvoetsluys as soon as he arrived, thereby presenting the Dutch with a fait accompli, Blake did not wait for royal permission. However, when he tried to get at his enemy the wind dropped, shore forts opened fire, and *force majeure* had to be abandoned for the tedious uncertainties of diplomacy. Blake had Charles Vane to act as his political agent and sent him to King John to open negotiations, reinforcing him with Vice-Admiral Moulton. The king rejected all three of Blake's alternative proposals: to hand over Rupert and his fleet, to allow Blake to attack it, or to order both fleets to sea. Meanwhile two French men-of-war arrived at the mouth of the Tagus and were quickly and peacefully 'bagged', the more peacefully because their commanders imagined that Blake's squadron was Rupert's flotilla. Blake felt he lacked the authority to make war on the French navy (although he was soon to receive it) and so he released them. They promptly sailed up the Tagus to make common cause with Rupert.

It was clear that Rupert could only be destroyed at the risk of war with Portugal. After a tedious period occasionally enlivened by such stirring incidents as an attempt by Royalist boat-crews to blow up one of Blake's ships and an occasional punch-up between the rival crews ashore, Popham arrived with reinforcements. The Commonwealth government had grasped the nettle, and decided that Rupert must be destroyed. Any Portuguese ships which tried to intervene would be fired on. As for the French navy, it was now considered an enemy to be attacked on sight. A few days earlier Blake on his own initiative had seized nine English ships, hired by the Portuguese, which formed part of the outward bound Brazil fleet. King John reluctantly prepared for war – the more reluctantly as his impoverished country was already at war with Spain and the vital Brazil trade depended on hired English ships. Indeed the Portuguese navy must have been instructed to do no more than go through the motions. Twice Rupert and Portuguese ships headed out to sea, twice the Portuguese vessels turned for home at the approach of the Commonwealth fleet, and Rupert had no choice but to follow them to safety. Finally, Blake, whose fleet had been much depleted by the necessity of sending ships home to refit and reprovision, seized the initiative by attacking the inward bound Brazil fleet, capturing seven ships and sinking another. Having triumphantly carried off his prizes to Cadiz for repairs and then sent them home under Vice-Admiral Badiley, Blake returned to the Tagus to discover that the bird had once more flown. King John sympathized with the Stuart cause but enough was enough. It had been made clear to Prince Rupert that he had worn out his welcome.

Rupert was now without a proper base and his days were numbered, although before he was scotched he could do damage. Disguising his ship as Blake's flagship he lured two prizes into his arms in the Straits and burned several other English ships in Spanish harbours, despite the protests of the port authorities. Then Blake, hot in pursuit, caught the Royalists early in November. The *Henry* (ex-*Roebuck*) surrendered without a fight, and five other ships were run ashore and burned. Only Rupert and Maurice, absent in pursuit of a prize, escaped. Rupert now sought refuge at Toulon where the French authorities were as eager to help the Royalists as by now the Spanish authorities were eager to help the Commonwealth Navy. However, the price of French support was Rupert's reluctant (and duplicitous) promise to harry Spanish rather than English shipping. The French saw Rupert only as a possible help in their war. They were rapidly losing interest in the Stuart cause, considering it hopeless. Rupert succeeded in patching together a flotilla of five vessels with French help but the client quickly betrayed the patron, for after a deceptive lunge eastward into the Mediterranean which succeeded in deceiving Admiral Penn, Blake's successor, as to his intentions, he abandoned the Mediterranean and for the next two years ranged down the African coast and across to the Caribbean. He was a spent force, however, helpless to injure his enemies whose superior gunfire kept him from the key trade routes. He quickly lost his flotilla, the largest ship being cast away with all hands in the Azores. He returned to France with his single remaining ship in 1653 but he had been of no significance from the time he fled the Mediterranean.[6] Blake had returned triumphantly to London in February 1651 where he was voted £1,000 by a grateful Parliament.

They had reason for their gratitude. Blake's busy fleet, potent and conspicuous whether in the Tagus, at Cadiz or in the Mediterranean ports of Spain, had made a powerful impression on the Spanish government. Spanish officials were amazed and bewildered by the number and size of the English warships which seemed to pass through Cadiz in an endless stream. Meanwhile Penn's squadron was cruising to Sardinia, Minorca and Leghorn, and Blake had detached yet another squadron to escort the Levant convoy to Aleppo. They were delighted to find so formidable a Commonwealth navy in existence; one capable of assaulting the French and which had already damaged the fragile economy of their other enemy, Portugal. It was England's naval might which brought official recognition of the new government along with a Spanish ambassador to make his bow shortly after an unofficial French negotiator had been booted out. Madrid was happy to receive the cooperation and friendship of even a Regicide regime against her old French enemy now that it wielded such a powerful naval weapon. Correspondingly, Mazarin's enthusiasm for continued naval hostilities rapidly waned in the face of the exploits of Blake and his fellow generals-at-sea.

Blake was given a rapturous welcome by the town of Taunton but he did not have long in which to enjoy his shore leave, for a new crisis the following month hastened him to sea. There were three centres of Royalist privateering which remained to be suppressed: Jersey, the Scilly Isles and the Isle of Man. Sir George Ayscue had been given command of a small but potent force of four ships and perhaps 500 or more infantry with which to secure the submission of the island of Barbados. En route he was to call at the Scillies and suppress that nest of pirates commanded by Sir John Grenville based at St Mary's. Blake was to be charged with the simpler and more leisurely task of dealing with the Isle of Man and was given a small force of fourth rates, with his flag in the *Phoenix*, and two larger armed merchantmen. Before either admiral had sailed news reached London that Tromp was on his way to the Scillies to deal with Grenville, whose privateers had taken several Dutch prizes. The Council was instantly alarmed that Tromp might have been ordered to seize the islands, which presented the horrid possibility that they might become an even more damaging base for Dutch privateers under the protection of the Dutch navy. Blake was ordered to the Scillies.[7] Ayscue would serve under him there before continuing on to Barbados. Blake must learn what were Tromp's orders and frustrate them if they involved his seizing St Mary's, while assuring Tromp that the English government had no objection to the Dutch regaining stolen property or seeking reparation from Grenville. Blake must then drive the Royalists from Scilly and make safe the Western Approaches.

Sir John Grenville appears to have combined insolent stupidity with an incapacity to face reality. Permitting his privateers to prey on Dutch shipping when Charles II desperately needed the friendship of the Netherlands is sufficient evidence of stupidity; refusing to pay compensation or restore prizes to the Dutch government demonstrates his insolence; his belief that he could hold out in St Mary's against the Commonwealth navy, not to mention the Dutch fleet, and his hope that he might soon be relieved, demonstrates his flight from reality. When Tromp arrived at St Mary's with only three ships Grenville released two batches of Dutch prisoners but refused to negotiate any return of prizes or payment of compensation (he had already sold both ships and cargos for much less than their worth). Tromp had barely departed in search of the rest of his fleet when Blake and Ayscue arrived. Ayscue had served there years before and knew that the key to St Mary's was the island of Tresco. With Tresco in their hands the victualling ships could lie safe from storms in the channel between Tresco and Bryther, St Mary's could be close blockaded, all privateering would necessarily cease for the ships in harbour could not get out and those at sea would fall into their hands as they returned. The point of Grenville's resistance would then be at an end and he might be induced to surrender on terms or St Mary's could be stormed in a combined operation and his garrison put to the sword. The capture of Tresco required an armed assault because Grenville, well aware of its significance, had garrisoned it with soldiers and artillery. The latter was taken from two frigates which Grenville had stationed to guard the entrance to the channel on which lay New Grimsby, where Blake had hoped to moor his victualling vessels. If this weakened the frigates they still proved too much for Blake's fourth rates because of the narrownesss of the channel, so Blake decided to attack the island's other side. Colonel William Clarke, who commanded the soldiers embarked for the Barbados expedition, launched an unsuccessful two-pronged attack. Major Morris's assault was led astray by local pilots influenced by fear rather than Royalism. Clarke's assault failed when his men were driven back despite all his efforts to rally them. The crews of the overcrowded boats, packed with inexperienced men, could not face the volleys of Grenville's soldiers. In the morning Blake rallied the soldiers with hot food and drink and a stiffening of 200 sailors to get them ashore. After a hard fight the defenders broke and 176 surrendered. Clarke lost four men killed, the defenders about a dozen. That night Grenville and some officers escaped to St Mary's, but forty Royalists were drowned. Tresco and the two frigates surrendered. Grenville's position was now hopeless.

Blake, knowing that heavy casualties must accompany an assault on

St Mary's Castle, negotiated a surrender on generous terms by which the Irish would be returned to Ireland, the English to Scotland. Grenville went as a prisoner to Plymouth until the government ratified the terms, but would then be permitted to depart for the continent. It was a remarkable triumph for Blake and his sailors. Lacking the navy's capital ships, with only a scratch flotilla together with Ayscue's support, he had captured the Scillies for the loss of only four men. He had rooted out a base of privateersmen, conciliated the local inhabitants by the generosity of his terms (liberty of person, immunity for their property, retention of all their old privileges), and taken prisoner along with Governor Grenville '300 Irish, 120 English, thirteen colonels, four lieutenant-colonels, nine majors, ten lieutenants, six ensigns, thirty-two gentlemen, one bishop, two doctors, two parsons and two Popish priests', as a contemporary account listed them. (Either St Mary's had become a nesting place for a ragbag collection of refugee Royalist officers or Grenville's little 'army' was somewhat top-heavy.) Blake had also set free three colonels of the parliamentary army in Ireland captured while on passage from Ireland to London. In addition he had shown some diplomatic skills in his dealings with Admiral Tromp who turned up twice with his fleet, first during operations and then after the surrender. Tromp did not recover his prizes or extract compensation but at least Blake seems to have soothed Dutch sensibilities. All these achievements were warmly appreciated by his masters when he returned to the mainland on 28 June.

It shows the confidence the government now had in Robert Blake that when they were faced by the crisis of the invasion of England by a Scottish army with Charles II at its head, the government sent him ashore to take command of the regiments still in the western counties, the local commander, General Disbrowe, having been despatched to the Midlands. He was not to be a 'sailor on horseback' for long, because only twelve days later he received orders to return to sea. This alteration was occasioned by the death of his old friend Popham. He hoisted his flag in the *Victory* in the Downs charged with emphasizing to foreign observers that the crisis had in no way left the country vulnerable to foreign enemies. On 3 September the defeat of Charles at Worcester freed Blake for his last task of an eventful year. He must reduce the last Royalist privateering stronghold: Jersey.

The Isle of Man had been taken by an expeditionary force led by Colonels Thomas Birch and Robert Duckenfield. Now only Jersey was left. The island was held by Sir George Carteret, a capable Cavalier commander whose firm control of his privateers had prevented any of the follies permitted by Grenville. The season was far advanced for campaigning, the waters around Jersey rock-strewn and dangerous. Blake hastened to put together a scratch squadron from the ships which were fitting out for the Winter Guard.[8] The *Victory* retired to Chatham for rest and repair while he hoisted his flag in the

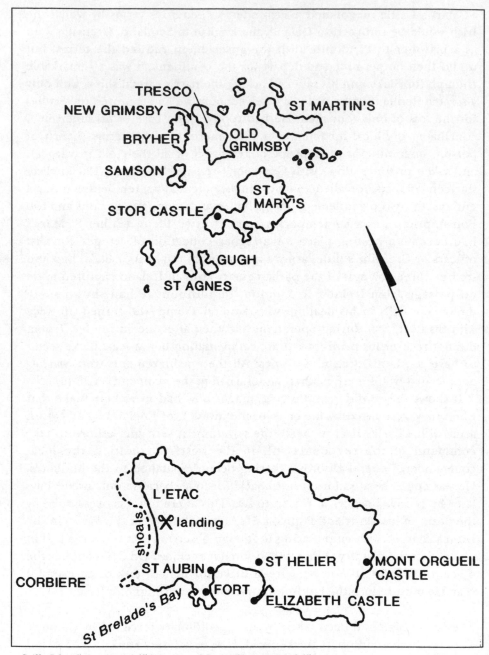

Scilly Isles Operation, 1651 (top) and Jersey Operations, 1651

38-gun *Happy Entrance.* On 17 October Blake sortied from Weymouth with about 2,000 soldiers, including Colonel James Heane's infantry regiment, six companies of Hardress Waller's infantry and two troops of horse. His fleet had now grown to eighty sail, many of them transports and victuallers, together with thirteen men-of-war ranging from the *Happy Entrance* down to the 10-gun *Hart.*[9]

Blake was pressed for time, for not only was this expedition setting out late in the season, but his ships were already earmarked for other duties. When the fleet arrived in St Ouen's Bay, Jersey, on 20 October Carteret showed his mettle by driving off a proffered flag of truce with musket fire. He had been aware of the task force's arrival off Sark late the previous evening and had mustered 2,000 foot and 300 cavalry and six small cannon. This was a formidable force to oppose the landing of an expeditionary force no more numerous, although it had the backing of the ships' guns, and its soldiers were more experienced and determined than Jersey's militia whose Royalist commitment was dubious. Blake sailed his fleet to St Brelade's Bay while Carteret marched his men across the neck of cliffs to oppose any attempt at a landing there. Blake soon saw that St Brelade's would not do but cruised up and down to keep his enemy guessing, sending his frigates into St Aubin's Bay to destroy shipping there. On 23 October the fleet returned to St Ouen's Bay to assault Carteret's positions. No sooner were the men in the boats than an approaching storm caused Blake to abort the operation because his chief ships would need to draw off into deeper water to ride it out. However, the delay was put to good use, the fleet sailing towards the far end of the bay where loomed the headland of Grand L'Etaquerel. This meant that Carteret, who had dug earthworks along the rising ground behind the beach, had to march his men in tandem with the ships in case Blake's army struck at the far end of the beach. Since they had already made a tiring counter-march from St Brelade's Bay to St Ouen's they were now exhausted, soaked by continual rain squalls, cold and hungry. Militia in better case would have found an Ironside assault a daunting prospect. These exhausted men had no stomach for a battle. Carteret knew this but his seamen assured him that Blake's transports were too large to get close enough inshore to land the regiments. He therefore sent his horse to forage inland and rested his troops on the foreshore. Soon, to their astonishment, in the failing light of an autumn evening the dim shapes of ships could be seen warping their way in by putting out their anchors and hauling up to them. Blake knew he could not get his large transports close enough inshore so he placed his smaller vessels in the van and, according to the accounts of Royalists present, constructed bridges from ship to ship, big to little, to get the men ashore. Remembering Tresco Blake sent in well-armed sailors with the van. Carteret did his best but most of the demoralized foot fled at the first touch, and he could muster only about a hundred of his horse for the rest had deserted. The dragoons charged bravely, trying to defeat the landing at the water's edge before it could consolidate. The engagement was hot until the dragoons' commander was killed, at which the rest retired discouraged. If Carteret had possessed reliable infantry the outcome might have been different. The following morning Blake completed the landing of stores and ammunition, which was as well because another gale soon drove him off shore. Only four or five men had been killed in the landing but heavy casualties were soon exacted by natural forces. When the fleet returned to anchor in St Aubin's Bay the Tresco frigate struck a rock and sank with 300 hands including her captain, William Blake, the admiral's cousin.

Blake now returned to Plymouth, arriving on 21 October, leaving Colonel Heane to subjugate the whole island. This Heane did very efficiently, persuading the garrison of Mont Orgueil Castle to surrender on generous terms over the protests of Sir Phillip Carteret, the governor's brother. The castle, which was too strong to storm and invulnerable even to mortar fire, contained forty-two guns and a thousand arms, with two months' provisions for seventy men. Governor Carteret, bottled up with his lady and a strong garrison in Elizabeth Castle, hoped to hold out, although Charles II had sent word he could surrender at discretion for there was no hope of relief. After a mortar bombardment had exploded a powder magazine the garrison lost heart and Carteret could no longer rely on them. He surrendered on 12 December and was allowed to sail for St Malo. His soldiers were offered the options of going to France, to Virginia or to England. Fifty-three guns, one hundred and fifty muskets and eight vessels sheltering under the castle's guns fell into the besiegers' hands. Blake's expedition had been a complete success. Since he went to sea his exploits, characterized by sound judgement, a shrewd use of available resources and flexibility of response, had demonstrated that not only did the Commonwealth have a navy, they had found an admiral.

During the three years from the summer of 1648 to the autumn of 1651 the navy had passed from a widespread mutiny, which took a substantial portion of the Summer Guard over to the Royalists in Holland, to a 'new-modelled', disciplined, greatly enlarged fleet, soon to be recognized as the most formidable in Europe. It had made the English sea-lanes safer by overwhelming the last Royalist privateering strongholds and in the course of pursuing and scotching the last Royalist squadron had become an important presence in the Mediterranean. The navy had made the King of Portugal see reason, and shown it was well able to wage a maritime war with Mazarin's France. Meanwhile, as the navy eliminated the danger of foreign invasion Cromwell and his legions had set out to challenge enemies nearer home.

CHAPTER FOUR

The Conquest of Ireland

I had rather be overrun with a Cavalierish interest [than] a Scotch interest;
I had rather be overrun with a Scotch interest than an Irish interest; and I
think of all, this is the most dangerous.

Oliver Cromwell to the Council of State, 1649[1]

Ireland represented unfinished business, indeed scandalously procrastinated business, to the Commonwealth government. The rebellion in
Ireland of 1641, which had helped to transform the constitutional struggle
between Crown and Parliament in England into a military conflict,
remained unavenged, indeed unsuppressed. This meant that Ireland was a
potential base and springboard for an invasion of England by Charles II and
a Catholic–Royalist army. During the Civil War and its aftermath Parliament
had been too preoccupied with its fight for survival at home and the
conflicts among the victors to be able to tackle Ireland. In the meantime
matters in Ireland had naturally not lain dormant. Protestants remained
garrisoned in Londonderry and some other Ulster fortified towns, in
Drogheda and Dublin and some towns in Munster, but the Catholics,
including the Irish Catholics and the Anglo-Irish ('Old English'), loosely
controlled most of the rest of the country. In view of the fact that the
Protestants were themselves divided between Royalists and Parliamentarians, it might seem surprising that the Irish were unable to conquer the
surviving Protestant enclaves.

The reasons for Protestant survival after 1641 are complex, and beyond
the scope of a study of the Interregnum.[2] Suffice it to say that the Protestants in Ireland tended to be divided between Royalists, Parliamentarians
and in Ulster the Presbyterian Scots. The Ulster Scots had received the
reinforcement of a Scottish army under Sir Robert Monro in 1642. They
naturally tended to side with parliamentary sympathizers although the later
quarrels between Parliament and Scots were echoed in Ireland. These
Protestant divisions would have helped the Catholic cause had they not
been bedevilled by their own bitter divisions. The Old Irish tended to look
with suspicion at the Anglo-Irish even though they were predominantly
Catholic, and with fear tinged with hatred at Protestant Irish (or English)
Royalists. This fear was well founded: the Protestant Royalists tended to find

their loyalty to the king sapped by their land hunger. If the king won his struggle in England with Irish help after the Irish had defeated the small parliamentary and Scottish forces in Ireland, what hope would there be of dispossessing the Irish Catholics of their land? The massacres of 1641 had been exaggerated but massacres had occurred and must be avenged, not least because land hunger could only be satisfied if they were.[3] Charles I ignored these predatory preoccupations of his Protestant Irish supporters because he dreamed of bringing to England an Irish army, enlisted from both races and creeds, to defeat the parliamentary forces. The price he would offer would be toleration (in practice though not in law) of the Mass and the guaranteeing of his Irish subjects' rights and title to their lands. This plan would alienate his English subjects, let alone the Protestant Irish, and many at his headquarters strenuously opposed it, causing the king to move towards it slowly and secretly.

The king had in Ireland a loyal servant, the Marquess of Ormonde, who was a better diplomat than a general, although his role demanded the skills of both.[4] Ormonde belonged to the Anglo-Irish aristocracy but had been brought up a Protestant as a ward of the Crown. A general in the royal forces which were supposed to crush the Rebellion, he had been kept largely inactive by the Lords Justices into whose hands the government of Ireland had devolved after the execution of Strafford and the death of Christopher Wandesford his successor. However, in 1642 Ormonde defeated a force of rebels and temporarily quieted Connaught. In 1643 the king ordered Ormonde to negotiate with the rebels and he won a twelve-month truce, although the Ulster chieftain, Owen Rowe O'Neill, ignored it. As a result Ormonde was able to send the king about 5,000 reinforcements through Chester, many of them English and the great majority Protestants. In January 1644 the king appointed him Lord Lieutenant and later that year he sent some Irish troops to aid Montrose's Scottish campaign. His prime task, however, from 1643 until his master's defeat, was to negotiate a treaty with the Catholic Confederation of Kilkenny, the clergy-dominated rebel government, which it was hoped would produce an Irish army large enough to invade England and restore Charles to power. Ormonde found this task hard going. The Confederation wanted guarantees for their religion which went far beyond the king's offer of 'toleration by neglect', guarantees of their rights and title to their lands, amnesty and oblivion for the excesses of 1641, and a more independent Irish Parliament – in fact home rule. The more the king yielded to these demands the more his support would ebb among his Protestant subjects. Nevertheless, Ormonde urged Charles to concede enough of them to get his army, and quickly too, for in 1646 the only port still in Royalist hands, Chester, was already besieged. However, Ormonde's problems were compounded by divisions between the Old Irish and the Anglo-Irish, and even within the ranks of the Old Irish themselves, and his situation had been made worse by the presence of the Papal Nuncio Rinuccini, a member of the Vatican faction which condemned treaties with heretics. (Rinuccini had even excommunicated the rebel government for continuing to negotiate with the king, at which his victims defiantly appealed to Rome against him.) Despite these problems Ormonde did achieve a treaty in 1646 although too late to help his master's cause.

However, if the Royalist cause was lost in England in 1646 the parliamentary cause in Ireland was far from won. The Protestant position had deteriorated after the Old Irish repudiated Ormonde's peace treaty in 1646 and Owen Rowe O'Neill defeated General Robert Monro's Ulster army at Benburb. This victory and O'Neill's close association with Rinuccini's extreme clerical party appeared to make his army a threat to Dublin. Ormonde thankfully handed over the city to the parliamentary forces in 1647. With the king in the hands of his enemies England's and Ireland's destinies now rested on negotiations between the two. Powerless to help the king further Ormonde left Ireland, had an interview with Charles at Hampton Court and then travelled on to long overdue recuperation in Paris, and so happily missed the second Civil War which might have brought him to the scaffold. Since the battle of Naseby, where the king's secret correspondence fell into the hands of Cromwell's cavalry, Parliament had been aware of what the king and Ormonde had been planning. The defeat of the king had averted the danger but England's rulers in 1649 felt great anxiety that the threat might revive on behalf of Charles II; all the more because Ormonde had returned to Ireland late in 1648. Following the king's execution in January and the horror and indignation it aroused among both Protestants and Catholics in Ireland, and with Rinuccini having departed for Rome early in February, Ormonde successfully negotiated another treaty with the Catholic Confederation and was preparing to lead some of their forces to expel the parliamentary soldiers holding Drogheda and Dublin. Although O'Neill held aloof from this alliance, preferring as usual to follow his own path, it was strengthened at least on paper by the defection from Parliament in 1648 of Murragh O'Brien, Lord Inchiquin, the Munster magnate.[5] On paper, because Inchiquin's change of heart was not echoed in the breasts of most of his army. Unable to swim against the Royalist current they awaited an opportunity to resume their parliamentary allegiance. Royalism was also encouraged by the appearance of Sir George Monro, the brother of General Robert Monro. An Engager in 1648 he was not at Preston and succeeded in retreating to Scotland and subsequently to Holland. Now he had come to serve his new monarch. Monro and Montgomery of Ards, another Ulster Scottish general, and their Scottish troops would serve under Ormonde, Royalism triumphing over religion.

Other Presbyterians, especially the clergy and elders of Belfast, perceived Ormonde as an Irish Montrose made even worse by his alliance with 'Papist malignants'. Their response to his growing army of about 13,000 men was characteristically impractical. They would not support the cause of an uncovenanted king yet they would not continue to assist the officers of a Commonwealth which had killed their king, rejected Presbyterianism and was maintained by an army infested with sectaries. Specifically they would not continue to support Colonel George Monck, stationed at Dundalk with large responsibilities and inadequate troops to discharge them. Monck's soldiers held several Ulster towns: indeed he was nominally in command of Ulster's eastern half. Many of his companies were Scots soldiers, and the Belfast elders sent word that unless he publicly took the Covenant, declaring himself a Presbyterian, they would withdraw his Scottish companies. Monck knew that a refusal would soon render his position untenable, for not only would he lose the Scottish companies, the Ulster Presbyterians would march against him, while the English companies, unreliable since the Regicide, would desert to Ormonde. However, if he took the Covenant he would be regarded as a traitor in London. Monck could only dissemble politely and hope that something would turn up. So while Ormonde's army grew more formidable the Presbyterians were busily undermining a commander who was prepared to defend Presbyterianism against Ormonde even if he rejected it for himself.

In this increasingly favourable situation the Marquess of Ormonde prepared to launch his campaign against Drogheda and Dublin. He hoped at first to win the campaign without firing a shot. The defection of Inchiquin and the conjunction of Monro, Montgomery and other Scottish commanders encouraged him to try to suborn the commanders of the parliamentary garrisons, Major-General Michael Jones in Dublin, Sir Charles Coote at Londonderry and Monck at Dundalk. Had these three men, and especially Jones, betrayed their trust the parliamentary reconquest of Ireland might have been thwarted before it began for lack of an invasion port. Coote, the son of a ferocious hammer of the Irish rebels in 1641, might seem an improbable defector but George Monck seemed a likely target. He was a professional soldier in the Anglo-Irish army which Ormonde had sent to England, only changing sides after his capture at Nantwich in 1644. He now faced insuperable difficulties and his English soldiers were already deserting to Ormonde. Monck ignored Ormonde's blandishments, instead making a truce with Owen Rowe O'Neill, and promising to despatch O'Neill's terms for a permanent peace to London. These included toleration for the Catholic religion, security of possession of Catholic lands, and indemnity and oblivion for the outrages of 1641. Monck knew his masters would never accept them and so delayed sending them as long as possible, lest a public rejection should end the truce. He even sent O'Neill a consignment of gunpowder. Monck informed Cromwell of what he had done, explaining that he was simply buying time. Cromwell in turn commended Monck's action to the Council of State as a stratagem of war. It was all to no purpose thanks to the Belfast Presbyterians: his Scottish soldiers marched away, his English soldiers deserted, his fief was overrun by Inchiquin's army and he retired to England. There he had a cordial interview with Cromwell at Milford Haven before journeying to London where, although he was officially reprimanded for his 'treaty', he was thanked for his services and suffered no other penalty.[6]

Ormonde also failed to suborn General Jones at the far more significant port of Dublin, despite some encouraging hints from the Protestant Bishop of Clogher, who was Jones's brother. Ormonde would have to take Dublin by force of arms, and quickly, before Cromwell arrived to render the task impossible. Encouraged by the capture of Drogheda and Dundalk, and with Dublin the only remaining east coast port open to Cromwell, he advanced on the capital. Unhappily for Ormonde Jones had received 2,000 reinforcements, Cromwell's advance guard, increasing the garrison to 8,000. This gave him parity with the forces Ormonde brought against the city. Ormonde could have been stronger but, influenced by rumours that Cromwell intended to invade through Munster, he made the commander's worst error: he divided his army in the face of the enemy. He sent Inchiquin to Munster with regiments needed before Dublin to resist a seaborne assault not destined to arrive and which Inchiquin would probably have been too outnumbered to resist if it had. Even worse he left Lord Dillon with 2,500 men at Finglas north of Dublin with orders to blockade the road although no danger could come from this direction. Ormonde soon showed that as he was no strategist so he was no tactician. He advanced through Rathmines to the small fort at Baggotrath, only a few miles south of the city. His mind fixed on assaulting the city when he was ready, it never occurred to him that Jones might assault him. Ormonde had so little thought of battle that his cavalry were away foraging when General Jones advanced to the attack. After defeating Sir William Vaughan's detachment on the Royalist right, Jones assaulted Ormonde with a pincer movement from north and south and the Irish army, taken by surprise, broke and fled. Its retreat was covered by Sir Thomas Armstrong with 1,000 cavalry, who arrived just in time to prevent a total rout.[7] Vaughan had been killed in Jones's first assault, Ormonde lost his artillery, his baggage, about £4,000 in gold and barely escaped falling prisoner himself. Dillon was urged to enter Dublin from the north while its garrison was campaigning to the south but discretion overrode valour and he withdrew. Rathmines was a disaster for Ormonde's army. Never again would it dare to confront the Ironsides in the field. For eight lean years Parliament had barely been able to hold a handful of towns outside the Pale. Now with the Confederation army retiring discomfited it disembarked at Dublin one of the most effective armies in Europe.

Parliament had been impatient to settle the problem of Ireland by such an expeditionary force since 1642 but had lacked the means to fight a war in two kingdoms. Even when Parliament was finally free to turn its attention to Ireland after the Regicide the struggles with Levellers and radical soldiers had caused more delay. The Commonwealth had endured frustration and anxiety, fearful that Charles II might descend on Ireland in the wake of his cousin Rupert, who had occupied Kinsale with impunity. If Charles captured or expelled Ireland's parliamentary garrisons he might launch an invasion of England. The Confederation would be happy to help Charles regain the throne in return for the guarantee of a Catholic Ireland ruled by an Irish Parliament. The chief priority must be to defeat the Confederation, preferably before Charles could arrive to inspire his followers and indeed before all the Republic's Irish enemies could unite against it. From the beginning the government had wanted Cromwell in command. Fairfax would not go and was in poor health. Cromwell himself had no desire to go to Ireland, that morass which had swallowed so many English military reputations. Almost fifty, and thus by seventeenth-century standards entering on the autumn of his days, the strenuous exertions of field and camp could have held few attractions. Moreover, he was a politician-soldier and could hardly relish being so far from Whitehall Palace. However, since his soldiers were at least as reluctant to go as their general, Cromwell must lead them, for the soldiers would hardly serve under anybody else. The soldiers gloomily referred to the pending Irish campaign as 'the cut-throat war', not because they wished to cut Irish throats but because they believed the Irish would cut theirs. The Council of the Army had first chosen regiments for Ireland but then abandoned this list in favour of choice by lot with a child pulling slips from a hat. This placed the responsibility for the choice in the hands of God. Ironically His choice tended to fall on the regiments of the politically respectable like Ireton, Scrope, Horton and Hewson which the Commonwealth would rather have kept at home, and to pass over regiments noted for their intense radicalism which they would have been happy to send abroad. However, since the Republic and the officers had directly sought God's intervention they could hardly disagree with His judgement, although some of their men displayed an impious resentment.

Because Cromwell was the necessary man, he was able to exact a long list of conditions. He was appointed Chief Governor in March 1649, and by July was already referred to as Lord Lieutenant. Foreseeing correctly that sieges would dominate his campaign he demanded an elaborate train of heavy guns and a record quantity of shot. He promised his soldiers that not one should embark until he had a full pay-chest, although the government at first had difficulty in satisfying his minimum demand of £100,000. Finally Cromwell himself led a delegation which extracted a loan of £150,000 from the City and Parliament enacted that £400,000 should be charged on future excise receipts. Cromwell also high-handedly seized £10,000 which was on its way to Bristol for the navy. He finally departed for Milford Haven on 9 July. Those who suppose that Puritans were austere men who shunned ostentation in their public concerns would have found that departure surprising, heralded as it was by fanfares of trumpets, the coach drawn by six grey Flanders mares and with eighty gentlemen and officers, well armed and mounted, as a lifeguard escort. A great white banner floated above the entourage, apparently symbolizing his mission to pacify Ireland, the same objective so strenuously sought by Mr Gladstone two centuries later although by an alternative method. Parliament was too relieved to see Cromwell depart to accomplish an objective so dear to their hearts to care about the manner of it, although sterner republicans might have considered it disquietingly regal.

Cromwell had not been idle during the weeks of military and financial preparation. One evening he had slipped quietly into a London inn seeking a furtive guest. Roger Boyle, Lord Broghill, younger son of the Earl of Cork, was en route for France to offer his services to Charles II.[8] Cromwell warned him that he might soon be in the Tower unless he chose to join his standard. It says much for Cromwell's capacity for making improbable friends that Broghill accepted the offer. It also shows what unreliable Royalists Anglo-Irish Protestants could be. Broghill's only demur was that he only be required to fight against the Irish, which Cromwell readily conceded. Broghill, who had earlier served under Inchiquin against the Catholic Confederation, was to prove a first-class artillery commander, and would do valuable service in persuading Protestant Royalists in the south-west to defect. Meanwhile Cromwell established contact with several officers in Inchiquin's army who were outraged by their leader's switch to the Catholic Confederation and were plotting to desert, and persuaded them to remain outwardly loyal until a more opportune time. Well prepared diplomatically, well furnished technically and financially, Cromwell embarked with an expeditionary force of 10,000 men, nearly 4,000 horses, artillery, ammunition and supplies, borne by three fleets amounting to 130 sail. In London there had been great fear that Jones would be unable to hold Dublin against Ormonde's assault, and Cromwell had planned to invade through a Munster port if Dublin fell. The news of Rathmines blew away all anxieties, Cromwell considering the victory 'an astonishing mercy, so great and seasonable that we are like men that dreamed'. Even so he ordered Ireton to lead part of the expedition to Munster but either because Inchiquin crushed a plot to betray Youghal to the invaders or because of unfavourable winds, Ireton joined his father-in-law at Dublin.

Once ashore and soon recovered from his first sea-voyage Cromwell acted with his usual brisk decisiveness. He knew that he needed civil as well as military policies for he must win the cooperation of as many Irish as possible. First he forbade his soldiers, under threat of severe punishment, to take free quarter from the inhabitants or to plunder them. He promised that all provisions supplied by the Irish would be paid for in cash, and instituted a market in his camp which would accompany his army wherever it marched. Although this policy did not survive his departure it won the cooperation of the people of Munster and Leinster for several months. On 24 August he ordered that no violence was to be offered to the life or property of unarmed civilians. Those who wished to remain in their homes would be protected on paying a fairly assessed contribution until 1 January 1650, at which time they could apply to the Attorney General for further protection. Militarily he had determined that his prime task was to seize all the east and south coast ports from Drogheda in the north to Cork in the south-west. The Marquess of Ormonde's deficiencies as a general were combined with an optimism in the face of adversity (particularly his poverty of money, ammunition and provisions) which would have compelled the admiration of Mr Micawber. Prior to Rathmines, although recognizing his army's deficiencies, including its high desertion rate, Ormonde had assumed he would take Dublin before Cromwell arrived. Defeated, he had turned north determined to pursue two objectives which he should have realized were mutually contradictory. He sought both to unite his forces in the hope of a decisive victory (although it was unlikely that he could feed so large a throng) and to hang on to all the ports in his hands. The second objective would deny Cromwell any ports through which to supply his army as they advanced from Dublin, but it divided the army he wished to unite into vulnerable bite-sized chunks which the Ironsides could advance to consume in the certainty that they would wait to be eaten. The medieval fortifications of towns like Drogheda and Wexford, however impressive to civilian eyes, might as well have been sand-castles when confronted by Cromwell's siege guns and assaulted by his disciplined soldiers. Once such towns were invested and the sea-borne siege-train put in position the outcome was certain.

While Cromwell reorganized his forces in Dublin Ormonde reinforced Drogheda on 17 August and installed Sir Arthur Aston as governor. Aston, a Catholic, had been notorious for his harshness while governor of Oxford during the first Civil War, even hanging innocent travellers suspected of parliamentary sympathies. To the gratification of Oxford's townsfolk Aston had lost a leg in an accident but had not allowed a wooden leg to force him into retirement. By 30 August Drogheda's garrison had risen to 2,871 and included the cream of Ormonde's army. Sir Edmund Verney commanded Ormonde's own regiment and Inchiquin had left an English Protestant regiment there with two regiments of mainly (but not exclusively) Irish Catholics. Ormonde withdrew with his remaining 3,000 men, including

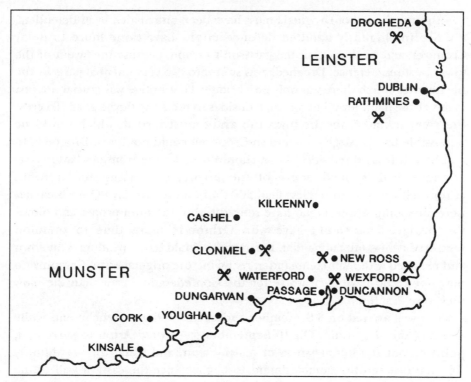

Cromwell's Irish Campaign, 1649–50

1,000 horse, to Tecroghan south-west of Drogheda and called for reinforcements from O'Neill in Ulster and Lord Clanricarde in Connaught, hoping with their aid to relieve Drogheda. He called in vain. Clanricarde did not come and O'Neill was seriously ill. His enemies subsequently accused Ormonde of cowardice in not doing more to assist the beleaguered town after the Ironsides arrived, but this charge was absurd. What could 3,000 unpaid, hungry men, ill-disciplined to the point of disloyalty, do against a well-fed, well-paid, experienced army of 10,000? Indeed Ormonde was more fearful of his own army than he was of Cromwell's, and with reason. As the Ironsides advanced some of Inchiquin's officers with 150 horse seized the opportunity to desert to them. Ormonde's real blunder was at the council-of-war in Drogheda before his withdrawal. There the vote to hold the place was six against four, but significantly three of the four were the three colonels who would actually have to defend the town and of the six in favour only the indomitable Aston would be present when the Ironsides made the assault. Ormonde should have overruled the council, withdrawn all his forces from Drogheda and avoided a pointless sacrifice.

Although the fall of Drogheda must have been anticipated by its defenders, a more intelligently handled defence might have done more to delay Cromwell and finally permit the garrison's escape, because the layout of the town favoured defence. Drogheda was split into two very unequal parts by the Boyne, over which there was only one bridge. That bridge was crucial not just to get at the main town but for the Ironsides to cross the Boyne at all. To cross the river inland from the town the army must ford it, which would be impossible for the siege-train and so Cromwell could not invest Drogheda to bombard it from three sides. Aston should have let the Ironsides batter away at the walled 'suburb' south of the Boyne, consuming ammunition. (Cromwell's guns fired not less than 200 shot on the first day.) Once breaches were appearing Aston should have retired within the town proper and blown the bridge. This would have won Ormonde more time to summon reinforcements and, failing that, the garrison could have abandoned the town and reunited with their commander, rectifying the original error. Certainly no outcome could have been worse for the Confederation army than the blow they were to suffer.

Cromwell arrived on 3 September and began to dig entrenchments while awaiting the siege-train. On 10 September he invited Aston to surrender, pointing out the hopelessness of his position, and when this was bluntly rejected ordered the bombardment to begin. Since the eastern wall of the 'suburb' was protected by a deep ravine, and the western wall was overlooked by an artificial hill known as the Mill Mount, fire was concentrated to make two breaches in the southern wall. Aston's last letter to Ormonde, asking for speedy help, shows that he knew the breaches would be carried the following day. The same day Ormonde heard from O'Neill's camp that no help could be expected from Ulster while neither Inchiquin in Munster nor Clanricarde in Connaught were sending reinforcements. During the continued bombardment on the 11th the defenders threw up a triple line of earthworks as a counter to the breach. This would have made more sense if Aston's infantry had not been very low on ammunition. 'My ammunition decays apace', Aston reported. In fact Colonel Trevor was advancing south from Dundalk with desperately needed ammunition, but the siege was over before he arrived. At five o'clock Cromwell ordered the assault. The regiments of Ewer, Hewson and Castle rushed the main breach, but were hurled back by the spirited resistance of the defenders and Castle was killed at the head of his men. Cromwell himself then crossed the glacis to rally the discomfited regiments and the troops followed him through the breach with such elan that in their rush they carried the earthworks as well. Although characteristic of Cromwell's fearlessness in battle it seems reckless of the Lord Lieutenant of Ireland to expose himself in this way. Certainly one stray shot could have altered the course of English history. Aston, his principal officers and about 300 of the

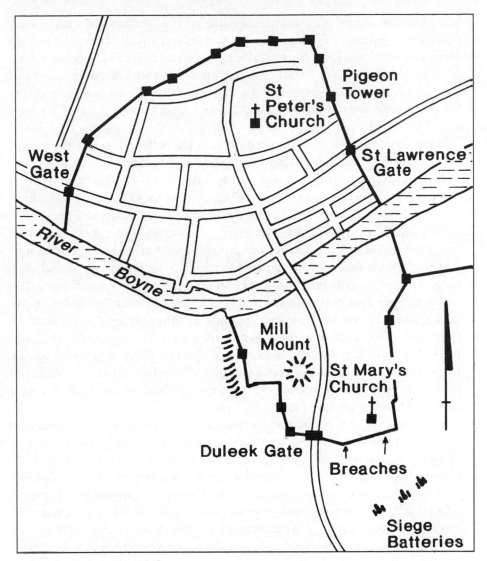

Drogheda, 10 September 1649

garrison took refuge at the top of the Mill Mount, perhaps hoping to make a last-ditch fight while the bulk of the garrison escaped across the bridge into the upper town. Cromwell, reaching the foot of the Mount, his blood up and his imagination no doubt wrought upon by the massacre stories of eight years earlier, pointed up the slope with his sword and cried out to his men to kill all with arms in their hands; in other words, take no prisoners. This was customary where garrisons had rejected an opportunity to surrender on terms, but what makes the taking of Drogheda a stain on Cromwell's reputation is that quarter was several times offered to induce groups of soldiers to surrender and after they had accepted they were then or later killed. Colonel Axtell climbed the Mount with a dozen men and demanded its garrison surrender. Aston, seeing that all was lost, agreed that his men would lay down their arms. Nevertheless, he and most of his men were butchered.

Meanwhile, the Ironsides pursued other soldiers fleeing across the bridge which they had lost the chance to destroy, and invaded the upper town, killing all armed men they found in the streets. It is claimed that about a thousand perished who had sought refuge in St Peter's Church. Some 'three score' barricaded themselves in the steeple and when Cromwell arrived he called on them to 'surrender to mercy'. However, the scenes they had already witnessed were hardly encouraging and they refused. Colonel Hewson and his soldiers, having failed to blow up the tower with gunpowder, built a fire of pews below it to smoke them out. Some took refuge on the roof and were shot down, others perished in the resulting fire and collapse of the tower. Finally the only strong-points holding out were two towers on the town walls, although their garrisons were not discovered until the following day. When these towers surrendered Cromwell ordered the transportation of most of their garrisons to the Barbados, although the officers in one tower were shot because their men had shot and killed several soldiers who were guarding it.

The massacre of the soldiers who had surrendered or were surrendering was Cromwell's responsibility and although that order was given in the heat of battle it was not rescinded in the calm of victory. Many soldiers were killed in cold blood the following day. Even that popular figure, Colonel Edmund Verney, who was interviewed by Cromwell, was stabbed to death immediately after leaving his presence; Colonel Boyle was called from his dinner and shot as soon as he emerged from the room. If these crimes were committed without Cromwell's consent there is no evidence that he sought to punish the murderers. Inchiquin wrote to Ormonde that many soldiers and some officers had escaped out of Drogheda, and all reported 'that no man had quarter with Cromwell's leave' but that many had been 'privately saved' by officers and soldiers and spirited beyond the walls. The story that on Cromwell's orders every man, woman and child within the town was slain is a fantasy, although it is still widely believed. Some unfortunate friars and some civilians certainly were killed, usually because they had armed themselves to assist the defence and were as liable to Cromwell's order as the soldiers. Others were saved by Cromwell's officers. However, there is no record of women or children being killed and nobody at the time claimed that they were, despite the propaganda value of such an accusation.

Although it has been claimed that the prisoners would not have been slain if they had not been Irish Catholics, it should be remembered that the soldiers in one regiment were English Protestants, and there were more Protestants among the mainly Irish Catholic regiments. Nor is it true as is sometimes alleged that quarter was never refused to the enemy in the English Civil War, for both sides were guilty of cruel excesses. Far more civilians, and they included women, were slain when Prince Rupert took Leicester shortly before the battle of Naseby than perished at Drogheda. However, it is true that with the single exception of the siege of Basing House Cromwell had been more remarkable for his merciful treatment of obdurate defenders than for his harsh application of 'the rules of war'. These rules encouraged the besieger to spare the lives of defenders who made no resistance and to put to death garrisons who fought it out in order to discourage resistance and useless loss of life in the future. Cromwell certainly claimed that his severity at Drogheda would encourage other towns to surrender at summons. This may have proved optimistic in the long run, but Dundalk and Trim were abandoned and Carlingford and Newry soon fell when Cromwell sent a strong detachment north to neutralize the threat from Ulster. Similarly New Ross was shortly to surrender at Cromwell's demand. Events at Wexford, a stronger, even more defensible place, were also influenced by the fearsome news from Drogheda, as we shall see. Ormonde reported that his army was as if paralysed by the shock of Drogheda just when it most needed to be active and resolute. Indeed the Confederation armies grew weaker, for many Protestant officers and soldiers deserted to the Ironsides, and many more Catholics decided that the only safety lay in flight abroad, chiefly to Spain. As a result of the defections a barrier of suspicion and distrust still further divided Old Irish, Old English and Protestant Royalists in the only army the Irish could field against the invaders.

With Drogheda secured Cromwell could launch his offensive south and west of Dublin. He wrote to Bradshaw on 16 September that 'we are marching our army to Dublin and then shall, God willing, advance towards our southern design', by which he meant the succouring of friendly towns and districts in Munster. Along the way Wexford must be taken for not only was it a notorious nest of privateers, its port facilities were necessary to supply the army during its south-west campaign and its garrison could not be left in the army's rear. Meanwhile Hewson was appointed Governor of Dublin, Michael Jones was rewarded for Rathmines with promotion to lieutenant-general and Ireton to major-general. With Carrickfergus the only substantial northern town still in Royalist hands by November Cromwell could march south knowing his Dublin base was secure from any northern threat, while his capacity to pay his men and his army's reputation for paying its way attracted material support and even recruits. Recruits he would certainly need. If the Irish could not defeat his army disease was another matter. Dysentery struck down more than 4,000 soldiers; many died, more were too weakened to fight and at best were only fit for garrison duty. It made no distinction of rank. General Jones would die in December. Moreover, the army suffered the debilitation which is the lot of invaders: the further it advanced the more troops it had to leave behind as garrisons in towns it had taken and to guard its lines of communication. Speaker Lenthall promised Cromwell he should have 5,000 reinforcements but it was to be months before they arrived.

By the time he reached Wexford Cromwell found himself in the uncomfortable position of having to besiege a well-fortified town, its eastern side protected by Wexford's expansive harbour and its western by a 20-foot masonry wall backed by an earthen revetment, and with only about 6,000 fit men out of a force of 8,000. Wexford's garrison was also much stronger than Drogheda's had been. Ormonde, although tempted to abandon the town before Cromwell arrived, had finally resolved to send in 1,500 reinforcements. The garrison numbered about 4,800 men. None of them was afflicted with dysentery but they were afflicted with doubt and division. The Irish soldiers were of the Rinuccini faction and wished to rid themselves of Colonel Synnot, the Anglo-Irish governor, and surrender the town on favourable terms. Colonel Synnot and other Royalist soldiers hoped to hold it. The council and citizens of Wexford had no desire to see their garrison or their priests suffer the fate of their Drogheda colleagues and wished to surrender, an attitude encouraged by the sight of Colonel Deane's menacing twenty-ship squadron anchored in their harbour. Unimpeded by the Rosslare fortress at the entrance whose garrison had fled at the approach of General Jones's regiments, the squadron had brought Cromwell badly needed provisions and the siege train. If Cromwell was worried by the depletion of his army, the garrison within Wexford was ripe for surrender or betrayal. The governor, however, replied evasively to Cromwell's first summons so that his reinforcements could enter the town from the north. Synnot may have hoped that Ormonde could advance to his relief if he gained more time but with Jones moving to block any approach Ormonde could do no more.

On 11 October Cromwell began his bombardment with eight heavy guns and two mortars. His batteries were to the south where the way into Wexford was blocked by a castle. Although well sited on high ground its walls cannot have been reinforced with earth and a breach was soon effected. Before Cromwell could launch an assault the magistrates, terrified by the fire-power brought against them and with the governor's agreement, sent commissioners to treat for surrender. Synnot sought liberty of worship and maintenance of clerical privileges, conditions which Cromwell could never accept. In turn Cromwell offered to protect the lives and property of the citizens and allow quarter to the officers while the private soldiers could return to their homes peacefully if they undertook never again to take up arms against the Commonwealth. Before Cromwell's terms had been conveyed to Synnot Captain Stafford, who commanded the castle and was perhaps unaware of the negotiations, surrendered the castle on his own initiative. Cromwell's soldiers moved quickly to exploit this unexpected advantage. The town wall's defenders, panic-stricken at the loss of the castle, the guns of which were soon trained on them, fled from their posts into the town. The Ironsides in the castle, seeing the town's ramparts denuded of troops, seized the initiative and rushed to the assault: some thrusting pikes into crevices in the ancient walls and hoisting themselves up, others mounting scaling ladders, they swarmed over the ramparts largely unresisted and took the town in no more than thirty minutes.

The panic-stricken citizens with their wives and children sought safety by embarking on boats to cross the harbour. Some soldiers and armed mariners from the privateering fleet tried to make a stand in the market place, perhaps to cover the escape of the women, but were soon overwhelmed by superior numbers and most were butchered on the spot. Priests and friars discovered in the streets or taking refuge in the churches were cut down. Others naively sought to win mercy by displaying crucifixes; since the iconoclastic Puritan soldiers considered such images the devil's work this brought them instant death. Meanwhile the press of terrified people seeking to escape by water was such that several boats were swamped and many of their passengers were drowned, among them women and children. For these deaths the Ironsides were not directly responsible but the killing of the soldiers and armed civilians, even though it has been justified on the grounds that this was normal where a garrison resisted after its defences had been taken, could not be justified at Wexford. Negotiations for surrender were in train and no assault on the town should have been launched before their outcome was known. The soldiers were temporarily out of Cromwell's control and the fact that he never so much as rebuked them later suggested that he approved the result even if he deplored the undisciplined attack without orders which produced it. Certainly after Drogheda soldiers who killed men trying to surrender could hardly be blamed for supposing that their actions would meet with their general's approval. Equally certainly the soldiers were incensed against Wexford's inhabitants, especially the mariners, because of the depredations and cruelties of its privateersmen against English merchant seamen in the recent past.

An anonymous letter writer of the time reported that while more soldiers were spared than at Drogheda about 1,500 soldiers and civilians perished, including more than 300 civilians who drowned in the capsizing of the boats. This death toll, which is supported by at least one Irish source, meant that up to 3,000 soldiers must have been taken prisoner along with most of about 2,000 'able men, mostly mariners' which Wexford is reported to have contained. The report that Cromwell slew every man, woman and child in Wexford is another fantasy. Cromwell was one of those fortunate people who are spared troubling reflections by their faith in the workings of God. He reported to Speaker Lenthall that while it had been his hope to take the town peacefully and preserve it harmless for the benefit of his army and the government: 'yet God would not have it so, but by an unexpected providence, in His righteous justice, brought a just judgment on them, causing them to become a prey to the soldier, who in their piracies had made preys of so many families . . .'.[9] Naturally he did not punish these instruments of the Almighty for what might appear to less confident eyes their undisciplined and murderous behaviour. Ever one to see English interests in their broader scope he did hint in his report to the Speaker that since the civilian deaths and the much larger number of inhabitants who had fled had left only one in twenty householders in the town, 'it were to be wished that an honest people would come and plant here'.

Once Cromwell's army had recovered from these excesses it began the 35-mile march along the coast to Waterford. The first obstacle was New Ross, a fortified town commanding the ferry across the Barrow river. Cromwell summoned the governor, Sir Lucas Taaffe, observing that it had been his principle to avoid 'effusion of blood' and 'that the people and places where I come may not suffer except through their own wilfulness'. The example of Drogheda, and Wexford's fate when it had consented to surrender at too leisurely a pace, had its effect at New Ross. After only two days Taaffe asked leave for his soldiers and such townsfolk who wished to accompany them to leave in safety, and for 'liberty of conscience' for such as chose to remain. Cromwell replied firmly that he meddled with no man's conscience but if Taaffe was asking for the Mass to be tolerated Parliament would not permit that where it held sway. In the end it was agreed that the soldiers should march away, abandoning their ammunition and artillery. All townsfolk who chose to depart within three months would be permitted to do so while those who elected to remain would be protected in their lives and property. These generous terms bore instant fruit, for when Taaffe's soldiers marched out of the gate 500 of them, all of English birth, took service with the Ironsides.

Cromwell certainly needed such timely reinforcement for the depletion of his ranks was continuing, with Wexford to garrison and now New Ross, and with a bridge across the Barrow to build – and then guard – before the advance on Waterford could be resumed. During this delay Cromwell sent Lieutenant-General Jones with 2,000 men to take Fort Duncannon which commanded the access to Waterford by sea. So long as it and Passage Fort on the opposite bank were in Irish hands he could not get his ships up the River Suir. This meant that provisioning a siege would be very difficult and he would be unable to bring up his siege-train. There was no possibility of bringing the heavy guns by land in view of the continuous rain which turned already vestigial roads into swamps. Ormonde knew he must hold Duncannon and Passage if he was to hold Waterford, especially the former. Passage, on the west side of the river, was under no immediate threat, although the Earl of Castlehaven was sent to reinforce its garrison. However, at first it appeared that Duncannon would be the one most likely to crumble. The Irish soldiers in it, with Drogheda and Wexford on their minds, deserted in scores at the news of General Jones's approach and Thomas Roche, its governor, informed Ormonde the place could not be held. Ormonde promptly sacked Roche in favour of Colonel Edward Wogan, who arrived with Ormonde's own lifeguards to give its garrison heart. Wogan had once served under Fairfax but had deserted to the Scots with his troop in 1648 so would not have been particularly eager to surrender to an Ironside army, even if he had not been a resolute soldier with considerable military flair.

While Cromwell was inspecting his subordinate's siege works at Duncannon he received the good news that at Cork on 16 October the English component of the garrison, supported by the town's English inhabitants, had declared for Parliament and after a brisk affray had driven out the governor and their former Irish allies. This body blow for the Irish cause had an immediate effect on Inchiquin's long-wavering soldiers who deserted so fast that he had soon lost all but 200 of his infantry. Useful though these soldiers were, Cromwell knew the fall of Cork had a much greater significance. The division between the two chief components of the Catholic Confederation army now became an unbridgeable gulf. In future the Irish would place their trust only in their fellow Irish and not in Royalist Protestants. Meanwhile at Duncannon the defenders resisted with such a will that Wogan, having had eighty horse ferried across the river, boldly sortied against Jones. The latter, deceived by the unexpected presence of cavalry into thinking Ormonde's army must be relieving the fort, withdrew on 5 November in such haste that he lost two cannon to the enemy.

Cromwell had been so eager to take Waterford, the second city in Ireland, grown wealthy and populous on trade and industry, that he had continued far beyond the normal campaigning season. He now paid the price. Waterford was to be the only Irish city which he besieged but did not take. The news from Cork misled him into supposing that divisions within the town would bring about its easy conquest. The inhabitants, learning how divisions had enfeebled resistance elsewhere, were determined to remain united. When Ormonde sent Lord Castlehaven with some reinforcements Waterford refused to admit him, for, although a Catholic, he was an Englishman. Instead they demanded a strong detachment of Ulster Catholics from O'Neill's army, and, although outraged at Castlehaven's rebuff, Ormonde had to consent.

Lieutenant-General Farrell arrived with 1,300 soldiers on 24 November. Ireton captured the Passage fort the very same day but it was a meaningless victory: the ships still could not come up the river while Duncannon held out. This left Cromwell with no heavy guns, an army diminishing daily by disease and the cruelties of the weather, and himself, as he reported, 'crazy in my health'. His officers were insisting that the army must retire to winter quarters. Although Cromwell tried to hang on, sending for 1,200 horse and foot from Cork to assist him, it was hopeless. Losing ten men a night to disease – they included two valuable officers, his kinsman Major Cromwell and General Jones, the victor of Rathmines – he would soon be outnumbered by the garrison he was besieging. If Ormonde launched a thrust with the remainder of the Confederation army the Ironsides would be in trouble. On 2 December Cromwell raised the siege and marched off. He had suffered one of the few setbacks of his military career. The terrors inspired by Drogheda and Wexford had ebbed. The resistance of the Irish had stiffened. Having lost faith in alliances they had resolved to fight with their own resources. This might mean that they would never be strong enough to confront the invader in the field but they had only once been able to do so when they had Royalist allies and then, at Rathmines, the Confederation army had been defeated. The war would continue for a time to be a war of sieges but when the invader had won this round painfully and at heavy cost in blood and treasure, the Irish would turn to the guerrilla warfare for which their country's topography, their resources and their skills were so suited.

In January 1650, despite his reverse at Waterford, Cromwell could contemplate the achievements of the Commonwealth forces with some satisfaction. Sir Charles Coote's capture of Carrickfergus in December had brought the government control of the entire eastern and southern seaboard, with the sole exception of Waterford. The revolt of Inchiquin's seasoned troops, no strangers to Irish conditions among which most of them had been bred, besides being an invaluable addition to his strength, had also painlessly delivered the Munster towns. These furnished comfortable winter quarters for his men in which they speedily recovered their health and their morale, both sorely tried by dysentery, Irish weather and Irish mud. Their effective numbers amounted to between 6,000 and 7,000 and Cromwell knew that Sir Hardress Waller would soon arrive with 3,000 reinforcements. Cromwell still retained his enormous advantage in money and supplies despite the financial difficulties of the Commonwealth government. Ormonde was in no such happy position. Irish towns still in Irish hands did not want his hungry troops within their walls even if their loyalty had been unquestioned, which it decidedly was not. Not even Waterford, buoyant in victory, would admit them and Limerick followed suit. Ormonde finally quartered his hungry, ragged army at Kilkenny, but his problems of pay, forage and food remained extreme and the townsfolk were soon regretting the generosity of their city fathers. The Old Irish were increasingly convinced that no Royalists were to be trusted, especially if they were Protestant, and would not trust even a Catholic if he was English. There were too many Royalists who had found Cromwell's service more attractive than the king's. This increasing suspicion, the belief that not even Ormonde could be trusted and that no heretics should be accepted as allies, was reflected in the contrast between Waterford's rejection of Ormonde's army and Clonmel's enthusiastic welcome for Major-General Hugh Dubh O'Neill with an army of 1,600 Ulster Catholics which arrived to reinforce its garrison.

In an effort to arrest the decline in the morale of the Irish and revitalize the fractured Confederation, the bishops gathered at Clanmacnoise and called for unity. The enemy was Cromwell, they reminded their forces, a mortal enemy from whom they could expect neither toleration for their religion nor mercy for themselves. Cromwell rather helped than hindered their efforts by a ferocious counterblast entitled a 'Declaration . . . for the Undeceiving of Deluded and Seduced People'. The clergy were guilty of pride, ambition, and cruelty, of keeping the people ignorant and seducing them into taking part in a 'horrid rebellion'. He declared that Ireland had prospered under English rule until the eve of that rebellion. (Strafford's ghost might have found this confident declaration somewhat ironic considering that his 'misgovernment' of Ireland was one of the charges brought against him by the Pym junta which Cromwell had enthusiastically supported.) Cromwell assured the Irish that he had no intention 'to massacre, banish and destroy' the Catholics in Ireland unless they warred against him, but if they followed their priests and took up arms against him he would exercise 'the utmost severity against them' and would accept no responsibility for the 'misery and desolation, blood and ruin' which would befall them. Cromwell's inveterate hostility to priests was not due to their religious beliefs but to their willingness to preach rebellion and war against the Commonwealth government. In Cromwell's eyes they were 'men of blood', responsible for the deaths of his soldiers and of many civilians just like that 'man of blood', Charles Stuart. He had tried and executed the king for that crime and he would not spare them.

In the spring of 1650 Cromwell moved against Clonmel, a well-fortified town on the Suir about 25 miles north of Waterford. A cavalry general of genius, but less experienced in handling infantry in the highly technical processes of siege-craft despite his Civil War experience, Cromwell was to find Clonmel a bloody frustration. He took the town but thanks to the skill and ingenuity of General Hugh O'Neill the cost was appalling. After three weeks encamped before Clonmel, hoping to persuade it to surrender peacefully, Cromwell ordered the bombardment to begin. As a breach began to appear O'Neill mobilized every able man to construct a 'lane' 80 yards deep with makeshift walls of timber and rubble running straight back from the widening breach. He closed the end with a rampart armed with cannon while soldiers with muskets were packed into houses whose upper stories commanded the lane. Knowing nothing of O'Neill's fearsome trap Cromwell ordered the assault on 16 May and with the enemy disquietingly silent the forlorn hope led by Colonel Culme advanced through the breach lustily singing a hymn. Troops poured after, some horse among them since the infantry were claiming that the cavalry escaped all danger in sieges, and the lane was soon packed with soldiers who were too crammed to be able to withdraw when they finally realized their peril. Then a party of O'Neill's men swung in behind to close the breach and the killing began, with cannon firing chain shot, with muskets, stones and scythes. Cromwell lost close to 1,000 men in less than an hour. He had been so unaware of danger that he had ridden with other troops to the town gate expecting it to be thrown open by his victorious soldiers. When he realized the attack had mysteriously gone wrong he sent reinforcements, suffering a further 500 casualties. When the attack was called off he was as far from carrying the defences as he was at the beginning. Ireton considered this disaster the heaviest the parliamentary army had ever endured either in England or Ireland. The courageous defence could not last, however. O'Neill had the best part of 2,000 men in the town but his ammunition was by now all but exhausted. That night he and his garrison stole from the town on muffled hooves, slipped past the besiegers unaware and headed for Waterford. Stunned by his losses, Cromwell was overjoyed when news was brought to his tent that the town was willing to negotiate a surrender. He quickly offered easy terms and his fury can be imagined when he discovered that the soldiers, a greater prize than the town itself, had escaped him. Despite feeling that he had been villainously tricked by the town's emissaries, he kept to the terms and when the chastened Ironsides finally marched into the town they committed no depredations. Their vengeance was reserved for the tail-end of O'Neill's army which Cromwell's cavalry pursued, killing many wounded, stragglers and women among the camp followers. O'Neill and his army, however, successfully escaped although Waterford, now stricken with plague, would not admit them.

A week later Cromwell left Ireland for ever. In the nine months he had been there he had achieved many military objectives, although it had all taken longer than the short, sharp campaign he had planned and the losses his army sustained had been far heavier than he had hoped, particularly deaths from disease. Dysentery had depleted his strong expeditionary force, and the necessity of garrisoning the towns he took depleted it further. Wisely the

Confederation forces had never faced him in the field for their army would certainly have been destroyed if they had. However, this meant that while Cromwell had taken every town he besieged apart from Waterford, the Irish still had the resources to put an army in the field if ever the Commonwealth army became sufficiently weak to offer a chance of victory. Moreover, although Coote in Ulster, Colonel Michael Jones and General Ireton would continue to besiege and take castles and fortified towns until there was hardly a strong-point left to capture, between 350 and 400 in all, the process still continued by which every success brought a further weakening of the Ironside army by garrisoning the captures and a strengthening of the Irish field armies by the addition of the troops released from garrison duty. Meanwhile the Irish now turned to guerrilla warfare. The word 'guerrilla' was unknown to our seventeenth-century forebears, Irish or English, but the Irish understood its possibilities very well and were to display great aptitude for this hit-and-run warfare, emerging from the mists for swift assault, never staying long enough in one place to form a target. The war in Ireland would be all the longer and all the more devastating because of it.

It would last until the summer of 1652 when the Irish signed the Kilkenny Articles with the exhausted, frustrated Parliamentarians and laid down their arms in Leinster, Munster, Connaught and Ulster. Prisoners of war were to be exchanged, and there was a general pardon for all save those guilty of massacring the Protestant settlers in 1641 and 'priests and Jesuits'. By that time both soldiers and civilians were heartily sick of the war and its costs. Certainly it was a bleeding wound for the Commonwealth treasury which nothing seemed capable of staunching. By now the Commonwealth army, despite the loss of fully a third of the soldiers Cromwell had commanded in 1649, had swelled to 33,000 men. Nevertheless this imposing force was still confronted by forces scattered among the provinces which totalled more than 30,000. In February 1652 the parliamentary commissioners in Ireland had to admit that the enemy still controlled large tracts of all four provinces and shortly after were complaining that they were contending with forces as large as or even larger than their own.[10] These men did not, however, ascribe their problems to any injustice or lack of statesmanship on their own part. Rather the stubborn resistance could only be ascribed to 'the wickedness and malice of the generality of the people'. During the period 1641 to 1652 the Irish population fell from about 1,500,000 to no more than 850,000. While large numbers died in the terrible winter of 1641/2 the majority of the 600,000 missing perished during the period between Cromwell's departure and the Articles of Kilkenny, that is, between 1650 and 1652. Most of these unfortunates perished of famine or disease, those dismal camp-followers of armies, as the parliamentary commanders struggled to come to terms with the unfamiliar weapon of guerrilla warfare. Their struggle inevitably visited terrible sufferings on the civilian population. The onset of disease was not selective, visiting the camps of the invader and careless of rank. An early casualty was the commander-in-chief, Cromwell's son-in-law, Henry Ireton. A chill picked up in the dismal, five-month siege of Limerick turned to a fever which carried him off on 26 November 1651.

All this misery could have been avoided and the commanders in Ireland knew it. All that was necessary was to guarantee the Irish liberty to practise their religion and to guarantee them quiet possession of their lands and farms. In summer 1651 parliamentary commissioners, supported by Lord Deputy Ireton, urged the Commonwealth government to give the Irish the assurances they sought. If this was not done, they concluded, the war would drag on, the land would not be tilled, sheep and kine would be destroyed, and the cost to the Commonwealth would be beyond their capacity to compute. This recommendation was not ignored but after lengthy debate in the Purged Parliament and in the Council of State it was rejected. The corrosive impact of their own 'massacre' propaganda, which they all accepted unquestioningly, inhibited common sense. Rather the government would adopt another, grimmer solution fraught with poisonous long-term consequences: the Act for the Settlement of Ireland of 12 August 1652. This 'solution' involved dispossession of Catholic landowners and their forced migration westward while English speculators, adventurers and settlers would buy their lands and so meet some of the war's mammoth cost. The act insisted that it was not its intention to destroy the Irish nation and extended pardon 'both as to life and estate' to all of the 'inferior sort', but excluded all who had taken part in the Rebellion of 1641, all Jesuits and priests who had abetted or encouraged the Rebellion and the war, 105 prominent Irishmen, and all who would not lay down their arms within twenty-eight days. Gardiner estimates that this meant that about 80,000 people faced the death penalty if they could be arrested, although in fact little effort was expended in doing so. Catholic gentry would lose one-third of their land and an amount equal to the other two-thirds would be assigned them in whatever part of Ireland Parliament designated. One of history's gargantuan land-grabs, it was made necessary by Parliament's reckless commitments in the past. The Irish Adventurers would need 1,000,000 acres to satisfy such promises and £1.75 million was owed to soldiers for arrears of pay which it was hoped to satisfy in land-grants. Catholic landowners with few exceptions were transplanted to Clare and western Connaught. More than half of all Irish land passed temporarily into the hands of soldiers and adventurers. Such a settlement was a recipe for disaster both in the short and long terms. It caused violent resistance to persist and the expense mounted as a consequence of the solution adopted to reduce it. Plague, pestilence, famine, the destruction of farming where people had eaten their very plough-horses and cattle in an effort to stay alive, had transformed an agriculturally rich society where bread was cheaper than in England, into one in which land was almost valueless. The soldier-settlers soon sold their entitlements to officers and returned disgustedly to England. No more than 12,000 new settlers took up Irish land. The dream of Protestant English yeoman farmers replacing the Irish was never fulfilled. Catholic Irish peasants had to be permitted to live even within the Pale or much of the soil would remain untilled. The idiotic insistence on solving Parliament's Irish problem on Parliament's own terms rather than on the very minimal and reasonable terms which the Irish would have accepted merely resulted in an expensive continuation of the problem and a situation in which everybody lost. Certainly the government's fear that Charles II would succeed in invading England with an Irish army was now removed. However, that danger, if it had ever existed, evaporated during Cromwell's nine-month campaign. Its achievement did not require the destruction of more than a third of the Irish population, or driving thousands of its most potentially productive and able men into exile, or for the government to incur massive debts, or for its soldiers to suffer such dolorous losses.

CHAPTER FIVE

Scotland: The Pre-emptive Strike

We did sinfully both entangle the nation . . . and that poor prince . . . making
him sign and swear to a covenant which we knew . . . he hated in his heart.

Alexander Jaffray, Covenanter, Breda, 1650

. . . the enemy's horse and foot were made by the Lord of Hosts as stubble
to our swords.

Oliver Cromwell, Dunbar, 4 September 1650

As we have seen, the Commonwealth from the first faced hostility abroad
and enemies at home, in Ireland and in Scotland. All danger of an Irish
invasion had evaporated as a consequence of Cromwell's campaign in
Ireland. The danger of a Scottish invasion and the dubious loyalty of home-
grown Presbyterians now became the principal anxiety of the Commonwealth government. Their most formidable warrior was needed at home to
advise on and deal with this danger. Above all he was needed to bolster the
government by his by now enormous prestige. Fairfax still commanded the
New Model Army and in a war against Scotland Cromwell might serve as his
second-in-command, but nobody doubted who would be the crucial figure.
From at least as early as January 1650 the Commonwealth government had
anxiously awaited Cromwell's return. In May he at last handed over to
Ireton and embarked for Bristol, where thunderous salutes from the
garrison's heaviest cannon greeted him. The journey to London was a
triumphal progress. He was met at Windsor by 'many volleys of shot' and by
'many persons of eminency' and then hastened to London, pausing only to
review with Fairfax massed regiments on Hounslow Heath. He pressed on to
Westminster as artillery and infantry fired congratulatory volleys in Hyde
Park. If the politicians remembered the Roman Republic's fate at the hands
of a successful general they were too relieved at his return to worry about
that unhappy precedent. When Parliament met a few days later it heard
Speaker Lenthall greet Cromwell with 'an eloquent oration' on his 'great
and strange works' in Ireland before resuming more mundane business and
thankfully leaving the Scottish peril to the Council and its laurel-wreathed
hero.

The Scottish situation had changed since Cromwell embarked for Ireland. During 1649 the Scots had remained hostile to the Republic but declined to take advantage of its Irish preoccupations. The Scots had been outraged by the execution of a Scottish monarch without any consultation with the Scottish government and over the protests of the Scottish commissioners sent to London to prevent it. However, they had no immediate intention of going to war. They had proclaimed Charles II in Edinburgh in February 1649 as a calculated slap in the face for any Englishmen who supposed they could compel them to become part of a Republic by a fait accompli. Nevertheless, this proclamation was very cautiously worded, containing a vital proviso that before they would consider restoring Charles II he must take the Covenant and undertake not only to guarantee to the Scots their Presbyterian worship but that his English subjects would adopt the same discipline. In its hour of need in 1643 the Long Parliament had given such an undertaking and the Scots were determined that it should be honoured. As the Rump, purged of most of its Presbyterian members, dominated and sustained by an army infested by heretical sects, would never honour that commitment the Scots reluctantly began to consider the possibility of a Presbyterian–Royalist counter-revolution. A commission had visited Charles at The Hague in 1649 consisting of a peer, three commoners and two ministers (the last doubtless to check any deviationism in the impressionable laymen while they were exposed to the king's dangerous charm) and had besought Charles to adopt the Covenant, warning him of the fatal consequences of any association with Irish Papists. At the time Charles, who must have wished to kick downstairs these representatives of those who had sold his father to the parliamentary forces when he had refused to do precisely what they were now trying to force upon his son, was courteously evasive. He still hoped that Ormonde's army of Catholics and Royalists would restore him, assisted by a Scottish rising inspired by the Marquess of Montrose. Then he could dismiss all Presbyterians to the devil for he would be enthroned without their help. Unhappily the Montrose expedition proved a total failure with its charismatic leader captured and executed, while in Ireland Cromwell's legions had ensured there could be no hope from Ormonde. The penniless king, living on the charity of his cousin, the Prince of Orange, was reduced to desperation.

In the spring of 1650 Charles again met the commissioners at Breda. There as one former Covenanter, Alexander Jaffray, was later to confide to his diary, they sinfully entangled 'that poor prince' compelling him to swear to a covenant which they knew he 'hated in his heart'. Charles persuaded the commissioners to agree that the English would only have to adopt Presbyterianism if a free Parliament voted in favour of the measure, but this agreement was broken as soon as the Kirk Party led by the Marquess of Argyle had the king in their clutches.[1] In Scotland, which he reached three weeks after Cromwell had arrived in London, Charles found himself as much a prisoner as his father had been, and feared he might share his fate of being 'sold south'. Helpless, subjected to daily insult from a parcel of elders and clergymen with neither tact nor compassion, Charles smarted and bided his time. The Kirk Party had much to answer for. Not only were they in the short run earning the implacable hostility of the Commonwealth government and its fearsome army, but in the long run they were making an enemy of a man who never forgot an injury and who could wait long and patiently for the opportunity for revenge. The Kirk Party could argue that there would be no advantage for the Scots in helping Charles to regain his throne if once on it he allowed a free Parliament to re-establish Anglicanism. Would they not then be back to the position of 1638? Once more they would have an Anglican king ruling in London who would soon be tempted to meddle in the religious settlement of Scotland. There would be no security for the Covenanters, as indeed there was not after the king's restoration without Scottish help in 1660 which was followed by twenty-eight years of persecution and proscription. (An early victim was Argyle, beheaded in 1661.) However, this was not an argument for compelling a desperate young man to forswear himself and agree to impose a form of worship which an overwhelming majority of his English subjects detested. It was an argument for leaving him well alone in his indigent Dutch exile and proclaiming Scotland a republic. The Republican government in London would have been happy to extend the hand of friendship, and interfering with the Kirk would never have crossed its mind. Yet the Kirk Party in their addle-pated way refused to see this. They had persuaded themselves that safety for Scottish Presbyterianism required an English Presbyterian polity, and that the only way to achieve this was to impose the king on the English along with a policy of relentlessly persecuting all who objected, whether Anglicans or radical sectarians. 'Whom the Gods wish to destroy they first make mad.'

Meanwhile the Commonwealth government was well aware from its agents in Scotland of the Scottish government's intentions and from its agents in Holland of the progress of the talks. It knew that the king would soon be among his Scottish subjects and that a Scots army might invade England after the harvest. The question was, should the Ironsides be concentrated in the North to await the invader or should there be a pre-emptive strike to crush the Scottish army within Scotland? Once returned Cromwell was heavily involved in the decision making. There were nineteen meetings of Council after Cromwell reached London and of these he attended seventeen. The Purged Parliament insisted that Fairfax should lead the army accompanied by Cromwell as his deputy, but while Parliament proposed the Lord General's conscience disposed. Fairfax was willing to take the field if the Scots invaded England but on 20 June the Council fatefully decided to strike before they could do so. As Cromwell observed, if a country had to go to war it was far better to fight on the enemy's territory than on its own. Fairfax, that man of strong principles and tender conscience, would have none of this. On 22 June he informed the Council that he would not command the expedition, refusing to accept that this was a defensive war. He still took seriously his own and Parliament's commitment to the Solemn League and Covenant of 1643. He probably foresaw that while the short-term objective might be to smash the Scots army and prevent it restoring the monarchy, the campaign's long-term objective would become the conquest of Scotland. The resignation of Fairfax produced a crisis because it was important that the Republic appeared united when going to war, and if Englishmen could not even unite against the unpopular Scots the situation was desperate indeed. Fairfax the moderate Presbyterian and Cromwell the Independent together leading the New Model Army would symbolize unity within the Commonwealth. Cromwell tried for a whole night to persuade Fairfax to change his mind, but his commander, who had been unhappy about the course of events since 1648, and would have welcomed a restored monarchy if constitutional rights could be guaranteed, seized this opportunity to retire. On 26 June Parliament appointed Cromwell as 'captain general and commander-in-chief of all forces raised or to be raised within the Commonwealth of England' and confirmed the Council's declaration of war on Scotland.

Cromwell, who had been heavily involved in preparing for the expedition, then set off for Newcastle, the rendezvous of the army. Once there he did not neglect the gentler arts of political diplomacy, hoping the divisions between Engagers and Kirk Party would simplify his task. He could not believe that the Covenanters were any more devoted to their Royalism than Charles was sincere in his Presbyterianism, and so sought to undermine his enemy by writing to leading political figures urging them to abandon this unnatural allegiance. Such correspondence had to be clandestine but he could openly address the hearts, minds and morale of the Scottish people. He issued two declarations from his Newcastle headquarters, the first addressed to 'the people of Scotland', the other to 'all that are saints, and partakers of the faith of God's Elect in Scotland'. The address to the people was designed to counter the Kirk's propaganda that the Ironsides would slay, torture, mutilate or rape all men, women and children who fell into their hands. Cromwell pointed out that no such horrors had been visited on the Scots when his army had entered Scotland in 1648 at the invitation of the very people who were now in power. They had stolen from nobody and preserved the 'best affected' from the enemy. He reminded his audience that Charles Stuart, now harboured by their government, had sought to enlist foreign powers to invade the English

Commonwealth, commissioned pirates to slay its mariners and seize their ships, and had seduced the Scottish government into rejecting the Commonwealth's hand of friendship. All this had led Parliament to the 'unavoidable necessity' of invading Scotland. Nevertheless they would not injure the persons or goods of the Scots and would recompense any who were damaged by the passage of his army. They should 'abide in their own houses' and not allow themselves to be misled by anyone's 'craft or subtlety'.

The declaration to the 'Saints' was more argumentative, reminding his audience that they were pursuing the same disastrous policy for which they had condemned the Engagers: conspiring with Royalists to invade England and overthrow a Godly government on behalf of a treacherous monarch. As for the Kirk's hostility to the religious views of his soldiers and other Englishmen, blasphemies had already been repressed, and the Scots should consider that the fundamental views of English Puritans and Scottish Covenanters were compatible and the difference of form unimportant. 'Is all religion wrapped up' in Presbyterianism 'or in any one form? We think not so.' These declarations could not persuade the Kirk party to abandon Charles, nor did their author expect they would. He knew they would stir the consciences of many and the doubts and fears they raised might separate many from the Kirk Party during the succeeding months.[2] For now Cromwell let these medicinal draughts work on the Scottish psyche while he marshalled his forces for the arduous campaign which confronted him. Having experienced Scottish roads before, Cromwell planned to move his provisions by sea and assembled a flotilla of eleven supply ships and four men-of-war under Rear-Admiral Hall. Over the summer this grew to a fleet of 140 merchantmen, transporting arms, munitions and food from London, Lynn, Harwich and Newcastle. Scores of shipwrights in Lynn and Newcastle built flat-boats to transport men, horses and supplies on the Firth of Forth. Cromwell lacked a siege-train of heavy guns, but had at least fifty field guns with 1,300 draught animals to draw them. Since Cromwell anticipated that the Scots would drive off their cattle and sheep, every soldier would have to carry several days' rations. A day's ration was just under a pound of biscuit, half a pound of cheese and a pint of small beer. This is inadequate provision for a soldier on the march. It must have been intended to supplement it from provisions carried in waggons or by sea, although it would have kept the men from hunger for several days.[3] Cheese was shipped from as far afield as Holland and Hamburg, while during the campaign 2,800 tons of oats and 11,000 tons of hay were hastened up from East Anglia, Surrey and Kent for the horses. However, Cromwell was to find that even preparation on this scale was not enough and supply did not run smoothly. There was no port comparable with Drogheda or Wexford, let alone Dublin, between Berwick and Leith and until they captured Leith the soldiers were certain to experience hungry marches. Moreover, too few ships during the opening weeks, and adverse winds delaying those he had, frustrated his logistical planning. Cromwell hoped to pick up some supplies from the countryside through which he marched, certainly fodder for his horses, and expected supplies from Berwick on waggons. In both he was largely disappointed.

The Ironside army was even larger than the Irish expeditionary force. By mid-July there were eight cavalry and eight infantry regiments at Newcastle, 16,000 strong, which would receive reinforcements of 8,500 during the succeeding twelve months. However, Cromwell was to find that the old enemy dysentery could enfeeble his army as efficiently in Scotland as in Ireland and he was not to command 20,000 effective men until 1651.[4] He was confronted by a numerically superior enemy, probably 26,000 strong by July, commanded by a general who had nothing to learn from Quintus Fabius about the most effective tactics to employ against an invader. Among the officers Cromwell selected for the expedition was George Monck, who had so favourably impressed him when they met at Milford Haven in 1649. Cromwell summoned him from retirement as a debt-burdened Devonshire squire and gave him command of a new regiment cobbled together from companies drawn from Newcastle and the Berwick garrison. It would one day become the famed Coldstream Guards.

When Cromwell entered Scotland he found, as his spies had warned, that David Leslie had stripped all the country between Tweed and Edinburgh of forage, food and people, pressing many into his army, and withdrawing the remainder behind the fortified line he had built from Edinburgh to Leith. Cromwell knew he was not confronting another Ormonde even before he inspected Leslie's dispositions. Leslie had learned his trade under that master of the field, Gustavus Adolphus. He had served under Alexander Leslie, Earl of Leven, in the Bishops' War of 1640, had defeated Montrose at Philiphaugh in 1645 and had served under Cromwell at Marston Moor. Cromwell knew that the defences Leslie had built were too strong for his army, at least until he had taken Leith, which anchored one end of them, and he could land some heavy guns there. The alternative of trying to work around Edinburgh to the west would expose his flank, and even if Leslie declined to attack it he could raid their lines of communication. Although the invaders snapped up Dunbar, Haddington and Musselburgh fewer supply ships arrived than expected at Dunbar thanks to adverse winds, and when the overland route from Newcastle was unexpectedly cut by armed civilians swooping down from the hills, the soldiers grew hungry. An attempt to take Leith beginning on 29 July failed. Four men-of-war off the harbour bombarded the town but did no damage to the fortifications confronting the infantry. The rain was as torrential as in Ireland. Since

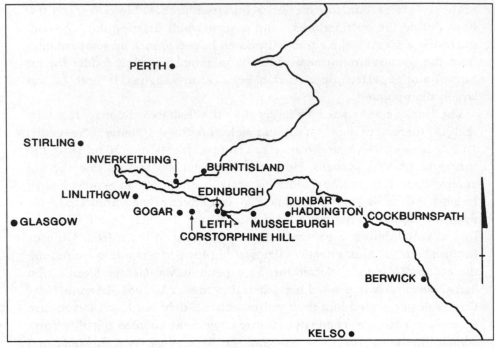

The Dunbar Campaign, 1650–1

Leslie would not come out to fight, Cromwell withdrew his hungry army to Musselburgh, Leslie's cavalry snapping at their heels. In one skirmish Lambert was wounded and briefly taken prisoner. Even at Musselburgh the exhausted regiments could not relax for Leslie sent the cream of his cavalry, 800 strong, to raid it. After a fierce struggle they were driven off with the heavy loss for the Scots of General Montgomery killed and Colonel Strachan wounded. Subsequently Cromwell fell back to Dunbar.

The Ironsides seemed further from conquering the Scots than ever but Cromwell was undaunted. He had never supposed the campaign would be easy. He rested his soldiers while labouring to provision them, heartening their morale with prayer-meetings and impassioned preaching. He also reverted to the less strenuous arts of propaganda. He returned sixty wounded prisoners of war, even lending his own coach to assist their journey. He also wrote to the General Assembly of the Kirk censuring their unnatural alliance with Charles Stuart – 'a covenant made with death and hell' – and bade them consider 'in the bowels of Christ' that they might be wrong. This was no mere exercise in propaganda: Cromwell sincerely believed that this war between Protestants was unnatural. All that was needed to end it was for the Scots to abandon Charles Stuart, a man who detested them and who would surely seek their destruction if he was ever restored to his throne. Cromwell's rhetoric had no effect. The Scottish Covenanters seemed determined to fulfil a melancholy destiny. With his army at last supplied he was ready to try what hard knocks could accomplish where eloquence had failed. Once again his army lunged westward, this time abandoning the coast and marching well to the south of Edinburgh. If Leslie launched a flank attack the Ironsides would have time to deploy to meet his assault. However, as it was Cromwell's strategy to bring Leslie to battle, reckoning that his trained, experienced army would certainly defeat Leslie's inexperienced, unenthusiastic conscripts, so it was Leslie's strategy to avoid this encounter until the enfeebling of Cromwell's army from hunger and disease compelled him to retreat to the Border. However, when Leslie saw that Cromwell intended to work his way round Edinburgh to cut off the Scottish army from the sources of its supplies he edged his army westward to match Cromwell's movement. On 20 August Leslie concentrated his army at Corstorphine Hill, protecting the Stirling road and preventing Cromwell turning north to the Firth of Forth and his supply ships. Finding that Leslie would not come down the hill to attack him (despite the bitter reproaches of accompanying Presbyterian ministers) Cromwell advanced further west and again Leslie matched his movement, the two armies confronting each other at Gogar. Here Leslie had picked a position so broken by swamps and easily defended obstacles that once more he was all but unassailable. Cromwell, often a hot-head in battle but cool and calculating before it began, recognized he had been foiled again. He could advance no further for his hungry troops would soon be starving if he did not fall back on his supplies. He gave the order to withdraw eastward.

The retreat was a nightmare for both armies but worse for the Scots. Cromwell wished only to withdraw to Dunbar unmolested. Leslie wished to harry his foe. Torrential rain and gales strong enough to tear down trees across their roads made both armies miserable but helped the Ironsides by impeding the Scots. The withdrawal continued to Dunbar, the nearest approach to a port and base they had. The Dunbar campaign was now entering its final, decisive phase. It appeared that Cromwell was facing humiliating failure. He had failed to draw Leslie into battle, yet destroying Leslie's army was essential for winning the war. Like the Duke of York of a later age he had 'marched his army to the top of a hill' and he had 'marched it back again', and all he had achieved were heavy losses from dysentery and 'fevers'. The high morale which Cromwell had generated was dissipating, desertion was increasing. Nevertheless, his soldiers were full of fight if only their commander could produce his battle. Their circumstances seemed so desperate, with so many of the men unfit and all hungry, and the Scots army at their heels, that it appeared certain Leslie would refuse battle no longer.

Leslie's army now found itself on the crest of Doon Hill, which lowers over Dunbar. Occupying the high ground is usually a sound military manoeuvre but it has its drawbacks when your infantry are under-fed, ill-clothed, without shelter, and the majority resentfully conscripted into an unfamiliar army life. The weather was vile, with strong easterlies and heavy rain squalls. The Scots were cold, racked by the same fevers as their opponents and, heedless of danger, longed to descend to the plain. Cromwell was as resolute as the most pugnacious of his troopers. Talk by some faint-hearts of evacuating the infantry at Dunbar by sea and letting the cavalry break through down the Berwick road had no appeal for Cromwell even if it had been practicable – which it was not. There were not enough ships and the enemy was too close. However, he was at a loss. He could not attack Leslie up a steep fell-side. If Leslie did not come to him, and soon, Cromwell would find his army withering before his eyes. It had already shrunk to about 11,000, or by approximately a third, during the campaign. A further 500 desperately sick soldiers were now embarked. Some effort was made to fortify the outskirts of Dunbar. Otherwise the army held a line on the plain, roughly facing the enemy, protected from any sudden descent of the Scots on the left by the Brock Burn, which was fordable towards the sea but further south was a formidable ravine. Since the decisive move must be Leslie's Cromwell's soldiers did what they customarily did in adverse circumstances: they sang hymns, listened to inspired preaching about smiting the Amalekites, joined in heart-felt prayers, and kept their powder as dry as their tents and the elements would allow. From defiant but indiscreet prisoners Leslie learned that the infantry had not been embarked, the prisoners assuring him that if the Scots advanced down the hill they would find men enough there to fight them. Leslie probably never believed that whole regiments had departed, although, peering through the gaps in the rain showers, he had distantly observed the embarkation of the sick.

The problem Leslie faced was how to accomplish his enemy's destruction. Their camp was out of range of his guns. If he descended the hill on his right, the option he actually chose, the Brock Burn hindered the deployment of his left wing because the area between the mountain and the burn was not wide enough for him to form a complete line of battle so as to strike Cromwell on the flank as the Englishman retreated eastward. Another dubious option was to attack down the steep hill on the western side of the burn, which was what Cromwell had at first expected, drawing up the Ironsides parallel with the coast road to receive it. Nothing could have proved worse than the option he chose, but that we only know from hindsight. The clergymen commissars who infested his headquarters constantly besought him to descend and smite the enemy in his wickedness but they had no understanding of the difficulties. For them numbers – and Presbyterian orthodoxy – were all. However, although they would be blamed for Leslie's descent from the crest, Leslie never made that excuse for himself. It was his plan which was put in train. He would descend to gently sloping ground just south of the Berwick road and there draw up his army facing north. Since the ground between the Brock Burn and the hilly area to the east was too narrow to deploy his whole force his left wing and part of his centre would have to be left straggling up the hill along the burn's eastern bank. His line-of-battle would as usual have the cavalry on the wings and the infantry in the centre. However, to avoid leaving his left wing cavalry largely useless up the slope, he transferred some to strengthen his right wing, making a united cavalry force of about 6,000. He also sent some of the remaining horse from the left to hold a pass, Cockburnspath (or 'Cockerspath') several miles down the Berwick road, a narrow way where as Cromwell ruefully remarked, ten men could hold off forty. Cromwell estimated later that Leslie cut his left wing by two-thirds to no more than 1,500 or 2,000 horse.[5] This reinforcement of the right meant that there was even less room for the infantry of the centre, so that clumps of both infantry and horse were left straggling down the burn's east bank where at least they might resist any attempt of the Ironsides to cross it. Leslie calculated that his battle-line above the road still outnumbered the Ironsides and his strengthened right wing would be able to deliver a devastating assault down the shallow slope against Cromwell's army if, as he expected, it tried to escape the Dunbar trap down the Berwick road. If Cromwell did not try to break out Leslie would pivot his army round at right angles with his centre now on the road and advance west across the burn towards the Ironsides and Dunbar. In the meantime Leslie sent a mixed force north of the main body to hold the ford. There was nothing foolish about Leslie's battle plan, which was well designed to overcome the problem of a battlefield which was too cramped for the size of his army. Its only flaw was that it did not occur to him that his sick, hungry and outnumbered enemy would dare to attack him.

All that day, 2 September, as the Scots moved in great streams of horse and foot down the slopes, gimlet eyes watched them from over the burn and observed Leslie drawing up his army in the cramped area below a farm called Little Pinkerton. Cromwell, his son-in-law Fleetwood and Lambert rode out at four o'clock to view their enemy. According to an improbable legend Cromwell cried 'the Lord has delivered them into my hands'. In fact he simply declared that the enemy had unwittingly left open the possibility of an assault and they should seize it. To this Lambert enthusiastically agreed. Cromwell then sent for Colonel Monck, who also counselled an attack. Shortly after they retired into his headquarters, Brockburn House, to hold a general council of war at which several officers, alarmed by the enemy's numbers, urged Cromwell to embark the foot while the cavalry cut its way south. This was the course which Leslie expected and which his dispositions would turn into a disaster. However, Lambert rallied the doubters, pointing out that the Scots would be down on them while they were still embarking the infantry, and the cavalry could not cut its way through the whole Scots army unaided by infantry and artillery. On the other hand they could attack Leslie's chosen battle-line with all their army while Leslie could not deploy all of his. If they smote the Scots on the narrow front below Little Pinkerton and also took them in the flank across the fordable reaches of the burn which Leslie had done little to defend, the Scots would have no room to manoeuvre. It was a situation in which inexperienced troops were likely to panic, and if they panicked they were doomed. 'If we but beat their right wing', Lambert argued 'we hazard their whole army, for they will be all in confusion.' The heartened officers made no further demur and the senior officers settled down to refine their plan of battle. (What follows must necessarily be a partly conjectural reconstruction because Cromwell's report of the battle was not detailed.[6]) Under cover of darkness Cromwell's army must cross the Brock Burn at three points because they must quickly take up their positions or Leslie might crush the Ironsides piecemeal before they had formed their line. Lambert's regiments had the vital role: to seize the ford on the Berwick road, disperse Leslie's advanced force on the other side and deploy along the road facing up the slope. Cromwell would lead one cavalry and three infantry regiments across the burn further north and wheel south to take position on Lambert's left. Monck's infantry would cross the burn south of the road and attack Leslie's flank as he moved to counter-attack. Meanwhile the artillery would continuously bombard Leslie's straggling left wing across the ravine.

Soon after midnight the regiments began to move inconspicuously into position. The over-confidence of some senior Scottish officers and the inexperience of their juniors made this easier than it should have been. Both armies had been ordered to keep in battle order overnight. Only one army wholly did so. The Scottish soldiers endured a night of frequent rain squalls with neither tents nor fires. A senior officer had ordered them to extinguish the fuses for their matchlocks lest the gleams betray their positions. Their regimental officers, expecting no peril from the enemy in such weather, had fled to the shelter of neighbouring farm buildings. The Scots were about to pay a heavy price for the Kirk's reckless purging of Engager officers and men early in the campaign. By contrast the English soldiers, led by men as experienced in war as any officer corps in Europe, were early in motion. Cromwell rode among the regiments all night on 'a little Scots nag, biting his lips till the blood ran down his chin without his perceiving it', for his concentration was total. To order 10,000 half-starved, disease-depleted men to attack 23,000 led by an experienced commander displayed breath-taking moral courage. He had lost 8,000 men from his 18,000-man army and defeat would destroy the remainder. Nevertheless

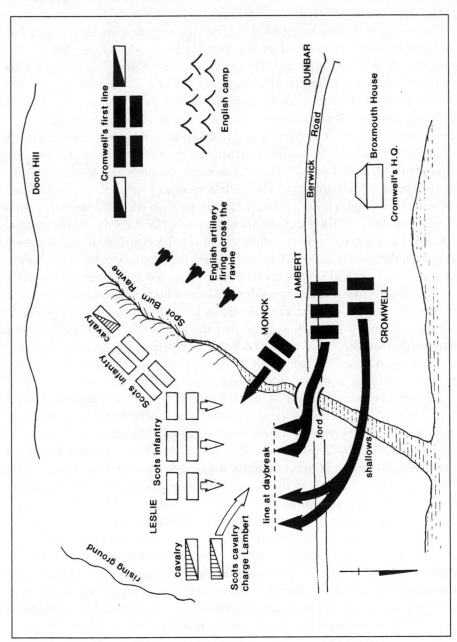

The Battle of Dunbar, 3 September 1650

with Lambert's help he calmly moved the regiments into position, two artillery pieces in the midst of each, quietly encouraging the men. At four o'clock trumpets from the Scottish lines sounded a belated alarm but by then Cromwell was ordering the advance.

The vanguard, consisting of three cavalry regiments and two of foot, crossed the burn by the ford on the Berwick road. Moonlight flooded the scene as Lambert's men quickly drove off the Scots' bridgehead and deployed along the line of the road. Meanwhile Cromwell himself was crossing the burn further north with his own cavalry regiment and three foot regiments of Pride's brigade and turning south to the Berwick road. Before he could arrive the real battle had begun with a charge at Lambert's regiments by several thousand Scottish cavalry, the cream of them in the front rank all armed with lances. The Scottish infantry also advanced down the slope. This was the most dangerous moment because Leslie's forces were already disposed for an attack on the line on which Cromwell wished to mass the bulk of his forces. At first driven back by the force of the charge, Lambert's cavalry, no more than 2,700 strong, rallied and vigorously assaulted the enemy in what Cromwell later described as 'a very hot dispute at the sword's point'. They were now reinforced by Cromwell's cavalry regiment and more infantry under Monck, which had crossed the burn further south, and now attacked the Scots infantry on the slope. Cromwell, having led Pride's infantry into the line on Lambert's left, launched them against the Scottish infantry (on Leslie's right) who were desperately trying to form up. As the sun cleared the horizon at about half-past five Cromwell shouted, 'Now let God arise, and his enemies shall be scattered!'

The action now became general with the superior discipline and readiness of the Ironside infantry more than offsetting their inferior numbers. A charge was mounted on the right by the cavalry of Lambert, Fleetwood, Whalley and Twistleton, with the infantry regiments marching resolutely alongside. Monck's infantry brigade made a decisive lunge across the burn into the flank of the struggling enemy, and suddenly resistance from Leslie's massed regiments fell apart. As Lambert had predicted panic seized the untrained levies and Cromwell was heard to shout in delight: 'I profess they run!' One Highland regiment distinguished itself by its refusal to panic, but its stubborn resistance was broken by a cavalry charge through its ranks, and the Ironside pikemen then moved in to kill or seize the soldiers, rank by rank. All the best Scottish infantry regiments were defeated by Cromwell's foot advancing behind their pikes. Since this main part of the action seems to have lasted no more than an hour, the battle must have been won by seven o'clock. Seeing the most resolute and experienced soldiers overrun and either killed, captured or in flight the remainder of the army melted away. The gunners abandoned their artillery and fled with the rest. The fleeing Scottish horse trampled down many of the hapless infantry on the left, and as Colonel Hodgson observed, 'they routed one another after we had done the work on their right wing'. Horse and foot fled in a heedless rabble which was pursued by the Ironside cavalry, smiting down fugitives on either hand: '. . . the enemy's horse and foot were made by the Lord of Hosts as stubble to our swords', Cromwell was to report in a grim image which haunts us still. Quarter was given to those who surrendered, however, and the number of prisoners taken, about 10,000, almost equalled the entire Ironside army. Briefly Cromwell halted his cavalry regiment to join him in singing the 117th Psalm. The psalm is very short.

> Oh Praise the Lord all ye nations,
> Praise him, all ye people.
> For his merciful kindness is great towards us,
> And the truth of the Lord endureth for ever.

No doubt the tired horses could have wished it were longer but they were quickly spurred on in pursuit.

Finally it was over. As the English soldiers, breathless, wearied with their exertions, halted and, leaning on their long pikes, peered after their fleeing enemy they could scarcely believe their own success. Their brethren in the cavalry, finally returning after an eight-mile pursuit, shepherding flocks of prisoners as they walked their tired horses, peered incredulously at the windrows of corpses lying across the slope. There were at least 3,000 of them. (Some authorities claim that even this horrifying estimate is too low and that the slain numbered nearer 4,000.[7]) More astonishing was the fact that all the bodies they saw lying beside the Brock Burn and spreading up the slopes of the hill seemed to be Scots. Cromwell had routed an army of 23,000 men with 11,000 men and, as he reported to Speaker Lenthall, 'I do not believe we have lost twenty men. Not one commissioned officer slain that I hear of, save one cornet and Major Rookesby . . . and not many mortally wounded.' These were all killed early in Lambert's assault.[8] As astonished as anyone, Cromwell had no reason to minimize his losses, rather the reverse for he badly needed reinforcements. It must be remembered that most of the Scottish infantry armed with matchlocks were unable to fire because of their extinguished matches. Nevertheless it is little wonder that Englishmen spoke for years afterwards of the 'miracle of Dunbar', Cromwell himself ascribing the victory to 'Wonder-Working Providence'. At the time, however, he simply exulted. Standing in his stirrups, his plumed hat in his hand, Cromwell watched the rout 'laughing excessively as if he had been drunk' (as John Aubrey later wrote) and 'his eyes sparkled with spirits'. The relief must have been enormous. Providence or no Providence, he had been in a corner, pressed against the sea, with no secure road out and his hungry army outnumbered by more than two to one. His response had been to attack. He had hazarded all and had won all. In addition to the 10,000 prisoners in their hands the Ironsides had taken all the Scottish artillery and baggage and 180 standards which would soon be hung triumphantly in Westminster Hall.

Why did Cromwell win? The legend is that he won because Leslie abandoned the high ground at the urgings of the Presbyterian clergy and descended to where Cromwell could get at him. This will not do. Cromwell was not besieging Leslie on his mountain; it was the other way round. Had Leslie remained where he was a day or so longer his own army would have deteriorated further and once desertion gathered steam it would have been unstoppable. Disease was already at work among his exposed and hungry men. You cannot defeat an enemy by sitting on a mountain and looking at him. He had trapped his enemy but to take him he had to descend and engage. He had to concentrate on his right wing because that was where the only escape route to Berwick passed. Cromwell demonstrated beyond all doubt that he was a 'master of the field' by perceiving that the conformation of the battlefield could be turned to his advantage. It allowed him to smite with all his regiments while Leslie could not deploy all of his to parry the blow. He had the courage and the experience to strike at the vital point even though it meant assaulting the toughest, not the weakest, part of the enemy's line. The numerical inferiority of Cromwell's cavalry and infantry was counter-balanced by their superior quality. The Ironsides were soldiers, not civilians clad in buff coats. Too many of the Scottish army had been snatched from their farms and trades, unfamiliar with their weapons, commanded by strangers. It could be said of them as Churchill said of the Kaiser's men: it was not their fault. It was their fate.

Dunbar was not to be Cromwell's last battle, but it was the crowning achievement of his military career and he knew it. It was his one victory against odds, and the odds had appeared overwhelming. Leslie's army had not simply been defeated. As a coherent force it had ceased to exist. Well over half were dead or prisoners. Those who escaped vanished in all directions, even south to the Scottish Border. One of Cromwell's first acts was to release 5,000 of the prisoners, most of whom were wounded or worn down by privations and exertions, and send them home or into the care of local people. The remaining 5,000 prisoners were sent south to Sir Arthur Hesilrige at Newcastle. Their fates were mixed. Some weavers were permanently settled there, some prisoners escaped, some were even transported to New England where they were well treated, becoming independent farmers after a period as indentured servants. The majority died of fevers brought on by privations, ill food and worse accommodation. Hesilrige did his best to keep them alive but when the Council demanded a thousand to send to Ireland he had to report he only held 600 fit men. Whatever their destinies, none fought against the Commonwealth again.

The battle transformed the political situation in two countries. In England the Presbyterians, held in check by the military control of the Independents but still a formidable if frustrated force within the Commonwealth, were now discredited. The prestige of the Commonwealth government had never stood higher. The 'Lord of Hosts' had been the watchword of the Ironside army at Dunbar, and it appeared that He did indeed confound their enemies. In Scotland the defeat had a shattering impact. While the extremists among the clergy and the Kirk party blamed David Leslie (and any among his army whose orthodoxy was suspect) for the disaster rather than their own futile policies, the Scottish people were not deceived. The prestige of the Kirk would never stand as high again during the lifetime of the survivors of Dunbar. Never again would the extreme Covenanting party produce statesmen and generals, conjure armies into existence or seek to compel the religious orthodoxy of the English. In the short term they would vainly resist compromise and the creation of a truly Royalist army. In the long term they had to endure the conquest of Scotland by an English army of heretic Independents, and when the Ironsides passed from the scene they would be under the heel of the very monarch they had sought to use as the tool of their sectarian ambitions and who had vivid memories of the humiliations they had heaped on him and on his martyred father.

Meanwhile Charles Stuart soon found his status changed for the better in Scotland, a change he probably anticipated. According to one hostile observer Charles had fallen on his knees to give thanks for the destruction of his enemies when he heard the news of Dunbar.[9] The story may be exaggerated. The picture of that cynical voluptuary falling to his knees to praise God demands a voluntary suspension of disbelief which may be beyond us. Nevertheless he doubtless rejoiced in his heart for now as the Kirk's prestige plummeted his status must rise, and with it the political fortunes of 'repentant' Engagers, old unrepentant Engagers, even Montrose Highland Royalists, 'malignants' of the deepest dye. Hamilton and Lauderdale, long excommunicate, hated and loathed for their royalism and betrayal of the purity of the Covenant, would be received into the Committee of Estates while Argyle, despite demeaning efforts to maintain his influence, would decline into impotence. Dunbar wrought a surprisingly peaceful revolution in Scotland during the coming months.

David Leslie reached Edinburgh by nine o'clock in the morning. The seventy-year-old Earl of Leven came wearily through the fortifications five hours later. The city had already learned the dreadful news from a humbler source. As a preacher promised his packed congregation a great victory, with terrible destruction to be visited on the horrid sectaries that day, he stopped in full flight, gazing in horror over the heads of the faithful. They turned to see leaning in the doorway a battered cavalryman whose distraught face spoke more eloquently of disaster than any words he could have uttered.

CHAPTER SIX

The Last Campaign: Worcester

This hath been a very glorious mercy, and as stiff a contest, for four or five hours, as ever I have seen. Both your old forces and those new-raised have behaved themselves with very great courage, and He that made them come out made them willing to fight for you.

Cromwell to Speaker Lenthall[1]

Dunbar did not end the war but it was slow to resume. Leslie, knowing that he could not hold his Edinburgh lines with the barely 5,000 men he had gathered up after his flight, fell back to Stirling to rebuild an army. The Scottish government fled to Perth. Cromwell also needed to rebuild, for he was scarcely in a position to overrun Scotland with 10,000 weary men. However, Leith and Edinburgh fell like ripe plums as the Ironsides once more marched west along the coast, although Colonel Dundas continued to hold Edinburgh Castle, deaf to the honeyed propaganda with which Cromwell bombarded him. More potent bombardment was beyond Cromwell's capacity until he received a siege-train of heavy guns and mortars. Meanwhile supplies poured ashore at Leith; the flat-bottomed boats which Cromwell had ordered from East Anglian ports during the summer could at last be delivered for operations on the Firth of Forth; and in response to Cromwell's urgent request 6,000 reinforcements arrived with more regiments promised as soon as they could be found.

Baffled like many before him by Edinburgh's rock-girt castle, Cromwell had advanced to Stirling by 14 September but despite his numerical superiority he realized Stirling would need heavier measures than he could mount. The river was too shallow to float his ships which he was accustomed to use as mobile gun-platforms, and the autumnal roads would not bear siege cannon. He soon fell back on Linlithgow, awaiting his siege-train and reinforcements, while his subordinates, Monck especially, busily reduced castles to the south of Edinburgh. These were a thorn in English flesh because from them moss-troopers raided supply trains on the Berwick road. Meanwhile Cromwell resumed the arts of propaganda. He hoped to detach any Scots whose Presbyterian orthodoxy might persuade them that their attachment to Charles Stuart had brought divine chastisement at Dunbar. Deep divisions there were among his enemies. Indeed, they led David Leslie twice to resign his command of the Scottish army although he was twice persuaded to stay on. Three extreme Kirk Party officers, including Colonels Strachan and Ker, eagerly accepted a commission to raise a new army in the western counties, but they were determined that it would not fight on the side of Charles Stuart. These extremists would soon be known as the Remonstrants because they published a 'remonstrance' against fighting for a king who had no sincere attachment to the Covenant and who wished to bring back the Engagers and even Montrose Royalists. Pledged to expel the Ironsides from Scotland they were quite prepared to accept the ascendancy of the Independents in England. Cromwell pursued them to Glasgow, anxious either to seduce them into his service or to disperse their forces before they became dangerous. Failing to do either, Cromwell left it to Lambert and Whalley to crush the western army which they did comprehensively in a night action on 30 November. The commander, Colonel Ker, was captured and Strachan, taking the safer option, soon surrendered to Lambert. Meanwhile Sir Walter Dundas in Edinburgh Castle who had appeared as granite against Cromwell's blandishments, surrendered after only four days' bombardment after the siege-train at last arrived in December. This maintained Cromwell's record of always capturing any castle his artillery bombarded, but probably Dundas had simply needed a respectable excuse to surrender. He was no enthusiast for the Stuart cause.

The year 1650 ended with the Kirk Party and its cause in ruins. By military victory, by relentless propaganda, by exploiting the divisions among the Scots of which his busy spies kept him informed, England's supreme general-politician had accomplished the destruction of the Common-wealth's Presbyterian enemies. However, this victory contained a disadvantage. On the see-saw on which the Kirk Party declined the king's supporters naturally rose. On 1 January Charles was crowned at Scone. He was now able to recruit an army which, although under Leslie's command, would owe its loyalty to him rather than to the Covenanter hierarchy. The objectives of this army showed this precisely: its function was not to drive Cromwell from Scotland and enable Charles to enjoy his Scottish kingship undisturbed. It was to advance on London, attract Royalists and all the Republic's other enemies to its banners, and restore Charles to his English throne. Royalist agents were despatched to organize risings in Chester and Liverpool in the west, Hull and Norwich in the east and in that old Royalist hotbed, the West Country. Royalist risings would complement the king's invasion and divert Ironside regiments from their prime task of trying to halt his advance through the north-west and the Midlands. They hoped the advance would be so swift, the English response to Charles's arrival in their midst so overwhelming, that London would be taken and the king enthroned before Cromwell could gather his scattered legions and head south in pursuit.

Meanwhile the army must first be created which was to accomplish these wonders and in the aftermath of Dunbar this was a lengthy process. In any event the Scottish winter is not a campaigning season, as Monck found when he tried to launch an incursion by flat-boats across the Firth of Forth in January. He retired discomfited by spirited local resistance and bitter weather. Similarly, Cromwell was repulsed by the elements when he sought to invade Fife, Scotland's richest agricultural region. 'General Winter' proving more formidable an opponent than General Leslie, there would be no more campaigning for almost half a year. Moreover Cromwell fell so seriously ill that it is a marvel he survived. Even in the euphoria of victory after Dunbar he had confided to his wife: 'I grow an old man, and feel infirmities of age marvellously stealing upon me.' Now, on top of a severe chill, he was attacked by the dysentery which had felled so many of his soldiers, and was also troubled by that intermittent fever or ague (perhaps malaria) which he had often experienced when young. He was also racked by severe internal pain. Although the government had largely suppressed the threatened Royalist risings, it was horrified to think that by the time Charles launched his invasion their great commander might be in his grave. Cromwell, who was feeling better, dismissed their fears and claimed to be fully recovered. Unfortunately he behaved as if this were true, quitting his sick-bed too early. In May he relapsed, with five fits of high fever in three days and those closest to him fearing for his life. The anxious government ordered him home as soon as he was strong enough to travel and despatched his two personal physicians to help to bring this about. Remarkably, considering his age and the privations he had recently endured, Cromwell recovered. He refused to quit Scotland, for it was time to take hold. His army's morale and discipline had declined while he lay stricken, with discontent and desertion increasing during these months of inactivity. The army too needed restoratives.

Cromwell's recovery improved his decisiveness. Having concentrated most of his forces at Queensferry, in late July he summoned Harrison and ordered him to be ready to march his 3,000 men south as soon as he heard of a royal invasion of England. Cromwell now had 21,000 men under his command and so could afford to divide his forces and even offer Leslie a tempting bait. Lambert and Overton crossed the Forth with 4,000 men and established a base on a narrow defensible peninsula. Leslie could attack them or he could swing south to assault Cromwell's army south of the river. He chose to send a strong force led by Sir John Brown and Major-General Holbourne against Lambert. At once Cromwell feinted towards Stirling with his main force, causing Leslie to order Brown and Holbourne to return. Lambert struck west and caught up with their army at Inverkeithing.

Although both armies were of equal numbers the victory was even more one-sided than Dunbar, despite its smaller scale. In a headlong assault Lambert's regiments slaughtered 2,000 of the enemy and took 1,400 prisoners for the loss of only eight men killed. Cromwell retired his main body and rejoined Lambert. Leaving only eight regiments south of the river he crossed Fife unopposed and compelled Perth to surrender the following day. Within a fortnight Cromwell and Lambert had once more transformed the situation. Their army's morale was restored, the Scottish army had suffered losses it could not replace, the Scottish capital was in their hands and while the king and the remainder of his army still held Stirling, they were cut off from all hope of reinforcement from the north. Their situation was melancholy indeed. They could take refuge in the logistically inhospitable Highlands where they would be hunted down in time. The king could take flight for France and his army surrender at discretion. Or they could take the desperate gamble of invading England, even though they knew that a larger army which they dared not face on their own ground must soon turn in pursuit. In these desperate circumstances Charles turned south for Carlisle, which was exactly what Cromwell had hoped for. Game cannot be killed until it is flushed.

Charles himself was eager to get to England if only because it was bound to be more agreeable than Presbyterian Scotland for which he had early developed a profound loathing. However, his senior officers entertained few illusions about their situation although they may have believed they held some cards. The best Ironside regiments lay behind them and so could not oppose their advance. In England they should mainly encounter militia, and any New Model regiments that appeared would be filled with inexperienced soldiers, even raw recruits, for the veteran regiments were in Ireland with Ireton, or had invaded Scotland with Cromwell or had reinforced him since. The Republic supposedly had few friends among the general population so Charles might expect considerable reinforcements from various well-wishers, including former Royalist soldiers and gentlemen's sons who had been too young to serve in 1642 but who would be eager to fight now. Then there was the Micawber principle which asserts that something is bound to turn up. The Duke of Hamilton had a far-sighted notion of what was bound to turn up: Cromwell and his Ironsides. As he confided to a friend, 'I cannot tell you whether our hopes or fears are greatest: we have but one stout argument – despair'. His gloom was well founded. The soldiers of the Royalist army melted away, first in Scotland through simple desertion, then in England thanks to that familiar haunter of the camp, dysentery. By the time the army had reached Westmorland it was shrunk to about 14,000. Hamilton might be gloomy but at least he was resolute. Loudon and Argyle quietly slipped away from a cause they saw as doomed. The losses to desertion would have mattered less if Royalists had flocked to the royal standard, but they did not. The Earl of Derby and Sir Philip Musgrave put a force of 1,500 men into the field but it was crushed in Lancashire without ever catching up with the main body. Cromwell had ordered Lambert to leave Colonel Robert Lilburne's cavalry behind in Lancashire and during his own march south sent an infantry regiment across the Pennines to reinforce him. However, Lilburne succeeded in destroying Derby's command outside Wigan on 25 August before they arrived.[2] The king's cause had been lost before it was launched. After the crushing of the Norfolk conspiracy in December came the arrest of Royalist agents in March who had betrayed all they knew to save their necks. Most damaging was the appearance of the king with an army of the hated Scots. The Royalist risings never occurred. With them a restoration would have been highly improbable – without them there was no hope at all. Reassured by Cromwell that all would be well, the government did not panic and swiftly implemented the measures he urged upon it. Hundreds of horsemen poured out of London to the county capitals to mobilize resistance. London also prepared itself with Speaker Lenthall and other MPs reviewing 14,000 men of the London trained bands on 25 August. The addition of this new emergency to the large military operations in Ireland and Scotland drove up the monthly tax assessment in August to £157,000. In hindsight such efforts were hardly needed to destroy Charles's depleted army but the government needed to keep the Royalists everywhere in awe, for they could not be certain that there would be no Royalist risings. Usurpers ever live with the nightmare of being usurped themselves.

One writer has described Cromwell's conduct of what became the 'Worcester campaign' as 'the most brilliant pursuit in the history of British arms'.[3] If at Dunbar he had shown himself master of the field August 1651 showed him a master of strategy, moving weighty pieces across the chess board of the two republics. He had ordered Harrison south at the first alarm with 3,000 infantry and 4,000 cavalry and dragoons. He was to do what he could to harry and delay the Scots from in front, while Lambert with several cavalry regiments hastened south to join him. They were to fend off the advance on London, push the Scots towards the west and hopefully bring them to a stand. They were the hounds which would bay at the stag but Cromwell would slay it. Meanwhile Cromwell drove south to join them by forced marches with a mixed force of infantry, horse and field artillery, 10,000 strong. Behind him he left George Monck, who was now a lieutenant-general, commanding a field army of 6,000 men with which he took Stirling peacefully on 6 August and Dundee by bloody storm on 1 September. Late in August, by a happy stroke, he also contrived to 'miserably surprise' and capture the Committee of Estates at Alyth, depriving Scotland of its last vestige of central government. Monck's conquest of Scotland was then merely a matter of mopping up a few isolated castles and strongpoints. On 13 August Lambert and Harrison joined forces in Lancashire slightly in the van of the advancing Scots. Falling slowly back they rendezvoused on the 15th with the infantry of Cheshire and Staffordshire at Warrington Bridge on the road to Worcester. They now controlled an army almost as large as the king's, between 12,000 and 13,000 men, and Cromwell had yet to arrive. The Scots arrived first and although the militia briefly held up the royal army it was deep country with high hedges, unsuitable for cavalry. Lambert and Harrison again withdrew to Knutsford to block the London road. Charles drifted south-westward to Worcester and the traditionally Royalist Welsh Borders. Meanwhile Cromwell had entered England by the eastern route. Fairfax hastened to join him as his army traversed Yorkshire, conferring with Cromwell for three hours in his coach. Fairfax had raised Yorkshire for the Republic, his earlier doubts resolved by the Scots invasion. The conduct of less exalted Yorkshire folk also belied Royalist claims of English disaffection from the Republic. They flocked to the army and accompanied the column for miles, helping to carry the foot-soldiers' burdens and relieving their thirst with beer and spring water, for baking heat continued throughout their dusty march. By 22 August Cromwell was into Nottinghamshire and two days later reached Lambert and Harrison at Warwick, where he also found Lord Grey of Groby commanding the Midlands militia. Once more one can only marvel at the New Model Army's ability to strike swiftly across great distances. Lambert's force had covered 200 miles in only ten days, but at least he commanded cavalry. Cromwell's army covered 300 miles in three weeks with only one day's rest, despite being hampered by artillery, by his nine infantry regiments, and unmounted militia picked up along the way.[4]

Cromwell, who now commanded an army of 30,000 men, the largest he had ever had under his immediate control, advanced west to Evesham and thence to Worcester where his stag was at last brought to bay. Charles and his army had reached Worcester on 22 August. His disheartened, exhausted troops would go no further. Charles and his senior officers had no doubt that they and their army faced a common fate. If Cromwell had not outnumbered them by at least two to one they would have been in a position of some strength. Cromwell needed to assault the Royalists in a pincer movement from both west and east or they might escape into Wales. To do this he must divide his army in the face of the enemy, and on ground itself divided by a river. Aware of his numerical superiority, Cromwell was unworried, but his preparations were meticulous. Lambert commanded the eastern wing, bombarding all morning the Royalists' new earthworks outside the city wall (called Fort Royal). The first phase of the battle, however, was confided to Fleetwood who crossed the Severn by a bridge a few miles south of Worcester and then advanced north along the western bank. Beside him a bridging train worked its way slowly up-river with

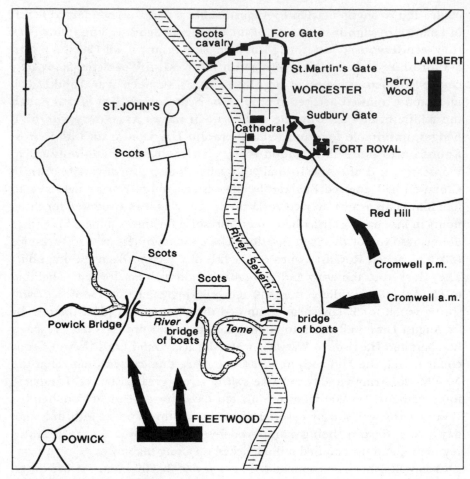

The Battle of Worcester, 3 September 1651

pontoons to give Fleetwood a bridge by which his right wing could cross the Teme, a river which flowed west to east and entered the Severn below the town. His left wing would force a passage over the Teme at Powick Bridge a few miles inland. The engineers would also build a bridge across the Severn just to the north of the Severn–Teme conjunction. This would give the divided army its vital link, enabling Cromwell to cross the Severn with his infantry and horse to assist Fleetwood and then pass back for the second, eastern, phase of the battle. By two o'clock the engineers had the two bridges in position and all was now ready on this first anniversary of Dunbar, a day as cloudlessly hot as any that blazing summer.

Fleetwood's two wings crossed the Teme successfully, although at Powick against fierce resistance, and engaged the enemy foot and horse amid the orchards and water-meadows. Cromwell himself, as reckless as ever of his personal safety, was the first across the Severn, leading his horse and foot to assail the Scots' flank. Brandishing their long pikes his men cried 'the Lord of Hosts', for the watchword of Dunbar had become the battlecry at Worcester. By a strange coincidence Fleetwood's left wing was engaged at the very place where the first blood of the Civil War was shed in 1642, so the war was fated to end close to the obscure field in which it had first begun. The meadows and orchards were cut up by hedgerows which enabled the Scots to defend resolutely. Charles, who from the cathedral tower had watched with interest the Cromwellian engineers at their bridge-building, now led a cavalry charge to assist the Scots infantry. However, although fighting with the courage of despair, the Scots were overwhelmed by superior numbers. Some fled west into the countryside. Most retired across the bridge into Worcester. On the west bank the Ironsides halted, blocking any sally or escape across the Severn.

The summer afternoon was spent but there was to be no respite, for a long and bloody evening would ensue. The Royalists had one last throw: to try to defeat Cromwell's right wing, left hanging while he was still engaged across the Severn. Lambert had bombarded the city's defences all day from the crest of Perry Hill where his army waited to repel any sally by the enemy or to launch an assault on the city with Cromwell's forces when they rejoined him. The Royalists arrived first. Led by Charles and the Duke of Hamilton, the Scots poured out of St Martin's and Sudbury Gates to be joined by Leslie's cavalry which he had so far held inactive at Pitch Croft, immediately to the north of the city. The Royalists hurled themselves up the hill while shot roared overhead from Fort Royal's guns. Lambert and Harrison met them with the regiments of Pride, Whalley, Disbrowe, Cooper, Thomlinson and Cobbett together with some militia units, but the Royalists fought so desperately that the Cromwellians were driven slowly back almost to the crest. Had their defence been less dogged Charles and Hamilton might have defeated Cromwell's right wing. However, the Ironsides bought sufficient time for Cromwell to lead his regiments back over the bridge of boats and across the slope into the Royalist flank. It still took three hours' hard fighting at push of pike before the Royalists were finally driven back into the town, the Ironsides so close at their heels that there was no time to close the gates in their faces and the fight continued in the streets. Cromwell's infantry swarmed over the rampart of Fort Royal and slew most of its defenders, for they would accept no quarter.

That should have been the end of it, but the Scots were without hope and determined to sell their lives dearly. The struggle continued long into the evening, street by street, with the young king leading charge after charge with a suicidal disregard of his life. He was determined not to fall alive into the hands of his enemies. Less understandably Cromwell was often equally reckless, on one occasion riding up quite close to the Scottish infantry jammed in the street to offer them quarter to which they replied with shots which he was lucky to hear whistle harmlessly past him. Finally the foot threw down their arms and tried to flee. The Royalist horse with the king still at their head fought on briefly, but Hamilton fell with a shattered leg, General John Middleton was wounded, David Leslie lost all capacity to command, riding 'up and down as one amazed, or seeking to fly he knew not whither'. Later the Scottish horse fled through the Fore Gate, the only exit still unblocked, and poured up the Bewdley road. They would not reach Scotland. Cromwell's careful dispositions had placed Colonel Lilburne's detachment, fresh from its victory over the Earl of Derby at Wigan, to block that escape route.

Finally even the king realized that flight was all that was left. Charles improvised a hasty life guard from his remaining horse and followed the Scots. The king who had just commanded nearly 14,000 men would by morning be reduced to a single companion. (The companion was Henry, Viscount Wilmot (1612–58), later Earl of Rochester, the father of the poet whose uninhibited life attracted notoriety even at the Restoration Court. He travelled sometimes with, sometimes separately from, his royal master until they sailed together for France.) Charles would be a hunted outlaw during the next six weeks, his eventual escape disguised as a gentlewoman's servant first to the south coast and thence to Fécamp more improbable than anything conceived by a romantic novelist. Certainly his father could never have accomplished it, for his inflexibility, sense of dignity and propriety would never have allowed him to adopt the subterfuges and disguises his son readily embraced. Charles showed a ready wit and skill as a masquerader, and probably enjoyed those exciting weeks more than any other period of his life. Certainly it was a story he loved to retell once his restoration had made it safe to reveal the identities of his helpers. Luck, of course, was with him. Lord Derby had placed him in the hands of Catholic families who were schooled in secrecy and experienced in concealing priests from prying eyes. Extraordinary loyalty was shown him by several ordinary folk who recognized him on his travels and declined to betray him despite the immense reward of £1,000 offered for his capture. Some posters, oddly to our eyes, described him as 'a black man above two yards high', referring to his swarthy complexion, very dark hair, and by seventeenth-century standards, unusual height.

In the city, with the looting beginning and some killing still going on into the darkness, Cromwell was able to write a hasty letter to Lenthall reporting on what he was to term 'the crowning mercy' of Worcester. Dawn illuminated a horrid scene with the streets choked with the dead and dying and hundreds more up the slope of Perry Wood, and in the meadows west of the Severn. As usual the casualties of the defeated were out of all proportion to those of the victors. The Royalist dead were measured in thousands. Cromwell lost about 200 killed, with Quarter-Master General Moseley and a Captain Jones the only officers. Hamilton, now a prisoner, died of his wounds a few days later. With him was the more fortunate Earl of Rothes. Other captives would soon be caught in Cromwell's net: David Leslie found himself conveyed to the Tower which already held his old commander, the Earl of Leven. Both, together with Lord Lauderdale, would remain there until the Restoration set them free. Cromwell reported on 4 September that between 6,000 and 7,000 ordinary soldiers were prisoners, but he meant infantrymen; this estimate must have climbed steeply as the 3,000 to 4,000 cavalry which had fled through the Fore Gate were rounded up. The Earl of Derby paid heavily for his readiness to share the adventure. Despite Cromwell's protests, for he was anxious to promote reconciliation now that victory was complete, he was beheaded at Bolton, and so were some of his followers, including the Cumbrian gentleman Timothy Featherstonehaugh who died on the scaffold at Chester. Lieutenant-General John Middleton, early a prisoner, added another adventure to a life crowded with incident when he escaped from the Tower in his wife's clothing four months later, much to the government's embarrassment.[5] In general the Commonwealth showed itself merciful to the defeated. Few Grandees were executed or even tried, and plans to ship some of the prisoners into virtual slavery in the West Indies were abandoned.

The defeat of the Scots army completed the extinction of that ring of dangerous enemies which had caused the Commonwealth such anxiety in the early months of 1649. The threat of foreign intervention had proved only a nightmare. The New Model Navy had dealt with Rupert and his flotilla of privateers, and commanded the sea-lanes around England to a degree which would have astonished even a Drake or a Hawkins. The threat from Ireland was totally gone even if the war of subjugation dragged on. Now the most potent threat of all, the Scots, their army and Charles Stuart, had been scattered in a defeat from which they could never recover. Scotland was safely in the grip of General Monck and his regiments. Moreover, the Commonwealth could draw comfort from an extraordinary and unexpected phenomenon. They knew that their regime was unpopular. How could it be otherwise when it only survived thanks to a huge army whose very existence burdened the people with taxes while it outraged their sensibilities by its religious radicalism? Yet when a young king appeared in their midst to save them from these afflictions they regarded his appearance with passive hostility or flocked in large numbers into the militia to vent their hatred on the Scots he brought with him. Because Charles had tried to regain his throne by invading with a foreign army the Commonwealth government and its victorious hero appeared as saviours of their country. The English might have preferred a monarchy to a republic but they had made it clear that they would never permit Charles to regain his throne on the back of a foreign army. This makes a very striking contrast with 1639. Then the invasion of the Scots was regarded with apathy – or even welcomed by those who realized it would compel the king to summon a parliament which would call his government to account. When the king called for his people to rally to him to expel the invader he called in vain. In 1651 the Republic called for help to defeat the new Scots invasion and the response was overwhelming. However unpopular the Commonwealth government might be it was apparently more popular than that of Charles I a dozen years earlier. After what was to be Cromwell's last campaign the government had a moral authority it had previously lacked, while Charles Stuart was a discredited exile. However, it was as well the Commonwealth was now secure on land, for within a few months it would face new perils at sea, and from the most experienced naval power in Europe.

CHAPTER SEVEN

War with the Dutch

The English are about to attack a mountain of gold; we are about to attack a
mountain of iron.

Adriaen Pauw, Grand Pensionary of Holland

About ten o'clock on a fine but blustery May morning in 1652 excited
shouts came from shepherds tending their flocks on the downs near Dover.
A Dutch fleet of more than forty sail was approaching the English coast.
Those nearest the cliffs and soldiers on the keep of Dover Castle could also
see a flotilla of nine English warships, a detached squadron commanded by
Admiral Bourne, anchored behind the Goodwin Sands to the east. Admiral
Blake with a further thirteen ships lay several miles beyond the South
Foreland to the west. The Dutch fleet hove to on the outer side of the
Goodwin Sands and two of the smaller Dutch vessels steered towards
Bourne's flotilla with flags courteously dipped. After a brief conference the
frigates returned and the fleet moved westward to drop anchor off Dover.
The Dutch flagship, conspicuous by its size, did not dip its flag in salute and
a cannon boomed indignantly from the castle in response to this neglect.
Meanwhile Bourne had his ships haul up their anchors ready to weigh at
the first hint of danger.

The Dutch were commanded by their best admiral, Marten Harpertszoon
Tromp, Lieutenant Admiral of the United Provinces from 1636 to 1653. He
had been sent to sea with stern instructions not to lower his flag at the
demand of English warships and to protect Dutch merchant convoys from
being stopped and searched for alleged 'contraband' (that is, goods
intended for France, a country with which the Commonwealth was still
carrying on a maritime war). He had no warlike designs against the English
navy, still less against the English coast. However, although he was not
supposed to begin a war his instructions were likely to have this result if he
carried them out. A proud man of great ability, famous for his victories
against the Spaniards, if he would not recklessly cause a war, he would not
disobey his orders to avoid it. While the English later were to refer to his
'braving it' on the English coast (that is, throwing down a challenge) he had
only appeared off Dover in search of shelter as he had at once made clear to
Admiral Bourne. Alerted by a vessel which had been in Dover road when

the Dutch arrived Blake upped anchor the following morning and began
the slow process of working up towards Dover in the face of a stiff breeze,
meanwhile sending orders to Bourne to bring down his flotilla as
reinforcement.

The next morning the Dutch remained at anchor, watched by Dover's
inhabitants with interest and an apprehension which was only increased
when Tromp tactlessly had his men engage in noisy musket practice. At
noon they sailed once more, standing off for the French coast in sight of
Blake's fleet, still laboriously tacking up towards them. While crossing the
Channel two Dutch warships, coming up-Channel, one much shot about,
brought Tromp the alarming news that they had been engaged in a skirmish
with three English warships while conducting a Genoa convoy. Later they
had espied another Dutch convoy apparently surrounded by Blake's
warships. Believing that these ships were being searched or impounded,
Tromp put his fleet about and headed back across the Channel to rescue
them. In fact Blake had ignored the Dutch convoy which, like Tromp, had
simply sought shelter. Seeing the Dutch coming down on him Blake also
turned his vessels downwind. His ship *James*, formerly in the van, was now
the rearmost of the column. His fleet took in sail so that both Bourne's
flotilla and the Dutch could catch him up. The Dutch fleet arrived first,
streaming behind Tromp's *Brederode* which was within musket shot by half-
past four. The *James* fired three shots, the last through Tromp's flag as a
signal to take it down. At this the *Brederode* fired a broadside and the action
soon became general with Bourne's flotilla steering into the rear of the
Dutch column and firing broadside after broadside at the Dutch ships.
Despite the division of Blake's fleet, prolonged by his turn downwind, the
outnumbered English ships had rather the better of the encounter. Two
Dutch ships were captured and their crews carried off prisoner, although
one ship was abandoned, apparently sinking, in mid-Channel, and was
salvaged by the Dutch as they withdrew. No English ships were lost although
the *James*, which was in the fiercest part of the fighting, was severely
damaged by seventy shot in her hull and more in her rigging. Several of her
crew were killed, including the master and a master's mate. In this odd,
muddled and unplanned way began the First Dutch War.[1]

It might seem strange that the new enemy was the Dutch Republic because,
as a Protestant Republican power, it might appear a natural ally of the
Commonwealth despite the Regicide. Certainly Cromwell believed this.
However, this notion of ideological solidarity ignored the commercial
interests which divided England and the Netherlands which were both
maritime powers and inescapably rivals for the foreign trade on which their
prosperity depended. This rivalry went back half a century and indeed it
might be asked why war had been so long delayed rather than why it broke

out in 1652. As early as the 1590s the Dutch had begun to make alarming inroads on England's trade to Baltic markets and to encroach on other English markets. To their traditional sphere of dominance, the bulk carrying traffic in grain, salt and timber of northern Europe, the Dutch were seeking to add the 'rich trades' which included the trade in spices, Dutch woollen textiles, the products of whaling, West African gold, silks and sugar. The war of independence against Spain led to the closing of the Scheldt which starved Antwerp and caused a massive population shift of tradesmen, artificers, weavers, merchants and mariners, together with their capital, to northern ports. As Antwerp declined, Amsterdam rose. This concentration of capital, industrial skill and commercial expertise gave the Dutch by the first decade of the seventeenth century that stranglehold on the rich trades which they had so long enjoyed over the bulk trades, an unprecedented combination. The speed and magnitude of the Dutch success was viewed with awe and alarm by such rivals as the cities of the Hanseatic League, the Danes, the Portuguese and the Venetians, but by none more than the English. In Elizabeth's reign the Dutch and the English faced a common enemy, Philip II's Spain. This muffled the tensions of trade rivalry. After 1603 James I made peace with Spain to the great advantage of English merchants and the brake on English hostility was removed.

During the second decade of the seventeenth century war clouds gathered. At Amboyna a psychopathic Dutch governor tortured and executed several English traders charged with an imaginary conspiracy to overthrow his government. There were other disputes: over the whaling off Spitzbergen, over the Muscovy trade, even over the dyeing and finishing of England's textile exports. The two countries tottered on the brink of war but, despite armed clashes at sea, somehow war was averted. Then in 1621 the situation changed in England's favour and tensions dissipated as the Dutch and Spanish resumed hostilities and the Dutch were once more excluded from Spanish, Portuguese and Flemish ports, from Spanish-controlled Naples and Sicily, and from Genoa, which took its lead from Spain. Their favoured position was swiftly taken over by English merchants. Often ascribed to England's neutrality during the Thirty Years War, the English advantage derived not simply from England's peace but from the Spanish–Dutch war, which brought wholesale privateering against Dutch shipping. Not only were the Dutch excluded from profitable Spanish and Portuguese markets, but their freight rates to other markets were driven higher by the expense of increasing their crews and arming their merchantmen against privateers and by soaring insurance premiums. They still commanded superior resources to their rivals in finance, shipping and whaling, but they could not hold their position against eager English merchants during the war. The dislocations of the Thirty Years War and the competition of the Danes and the Hanseatic towns prevented the English

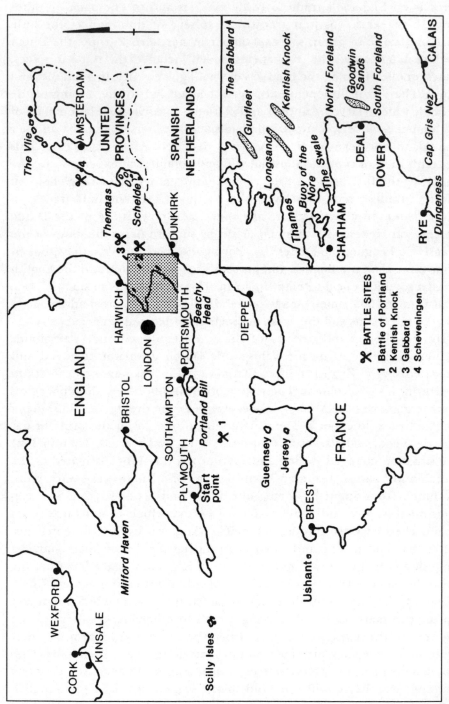

The Battles of the First Dutch War

from controlling the northern trade, but they monopolized the trade in Baltic products, particularly tar and timber, to the Spanish Netherlands. In the south and the Mediterranean the English could trade undisputed to Iberian ports, not only with English wares but also with the 'rich trades' brought home by the East India Company. Moreover, that company had a virtual monopoly of spices at Genoa. Even in the Levant the Dutch suffered in competition with the English because they were cut off from the Spanish silver with which they had formerly settled their balances at Aleppo.

Of course, the Dutch could still out-trade the English in East India spices, especially pepper, in France and northern Europe, for their East Indiamen, well-armed floating fortresses, had no fear of privateers so need not raise their freight rates. Nevertheless, a dozen years which would have been very bleak for English merchants and their cloth manufacturers proved instead a period of substantial prosperity. Not even the dislocations of the first Civil War entirely destroyed this commercial advantage. However, merchants who could turn their eyes from bulging ledgers to look beyond their counting-house walls must have realized how precarious their prosperity would be when the Dutch and Spanish made peace. They were given an unpleasant foretaste in 1640 when the Portuguese re-established their independence from Spain and promptly threw open their ports to the Dutch. Within a year more Dutch ships than English berthed at Lisbon. In 1648 the blow fell when Spain and the Netherlands signed the Treaty of Munster. It was widely resented in the Netherlands but appeared so precarious that many Dutchmen believed it would not last. English hopes of its speedy collapse were vain: this peace proved long-lasting. All the old Dutch advantages resumed: Amsterdam's formidable financial power, low Dutch interest rates, cheaper freights, the sheer volume of Dutch shipping. The Dutch not only had more ships, they could operate their ships more cheaply. The Dutch 'fluit' was the container vessel of its day. Large, rounded, simply rigged, it required fewer crewmen and carried more cargo than its English equivalent because, unlike large English merchantmen, fluits were not warships in embryo: carrying few or no guns they did not need a large crew. Moreover, the lack of men and artillery meant that stores to feed both were not competing with cargo for space.

Soon there was a forest of Dutch masts in every major Spanish or Flanders port, and the embargo at Genoa ended. Of course, English trade to northern and southern Europe was too well entrenched to be thrust back to the levels of 1621, but the impact of Dutch competition was everywhere traumatic and in some markets devastating. The number of English voyages to the Baltic fell every year successively from 1647 to 1652 despite an upsurge in demand for northern grain in western Europe. In Genoa the Dutch re-established their pre-war dominance in Baltic products, grain, timber, naval stores. England's domination of the trade in fine Spanish wool evaporated with the Dutch reported to carry 80 per cent of it by 1650. This revived the long depressed Dutch textile industry which now challenged English fine cloth in Iberia, Flanders and the Baltic markets. This in turn led to a revival of the Dutch Levant trade.

It was a particularly humiliating symptom of the changed situation that some Mediterranean goods now arrived in English harbours in Dutch ships, since English wholesale merchants found their cheaper freights as attractive as any other customer. Here at least the Commonwealth government could act decisively. The Navigation Act of 1651 restricted such produce to the holds of English ships. The act hurt the Dutch and they objected to it, but it could not check their resurgence. There were other sources of anger closer to home. Inward-bound English vessels often found the Thames estuary thronged with Dutch herring busses which had followed the herring shoals south from the Shetlands. Wherever English mariners looked, there were the Dutch, usually in greater numbers. English merchant shipowners everywhere felt the constriction of Dutch competition. The Dutch were now embarked on their greatest phase of commercial expansion, making the Low Countries the centre of a great empire with bases, trading posts and colonies in North America, the Caribbean, West Africa, around the Indian Ocean and through the Spice Islands. Of course, others suffered from this Dutch expansion, the Hanseatic towns and the Danes among them, but they were too weak to challenge the Dutch. England's Republican government was another matter. Its civil wars over, its navy 'new modelled', its army powerful, it could not suffer such heavy blows to its trade without being tempted to seek a military solution.

Intertwined with commercial rivalries were more political reasons for war. The Commonwealth was engaged in a desultory privateering war with France from 1649 to 1655. Claiming the 'sovereignty of the seas', initially in British waters but increasingly throughout the North Atlantic and even in the Mediterranean, the English asserted that they had the right to stop all neutral vessels to ensure they did not carry contraband, that is, French goods. (Since privateers as well as naval vessels asserted this right some Dutch seamen were even tortured to make them declare goods to be French when they were not.) These activities dislocated Dutch trade because they carried the goods of all nations. The Dutch countered with the claim that the flag covered the cargo. If the ship was neutral so were its contents. Refusing to concede a claim so inimical to its interests, the English continued to seize Dutch ships and cargoes. The Dutch retaliated but their gains could not balance their losses, even when the French permitted Dutch privateers to use the sanctuary of Dunkirk. The heavily armed English merchant ships, designed for war as well as trade, could resist privateers much more effectively than the under-gunned fluits. There were other political complications. Charles I had married his daughter to William of

Orange, who as William II was Stadholder from 1647. The Dutch had given shelter to the revolted fleet in 1648 and to Charles II's court-in-exile in 1649–50. They allowed to escape the Cavalier murderers of a Commonwealth diplomat and refused to recognize the Republic. The Orange party dreamed of restoring Charles II with the help of the French. However, the Orange party was only one element in the deeply divided Netherlands, where republicanism was always strong and suspicion of monarchist aspirations never slept. The merchant oligarchy of Holland, far the wealthiest province, sent its own agent to London and the States General steered a middle course, avoiding war and offering the Stuart cause only sympathy. After launching a military coup against Amsterdam which was a complete failure, William II died suddenly in November 1652, a week before the birth of his son, the future William III.

This transformed the situation so dramatically that Holland succeeded in persuading its fellow states to recognize the English Republic, and early in 1651 an English delegation led by Oliver St John and Walter Strickland arrived to negotiate a treaty. If St John and Strickland hoped to persuade the Dutch to abandon their claim to freedom from search they were disappointed. Nothing came of their proposed political and military alliance, nor of their extraordinary suggestion that the two Republics should combine into a single commercial and diplomatic unit. The Dutch had no desire for too close an alliance which might involve them in English wars with their customers. The Navigation Act of 1651 was in part a reflection of the Commonwealth's naive disappointment at this refusal. Meanwhile the English seized 140 Dutch ships during 1651 and a further 30 during January 1652. In the face of such provocation it may seem surprising that the Dutch did not themselves declare war during 1651. After all the Dutch had, during a series of military and naval campaigns which lasted from 1567 to 1648 (save for the interruption of the Twelve Year Truce of 1609–21), successfully fought for independence from the greatest power in Europe, the Spanish Empire. Their navy was large and commanded by experienced admirals. Their armies had enlarged the United Provinces by conquering part of the Spanish Netherlands during the Thirty Years War. From that European catastrophe the Netherlands were the only participant to emerge wealthier and more powerful than when they had entered it, having obtained not only Spain's acknowledgement of their independence but also the right to trade with all parts of the Spanish Empire. On the other side the English navy had not fought a fleet action since the Armada. Defeating Rupert, conquering the Scilly and Channel Isles, blockading Lisbon and establishing a Mediterranean presence, although impressive, were hardly comparable to the past exploits of the Dutch navy. Contemplating the astonishingly successful Netherlands confederacy, with Amsterdam the financial capital of Europe, the Dutch clearly Europe's most industrious and sophisticated people, sustained by a powerful army and navy, foreign observers considered that humiliation and defeat would be the likely outcome if the Regicide state went to war with the Netherlands.

This sanguine view was not shared by Dutch statesmen (although it increasingly appealed to the aroused Dutch people). When war became official in the summer of 1652 the Grand Pensionary of Holland, Adriaen Pauw, gloomily observed: 'The English are about to attack a mountain of gold; we are about to attack a mountain of iron.' More aware of strategic realities than non-naval-minded neighbours, the Dutch were conscious of England's advantage in lying beside the beginning of their chief trade routes, its south-eastern and southern coasts well furnished with ports and bases from which to assault the immensely valuable Dutch convoys. The English merchantmen which would be taken by Dutch privateers and warships would not counterbalance the much larger number of Dutch vessels which would fall victim to English vessels in the Narrow Seas. Moreover, although the Dutch navy had large ships, their first rates were neither as large nor as heavily armed as the first, second or even third rates of their opponents, which, if commanded by resolute admirals, would prove formidable in a sea battle. Finally even if the Dutch were victorious at sea, as many Dutchmen and neutral observers expected, what could they hope to gain from expensive naval victories that they did not already possess?

All this explains why Dutch negotiators had arrived in London in December 1651 to negotiate a general settlement of grievances, although hampered by their masters' demand for the repeal of the Navigation Act. However, the Dutch had no intention of going to war over the Navigation Act. More vital to them was stopping English assaults on their ships, and above all to establish the principle that the flag covered the cargo, otherwise Dutch neutrality would not protect her trade, the very life-blood of her economy, when other countries went to war. While the ambassador was seeking damages for English depredations on their commerce, the English brandished a long list of claims for damages, real or imagined, committed by the Dutch from Greenland to the East Indies during the previous half-century. In February 1652 the Commonwealth learned that the States General had voted to fit out a fleet of 150 sail, which they interpreted as a threat. By May, despite all the efforts of the ambassadors, the government had stiffened its non-negotiable demands: the recognition of England's sovereignty of the seas, the payment of tribute for fishing in British seas, and the Dutch to relinquish their claim to carry a belligerent's goods under the protection of their flag. Admiral Blake was ordered to collect a strong Summer Guard in the Downs while the Estates ordered Tromp to sea. The Dutch navy was divided into three squadrons, one to protect the trade route to the Baltic and the north, one to meet and convoy safely home the East Indies fleet, and the third to station itself with the 'great fishery'. Even after that first, half accidental, engagement between Tromp and Blake off Dover, the Grand Pensionary Pauw was sent to England in June in a last ditch attempt to avoid war. It was in vain. The Commonwealth would not back down while the Dutch government feared that signs of weakness in the face of English intransigence would strengthen the Orange party, for the Dutch people were now strongly Anglophobe. Pauw and the other commissioners were ordered home and on 6 July the States General ordered Tromp to lose no opportunity to attack the English fleet and do it 'all imaginable damage'.

The English government saw the Dutch merchant marine, not the Dutch navy, as the first priority of their fleet. Destroy or capture that immense asset and their enemy would be brought to his knees. The Dutch herring fleet was in the North Sea and the Dutch East Indiamen, with their mouth-watering cargoes, were expected to come home by the northern route around Scotland. Admiral Blake was to steer north and destroy all he could not capture. Strangely Tromp's fleet was not perceived as a serious threat to Blake's expedition or to England's shores during his absence. Greed for plunder led to a myopic disregard for perils which would have been obvious to British admirals of a later age. The Council happily allowed Blake to choose how many ships to take with him and how few to leave with the flotilla then anchored in the Downs. This flotilla, commanded by Sir George Ayscue, lately returned from capturing the Barbados, remained as an inviting target for the huge Dutch fleet cruising off the Dutch coast. Blake's fleet headed north leaving Ayscue vulnerable. Blake was, of course, aware that Tromp was at sea but assumed his first priority would be the convoys, that Tromp must therefore pursue him and that Blake could then bring on a fleet action which he expected to win. However, he left Ayscue in a parlous situation if Tromp preferred to snap up this tempting morsel before beginning his northern pursuit. Meanwhile, far from maintaining a discreetly low profile in the face of the menace of a fleet of more than eighty ships just over the horizon, the pugnacious Ayscue sallied out with nine ships to attack a convoy of thirty to forty Dutch merchantmen homeward bound from Portugal with only four escorts. In the event Ayscue took five, burnt three and twenty-six ran themselves ashore on the Calais sands. Of these Ayscue managed to refloat two despite every French effort to prevent him. Eight further ships fled of which one, 'a rich ship very strongly defended', was captured. Tromp could hardly ignore this provocation and soon appeared off the Downs with eighty-three men-of-war and nine fire ships, although the latter were incapable of weathering a heavy sea, and his fleet was poorly provisioned for a lengthy voyage. Ayscue, hopelessly outnumbered, stoutly put his ships in a posture of mutual defence and erected shore-batteries for added protection. However, with

Ayscue bottled up behind the Downs, Tromp, uncharacteristically sluggish, wasted a week preparing his assault. On 11 July, the eve of his attack, the wind suddenly changed south-easterly, rendering it impossible. Next morning watchers on the Kent shore saw a cloud of grey canvas streaming north-east. A scout had already learned from a captured Dover vessel where Blake was bound. Tromp could delay his pursuit no longer.

Blake's fleet had beaten vainly against northerly winds off the east coast for a week. However, the same southerly change blew a vanguard of Blake's frigates down on the Dutch herring busses off the Shetlands on 12 July. The small English flotilla overwhelmed their twelve escorts in a brisk fight, sinking three and taking nine with 900 prisoners. To Blake's relief the fishing fleet escaped during the fight. He had no desire to wage war on peaceful fishermen and could not have coped with so many prisoners. It was now time to seek the greatest prizes of all, the East and West Indies convoys. It appears that Blake nominated Fair Isle between Orkney and Shetland as the rendezvous. Judging that both the Dutch convoy and Tromp would do the same, he hoped to capture the one and defeat the other in battle. His reasoning was sound but the god of winds once more intervened. Tromp's van sighted distant ships off Fair Isle, and rightly assuming that Blake's main fleet was just over the horizon, Tromp prepared for battle. No sooner had he done so than both fleets found themselves in one of the most violent storms ever to smite battle fleets at sea. With the Dutch driving down on the Shetlands' menacing cliffs, it was every captain for himself and the fleet scattered. When the weather moderated on 27 July Tromp's fleet, which had numbered nearly one hundred sail, was down to thirty-four. Two found themselves off Norway, fifty-one found precarious shelter in the western fiords of the Shetlands. The English reported that ten were wrecked on the Shetlands and six foundered at sea. Another sank before Tromp's horrified eyes. The storm had also struck the Dutch convoys as they approached Fair Isle. Two were wrecked on the Shetlands, while at dawn others were amazed to find themselves amid Tromp's wallowing warships. Blake's ships had been more fortunate, finding shelter in Bressay Sound on Shetland's east coast, although none escaped damage and many were unfit for battle.

The storm might be considered to have robbed Blake of a double triumph. However, in a fleet action he would have done very well to have destroyed sixteen or seventeen of Tromp's warships with no loss of his own, and with hardly an English life lost. At Blake's great victory at Portland in 1653 the Dutch lost seventeen warships and thirty merchantmen but the English lost a ship and suffered hundreds of casualties, including some of their best captains. Certainly the Dutch knew they had suffered a disaster as their warships straggled home during the following weeks with many seamen injured, more afflicted with scurvy, all half starving. Of the fifty-one stragglers none could be refitted in time to take part in the autumn campaign in the Channel. There was another English gain. Republican enemies seized the chance to make Tromp, a monarchist, a scapegoat for the disaster. He resigned before they could dismiss him. The Dutch had discarded their best admiral just as Blake's talents were maturing.

Ayscue, now reinforced to twenty ships and with more joining him, had the advantage in the Channel once Tromp's great fleet had streamed north. Armed with two 60-gun ships, the *George* and the *Vanguard*, eight ships of between 36 and 40 guns, and about forty lesser vessels, he shepherded home two valuable East India and Levant Company convoys. Meanwhile the Dutch sent Admiral de Ruijter to bring home the West Indies silver fleet which was off Spain anxiously awaiting an escort. De Ruijter's task was formidable. He would have to fight Ayscue while tied to the convoy's protection, and even if he defeated him Blake might have returned to block the Narrows before he could reach safety. However, if Tromp was the genius of the past, de Ruijter was the man of the future. Ayscue found de Ruijter and his convoy off Brittany on 16 August. The Dutch had forty warships and sixty merchantmen, although to the English these proportions appeared reversed, because many of the heavily armed merchantmen took part in the battle. Ayscue had about forty warships and four fire ships, but his ships outgunned their opponents in number and weight. Ayscue hurled his fleet at the Dutch in a compact mass. A desperate fight occurred around the *Struisvogel*, whose crew were only prevented from surrendering by the master's threat to blow up the ship. Sir George forced his way through the Dutch with six other ships and then tacked back again so as to keep the weather gage, but the rest of the fleet failed to keep with him. In the fight the Dutch concentrated their fire on the sails and rigging of the English while the English concentrated their heavier guns on the Dutch hulls. The *Bonaventure* would have been lost if the English had not dispersed her adversaries with a blazing fire-ship and then towed her out of action. Darkness ended all. No ship was sunk or lost by either side (save the fire-ship), both sides suffering about a hundred casualties. The Dutch lost a rear-admiral to a heart attack after the action; the English rear-admiral, Michael Pack, died of his wounds. There can be no doubt who had the advantage, however. Despite Ayscue's fire-power de Ruijter had saved his convoy, while the damage to English rigging prevented any pursuit for a second attempt. Even worse, when Ayscue's fleet retired to lick its wounds in Plymouth, de Ruijter was able to follow him there only three days later. He planned to attack the English at their anchorage but again a sudden shift of wind saved Ayscue, this time from a peril of which he was not even aware. The fact that the Dutch admiral was prepared to attack a force of more powerfully armed ships in their own anchorage, and with every prospect of success, demonstrates his courage and resourcefulness. Ayscue, who may have been in poor health since his West Indian voyage, shortly after resigned.[2]

For the next month de Ruijter kept the Channel unmolested. Blake was inactive in the Downs probably repairing his ships from the wild northern voyage. Finally he sortied, but against a different enemy. The Duc de Vendôme had sent a seven-ship expedition to Dunkirk which must surrender to its Spanish besiegers if not immediately relieved. Blake's fleet snapped up six almost before they knew they were in danger and Dunkirk surrendered the following day. The Commonwealth ignored Vendôme's demands that Blake should be dismissed for this exploit, so he laboured down Channel against the prevailing westerlies in search of de Ruijter. They did not meet, although at one time Vice-Admiral Penn's eighteen-ship squadron would have lured him on to Blake's main body had they not been separated by heavy weather. De Ruijter finally sailed home, his provisions exhausted and with ten ships barely seaworthy. Foiled of engaging de Ruijter Blake retired to the Downs to await the next Dutch initiative and to watch for any Dutch convoys coming up-Channel. He was soon to have a new opponent. Tromp had been replaced by the Vice-Admiral of Holland, Witte Corneliszoon de With, a courageous commander with few skills at managing men. Hot-tempered, vituperative, intolerant, he did not suffer fools gladly and the timorous not at all. His sailors loathed him, rather unfairly, because they could not forgive the abandonment of Tromp. De With was innovative, dedicated, and impatient with the administrative incompetence of a state divided among several provinces which could not even agree on a common rate of pay for their seamen. Had he directed his aggressiveness solely against the enemy instead of too often turning it against his own subordinates he might have been one of the great admirals. It is difficult to imagine a more different personality from that of Blake, who was usually even-tempered, uncomplainingly loyal to his superiors and popular with his men. These two commanders were now to meet in battle.

Reinforced by de Ruijter on 2 October, de With's combined fleet of sixty-two sail was driven north by adverse winds towards the Goodwin Sands where they found Blake's fleet lying in the Downs. The fleets were roughly equal in numbers but Blake commanded seven great ships of 50 guns or more including the famous *Sovereign*, which still carried more than 80 guns although she had been cut down by a deck so that she could open her lower gun-ports when she heeled. Adverse winds prevented an action until the 8th by which time de With had been blown north, desperately trying to assemble his ships, until he was off the northern tip of the Kentish Knock shoal north-east of the mouth of the Thames. Blake pursued him but failed to concentrate his forces, so that Admiral Bourne's division was left isolated astern. Seeing his opportunity de With tacked towards Blake, the two fleets approaching on opposite courses. The Dutch had mislaid several ships

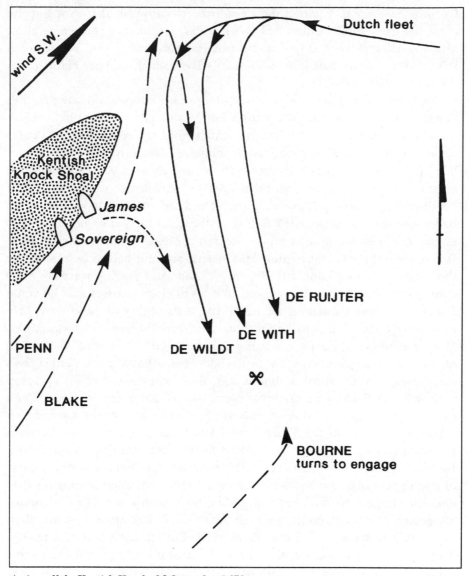

Action off the Kentish Knock, 28 September 1652

during the gales and had fifty-nine vessels in four divisions, de Ruijter on the larboard wing, de With in the centre, de Wildt forming the starboard wing but slightly to the rear. Cornelius Evertsen commanded a reserve behind. With Blake in the 88-gun *Resolution* in the van the English were in a ragged column about six miles long, for they had not yet perfected the disciplined line-ahead formation of later days. De With, seeing Tromp's old flagship *Brederode* had joined the fleet, tried to move his flag to it but the crew, intensely loyal to their old commander, mutinously refused to allow him aboard, and the outraged and furious admiral had to shift to the much less suitable 44-gun East Indiaman *Prins Willem*, which he later claimed was the worst sailer in the fleet.

The fleets opened fire as they passed on opposite courses, although neither Penn's *James* (66 guns) nor the giant *Sovereign* took part in the initial clash as they both grounded on the Kentish Knock, and the remainder of Penn's squadron waited while they extricated themselves. Meanwhile, the Dutch were bearing down on Bourne's dangerously isolated division on a course which must eventually take them past Penn's delayed squadron. When sufficient of his ships had closed up Blake wore round and tacked after de With. Captain Badiley, in the van of Bourne's flotilla, nothing daunted at seeing the entire enemy fleet bearing down on him, steered recklessly into the midst of the Dutch where he was immediately heavily engaged and had to be rescued by the *Speaker* and two consorts. His vessel's sails and rigging were so badly damaged by Dutch ships firing from all sides at close quarters that he could not work his vessel which for a time drifted at the mercy of the currents. He took nearly 100 shot into her hull and suffered at least sixty casualties. However, he succeeded in getting his crippled vessel into Yarmouth. Meanwhile, in a manoeuvre that proved decisive, Admiral Penn got his *James* and *Sovereign* off the shoal in time to hurl them and the rest of his squadron into de With's flank as it tacked past them. 'We fell pat to receive them,' Penn commented happily, 'and so stayed by them until night caused our separation.' Folk on the Kentish and Essex coasts could hear the guns rumbling continuously over the horizon as the fleets drew slowly southward. De With's manoeuvre should have richly rewarded him but the abrupt change of course past Blake on to Bourne threw off the poor sailers among his fleet and encouraged the faint-hearted among his captains to avoid the combat altogether. The Dutch crews, hopeless out of formation, often fired into their own vessels in trying to fire over them at the English yards and rigging. The English gunnery was more disciplined, broadsides being fired from some ships only at a signal on the ship's bell, and only when the enemy was in close range. The *Sovereign* engaged a score of Dutch frigates with terrible effect to both hulls and crews. Both de With's and de Ruijter's flagships were crippled aloft and two other ships were so badly dismasted that they were soon boarded and captured. One of them had been so shattered by cannon-fire that it had to be abandoned but the next day, with the same ingenuity they had demonstrated after the Dover action, the Dutch salvaged her and brought her to safety. De Wildt's flotilla suffered heavily, his own ship captured and himself made prisoner when the ship to which he had fled was also taken. One Dutch ship blew up. Apart from Badiley's vessel the English fleet suffered little except damage to upper yards and rigging.

The following day the two fleets were still only two miles apart. Nine Dutch ships had gone missing during the night, and apart from the three taken or sunk by the English, three more were entirely disabled. Although de With was still determined to engage Blake again, the fight had gone out of his captains and de Ruijter himself could see that to throw their damaged ships, reduced to forty-nine, their crews weakened by scurvy and their recent exertions, against Blake's almost intact and heavily gunned fleet would be to lose all. Reluctantly, breathing fire against captains whose timorousness he believed had betrayed him, and against those who would not resume the battle now, de With headed home. It was the right decision. De Ruijter had reported after his fight with Ayscue that the English artillery made their fleet far more powerful than the number of vessels had led him to expect. De With for all his bluster had learned the same lesson, reporting gloomily that 'the guns on their smallest frigates carry further than our heaviest cannon'. As for Blake, he wished to pursue but his vessels were too ill-provisioned for a blockade and too slowed by damage aloft to catch de With and bring him to battle, so the English celebrated a victory which might have been more decisive than it was. The mid-seventeenth-century English man-of-war was the most formidable single weapon then existing but, soldier at sea as he was, Blake had yet to learn how to employ it to best effect. His worst blunder was the failure to concentrate. Blake had the wind and should have advanced on the enemy with all his force, not left Bourne to face the brunt of the enemy's up-wind assault. The disorder of the Dutch fleet, the very varied sailing qualities of their ships (many of them converted merchantmen), the lack of spirit of many of their captains, and the ferocity of the English broadsides brought about their losses rather than de With's tactics which were well conceived or Blake's tactics which were not. Blake was never again to have as good an opportunity to destroy or capture the Dutch fleet.

Blind to such reservations, the English government rejoiced in a victory which unfortunately encouraged them to behave as if the war was all but won. This would have mattered less if the fleet had been ready for any eventuality, but it was not. Ships needed repair, all needed re-victualling, the sailors were mutinous because of their arrears of pay. Yet in their euphoria the government failed to vote more money for the navy, which was already over-budget by more than £400,000. Moreover the government, having resolved to spend £300,000 on new construction, neither cancelled the programme nor voted the money to pay for it. During the autumn the battleships *Kentish*, *Essex*, *Sussex* and *Hampshire* rumbled down the slipways with flags bravely flying, onlookers cheering, but these patriotic occasions only deepened the naval deficit. Victualling and repairs slowed as naval contractors grew cautious; they were only prepared to work on credit after the government had voted the funds for their eventual compensation. Meanwhile in other theatres the course of the naval war appeared less rosy than in the Narrow Seas. The Danes had contemptuously rejected an attempt by a small naval expedition to negotiate better terms for England's trade with the Baltic, so a new expedition must be mounted too powerful for the King of Denmark to brush aside. In the Mediterranean matters were worse. A squadron under Richard Badiley had been badly mauled by a larger Dutch squadron while a flotilla under Henry Appleton was bottled up in Leghorn enduring the unreliable hospitality of the Grand Duke of Tuscany. A fleet of at least twenty ships must be despatched to restore England's Mediterranean fortunes. Blake found his fleet gravely weakened by these distant priorities. The November elections to the Council of State brought a Council less responsive to the mercantile lobby and more inclined to make peace with the Dutch who, it was assumed, would now be in a more amenable frame of mind. Proposals for social and legal reform distracted the new Council from the sea affair. All this left Blake moored in the Downs commanding a mere skeleton of the force which had sortied against de With.

The Dutch who had already fought the greatest power in Europe to a standstill were far from beaten. Both Tromp, brooding in retirement, and de With, fresh from his experience of English fire-power, wanted to build ships which would match the English first, second and third rates. Their masters feared such ships would be too large for the shallows off the Dutch coast, unable to grasp that only ships able to meet the English men-of-war on equal terms could give them victory at sea. Only one warship of 150 feet was built, with ten third rates and nineteen lesser frigates. Tromp had wanted six of 150 feet, twelve of 140 feet and six of 134 feet. However, the Dutch as usual repaired and refitted their existing ships with exemplary speed, and to the joy of the fleet Tromp was restored to command. By late November he was struggling to get a fleet of warships and a huge convoy of merchantmen to sea. Blake, who was as unconcerned at his increasingly exposed position as Ayscue had been before the northern voyage, was rudely woken from his complacency by the appearance of a fleet of five hundred sail, of which nearly ninety were men-of-war. With the huge Dutch merchant convoy screened by his fleet Tromp sailed west down-Channel, tacking against the prevailing wind in an attempt to get to windward of his opponent. Blake sortied immediately, racing down-Channel much closer to the coast in an effort to gain the weather gage. The two fleets raced in parallel separated by shoals called the Rip Raps. This tacking duel could not continue indefinitely because the probing point and shingle ridges of Dungeness loomed ahead. There Blake must steer towards his enemy or ignominiously but sensibly in view of the heavy odds retire downwind to a safer haven. Characteristically Blake steered towards the enemy.

The position was hopeless. Blake's manoeuvring was hampered by the coast close behind him which negated his superiority in fire-power, and he would have been greatly outnumbered even if his ships had not been widely separated by the race to Dungeness. After an exchange of broadsides between Tromp's *Brederode* and Blake's *Triumph* the second English ship, the *Garland*, thrust between them and the *Brederode* quickly grappled and tried to capture it. The *Anthony Bonaventure*, an armed merchantman, boldly attacked the *Brederode* on her unoccupied side and it seemed as if the Dutch might lose their flagship. Instead Evertsen intervened against the starboard quarter of the English vessel and it was the *Anthony Bonaventure* which fell prisoner after the death of her courageous captain, Hoxton. The *Garland* also succumbed, following the death of her captain, despite an explosion, which may have been a desperate act of defence, which hurled the quarterdeck and poop clear off the ship. Blake could not assist his beleaguered ships for he was beset by other Dutch warships, including de Ruijter's. The *Triumph* was ably assisted by the *Vanguard* and others, but the straggling English warships, whose captains had had little confidence in this sortie from the start, only indecisively attacked the Dutch rear. In the end as the short autumn evening had saved de With's fleet, so the short winter afternoon saved the English, the battle having begun about three o'clock. The English gradually retired first to the Downs and then to the greater safety of the Thames estuary with Tromp pursuing as soon as his convoy was safely down-Channel. Tromp longed to pursue Blake into the Thames but none of his experienced pilots dared to guide a fleet where they had so often taken their own ships.

Blake was safe, but never can so small a battle have had such destructive consequences. According to unreliable legend Tromp lashed a broom to his masthead as a symbol that he intended to sweep the Channel of English ships. Certainly he did so over the following weeks. He even put boat crews ashore to seize the cattle and sheep of bewildered farmers. Moreover, having gained this overwhelming advantage the Dutch forsook their respect for neutrality when blockading English ports, for they seized any neutral vessel carrying naval stores from the Baltic and took them to the Netherlands. Indeed they piratically seized neutrals regardless of cargo or destination. In the euphoria of victory they promised to bring the Regicide government to its knees. It seemed that for the Dutch, as for the English, neither statecraft nor common sense could survive a victory. In fact the English were far from supine just because they were not vaunting in the field. In the post mortem after Dungeness several captains were sacked for lack of courage or competence, one of the victims being Benjamin Blake, the admiral's brother. Robert Blake himself took responsibility for the defeat, and offered his resignation but either because the Council was too wise, or because it was too fearful of the effect on the sailors who idolized him, his offer was firmly declined. The government had grasped that captains commanding ships which they owned would not vigorously assault the enemy: they were more concerned at the possible loss of their property than about the loss of the battle. Hired merchantmen were to be phased out of the fleet which would be composed increasingly of 'state's ships', that is men-of-war built for the navy. Better a smaller fleet of heavily armed naval ships than a larger fleet which included uncommitted, unreliable armed merchantmen. Blake and his captains declared to the Council that they were ready to tackle a ninety-sail fleet with only sixty of their own so long as the sixty were all men-of-war, of at least 26 guns and with at least forty armed with 36 guns or more. Several of the men dismissed the service were not merchant captains but naval commanders. Their sin was not cowardice so much as a determination to think for themselves. They had rightly believed the Dungeness race ill judged and did not wholeheartedly support their commander. In future the admiral's lead must be followed, his orders obeyed without question once the council of war had finished its deliberations. Laws of War were drafted, the basis of the later Articles of War, most of them carrying the death penalty for non-compliance. Some prescribed sober and reverent worship and refraining from profanity, others related to embezzlement and the treatment of prisoners, five were aimed at treacherously aiding the enemy, while most of the rest covered discipline in action, cowardice, negligence, and lack of zeal in supporting their fleet.

Meanwhile to check desertion and incipient mutiny, money was voted to reduce arrears and to increase the seamen's wages, while the shares of prize money were made to match those offered by privateers to lure away naval seamen. These reforms tightened discipline, made the fleet more effective, desertion decreased, more men enlisted. Nevertheless to man the giant fleet the Council was mobilizing to cleanse the Channel of its Dutch overlords seamen aged fifteen to fifty were pressed in most coastal towns. Moreover 1,200 soldiers were sent to the fleet to improve discipline and repel boarders, the foundation of the Marines.

With all these reforms and reorganizations in place, three 'generals-at-sea', Blake, Deane and Monck, left their Thames moorings on 10 February and headed into the Channel. Monck was an afterthought. He had been plucked from Scotland as a new naval commander but as a newcomer was supposed to stay in London to supervise naval affairs. Monck had no intention of navigating a desk while others saw all the action and so sailed as admiral of the White squadron in a second rate, the *Vanguard* (56 guns). The Blue squadron was commanded by Penn in the *Speaker* (56 guns), and the Red squadron by Blake and Deane, both of whom were aboard another second rate, the *Triumph* (62 guns). John Lawson, an ardent radical Baptist, was left without a squadron of his own but sailed as vice-admiral of the Red.

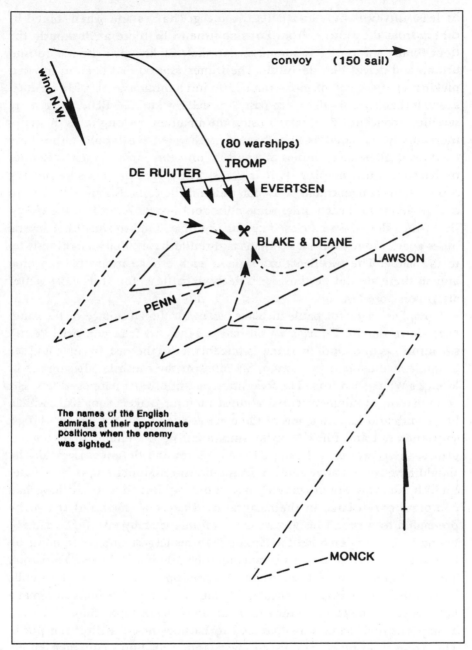

The Battle of Portland, 18 February 1653

At least fifty-two ships had sailed from the Thames and when joined by others from the Downs, from Portsmouth and by three at Plymouth, the fleet finally amounted to about seventy sail. Blake's priority was to find Tromp and defeat him decisively. The Dutch admiral had been in the west picking up a convoy of more than 150 merchantmen at the Isle de Rhé. Fearing that Tromp might slip past him, convoy and all, Blake once more sacrificed concentration, crisscrossing the Channel on long tacks, his ships increasingly extended as the Channel grew wider. He should rather have used his smaller, faster vessels as scouts to hunt the enemy, much as Rodney or Nelson would employ their frigates, while keeping his slow-moving capital ships concentrated ready for action. When on 18 February the two fleets stumbled on each other some miles south of Portland Bill, the eighty-ship Dutch fleet was well closed up and the three English squadrons several miles apart. Monck was most distant and would have to tack laboriously up to the battle. The two fleets had sighted each other early in the morning and so there should be time for a decisive battle before the short winter afternoon closed in.

Tromp, as eager for battle as Blake, and with the advantage of the wind, bore down on the *Triumph* which had only twenty-four consorts. Penn's squadron was due south of Tromp, while further to the east Tromp could see a flotilla commanded by Lawson. Six miles to the south lay the topsails of Monck's White squadron. The following account of what happened next is a combination of conjecture and reconstruction.[3] Blake's squadron, which, like Penn's and Lawson's, was heading across the line of the enemy's lunge, shortened sail and turned to the wind, awaiting the enemy in a compact group, their cannon bristling all ways for mutual defence. Logically he should have turned away and led Tromp down on Monck's squadron. Later English admirals would certainly have done so, but they would have had complete confidence in their captains. Blake may have felt that if he pretended to turn tail his weaker brethren might really take flight. He was bound to have a fierce fight as Tromp with his largest ships bore down on him, supported by squadrons commanded by Admirals Evertsen, Floriszoon and de Ruijter. Lawson in the 64-gun *Fairfax* appears to have led his flotilla around the rear of Blake to engage the enemy. Tromp and Floriszoon met a hot reception, the former losing his main and mizzen yards. Both Blake and Tromp saw their squadrons 'reduced to harmlessness', as Evertsen put it. The *Triumph* suffered damage to masts and yards and many men killed, including Captain Ball and Blake's secretary, Drue Sparrow, while Blake's leg was grazed by a bar-iron shot. Evertsen was a frustrated spectator of this hot fight as he worked his way around it trying to find Lawson, only to discover he had vanished into the smoke of the central engagement.

De Ruijter attacked Penn's ships which were not tightly bunched as they came to aid Blake and, his ships swiftly getting among them, his men boarded the *Oak*, *Prosperous* and *Assistance*. The *Assistance*, carrying Rear-Admiral John Bourne, was briefly captured but then recaptured when Lawson's squadron appeared through the smoke. The Dutch boarders were cleared from the *Oak* and *Prosperous* but the *Sampson* (an armed merchantman) was so shot up in the intense fire-fight that she was later scuttled. De Ruijter's own ship was dismasted and later had to be towed. Finally the Dutch ring around the *Triumph* and her consorts was breached and their bombardment died away. Dismayed, thwarted, Tromp had to withdraw his battered ships and return to the convoy, leaving four ships to fall into the hands of the enemy with four others sinking. The convoy had been slowly plodding up-Channel listening fearfully to the thunder of a fiercer and more prolonged cannonade than any seaman could remember drifting up from the south. Now the convoy was in danger, for Monck had sent his faster vessels to attack it. He himself had laboured up all through the long morning with his heavier ships until he was able to pour broadside after broadside into Evertsen's squadron which was still striving to engage Lawson's flotilla. Despite his late arrival Monck's *Vanguard* was so heavily engaged that she lost more killed than most of the other English warships.

In the fading light, with many of his ships in danger of sinking or capture, and all short of ammunition, Tromp strove to restore some order among his fleet so as to cover the precious convoy. In the rear, the English sent their worst damaged ships into dock along with several captives. Those damaged aloft hastily rigged new masts and yards, as the rest struggled to reform their squadrons in the fading light. Then they turned to pursue. The action grumbled on during the following two days. There was no general action on the 19th because Tromp, pinned by his responsibility to the convoy, could not turn at bay. Moreover he had too many ships that were largely passengers, unable to fight for lack of ammunition. He stationed them amid the convoy to stiffen the morale of the merchantmen by their appearance. Tromp drew his more serviceable ships into a long half-moon between the convoy and the pursuing English with the *Brederode* at the centre of the arc, Evertsen on the left 'horn' and de Ruijter on the right. This tactic saved the convoy in general, but from time to time the English got among them and snapped up prizes, and made hay with some ill-disciplined merchantmen who broke in panic and tried to steer away for French ports. The approaching Narrow Seas had filled them with dread for they found the possibility of seeking refuge in a neutral Spanish Netherlands port more daunting than capture by the Protestant English. Two men-of-war from Evertsen's wing were captured. Floriszoon also saw one of his squadron taken but could do nothing to save it. His own ship, the *Monnikendam*, had lost its main topmast and mizzen yard the day before. These had been repaired but were again shot down, while the remarkable capacity of the English gunners to strike Dutch hulls below the water-line had left his crew fighting to keep the *Monnikendam* afloat. With the convoy half mutinous, with several Dutch captains who had played little part in the battle determined they would desert the flag now that their admirals were in near sinking or badly damaged ships (de Ruijter was still under tow) and with the more resolute ships almost out of ammunition, the 20th (February) appeared certain to be a day of total disaster.

The dreaded English broadsides opened about nine o'clock, and after a brief and ineffective return of fire the Dutch fleet continued to flee eastward with the faster English frigates barking and biting at the leeward flank of the convoy. As the short winter afternoon closed in, with only thirty-five ships left of the more than seventy which had entered the battle, Tromp decided on a desperate throw. He led his fleet close to a lee shore in winter by steering his fleet and depleted convoy towards Cap Gris Nez. There in the falling darkness he found relief. The English with their injured masts and spars and their heavier draught dared not follow him. They believed him trapped, pinned by the north-west wind and the ebbing tide which was setting fiercely against him. They anchored to await his final defeat the next morning when Tromp would, they imagined, have to steer out into their arms to try to double the cape. In fact, as his pilots knew, there was some deep water under the cape and Tromp's fleet stole past its sombre loom during the night. Against all likelihood the veteran admiral had saved the bulk of his command. He was just in time. Snow flurries from a darkening sky warned of severe weather. Masts went over the side on the 21st (including Floriszoon's mainmast), and more vessels came under tow as the fleet struggled on to anchor off Dunkirk on 3 March. By then fleet and convoy totalled only 70 vessels out of approximately 220 in sight at the beginning of the action. (This assumes 150 merchantmen and at least 70 warships. Some merchantmen had found refuge in neutral ports or were scattered about the Channel mislaid by both sides.)

The English whether at sea or in London spent no time in repining a missed opportunity. However incomplete, they knew the victory had been devastating to their enemy. The navy claimed seventeen men-of-war sunk or taken, and about sixty merchantmen were either in their hands or sunk by gunfire. The number of seamen killed, wounded or captured must have amounted to about 3,000. The English lost only the armed merchantman *Sampson*, although many others were badly damaged and would be unfit for action for several weeks. They estimated their own casualties at about 600. More significant for both sides was the strategic situation after the battle. The English command of the Channel was re-established and the Dutch were compelled to order their convoys to take the longer and more dangerous northern route. They were well aware that the English had won this engagement without employing their first rates, the *Sovereign* and the *Resolution*. With the advantage of numbers and concentration, with the

English squadrons scattered across the Channel on the first day, the best
Dutch warships had been unable to overwhelm the English second, third
and fourth rates because of heavier guns better served by disciplined gun-
crews. Moreover, this victory over the best Dutch admirals combining
decades of sea experience, and with only de With absent, had been won not
by experienced admirals but by generals and colonels transferred from the
English army. It was a gloomy picture.

Nothing could more vividly demonstrate the remarkable resilience of the
Netherlands, despite the bickerings and jealousies of the states, despite the
divisions between republicans and monarchists, than that after such a defeat
in February a fleet of more than a hundred ships sortied into the North Sea
in early May. The intervening period, however, was dismal for Dutch trade.
Tromp himself advised the merchants to keep their ships at home, and
those abroad dared not attempt a run for home. It is said that grass grew
amid the cobbles of the Amsterdam streets, that 3,000 houses stood empty
and that there was widespread unemployment. In March de With
suppressed a mutiny on board his flagship and sortied with a small flotilla,
furious that he had only eighteen vessels and 'two galliots' instead of the
forty he had expected, and especially that not one was a first rate, for he
had no illusions about the capacity of small Dutch men-of-war to withstand
English broadsides. He sailed to attack the Newcastle coal fleet but it
sheltered under the guns of Scarborough Castle, which held de With out of
range. A council of war wisely decided that a closer attack in the face of
Cromwellian artillery would be suicidal. Bitter and frustrated, de With
retired to Schoonvelt declaring that without more and bigger ships the
Netherlands faced disaster. This need his masters and Admiral Tromp were
labouring to satisfy. On 5 May 1653, together with de Ruijter and de With,
Tromp sortied from the Texel commanding eighty men-of-war and five fire-
ships (he had asked for twenty-four and one of the five soon sank) and
headed north escorting a convoy of 200 merchantmen to the Shetlands.
Tromp was determined not only to escort the precious convoys inward and
outward, but also to bring on a decisive fleet action.

The English would be happy to oblige him if only they could track him
down. Since the three-day battle they had been grappling with their own
problems. First they had many wounded. In their report announcing the
victory Blake and his colleagues had pleaded for relief for the widows and
orphans of the 'divers both of honesty and worth slain', and for the
'languishing estate' of the wounded. Such relief might encourage others to
risk life and limb in the future. Parliament needed no urging, providing
payments to widows and pensions for the permanently disabled, while
organizing care for the wounded at Portsmouth and other ports. They even
despatched the most eminent physician in England, Dr Daniel Whistler, to

Portsmouth.[4] He ordered the removal of the worst wounded from the fetid atmosphere of cramped houses into hospitals and sought permission to construct an additional hospital in the ruins of Porchester Castle, while he sent the less seriously wounded back to their ships, which he considered healthier quarters than those ashore. His chief patient was the wounded Admiral Blake who had a fever and was slow to recover. Meanwhile the naval yards at Portsmouth, Southampton and Chatham were scenes of bustle and improvisation as badly damaged ships were made battle-worthy and as, at Blake's suggestion, forecastles were raised on the frigates so that their crews would be better able to defend them against boarders pouring over the waist. On 25 April seven Swedish ships arrived with masts, pitch and lead which the fleet soon devoured. London and other neighbouring ports were swept of able-bodied men, while incoming colliers and Indiamen were plundered of seamen. Slowly the flotillas were readied. Penn went to sea first in early April to convoy the Newcastle fleet to London, and then lay off the Suffolk coast where he was reinforced by Bourne arriving with twenty armed merchantmen. The two commanders took their force to join the main fleet off the Isle of Wight on 29 April. Monck and Deane now commanded eighty men-of-war, a figure which would soon climb to 105, and they could hope for further reinforcement when Blake got to sea. They were aware by now of the fall of the Commonwealth government but simply concentrated on the coming campaign.[5]

When they sailed the three admirals, Monck, Deane and Penn, were equipped with the new sailing and fighting *Instructions* which had been drawn up by Blake, Deane and Monck in March and from which some authorities date the tactic of steering into battle in line ahead formation. These declared that when a 'general' (i.e. admiral) was seen to engage the enemy, or when he fired two signal guns and 'hoisted a red flag at his fore-topmast-head, then each squadron shall take the best advantage they can to engage with the enemy next unto them, and in order hereunto all the ships of every squadron shall endeavour to keep in line with their chief, unless the chief of his squadron shall be either lamed or otherwise disabled (which God forbid)', in which event 'every ship of the said squadron shall endeavour to get in a line with the admiral . . .'.[6] Certainly during the earlier battles of the first Dutch War the English, like the Dutch, had tended to fight in the old-fashioned way: 'charging' (a word often used by participants) the enemy, in no distinct formation, firing at any hostile ship they encountered. Save for the action off Dungeness, when the English were scattered and outnumbered, this had worked reasonably well. The well-trained gun-crews and massed batteries of heavy iron guns had done terrible execution in the packed lightly constructed Dutch vessels. The Dutch ships were built for speed, for shallow waters, and for carrying large crews which would board and take the enemy. Their armament was secondary, intended to slow the enemy by bringing down his masts and yards so that he could be boarded. The new line ahead tactics should enable the English to take advantage of their fire-power by standing off from the Dutch at least 500 yards and battering them with a cannonade to which the Dutch guns could not effectively reply. If the English fleet had the weather gage the Dutch would be unable to close the range, still less come alongside and board. Both Monck and Deane had specialized knowledge as artillerymen and Blake had defended three besieged towns. They saw their warships as mobile artillery platforms and recognized that new tactics were needed to make the most of these formidable weapons. The new sailing *Instructions* provided for still primitive but more effective signals between ships, and for more effective sailing and tacking in a disciplined formation.

Meanwhile Tromp had been concentrating his forces. Having despatched his convoy he briefly visited Bergen and then sailed back to the Narrow Seas where Floriszoon joined him with sixteen warships on 20 May. They then sailed on to the Maas to pick up Evertsen's squadron. Tromp was full of fight for he now had ninety-two men-of-war, five fire-ships and six small vessels. The English had been unable to locate him, pursuing him to the Shetlands but arriving two days too late, and his Bergen visit ensured their paths did not cross. Finally, after a cruise to the Texel and the Vlie they retired to pick up reinforcements from Yarmouth. Tromp, as frustrated as his opponents, first sought them in the Downs and then passed on to Dover where he wasted valuable ammunition on a fruitless bombardment. Finally he learned of the English position from scouts and steered west to engage them. The English, equally informed, ordered all vessels between Long Sands Head and Orfordness to join them. The still ailing Blake had also assembled a squadron of ships from the Thames and was moving them to a secure anchorage in the Gunfleet, a deep channel south of Harwich and north-east of the mouth of the Thames, protected by the Gunfleet shoal. At six in the morning of 1 June Monck and Deane sortied from Sole Bay with 105 ships mounting a formidable armament of 3,817 guns – and Blake's squadron had yet to join them. Deane and Monck were both in the *Resolution*, leading the Red squadron in the centre. Penn commanded the White in the *James* (66 guns) on the starboard wing, while Lawson in the *George* (56 guns) led the Blue squadron on the larboard wing, and smaller frigates scouted ahead.

At noon the Blue squadron frigates let fall their top-gallant sails, which by the new signalling system meant that they had seen the enemy. Tromp was about four leagues to leeward as the fleet steered towards him. At four o'clock Lawson, whose wing was closest to the enemy, slowed to let the main body come up. At this point the English fleet was just south of the Gabbard Shoal, about forty miles due east of Harwich, and there the ships anchored in a misty, fading light. The Dutch lay all night several miles to the south east. Monck and Deane hoped to be joined by Blake's squadron and looked forward to a decisive battle in the morning. In fact Blake was still in the Gunfleet commanding his thirteen-ship flotilla in the 56-gun *Essex*. Hearing that his presence would be welcome and 'being desirous to put in for my share for the service of the Commonwealth in this present juncture', as he put it, and despite being far from fit, he sortied on the afternoon of 2 May. That morning Monck and Deane had decided to put into action the new fighting *Instructions*, and came down on the enemy in three parallel lines, although no doubt ragged and irregular by later standards. Having the weather gage they then turned to port in one roughly continuous line with Lawson in the van, Monck and Deane's Red squadron in the centre and Penn in the rear. Orders were given that no ship was to be boarded until she had been shattered and left derelict by long-range fire. The crews were solemnly assured that this tactic would not deprive them of their prize money of £10 per gun for every ship destroyed or captured. The winds were very light and it was eleven o'clock before the English fleet opened a long-range but damaging bombardment. The fleets sailed on roughly parallel courses with the English maintaining their bombardment from about 500 yards. This persuaded the weaker Dutch vessels to edge away from their main body.

About three o'clock in the afternoon the wind veered to north-east and Lawson's course began to converge with that of the enemy. De Ruijter in the van seized this opportunity to tack up towards Lawson's squadron while Tromp behind him followed suit, for he saw a gap had opened between Lawson and Monck. Monck hastened to the assistance of Lawson's squadron which was heavily engaged with several ships badly damaged. Monck's *Resolution* came under fire from sixteen ships. Deane was slain by a chain shot at Monck's side, drenching him with blood. Monck covered Deane's mangled body with his cloak and ordered it carried below lest the men be discouraged. He now found himself in sole command of a very hot fight, although Penn's White squadron soon came up and together he and Monck regained the wind and forced the Dutch to leeward. At dusk the Dutch were in full retreat, sweeping along the Dutch coast past Blankenburg, past their objective, the Weilings, until they were nearing the Maas. Some Dutch captains, their ships badly battered and still under fire from their pursuers, became panic-stricken and deserted in the darkness. By midnight the fleets were off Dunkirk. The Dutch had lost one ship to an explosion, and one or two sunk in the heavy engagement with Lawson's squadron. Monck had not lost a ship sunk or captured and the new tactics appeared to have worked better than could have been expected for a first trial. A dawn council of war on the *Resolution* decided that the squadrons would sail in parallel lines led by the flagships sailing abreast, with Monck in the centre, and pass through the enemy and disperse him. The Dutch were to be pursued hotly 'as far as the shoals would permit' and Monck urged any captains who had wavered 'to wipe out the past and do their best in the present'.

At the same hour Tromp was holding a gloomier council of war. The blunder at Dover had come home to roost: the ships were short of ammunition. Tromp and his admirals were angered by the lack of courage shown by some Dutch captains, but their complaints seem unjust: many Dutch ships were too small and frail to engage the English men-of-war in line of battle. Since the Dutch fleet could not fight for long Tromp ordered 'one more sharp attack' before a general retirement, but it was clear that the attack could only be defensive. Action did not begin until noon and was followed by what an English contemporary contentedly called having 'the harvest and gleaning of the vintage with less loss than ever before'. Finding that Monck had the weather gage Tromp by mid-morning had set course for the sheltering shoals of the Scheldt estuary, fighting a heroic rearguard action as he went. He ordered the weaker Dutch ships, which tended to huddle together for protection, to sail more dispersed but many had been badly damaged the day before, dropped behind and were snapped up by their pursuers. As Tromp's force shrank he was alarmed to discover a fresh column of ships heading into the fight on his port bow. This was Blake's squadron with his nephew, Robert, commanding the *Hampshire* in the van. Soon the Dutch heard distant cheers. The newcomers had called to their compatriots that Blake was back.

Towards evening the retirement degenerated into a rout which not even Tromp could control. The *Brederode* itself was only spared capture by desperate efforts from the vice-admirals. At one point a group of four or five Dutch ships fell aboard each other in hopeless confusion, and were captured. Other laggards were either sunk or taken. When Tromp finally gained the protection of the Scheldt out of 103 ships only 74 remained in company, many of them damaged aloft and holed below. The *Brederode* had nearly 6 feet of water in the hold. Another eight had fled to Goeree. Of the rest eight were on the bottom and eleven were captured, while all the five fire-ships had burned to no purpose. Monck had no intention of risking his fleet and his victory among the shallows off Ostend. As an Englishman with memories of the Scottish campaign wrote regretfully: 'The enemy will go where we cannot follow him, like the Highlanders to the mountains.' So the victory could not be as complete as Monck wished. The English sent home their prizes with a dozen of the worst damaged of their ships; the rest patched up their top-hamper and turned to blockading the Texel and the Zuider Zee. Tromp retired into his marshy fastness to lick his wounds and prepare for another day. Despite his losses, despite the English superiority in gunnery, he would not admit defeat. Only death could quench that resolute spirit.

For a month the English fleet haunted the Dutch coast, regularly seizing Dutch ships whose captains were unaware of the danger or desperate enough to risk a dash for home. The economic condition of the Netherlands grew worse. Banks were closed, their books of assets blank. Merchants had empty warehouses and hungry creditors. Sailors in ships full of exports consumed their provisions before they could even put to sea. All the Dutch longed for peace, but the statesmen recognized that to make peace now would mean a peace imposed by the victors on the vanquished. Only Tromp and his admirals could prevent this by breaking the blockade so that hundreds of Dutch merchantmen could reach foreign markets, and that needed a victory at sea. Both objectives Tromp was determined to accomplish or die in the attempt. He scoured the country for men and resources, had shipyards and wharves packed with ships under repair and demanded that the big ships still on the stocks should be completed. Once again the Dutch achieved a remarkable recovery, but they faced a problem. Since Tromp was fitting out in the Scheldt and de With's squadron was fitting out at the Helder at the entrance to the Zuider Zee, the two squadrons could not combine without first putting to sea where the lurking enemy might defeat them separately before they could unite.

Monck and Blake had their own problems. Bad beer, poor provisions and ships too long at sea meant sick crews. It was essential to return to Sole Bay to replace the sick, restore depleted stocks of ammunition and stores, and repair masts and yards. Yet it was vital to maintain the blockade or the Dutch would score a success without firing a shot; so Monck left a screen of frigates and smaller vessels which contrived to appear more numerous and stronger than they were, sailing so close to shore that Dutch scouts could not get out to discover the true position. Monck had returned on 14 July before Tromp learned that he had ever left. Blake was not with him. He was now so ill, partly with kidney stones, that his life was despaired of. He retired to Bath where he slowly recovered, but he had fought his last battle against the Dutch. Long before Blake recovered Tromp was at sea. At the beginning of August Tromp ordered de With to take station just outside the Helder. He could retire if the main body of the English fleet attacked him and could fall on the rear of the English fleet if Monck turned to assault Tromp as he took his course up the Dutch coast. Monck correctly interpreted de With's manoeuvres. Nevertheless, when his scouts reported Tromp's sails advancing from the south he abandoned de With and turned to fight the larger threat. With a westerly wind Tromp steered to gain the weather gage but the wind backed northerly to Monck's advantage. At this Tromp turned south once more to draw Monck away from the Texel and allow de With to bring his fleet into action. The English chased Tromp hard and some of the English capital ships were in action by early evening. Monck's flagship, *Resolution*, was so hotly involved that she lost seventeen killed and twenty-five wounded. Darkness ended the fight and Tromp managed to lead his fleet northerly while Monck, believing his adversary still to leeward and dropping down the coast, drifted south, making hasty repairs to spars and rigging. Tromp's adroit manoeuvre meant that the next day Tromp and de With were in sight of each other. They had also gained the weather gage.

If Monck had been out-manoeuvred by his more experienced opponents he was quite undaunted. He intended to attack at the first opportunity. However, high winds and a violent swell reminded the adversaries that they were dangerously close to a rapidly shoaling lee shore and both devoted the 9th to trying to remain a safe distance from land without scattering. The rising sun appeared to calm the storm on the 10th and the battle resumed early. Tromp and de With together commanded 107 warships and 9 fireships, Monck 104 men-of-war and 16 smaller vessels, for Blake's flotilla was yet to arrive. Tromp had his main fleet in a ragged line and turned his ships downwind towards his enemy, Monck tacking to meet him with his squadrons in line in accordance with the new fighting *Instructions*. As Monck later wrote *Resolution* and *Worcester* led the fleet 'in a desperate charge through the whole Dutch fleet'. As Tromp turned to follow there appears to have ensued a close-hauled tacking duel of the kind familiar to yachtsmen, but one involving horrors unknown to Cowes Week. Each time the two fleets passed through each other the English fired broadside after broadside into their opponents. To this the Dutch replied with what weight of metal they could but as usual the contest was very uneven. However, with both sides bound in their formations, it must have been more difficult for the Dutch captains of the frailer ships to flinch from the encounter. As Captain Cubitt of the *Tulip* observed: 'In passing through we lamed several ships and sunk some; as soon as we had passed them we tacked again upon them and they on us; [we] passed by each other very near; we did very good execution . . . Some of their ships which had all their masts gone . . . put out a white handkerchief on a staff and hauled in all their guns.'[7]

However, Cubitt would not permit his eager men to send boats to take the prizes and the *Tulip* and her consorts continued to fire broadside after broadside on each leg of their tack. The two fleets passed through each other on four occasions, doing 'great execution upon each', as the ships bombarded each other 'almost at push of pike'. When two Dutch ships engaged Monck's *Resolution* Cubitt reports that the 'very heavens were obscured by smoke, the air rent with the thundering noise, the sea all in a breach with the shot that fell, the ships even trembling and we hearing everywhere messengers of death flying'. The journal of the *Vanguard* reported that 'many of their ships' masts were shot by the board, others sunk to the number of twenty. At last God gave us the wind.'[8]

In fact the Dutch had had enough and fled before the wind for the

Helder with the English closely pursuing. This was not Tromp's decision. He had been shot through the breast by a marksman on the *Tulip* on the first pass. Carried below to his cabin his dying words to his anguished officers were characteristic: 'I have run my course. Have good courage.' He was spared seeing the scale of his fleet's defeat. The Dutch certainly lost between fifteen and twenty ships, burned, sunk by gunfire or captured, although Penn estimated the loss at thirty. Between 3,000 and 4,000 of their men had been killed, wounded or made prisoners. The English had lost a third rate, the 32-gun *Oak* and a fire-ship, *Hunter*, and suffered 500 casualties. To their delight they found they had recaptured the *Garland* and the *Bonaventure*, taken by Tromp off Dungeness, but they had been so battered they had to be scuttled.

The Dutch fleet at last reached the safety of the Zuider Zee and Monck, aware of the danger of trying to hold station with wounded ships on a lee shore, soon turned for the safer anchorage of Southwold Bay. The fierceness of the English bombardment at what became known as the Battle of Scheveningen may be judged from the fact that Monck needed 1,000 barrels of gunpowder and 80 tons of shot to recharge his magazines. However, the breach in the blockade should have been only temporary: by 29 August Monck sailed for the Dutch coast. Here he received intelligence that de With had sailed for the north with a large Baltic convoy only the day before. Strangely, Monck declined to pursue him, and since the horse was gone, declined to remain bolting the door with his great ships facing heavy weather on a lee shore. Leaving the frigates on patrol he returned once more to English waters. Unfortunately his intelligence was faulty. De With had not yet sailed but did so on 11 September with 340 merchantmen. He evaded the cruising frigates, and, with consummate seamanship, did so again on his return with another vast convoy of Baltic traders rescued from Scandinavian ports. Meanwhile, the English Parliament rewarded Blake and Monck and their vice admirals with gold chains and medals and struck more medals for their junior officers. The Dutch buried Tromp with the pomp and ceremony appropriate to his long and selfless service.

The two states were now moving slowly towards peace. Mercifully there would be no more pitched battles in the first of Britain's great naval wars, for the founding of the Protectorate brought to power a ruler who had always disliked this war between Protestants. However, the treaty signed in April 1654 must be considered later with the Protector's foreign policy.

CHAPTER EIGHT

The Swordsmen Take Power

England is not as France, a meadow to be mowed as often as the governors please: our interest is to do our work with as little grievance to our new people, scarce yet proselyted, as possible.

Thomas Scot to Oliver Cromwell, 2 November 1650[1]

Throughout the life of the Commonwealth there was tension between the Purged Parliament and the army. While its domestic policies had the broad support of men like Fairfax, more revolutionary grandees like Major-General Harrison and Ireton (and, after Ireton's death in Ireland, John Lambert) were dissatisfied by the slow progress of reform, or in some areas of government its lack of progress altogether. More junior officers and radical-minded soldiers (or former soldiers) found its apparent sloth in bringing about truly revolutionary reform deeply disillusioning. They had entertained such hopes in that dawn of 1649, and for many these hopes had persisted, although with increasing impatience and frustration, for several years. They might have exclaimed of 1649 as Wordsworth did of 1789 'Blessed was it in that dawn to be alive' but like the poet they were doomed to disillusionment, although in a different way. If the poet was appalled by just how revolutionary the French Revolution turned out to be, the revolutionaries of 1649 found the revolution not revolutionary enough. They had thought in February 1649 that they stood on a threshold, that revolutionary achievements lay before them. Slowly and sadly they discovered that all the revolution they were going to get, if the Purged Parliament had its way, was the revolution they had already had: the extinction of the monarchy and proclamation of the Republic, the abolition of the House of Lords and of episcopacy, and a grudging toleration of the sects.

We have seen why this was so. To blame were the Rump's desperate efforts to make their regime more acceptable by enlisting the support of men who were opposed to the revolutionary changes already in place, monarchists at heart, appalled by the Regicide no matter how hostile they might have been to Charles I in the past, anxious not to be associated with the guilt of the Regicides. Since the Civil War they had feared a social revolution which would assail their property, their status, their local power and privileges. To them the demands of the Levellers and soldiers were a worse threat than any posed by Charles I. These conservatives dominated the Purged Parliament by numbers, a dead weight against reform. The radicals were a minority, and even they, as Thomas Scot's remark to Cromwell in the epigraph reveals, were turned cautious and pragmatic. Yet the conservatives sat beneath a sword of Damocles. The Purged Parliament survived by courtesy of the Grandees. If the Grandees ever became as alienated from the Purged Parliament as were their soldiers Parliament's life would be brief. It survived as long as it did first because of the enormous tasks which it heaped on the army: the crushing of Ireland and Scotland; second, because of the decline of political militancy among the soldiers after the crushing of the Leveller-inspired mutinies of 1649. Thereafter the soldiers' prime preoccupation was their pay. Professor Gentles observes that, during the 1650s, 'the continuity of the army's political consciousness rested almost entirely on the permanence of its officer corps'. The rank and file came and went, the turnover of retirement and recruitment more rapid than earlier.[2] Once the soldiers trooped home after Worcester, the Republic secured from foreign and domestic enemies, the officers had more time to contemplate the Purged Parliament's dismal reform record. Unfortunately there was little progress during the next eighteen months in the four areas in which the radicals hoped for change: religion, social reform, parliamentary reform, the law. The Purged Parliament did make some effort at reform even if the enthusiasm of a majority of its members was at best lukewarm, but each time after a burst of energy there followed a relapse into somnolence, and the efforts petered out in committee or were talked to death or tabled.

Religious toleration as a legislative issue always faced difficulties because at least half the members were Presbyterians and a further 14 per cent were 'Presbyterian-Independents', that is, accepting a Presbyterian form of worship within independent congregations. Their Presbyterianism may have been Erastian, not belonging to the classic Scottish model, but they shared the Kirk's horror of heresy and fear of God's vengeance should heresy flourish. Nevertheless, there were some reforms. Some ministers were better maintained. Missionaries were sent into those 'dark corners of the land' where 'godly' preachers were scarcely ever heard. Parliament passed bills for propagating the gospel in Wales and the northern counties, as also in New England and Ireland, during 1649–50, although a general act for the whole of England petered out in committee. There were some gestures toward religious toleration. This was a vexed issue because even those MPs who most desired it did not wish to promote a flourishing of sects guilty of immoral excesses like the Ranters, while at least half the MPs did not approve of it at all. Indeed Parliament at one time declared it would never permit 'universal toleration'. In any event since the existing national

Oliver Cromwell, miniature by Samuel Cooper. By courtesy of the Buccleuch Collection, Drumlanrig Castle, Scotland.

Sir Thomas, 2nd Baron Fairfax of Cameron, engraving by William Faithorne. By courtesy of the National Portrait Gallery, London.

George Monck, 1st Duke of Albemarle, KG, unfinished sketch by Samuel Cooper. The Royal Collection © Her Majesty The Queen.

General Henry Ireton, Parliamentary General Lord Deputy of Ireland, 1649, bodycolour on vellum by Samuel Cooper. Reproduction by permission of the Syndics of the Fitzwilliam Museum, Cambridge.

General John Lambert, engraving. By courtesy of the Trustees of the Mansell Collection.

The ornamental stern of the Sovereign of the Seas, *designed by Sir Anthony van Dyke. By courtesy of the National Maritime Museum, London.*

General Robert Blake, portrait by Samuel Cooper. By courtesy of the National Maritime Museum, London.

The Swiftsure, 64 guns, 350 crew, a typical second rate of the Commonwealth navy, engraving by van de Velde. By courtesy of the National Maritime Museum, London.

Prince Rupert, portrait by Sir Peter Lely. By courtesy of the National Maritime Museum, London.

Lt Admiral Martin Harpertzoon Tromp. By courtesy of the National Maritime Museum, London.

Charles II, miniature by Samuel Cooper, watercolour on vellum. From Goodwood House by courtesy of the Trustees.

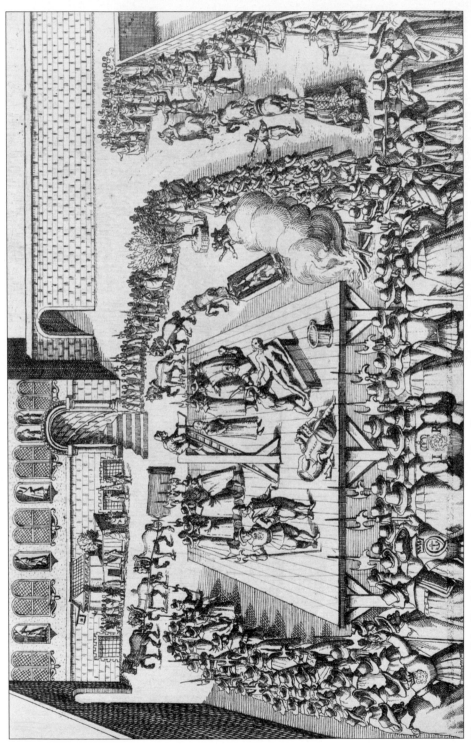

The Execution of the Regicides, *a contemporary engraving. By courtesy of Barnaby's Picture Library, London.*

church, despite its Presbyterianism, was powerless to repress the sects the demand for a legal basis to toleration was blunted. In August 1649 the Presbyterians tried to force through a clause in the proposed Declaration on Religion which endorsed Presbyterian government and the use of the Directory of Service, which was only defeated by the casting vote of Speaker Lenthall. Nine days later the Army Council petitioned for a repeal of the penal laws save for those against Catholics and Anglicans still wedded to the Prayer Book. The Purged Parliament responded with a bill which was twice read but again perished in committee. A bill to abolish compulsory church attendance also failed. The stinging reproach, at least by implication, which Cromwell sent to the Purged Parliament in his letter from the battlefield of Dunbar, cataloguing the ills of the nation and demanding their redress, spurred Parliament to revive the attendance bill and it was passed on 27 September 1650. This was to be the Purged Parliament's final achievement in religious reform. (There was in fact one other but it was hardly part of the radical agenda. In June 1652 Parliament enacted that recusants could not be compelled to attend Protestant services.) Other religious legislation was in favour of morality, not toleration of the sects. The year 1650 saw laws for stricter Sabbath observance, making adultery a capital offence, against profane swearing and against blasphemy. The last might have menaced some sects, but the Independents watered it down in committee so that it only forbade those sects which proclaimed that their leader was the reincarnation of Christ or asserted that any sin was permitted the Elect, so that less scandalous or eccentric sects had little to fear. Tithes, a bitterly divisive grievance, remained. Indeed the bill which improved the maintenance of ministers and schoolmasters strengthened tithes by applying impropriated tithes once owned by bishops, deans and chapters. The Council of State as early as June 1649 urged the abolition of tithes, but Parliament would not do so until an alternative method of funding the ministry was determined and it could never agree what that alternative should be.

It could hardly be expected that social reform would fare better from this socially conservative body. At least as early as 1642 landowning members of the parliamentary party had feared a social revolution or a descent into anarchy during which their lives and possessions would nowhere be safe and their anxiety never slept. Nevertheless the Purged Parliament did discuss proposals for reform, some of which can hardly have seemed threatening to squirearchal interests – for example, the proposal to give the northern counties a university at Durham. Nevertheless, despite the support of Cromwell and Sir Arthur Hesilrige, nothing came of this salutary proposal. The poor fared little better: 1649 was the last of a three-year cycle of poor harvests and dearth, and the homeless died of cold and hunger in the streets during the bitter winters of 1648/9 and 1649/50. Cold struck even at those who were housed because coal prices rose dramatically during the first winter of the Republic, partly because of the imposition of a heavy tax at Newcastle. Trade was depressed, unemployment high. During 1649, however, these 'revolutionaries' simply sought the traditional remedy of trying to bring down prices, and even in this they were slow and ineffective. The tax on coal remained until September 1649 and was soon to be reimposed although at a lower rate. Local authorities were encouraged to restrict brewing to increase the supply of grain for bread. The price of beer was regulated in September but a bill for a general control of food prices perished in committee, as it did when it was briefly revived in 1650. The most unpopular tax was the excise, for it bore most heavily on those least able to pay it. The *Agreement of the People* had proscribed it. The Purged Parliament, desperate for money to pay Cromwell's legions, stubbornly clung to it. An act setting up a scheme for employing paupers did reach the statute book but it only applied to London; a proposal to extend its benefits across the nation was never implemented. Although both trade and agriculture improved after 1649, which increased employment and decreased food prices, the plight of the poor remained desperate. The Purged Parliament's responses were inadequate or late, usually both. Meanwhile the benefits designed by the Leveller-inspired *Agreement* for the small manufacturers and traders were never translated into action. Great monopolistic companies like the Levant, East India and Muscovy were always sustained against the challenges of the less privileged.

In the sphere of law, perhaps surprisingly, progress was no better. Surprisingly because cheaper access to law, and an increase in the speed and efficiency of the courts, should surely have appealed to country gentlemen. However, there were only fourteen lawyers among the seventy or so members who comprised the revolutionary minority of the Purged Parliament while there was an increasing number of lawyers among the conservative majority which reinforced Parliament after the Regicide (twenty by February 1649, forty-four by 1651) and these included such single-minded defenders of the Common Law as Bulstrode Whitelocke, one of the Commissioners of the Great Seal, and Oliver St John, the Chief Justice. The lawyers showed great skill in delaying proposed reforms in committee, talking them to death in the House, or emasculating them at various stages of their crawl towards legislative enactment. However, the lawyers needed the support of the country gentlemen to frustrate the reformers and they received it because the latter saw law reform as the thin end of the wedge. The Levellers had frightened even those who would have welcomed some moderate reforms by seeking too radical a change. One radical would later write: 'The major laws made in this nation are founded upon principles of tyranny, fallacy and oppression for the profit and benefit of those that made them.'[3] The Levellers had wanted the Common Law swept away and replaced by a small book of laws, written in English and therefore easy to understand and apply (as they innocently thought), and they wished to see the re-establishment of courts in every hundred in the Commonwealth at which justice would be dispensed by twelve men elected annually, or the institution of county courts, again with local justices annually elected. This would have been a revolution indeed. The landowners feared that their hegemony over rural and urban England would soon be at an end, with a descent into an anarchic era wherein the many poor would prey on the affluent few. Landowners would resist any reform if the lawyers told them that this was the slippery slope down which interference with the Common Law would hurl them. As a result little was achieved before the dissolution of the Purged Parliament in 1653. As Cromwell later remarked: 'We cannot mention the reformation of the law but they presently cry out we design to destroy property; whereas the law as it is presently constituted serves only to maintain the lawyers and to encourage the rich to oppress the poor.'[4]

The little reform which was achieved was largely due to the promptings of the army, especially after some senior officers came back to take their seats after Worcester. Prior to that there had been some relief for debtors in three bills passed between September 1649 and April 1650, and a minor but useful speeding up of some formerly cumbersome procedures. However, a bill to establish badly needed probate, marriage and divorce administrations failed in May 1649. Cromwell's grim observation in his Dunbar letter that 'if there be any one that makes many poor to make a few rich, that suits not a Commonwealth' was correctly taken to refer to the lawyers. However, even this dig of the spur only produced an act for conducting court proceedings in good English rather than in a mixture of bad Latin and worse Norman French, a reform which should have been achieved two years earlier. Efforts to tackle 'the law's delays', to reduce high fees and salaries for law officers, to reform jury selection and for prison reform, petered out in committee. After Worcester the army pressure brought about an independent commission chaired by Matthew Hale, a distinguished jurist but in no sense a radical figure.[5] Among other members was the future Whig leader, Sir Anthony Ashley Cooper. There were five genuine revolutionaries on it, among them Hugh Peter, but their membership merely served to dampen radical agitation outside the House. Its cautious suggestions included abolishing imprisonment for debt, the establishment of county courts, and the reduction of some fees. Although welcomed by Parliament even these cautious recommendations perished amid its delays, sloth and verbosity. The only substantial reform enacted finally established the badly needed probate administration within Common Law courts in April 1653 which the Purged Parliament had been promising since 1649. Nothing was done to reform the Court of Chancery which, although it had not yet sunk to the depths plumbed by *Bleak House*, was already displaying symptoms of that capacity for wasteful and costly procedures combined with profitable delay which would become a sustained descent into corruption and institutionalized denial of justice during the next century.

The *Agreement of the People*, at Ireton's insistence, had initially contained a clause that the Purged Parliament should be dissolved at the end of April 1649. Cromwell had opposed this. With his old-fashioned respect for parliaments he felt that this should be left to Parliament itself. Ironically, it was the Purged Parliament's activities in 1653 to bring about its own dissolution which led him to expel it at musket point. The Purged Parliament knew that it could not rule indefinitely, but it displayed no impatience to be gone. At a time when the new Republic was beset by enemies at home and abroad, and when the country was at war in Ireland and against the Scots, this was excusable. Total victory brought greater pressure from the army for a dissolution, and the outbreak of the Dutch War did nothing to damp this. Many in the army, including Cromwell himself, were opposed to the war. Moreover it was a naval war, which left the army idle and so able to indulge its taste for politics. On 13 August the Council of Officers petitioned Parliament to implement the reform programme of 1647 and to provide for dissolution and succession of the legislature. For five years it had wanted this programme to be implemented, and its lack of success in getting what it wanted demonstrates the limitations of the Swordsmen's political power during that period. The MPs could not get rid of the army because they would not survive a week without it, but the army could not compel the MPs to realize its objectives. In part this failure was due to divisions within the army itself, especially between junior and senior officers, but also in the divisions between the senior officers, of which the latest was between the pragmatical Lambert and the religious zealot Harrison.

During the autumn and winter of 1652/3 Cromwell was to play a crucial role in relations between the army and Parliament and, oddly in view of what was to happen, Cromwell's role was that of mediator. Arch-Presbyterian Sir Arthur Hesilrige represented those MPs who wished to see the Purged Parliament continue indefinitely but with the places of the purged MPs filled by recruitment. General Harrison, convinced as a Fifth Monarchist that Christ would soon return to give mankind a heavenly government, wanted to replace the Purged Parliament with an assembly chosen from the 'saints' to ensure that England had a suitably pious government to greet Him. Positions divided by so vast a gulf certainly needed a mediator. Fortunately Cromwell had the prestige needed to sustain the role. He was set apart by his extraordinary series of victories. He was the army's commander-in-chief, a powerful and prestigious position, and he was an MP and a member of the Council of State. Men accustomed to obeying his commands, ranging in rank from captain to admiral, commanded at sea. Foreign ambassadors without exception regarded him as the most important man in the Republic, reporting every rumour, conjecture and speculation about him to their home governments. They tended, naturally although mistakenly, to see Cromwell's underlying hand in everything that occurred. Cromwell persuaded the officers to drop their demand for an early dissolution of Parliament; this may have had a good effect, for the Purged Parliament reversed its decision not to dissolve until November 1654 and formed a new Committee on Elections to devise an earlier dissolution. However, it only debated its new election bill (which was supposed to bring about a dissolution and an election under a reformed distribution and franchise) on one morning a week, and usually at a poorly attended House of no more than forty or fifty members. This leisurely approach meant that it was almost eight months later before the Purged Parliament had a bill nearing completion. At that point, on 20 April, Cromwell took a file of soldiers and abruptly dissolved it. Why did he behave so uncharacteristically?

We can only conjecture what Parliament's precise intentions were in its election bill because Cromwell carried it off with him and it was never seen again. Following Gardiner, historians uncritically accepted that the Purged Parliament was determined not to dissolve but rather to permit its members to retain their seats while recruiting new members to fill the vacancies left by the Purge of 1648; that this self-interested determination to hang on to office so angered the Swordsmen that Cromwell impulsively dissolved the Rump.[6] More recently it has been demonstrated definitively that the bill provided for a genuine election based on revised electoral boundaries, with increased county membership and a sweeping away of rotten boroughs – indeed that the bill which Parliament was debating on the morning of 20 April contained many of the features which the Council of Officers had long demanded.[7] This causes historians an immediate difficulty. If the bill for a new parliament was what the Council of Officers wanted why should Cromwell go to the length of a military *putsch* against Parliament to prevent its passage on the morning the House was to vote on it? Both Dr Worden and Professor Woolrych have devoted very sophisticated analysis to this problem.[8] Only the barest summary, which does justice to neither, can be attempted here.

It is likely that the army had changed its views during the past eight months. It wanted a new parliament, but not one which might be hostile both to the army and the sects. It therefore wanted to ensure that the qualifications for membership and the franchise would be supervised by men it could trust, and that did not include the current membership of the House. Its dislike of the Purged Parliament had deepened to a profound loathing. Since the Parliament was determined not to dissolve until after the new parliament had been elected and so keep control of qualification until after that election, the Council of Officers became increasingly disturbed. Such control would permit the Purged Parliament to ensure that members of the new body were as conservative as themselves, and even more hostile to the sects and to the army. Cromwell was as worried as any but wished to avoid a military solution. However, if he had been a brake on the army hotheads who wished to use military force against a body they perceived as corrupt, self-serving and godless, this was not because he did not share their hostile opinions. If he rejected a violent solution it was because he shrank from turning his back on the last surviving trace of legitimacy in government, and perhaps also because he still felt a nostalgia for the great days of the Long Parliament in which he had himself played a substantial role. (Significantly, when he spoke in the House the next morning he began with a sober rehearsal of the past achievements of the Long Parliament before the contrast between those achievements and the self-serving inaction of its purged remnant moved him to furious denunciation.) Moreover, he could not see what would follow such a *putsch*. However, Cromwell had grown to abominate a system of government in which the legislature was a perpetually sitting body which exercised executive as well as legislative functions. Like several other officers, including John Lambert who had become Cromwell's political and intellectual confidant since the death of Ireton, he inclined towards a nominated body of about forty members, men of unimpeachable morals and commitment to the Commonwealth. This body could be chosen by the Purged Parliament and the Council of Officers cooperatively and could have greater army membership than the current Council of State. Once this council of 'sage, grave men' was established Parliament could dissolve itself and the council would carry on the government acting as a permanent executive and also as a temporary legislature: temporary because Cromwell saw this conciliar government not as a long-term solution but as a bridge to a resumption of more traditional and constitutional institutions. When the country had become sufficiently reconciled to the Commonwealth the council would organize the election of a new parliament.

Although the motives for the actions of some participants and the precise details of the electoral bill before the House must remain conjectural, the sequence of events is clear. On the evening of 19 April 1653 Cromwell, with the consent of the Army Council, had invited the parliamentary leaders to confer with him and some other officers at his lodgings near the Whitehall Palace cockpit. Here he presented the argument for conciliar government. None of the parliamentary leaders favoured Cromwell's solution, not surprisingly, except Chief Justice Oliver St John. Whitelocke, as one would expect, was fertile in legal arguments against so revolutionary a proposal.

The discussion had no result except the exhaustion of the participants but they agreed to meet again the following afternoon. The parliamentary leadership undertook to delay the further progress of the bill until these discussions were concluded. However, when those leaders arrived at the House next morning they found the members busy discussing the bill. According to Gardiner the House itself had called for the bill, ignoring the leaders' promises, 'and sought to hurry it through before Cromwell could be informed'.[9] Harrison's warning of the risk they were running was ignored. Vane and the other leaders, helpless to stop proceedings, either joined in or silently watched. They were soon joined by another silent watcher, Cromwell himself. Having learned with astonishment and anger that despite the promises he had been given Parliament was likely to hasten to a vote, he rushed to the House with a file of soldiers which he left guarding the doors and took his seat. That he had been taken by surprise is shown by his garb, which was that of a casually dressed country gentleman rather than the military uniform he wore on formal or significant occasions. After listening to the debate for some time, and finding that the members were about to vote on the bill, he intervened and after first extolling the achievements of the Long Parliament since its first meeting in 1640, relapsed into a violent denunciation of the present membership, accusing some of being 'whoremasters' (gazing fixedly at Henry Marten) and many more of being corrupt. His general criticism was that they had had no heart to do anything for the public good, that they had 'espoused the corrupt interest of Presbytery and the lawyers, who were the supporters of tyranny and oppression . . . the lord had done with them, and had chosen other instruments for the carrying on of his work that were more worthy'. He then ordered Harrison to call in the soldiers and clear the Chamber. At one point Sir Henry Vane, one of his closest friends, cried out, 'This is not honest, yea it is against morality and common honesty.' To this Cromwell, who believed Vane had betrayed his undertaking of the previous evening, responded, perhaps more in sorrow than in anger, 'Oh Sir Henry Vane, Sir Henry Vane, the Lord deliver me from Sir Henry Vane!' Speaker Lenthall defiantly kept his seat but Cromwell ordered he should be taken down, and Harrison took his hand to help him from the chair. As the hundred or so members trooped out, stunned and disconsolate, Cromwell declared: 'It's you that have forced me to this, for I have sought the Lord night and day that he would rather slay me than put me upon the doing of this work.' Pointing at the mace he remarked: 'What shall we do with this bauble? Here, take it away!'[10]

Cromwell then returned to the Cockpit where he found the officers gathered, and threw the key of the chamber down on the table before them. When he told them what he had done they were almost as surprised as his parliamentary victims. When some objected that this way would lead to 'ruin and confusion' he assured them that he would do more good and more rapidly than could ever be expected from Parliament. However, despite this boast, he had no intention of establishing a military dictatorship. That afternoon several of the Purged Parliament, Sir Arthur Hesilrige among them, defiantly assembled to hold a meeting of the Council of State, but Cromwell had anticipated this. He turned up with Lambert and Harrison and calmly told them that if they met simply as private persons they should not be disturbed 'but if as a Council of State this is no place for you', and that they should take note that Parliament was dissolved. To this Bradshaw bravely replied that they had heard what Cromwell had done that morning, and 'before many hours all England' would hear it, but that if Cromwell thought Parliament was dissolved he was mistaken 'for no power under heaven can dissolve them but themselves'. They then sadly dispersed.

If Bradshaw was implying by his reference to 'all England' that the country would deeply resent Cromwell's coup he would soon be disillusioned. England received the news of the Purged Parliament's dismissal with enthusiasm, for it was a government with remarkably few friends. Indeed the action probably made Cromwell more popular than he had been since the victories of Dunbar and Worcester. Cromwell had spent several months in increasing isolation, albeit an isolation self-imposed. He had rarely attended either the House or the Council of State, both of which he regarded with contemptuous dislike because of their tardiness in reform. However, what he had done in his mediating role since August 1652, however beneficial its intention, had been seen as betrayal by the radicals in the army and by the Fifth Monarchists led by General Harrison. Ideologues dislike compromise and rarely forgive those who achieve it. Harrison had become the officer to whom the sects looked for protection and leadership. The *putsch* transformed this situation. Cromwell was once again the radicals' hero both in the regiments and in the sects. The sectarians of Hereford apostrophized their hero: 'Oh my lord, what are you, that you should be the instrument to translate the nation from oppression to liberty, from the hands of corrupt persons to the saints?' The enthusiasm of the 'saints' of Durham was tempered with candour. They rejoiced that 'the Lord had again quickened you', 'renewing a remembrance of your former engagements for this poor nation', because they had feared that 'God's presence withdrawing from you was the cause of your long silence'.[11] As for the much larger audience outside the army and outside the sects they rejoiced to see a deeply unpopular government dismissed. Many who wished to see monarchy restored may have perceived the *putsch* as the prelude to a restoration. If so they would be disappointed, for while Cromwell had no precise idea of what should happen next he had had no intention of restoring Charles Stuart. His action had been unpremeditated and his behaviour in the House supports Dr Worden's contention that he was acting in a mood of spiritual exaltation, as indeed he reported to the Council of Officers later.

In the immediate aftermath of the dispersal of the Purged Parliament Cromwell and the Council of Officers made it clear that since they had not acted with any concerted plan for the future government of the country they must put themselves 'wholly upon the Lord for a blessing'. That 'blessing' would turn out to be the small Nominated Parliament, known to Royalist propagandists as 'Barebone's Parliament' but this took time to emerge. Indeed when the pamphleteer Marchmont Needham wrote a vindication of recent events nine months later he thought that the best proof that the army did not carry out its *putsch* in order to seize power for themselves was their 'irresolution and unpreparedness' as to what to do next. The most informed analyst of the army, Professor Gentles, believes that Cromwell had been meditating a seizure of power for months, deducing that when Cromwell contemplated the obstructive Rumpers 'the thought must have crossed his mind that he could do a better job at the helm of government than any of them'. As evidence he cites Bulstrode Whitelocke's note in his *Memorials* of a conversation with Cromwell in about November 1652, during which they discussed the future government of the realm and in the course of which Cromwell asked: 'What if a man should take it upon him to be King?' To this Gentles adds the story that Cromwell tried to convince some London clergymen that a forcible dissolution was in the country's interests, and when the Revd Edmund Calamy replied that it was impracticable, the nation would be opposed, with nine out of ten against it, Cromwell is alleged to have replied: 'What if I should disarm the nine and put a sword into the tenth man's hand; would not that do the business?' Cromwell could be a tease and liked to shock the pious, so even if the story is true we need hardly take this as serious evidence of his intentions. However, the story is second-hand and Calamy hardly an objective source, as he had ardently desired the restoration of the purged members and was a bitter enemy of all Swordsmen.[12] Professor Gentles himself dismisses the idea that Cromwell planned to become a military dictator. The solution of a small council which could rule the country until the time was ripe for a general election, which Cromwell had advocated on the night of the 19th, had been knocked on the head by Cromwell himself. He had dispersed the government which was supposed to appoint the council. Nor could the Army Council call a general election on the spot. That would simply call into being a monster which would soon make the Council of Officers look back on the Purged Parliament at its worst with nostalgia. It would certainly be full of Presbyterians, those ancient enemies of the army, and, even worse, of men who were by now convinced monarchists, even if all former Royalists were excluded.

Nevertheless the Swordsmen acted like men who were determined to return government to civilian hands as soon as possible. The Council of Officers invited to their deliberations former members of the Purged Parliament on whom they felt they could rely. According to Edmund Ludlow Cromwell had already secretly begged two of these men to persuade Oliver St John, John Selden and a few others 'to draw up some instrument of government that might put the power out of his hands'. If true this reflected Cromwell's yearning for a constitutional solution, a natural reaction of this unrevolutionary-minded man to finding himself in a wholly unconstitutional situation.[13] He had to accept the fact, however, that the Swordsmen must settle the new government, for all power was in their hands, and therefore he could achieve any form of government to which he could persuade the Council of Officers to agree. There was the rub, for that body was as usual badly divided. After a good deal of hard arguing among the officers and their civilian allies, during which Cromwell was said to be 'at a nonplus', he characteristically plumped for a compromise between the Lambert position and that of Harrison. Cromwell appointed as a stop-gap measure a new Council of State which would do what the old Council of State had done: handle foreign relations and the ordinary administration of the country. It was a ten-man body, containing four generals (Cromwell, Harrison, Lambert and Disbrowe), four members of the old Council (Walter Strickland, Sir Gilbert Pickering, John Carew and Anthony Stapley), William Sydenham, a former parliamentary soldier who had recently been governor of the Isle of Wight, and Colonel Robert Bennet, a retired garrison commander. The council was a sop to Lambert, but for the legislature he rejected Lambert's suggested written constitution, moving closer to Harrison's solution of a nominated parliament (although rejecting his call for a legislature of seventy, the number derived from the Israelites' Sanhedrin). Rather there would be a legislature of about one hundred and forty members which would be chosen on a county basis by the Council of Officers (or perhaps only the senior members of it). The legend that the Council circularized the various congregations scattered across England inviting them to forward nominations is derived from a 'sheer conjecture' of Gardiner, which the leading authority on the Nominated Parliament has recently demolished.[14] When the officers debated how to select the members, calling for nominations from congregations was one of the options canvassed, 'much said sweetly (on) both sides', as Harrison reported. However, the officers would not relinquish the right to determine who should sit, and the legend of congregational participation seems to derive from the fact that some officers of their own initiative wrote into the country seeking suitable nominees, and some congregations of their own initiative sent in nominations, some of which were chosen and others not. Cromwell made some nominations himself but later claimed it was fewer than any captain in the army, doubtless an exaggeration.

Although the body was less than a quarter the size of a normal parliament, representation was based on counties but included members from Scotland, who were Scots serving with varying degrees of reluctance, and from Ireland, all of whom were English and included General Henry Cromwell, Oliver's younger surviving son. Thus the Nominated Parliament which assembled on 4 July could be called the first Imperial Parliament – if it deserved the name of parliament at all. It was not in fact called a 'parliament' until a majority of the members decided to do so on their first full day of business. (The forty-six who opposed the decision were an odd combination of extreme radicals who abominated the name and conservative traditionalists who did not think it deserved to bear it![15]) It has been unfairly known to history, thanks to Royalist sneers, as 'Barebone's Parliament' for no better reason than that one of the members was a London clergyman called Praise-God Barebone. He was an Anabaptist leather-seller whose name caught the fancy of Royalist propagandists, but was probably of Huguenot stock and his name really 'Barbon'. It was snobbishly dismissed as a gathering of country bumpkins and urban ignoramuses of no education, knowledge of government or experience of the world, and notorious for preaching extreme Puritan doctrines. The French ambassador with Gallic cynicism suggested that Cromwell had picked them because their unfitness for government would leave government in his hands, while Edward Hyde from a safe distance in the Low Countries dismissed them as 'a pack of weak, senseless fellows . . . much the major part of them consisted of inferior persons, of no quality or name, artificers of the meanest trades, known only by their gifts in praying and preaching.'[16] Some have uncritically accepted these contemporary but wildly distorted judgments. Certainly the assembly was on average of a rather less socially distinguished composition than the pre-Civil War parliaments, but that is merely to expose how unrepresentative even of propertied people parliaments traditionally were. Professor Woolrych defines the membership as seventeen 'greater gentry', twenty-two 'county gentry', sixty-six 'lesser gentry', seven 'professional gentry', nine 'merchant gentry' and twenty-three 'merchants and professionals', making 144 in all, although not every one of that number took their seat and several more were infrequent attenders or abandoned their duties well before the Nominated Parliament dissolved. Although almost half the members served in no other parliament (in itself no guarantee that they were unfit to be in this one) the great majority of them were drawn from the top 5 per cent of the population in wealth or status or both, and the traditional governing class was well in evidence. The septuagenarian Speaker, Francis Rous, formidably fit despite his age, a former Provost of Eton and Pym's half-brother, had sat in every parliament since 1626. His great reputation presumably outweighed his Presbyterianism in his selection. The Nominated

Parliament also contained two lords (Lord Eure, a peer, and Viscount Lisle, who held a courtesy title), four baronets and four knights. Among the greater gentry were three future earls. Among the lesser gentry was George Monck, who was born the son of a knight and would die a duke. He had been lately a lieutenant-general in Scotland and more recently an admiral like his fellow naval member, Robert Blake, who is classed as professional gentry.[17]

The story that the Fifth Monarchists, although a minority in the Nominated Parliament, quickly seized control of all the key committees, and thereby dominated its proceedings until a revolt by the conservative back-benchers brought dissolution to all, does not withstand close inspection, although it was widely propagated by pamphleteers later.[18] Fifth Monarchists were never more than 10 per cent of the Nominated Parliament, and even that figure includes members who rarely attended and others who appear to have played little part in proceedings when they did. Harrison himself, who was co-opted to the assembly along with Cromwell, Lambert and Disbrowe, was active early and late but abandoned the House for several weeks in between. (Cromwell and Lambert played no part at all.) In general the committees of the Nominated Parliament, which were devised at the beginning by a 'committee of committees', had a very wide membership because strenuous efforts were made to divide the labour up among all the members of what was a very small assembly. Far from dominating the work of the assembly it has been suggested that the early disappearance of several Fifth Monarchists was due to their realization that the conservatives in the House were too strong for them.[19]

The Nominated Parliament met on 4 July 1653 in the Council Chamber in Whitehall, a room inadequate even for this modestly sized body, and since when Cromwell entered to address them he was surrounded by a bevy of senior officers, the atmosphere quickly became stifling. The Lord General promised to cut short his remarks but in fact spoke extempore, as was his unfortunate practice, for fully two hours. The pith of his message was that his hearers had received a call from God to settle his People and that on behalf of the army he was formally handing over all power, executive as well as legislative, to them. The assembly then decided to adjourn and agreed, over some Fifth Monarchy and other radical opposition, to hold their meetings in the old House of Commons. After a day of prayer and fasting, in which prayers were led from among their own membership rather than by London clergymen, the members established a new Council of State, rather larger than the one which the Purged Parliament had employed, to carry on foreign affairs, the war with the Dutch and more routine public concerns. They then turned to reform. Whatever the lack of experience of many of the members it must be said that during the following six months the Nominated Parliament showed itself much more vigorous, energetic and determined to effect reforms than the Purged Parliament. Indeed one of the problems was, at least in the assembly's last weeks, that bottlenecks occurred, and days were lost in wrangling over which measures deserved priority of debate. Many of the reforms it pursued had been conspicuous among the problems addressed by the *Heads of Proposals* and the successive *Agreements of the People.* The old Hale Committee's recommendations were taken up but despite much industrious committee work and much determination to see the Hale Committee's reforms through only two made their way to the statute book.[20] The better known of these was the contentious 'Act touching Marriages' which provided for civil marriage. Other Hale reforms might have reached the statute book had the Parliament not self-destructed too early to bring them to a division. One of the prime targets was the Court of Chancery, which members perceived to be the legal system at its worst – protracted, needlessly expensive, a cesspool of featherbedding and greed. Here the reformers struck trouble since it was impossible for the committee to agree as to what body, if any, should discharge its functions. In the end the Nominated Parliament as a whole bolted and voted to abolish Chancery before their law reform committee had solved this crucial problem. Chancery was destined to resurface clinging to all its vices but not all its ancient virtues as a consequence of the failure to supply an alternative.

The issue which brought about the final destruction of the Nominated Parliament was religion. This might have been expected of a body whose majority was moderate to conservative but possessed of a substantial minority of religious enthusiasts, diverse in their religious persuasions but united in placing the imperatives of religion above the rights of property. The last has relevance because one of the most contentious issues was that of tithes, as it had been earlier for the Purged Parliament, and another was the right of lay proprietors to present to livings, and to regard that right (supported by the Common Law) as a form of property which could be bought and inherited or leased, like any other part of their estates. Both were divisive issues (although the hostility to presentment as a species of property was shared by many moderate members) and both were intermingled in the most divisive issue of all between radical and moderate opinion. This was the necessity for maintaining, whether by tithes or some system of national remuneration, a professional, university-educated ministry. Even those moderate-minded members who were opposed to tithes in principle were not prepared to see the system abolished until it had been replaced by some other form of remuneration because that would destroy the professional ministry to which they were committed. Other propertied members, like their predecessors in the Purged Parliament, were determined to maintain tithes because impropriated tithes were a species of property. For them the argument of some radicals that since Christ was a carpenter preachers should support themselves by manual labour was outrageous, false both in principle and fact.

Increasingly the landed members of the house began to feel that their enforced association with religious enthusiasts who were below them on the great ladder of degree was intolerable. The enthusiasts' interests, their attitudes, their vehemently expressed convictions were too alien from their own to be longer endured. In its final report the committee on tithes recommended retention and supported the view that impropriators had a legal title to their tithes – but only by a very small majority. On 10 December 1653 the Nominated Parliament rejected the report by a majority of 56 to 52. The vote is significant. Not only was it very close, which demonstrated how divisive the issue was, but the size of the vote demonstrated that the moderates were deeply concerned about the issue for increasingly they only turned up in strength when something they perceived as vital to their interests was to be decided. Nevertheless, the radical victory appeared to threaten a final assault on tithes and lay patronage even though many who voted on the radical side had no intention of seeing England deprived of a maintained and trained ministry. The defeated moderates moved quickly to kill the threat before it could do further harm. The previous month they had succeeded in erecting a High Court of Justice, an instrument for trying enemies of the state, by the expedient of assembling at the House on a Monday morning when they knew most of the radicals would be at a prayer meeting. (The radicals had opposed this measure, perceiving that it had been inspired by the jury's acquittal of John Lilburne in his recent trial for treason after his unlicensed return from abroad after the fall of the Purged Parliament which had exiled him.) The moderates now adopted this method again with a more drastic purpose. On 12 December a group of about forty conservatives reached the House very early and with the support of Speaker Rous, who as a Presbyterian naturally favoured a maintained ministry, agreed to resign their authority on the grounds that they were no longer able to prevent what they termed 'the confusion and despoliation of the nation'. The Speaker, fearing that as members came haphazardly to the chamber the plan might be voted down, did not put the proposal to a vote but came down from the chair and led the conservatives in a body to Whitehall to return to Cromwell the power he had bestowed upon them. Once there they hastily subscribed their names to copies of the motion of resignation which Sir Charles Wolseley had moved in the chamber. (Although the signatories only comprised about a third of the total membership other genuine conservatives or men with an eye for political opportunity turned up over the next few days to add their signatures, which brought the membership of the coup to about eighty.[21]) Cromwell received the deputation with his habitual courtesy but with surprise and head-shaking at the responsibility they had reimposed upon him. However, if he was surprised other senior officers were not. Before the deputation had even reached Whitehall two officers, Colonel Goffe and Lieutenant-Colonel White, with a file of soldiers, arrived to clear the chamber of the radical rump, now grown to about thirty, which had remained in defiance of the coup. They had been despatched by that old enemy of the Nominated Parliament, General Lambert, who had clearly been privy to the coup all along. The Saints argued that they had been called together by the Lord General and only an order from him could disperse them. (This rather undermined the force of the protest they were composing when the soldiers appeared, which had declared that they had been 'called by God to that place'.) When one of the colonels asked them what they did there, one replied that 'they were seeking the Lord'. To this one officer replied 'Come out of this place then for to my knowledge the Lord hath not been here this twelve years past', which for a member of the New Model Army was a curiously sweeping dismissal of the life and achievements of the Long Parliament. Sir John Carew, perhaps the most ardent of the Fifth Monarchists and certainly socially the most distinguished, declared that Cromwell 'took off the crown from the head of Christ and put it upon his own'. This description of what had occurred was neither impartial nor exhaustive.[22]

CHAPTER NINE

The Protector

My power again by this resignation was as boundless and unlimited as
before: all things being subjected to arbitrariness, and myself a person
having power over the three nations boundlessly and unlimited.

Oliver Cromwell, 1654[1]

The Saints were dispersed and the high tide of Puritanism was now on the
ebb. Power had indeed returned to the Lord General's hands. Cromwell
thought of himself as the only constituted authority that was left. Because
he had been appointed to supreme command over the New Model Army by
the Long Parliament he saw himself, and many others saw him, as the only
surviving repository of authority in the state. Of course, this was not strictly
true, happily for the conduct of routine affairs. The courts still sat, the
Chancellorship was still in commission, there was still a Chief Justice and
the departments of government, such as the Admiralty and the Treasury,
continued to function. This was as well considering that a titanic naval war
with the Dutch had not yet been brought to an end. However, Cromwell was
simultaneously if unconstitutionally head of state and 'prime minister', and
there was no legislature either elected or selected. There seems little doubt
that Cromwell, far from having plotted the overthrow of 'King Jesus', as the
Fifth Monarchists were soon alleging, was taken by surprise. He had lost
faith in his 'saintly' experiment well before its end, muttering that he was
'now more troubled with the fool than the knave', but had not planned its
demise. He still hoped it would reform its ways, cease quarrelling, and
produce reform legislation of a moderate kind which the political nation of
which he was a member would not perceive as a fanatical attack on
property. However, if Cromwell was surprised other Swordsmen were not,
and particularly General Lambert. He it was who had been so well prepared
for the Moderates' coup that the radical remnant of the Nominated
Parliament was tidied away before the Moderate deputation had arrived at
Whitehall to surrender its authority.

Major-General John Lambert was a man of a different stamp from Major-
General Harrison. He did not share Harrison's extremist views on religion.
Although he had been delighted by his commander's expulsion of the
Purged Parliament, he had strongly opposed the calling of the Nominated

Parliament, had no sympathy with the religious notions of the Fifth Monarchists, and wanted Cromwell to rule through a small, effective council until the country was reconciled to Republican rule and a proper parliament could be called. He and Harrison came from very different backgrounds. While Harrison was the son of a Staffordshire butcher Lambert was the son of the squire of Malhamdale, near Skipton in the Yorkshire Dales, a region where the Old Religion still clung tenaciously. Lambert's family was Protestant and opposed to the Arminian ritualism of Archbishop Laud and Charles I, but he had been well insulated in his remote rural manor house from the intense Puritanism which flourished in such Yorkshire woollen towns as Bradford and Halifax. Lambert was still only twenty-two when the king raised his standard at York, but Yorkshire gentlemen prepared to fight for Parliament were in a minority in 1642 and so his decision to join the parliamentary army of Ferdinando, Lord Fairfax, ensured his rapid promotion. In 1644 Lambert served in Sir Thomas Fairfax's northern army when it defeated the Anglo-Irish Royalists at Nantwich, where among their other prisoners was that man of destiny, George Monck. He fought at Marston Moor in 1644 and after the formation of the New Model Army took command of the northern forces. As a result he missed Naseby and the battles of the western campaign, but took part in the mopping-up operations in Devon and Cornwall in the winter of 1645/6 and was present at the siege and surrender of Oxford in 1646. In 1648 he was again in the north and the outbreak of the second Civil War saw him march against Sir Marmaduke Langdale's Royalist army which he defeated, and advance north to take Appleby and Carlisle. However, he was hopelessly outnumbered by the invading Scots under the Duke of Hamilton and fell back into Yorkshire where there had been further Royalist outbreaks at Scarborough and Pontefract. After Cromwell joined him at Knaresborough he took part in the rout of Hamilton's army at Preston as second-in-command. Lambert's command of the prolonged siege of Pontefract Castle meant that fortuitously he missed the trial and execution of the king. (As a consequence, at the Restoration he escaped the hideous penalty inflicted on such Regicides as Harrison and Vane, although he was convicted of treason.) He did not go to Ireland but took a leading part in Cromwell's Scottish and Worcester campaigns. In 1653, now thirty-three years old, able, ambitious, urged on by his beautiful, equally ambitious wife, uninhibited by beliefs in the imminence of the Second Coming or any other species of radical Puritanism, he saw before him a political prospect very different from that envisaged by Harrison. He was well prepared for the new political crisis. His faith had always lain in a written constitution dominated by secular considerations which would ensure the security of the army, and he had carefully drafted a constitution which he believed would achieve this. After expelling the Purged Parliament, Cromwell had besought men to provide an 'instrument' under which the country could be governed and which would relieve him of the *de facto* military dictatorship. Now Lambert and a few like-minded colleagues set such a document before him. The *Instrument of Government* formally relieved Cromwell of the powers which the defection of the Nominated Parliament had placed on him, but enshrined him as head of state as centrally as Charles I had ever been. Although the precise sequence of events is unclear it seems that Cromwell had already seen an earlier version of the *Instrument* before it was officially brought to him on 12 December 1653, and that in its earlier draft it would have made him king. ('Seven of them made an Instrument of Government [and] brought it to [me] with the name of king in it', he later reported.[2]) If Gardiner's reconstruction is correct, and it is certainly plausible, Cromwell had rejected the proposed *Instrument* because he never believed the army would accept a monarchy, and shrank from dismissing the Nominated Parliament despite his disenchantment with it.[3] Now the Nominated Parliament had dissolved itself and the *Instrument* had dropped all reference to kingship. The earlier text had offered Cromwell powers he neither possessed nor claimed. In December he found himself possessed of those powers willy-nilly and the *Instrument* was a means to restrict them constitutionally. After lengthy discussion Cromwell agreed to accept the *Instrument* on condition that there would be no Cromwellian monarchy and that he could modify certain details. This was agreed, and the next day Lambert and a large number of officers appeared in the Council Chamber. The civilians present were excluded while Lambert obtained the assent of the Swordsmen to the *Instrument of Government*. It appears Lambert rode roughshod over any general objections while any specific demurrals, such as the suggestion that the command of the army should be removed from the Protector, were brushed aside with an empty promise that they would be considered later. Further discussion on the following two days with Cromwell present produced the *Instrument* in its final form. Cromwell would become Protector governing with a council and a periodic parliament.

The *Instrument of Government* was the kind of constitution which is written by men conscious of living in dangerous times. They perceived social and political anarchy as a real threat, but believed it was vital to learn from the experience of the past and so avoid the perils of 'kingship', 'oligarchy' and 'democracy' as defined by Aristotle: the tyranny of the one, the few or the many. Lambert and his collaborators devised a constitutional monarchy although without the hereditary principle and with the title 'protector' substituted for 'king'. A monarchy which could rule without parliament until financial necessity compelled it to call one had failed under Charles I. Government by an unfettered Parliament, as devised by the *Agreement of the People*, with a council which was the creature of the legislature, had also failed. Cromwell later justified the *Instrument of Government* as seeking 'to avoid the extremes of monarchy on the one hand and democracy on the other' (he meant the Purged Parliament), and which had not been found in '*dominium in gratia*' (that is, rule by the Nominated Parliament). Now there would be a mixed constitution with various powers, responsibilities and functions divided between the executive, itself divided into the Protector and Protectorate Council, and the legislature.[4] The latter would be a triennially elected parliament of 460 members drawn partly from Scotland and Ireland (30 each) with the remaining 400 elected by English constituencies. These were redrawn along lines earlier proposed by Ireton and the Levellers, with some rotten boroughs suppressed, other boroughs reduced to one member and some counties gaining extra seats. However, the old 'forty shilling freehold' franchise for the counties was replaced by a qualification of £200 in real or personal property. The qualifications of borough voters were left to the boroughs, but borough members fell from 419 in the Long Parliament to 136, while county members would be 264 in 400 rather than 90 in 519. For nine years former Royalists, Engagers or Presbyterian adherents of Charles II in 1651 would be disenfranchised.

Although the *Instrument* divided responsibilities and powers between executive and legislature, with the latter a check on the former, the Protector potentially had immense power. Parliament would not meet until September 1654 and during the preceding nine months Cromwell and the Council were empowered to issue decrees which would have the force of law until Parliament should ratify or amend them. The 'power of the purse', which the old parliaments had had over the monarch, was theoretically missing because the *Instrument* provided for a peacetime income of £200,000 a year for the ordinary expenses of government, and further sums for the provision of a navy capable of maintaining security in home waters together with an army of 30,000 horse, foot and artillery. (The catch was that the army numbered between 50,000 and 60,000, so more funds would be needed until it was reduced.) The Protector was also to enjoy the income of the remaining Crown estates and other perquisites of royalty. Parliament was powerless to interfere with any of these government revenues so that it was not easy to see how it could prevent its own dissolution if it persisted in policies which the Protector disliked. Supporters of the *Instrument* such as General Lambert could argue that the Protector had to act with the advice of his Council, and indeed on paper the Council was a very effective brake on the Protector's initiative. It was a small body of men possessed of considerable experience of public life. Fifteen of its members were prescribed by the *Instrument* itself, and subsequent vacancies were to be filled by a method which could be manipulated to suit the wishes of the Protector. The maximum membership was to be twenty-one (although it never reached that figure), and the councillors were in a particularly strong position because they were appointed for life. Lambert, of course, was one of them; others were Lieutenant-General Charles Fleetwood, Major-General Philip Skippon, Colonel John Disbrowe, all serving army officers. Cromwell always liked to be surrounded by men closely connected to himself by professional or family links. Significantly Fleetwood was Cromwell's son-in-law, having married Ireton's widow, Bridget, and John Disbrowe was Cromwell's brother-in-law. Like Ireton he had been one of the original captains in Cromwell's troop of horse in 1642. A civilian councillor, Henry Lawrence, was another brother-in-law. The military did not dominate the Council in numbers for the remainder can be classed as civilians, although many had seen service during the war. William Sydenham had served in the Civil War but more recently had been governor of the Isle of Wight, an administrative post. Colonel Philip Jones, an increasingly wealthy administrator in South Wales, had only served locally during the war. Sir Anthony Ashley Cooper's military career had ended in 1646; Viscount Lisle had served briefly in Ireland and Edward Montagu not since 1645. His distinguished naval career both under the Protectorate and the restored monarchy lay ahead. Francis Rous had just served as Speaker of the Nominated Parliament, and other leading conservative members of that body on the new Council were Lawrence, Sir Gilbert Pickering, Walter Strickland, and Richard Major.[5] Into the hands of these men and the Protector were now confided the destinies of Britain.

The chief officers of state were to be appointed by the Protector 'with the approbation of Parliament', which suggests that their right to approve his choices was more real than their right to object. All other appointments were in Cromwell's hands. The continuity between the Council and the Nominated Parliament (only Skippon and Fleetwood had not been members, although Lambert had never attended) and the old Council of State or both was reinforced by many of Cromwell's appointments (or by those he left unchanged).[6] Parliamentary legislation which was in breach of the *Instrument* could be vetoed by the Protector but there was no body nominated to determine whether such a breach had occurred. Moreover the *Instrument* could only be amended if all branches agreed. Finally, while the country's militia could only be employed by the Protector with Parliament's consent if it was sitting and otherwise with the Council's consent, no reference was made to the standing army or the navy. The omission, possibly the result of hasty drafting, left the Protector in control of the regular armed forces. Thus Britain would now have a supreme Swordsman by the very constitution which was supposed to end a *de facto* military dictatorship, and the Swordsmen he led were themselves largely out of the financial control of both the elected and the nominated branches of government. This at least was the theory. In practice the Protector would have to keep the civilian administrative costs of government within £200,000 and since the *Instrument* only provided for funding a peacetime army of

30,000 he would need to reduce it from the 57,000 which were currently with the colours and reduce the navy from the gargantuan force still engaged in the Dutch War. Any constitutional lawyer who read the *Instrument of Government* would certainly recognize that a soldier wrote it.

On religion the *Instrument* modelled itself on the *Agreement of the People*, merely stipulating that there should be a public profession of Christianity, and that nonconformist congregations would be protected so long as they did not abuse this licence to the detriment of others or the disturbance of the peace, a qualification probably inspired by the public misbehaviour of some of the Quakers. Toleration did not embrace either Papists or Anglicans still wedded to the Prayer Book and to prelacy. On the vexed tithes question, while the *Agreement of the People* had asked that clergymen should be maintained from the public treasury and tithes abolished, the *Instrument* was more conservative, content to keep tithes for the present while decreeing that 'a provision less subject to scruple and contention and more certain than the present' should be employed to maintain 'able and painful' preachers. However, this was qualified by the procrastinating phrase 'as soon as may be'.

The Protectorate might have sprung up mushroom-like, but no effort was spared to launch the new regime with dignity and give it whatever aura of legitimacy solemn pageantry might provide. The New Model Army and various civilian allies, which included the judges and the City of London, displayed a remarkable capacity for speedily organizing the equivalent of a coronation. On Friday 16 December, only hours after Cromwell had formally approved the *Instrument*, a procession of dignitaries left Whitehall Palace for Westminster Hall to induct the new ruler, led by the Commissioners of the Great Seal, the Barons of the Exchequer and the judges in their robes. These were followed by the members of the old Council of State, soon to be superseded, and close on their heels the Lord Mayor, Recorder and Aldermen of the City of London resplendent in their scarlet robes. Finally came the Lord General himself, dressed in a plain black suit and cloak surmounted by a hat with a gold band, accompanied by an entourage of senior officers. Had it not been for the horse and foot lining the streets and the preponderance of military and naval officers at the climax of the procession it might have looked like a cross between an Oxbridge degree-giving procession and the opening of a particularly grand assize. Nevertheless it doubtless appeared ostentatious and savouring of monarchy to some Puritans. At Westminster in the Court of Chancery the Protector stood bareheaded between the Commissioners of the Great Seal while his oath of office was read, and then sat covered while Lambert knelt to offer him a sword, which Cromwell buckled on, surrendering his own (symbolically exchanging a military for a civilian sword) after which the

Lord Mayor presented him with a sword and cap of maintenance which Cromwell solemnly handed back. He was also handed the Great Seal, another portentous symbol of authority. The procession then returned to the Banqueting Hall at Whitehall where the Protector's chaplain, Lockyer, delivered an exhortation. The investiture ended with the firing of three volleys of shot by the soldiers, which can only have emphasized the military character of the affair. In general the country seems to have accepted the new regime with relief, although the Baptists were disgusted that any but God should bear the title of Protector, while the Fifth Monarchists were in a very frenzy of rage that the rule of 'King' Oliver should precede the reign of King Jesus. There were other recalcitrants. When heralds escorted by troopers proclaimed the new regime one ill-informed spectator, seeing a herald reading a proclamation at Temple Bar, asked what was afoot. Being told by a trooper that Oliver was installed as Protector, he responded, 'He protects none but such rogues as thou art!' When the trooper sought to cut him down he hauled the trooper from his horse and gave him a drubbing – to the entertainment of the spectators.[7]

The man who had been ceremoniously charged with these heavy responsibilities was now fifty-four years old, approaching old age by the standards of his own era. Arguably the most famous man in Europe, his latest transformation occasioned no surprise because Europeans had assumed that he was the true ruler of England, at least since the expulsion of the Purged Parliament. He had not only tried and executed a king but had conquered that king's other kingdoms, Scotland, now united with England, and Ireland. He commanded an army of close to 60,000 men, comprising disciplined reliable infantry and that rare phenomenon, disciplined reliable cavalry. The Protector commanded another weapon more immediately menacing: the largest navy so far seen in terms of combined numbers and fire-power. Probably the Republic's single most impressive and unexpected achievement in the eyes of European chancelleries was its victories over the Dutch navy which had acquired a reputation for invincibility during its long wars with Spain. It is not surprising that in a Western Europe which was delicately balanced after the end of the Thirty Years War the coming to power of this man of war, armed with such weapons and with nothing to fear from enemies abroad or at home, should arouse intense interest in the courts of France, Spain and Northern Europe.

The Protector was an enigma to his fellow-countrymen, still more to foreigners. Not even such sharp-eyed spies as the agents of the Venetian Republic or those assiduous Cromwell-watchers, Antoine de Bordeaux-Neufville and Alonso de Cardenas, respectively the ambassadors of France and Spain, could quite get him right.[8] The problem lay in the man himself.

Cromwell was as lazy in administrative affairs as he was active and dedicated in war, while in politics he did not plan ahead, rather seizing opportunities as they appeared. Yet once power was in his hands he held it with a bulldog's tenacity. Cromwell's well-known observation that 'no man goes further than he who knows not whither he is going' was apt and revealing. At critical periods he tended to drift with the current, not seizing control of events and shaping them to his will, but waiting to take charge only when he perceived that something was inevitable. Then procrastination, long silence, apparent bewilderment, indecision and anxiety would suddenly be cast aside in favour of swift, sometimes brutal, action which often took even his closest associates by surprise. The dismissal of Parliament astonished the Council of Officers. Even more typical was Cromwell's conduct during the crisis of 1648. A conventional man-of-destiny would have hastened to the capital after the victory at Preston to seize control and ensure that his Presbyterian opponents in the Long Parliament did not force a deal on the helpless king which would endanger congregational autonomy and the future of the New Model Army. This soldier-politician chose instead, as we have seen, to hang about the siege of Pontefract Castle, where his presence was not needed, while his son-in-law Ireton dominated events in the capital. There is no reason to believe that he controlled the course of events from this Yorkshire fastness or that he ordered or even foresaw Pride's Purge. Lukewarm in his support for the trial of the king he did not intend the king's death until the trial began. Then he abruptly threw off all indecision, as ardent for the Regicide as any vengeful soldier, brutally declaring: 'We will cut off his head with the crown upon it!' As was usual with him, once he had conquered indecision he was at his most boisterous, indulging in schoolboy horseplay with the court's inkwell and pen and an occasion of tragic significance derogated into a classroom jape.

Cromwell's apparent contradictions are often ascribed to his being a strange mix of practical soldier, millenarian Puritan and conservative country gentleman imbued with nostalgia for the Elizabethan age. All this he combined with what was then a very radical and unexpected commitment to religious toleration for Protestants, including beliefs he must have regarded as nonsense at best and dangerous at worst. When he told an Irish commander that he 'meddled with no man's conscience' but would not permit the Mass, he meant what he said. His forbidding the Mass reflected his determination to stamp out subversive preaching, not the tenets of the Catholic faith. Cromwell was a hero to the Congregationalists of Massachusetts since he not only protected them but protected their co-religionists in Britain. However, they would have shuddered in their meeting houses, those citadels of intolerant conformity, if they had grasped how deep was his commitment to toleration lest intolerance unwittingly suppress the truth. Like all Puritans he believed in the workings of Divine

Providence and there is no reason to doubt his sincerity in ascribing his victories not to his own ability but to God's will. However, it is surely not entirely coincidental that God's wonder-working Providence always seemed to increase Cromwell's prestige, influence and, ultimately, power. As one observer has noted, while it can be argued that Cromwell procrastinated because he was waiting to see which way the will of God was tending, it appeared that 'God clearly always wanted Cromwell to survive politically'.[9]

Fundamentally, like Napoleon, he never forgot that he 'rose from the camp'. Without the army he would have remained no more than a minor East Anglian gentleman. The New Model Army might be in large part his own creation, but it had also made him and he never made the mistake of ignoring its prejudices, although he successfully resisted the aspirations of its more radical soldiers. He never retired to civilian life after 1642, for even as Protector he remained Lord General. Thus despite the constitutional trappings of the *Instrument of Government*, despite Cromwell's longing for constitutional legitimacy and general acceptance by at least his English subjects, the rule of the Protector was the rule of the Swordsman.

First and foremost it was necessary to provide the Protector with the trappings of authority, which included decisions about protocol in dealing with foreign ambassadors and others, but above all with establishing a household. Cromwell had for years enjoyed the respect of foreign ambassadors despite the taint of regicide because the envoys of foreign governments always gravitate to where they believe the power resides. To them Cromwell had been that focus ever since his return from Worcester and his retirement from active soldiering. However, for the Protector as an office rather than a man to enjoy the prestige of other European governments, most of which were royal courts, a household which would also be a court was necessary. The Council in setting up the Protector's court very naturally took over the buildings and reinvented the bureaucratic structure of the court of Charles I. This involved a variety of outward appearances and inner realities which were disagreeable to the more austere Republicans and a turning back of the clock from the brave new world of 1649, when the English government strove to reinvent itself as the English Republic. Nevertheless, granted that a strong central government was needed to avoid confusion and chaos, and that the Protectorate was a likely way to achieve this, the Council's measures seem sensible, practical, appropriate and they worked.[10] The decaying, neglected Palace of Whitehall received a new lease of life as its chambers were redecorated. Hampton Court also revived for it was Cromwell's favourite among the royal palaces and it was the Protector's custom to pass up-river to it on Friday evenings and to return downstream to Whitehall on Monday mornings, giving him a claim to being the inventor of the English 'weekend'. In its extensive grounds the Protector could gratify his passion for hawking and for hunting with the buck hounds. Windsor Castle, Greenwich House, Somerset House, St James's Palace and the former 'King's Manor' at York were other royal residences which were allocated to the Protector's and his successors' use in perpetuity. However, Oliver spent little time at any other than Whitehall, which was the seat of government as well as his home, and Hampton Court to which he fled for recreation.[11]

The advent of the Protectorate provided a salutary period for many royal treasures and kept them safe from vandalism or sale until the Restoration. While the Commonwealth government had sold much of Charles I's magnificent art collection some had survived along with a very valuable collection of furniture, tapestries and sculpture. Cromwell's moderate pragmatism permitted him to enjoy works of art which would horrify ardent Puritans by their Papistical references or pagan 'lewdness', as in the nude gods and goddesses which caused some alarm and despondency when they were restored to the Hampton Court gardens. A Puritan lady, Mrs Mary Nethaway, wrote protesting about them, warning His Highness that God's wrath might strike him down at any moment if they remained. It was that the subjects were pagan, not their nudity, which disturbed Mrs Nethaway: '. . . whilst they stand, though you see no evil in them yet there is much evil in it, for whilst the groves and altars of the idols remained untaken away in Jerusalem, the wrath of God continued against Israel.' The Protector, like the statues, was unmoved.[12] Less blatantly offensive to the godly were the sets of tapestry which were now rehung, some involving as many as ten pieces to a set, depicting mythological, classical or biblical themes. They included *The Seven Deadly Sins* and two versions of *The History of Vulcan, Mars and Venus* (one of which adorned the Protector's bedroom at Hampton Court). Others featured *The Siege of Jerusalem, The Triumph of Julius Caesar, The History of Charlemagne* and *The Story of King Hezekiah. The Glory of Meleager* adorned the Hampton Court apartment of Cromwell's daughter, Frances. The ten-piece set *The Life of Abraham*, which had belonged to Henry VIII and was of suitably gargantuan dimensions (each piece 15 to 16 feet high and from 25 to 30 feet long) and valued at £8,260, decorated Hampton Court as it still does. Another set of tapestries with a strong appeal for the Protector was that depicting *The Defeat of the Spanish Armada.* Unhappily they perished in the destruction of Parliament by fire in the nineteenth century.

Two paintings from Nonsuch, a palace the Protector did not use, were surely unsuitable for a Puritan, for they were both devoted to the Madonna. Others included Van Somer's *An Ambassador of France* and Titian's *Herodias with the Head of John the Baptist.* The two greatest surviving works, outstanding products of the High Renaissance, were, first, Mantegna's *Triumph of Julius Caesar,* a work almost as immense as it was renowned (nine canvases each nine feet square), and secondly, the even larger and more valuable Raphael cartoons of the *Acts of the Apostles* which Leo X had commissioned for tapestries for the Sistine Chapel and which Charles had purchased in 1623. Both are still in the royal collection. To complete the furnishing of the Protectoral suites the Council delved into the spoils lately seized from Stirling Castle, including chairs of state, high stools, a bed's red velvet furnishings, silk curtains and canopies. In October 1654 Clement Kinnersley, the official decorator, claimed £500 for gathering the late king's possessions and decorating and furnishing Whitehall with them. When John Evelyn revisited Whitehall in 1656 after a lapse of years he found the palace 'very glorious and well furnished'.

The Protector sought to cultivate a special relationship with the City of London whose wealth his government would need to draw upon in the future. There can be little doubt that the coming in of the Protectorate court warmed this new relationship, for it brought badly needed business for many trades, crafts and commercial companies which had languished ever since 1642. The extinction of the court and the decline of so many noble households, reduced by deaths, exile and 'malignancy' fines, had cut off valued custom. Now a stream of orders poured out to pewterers, braziers, gilders, plasterers, upholsterers, refurbishers of tapestries and hangings, cabinet-makers, musical instrument makers, carpenters, picture restorers, silkmen, linen drapers, jewellers, gold and silversmiths, importers of Turkey carpets and Eastern porcelain. The Council purchased two sets of plate for the Protector's use from the Lord Mayor which cost more than £3,000, and the expenditure on various London craftsmen and merchants for decorating the palaces amounted to a further £3,000. The City must have hummed in a way which it had not since the calling of the Long Parliament in 1640. Like the raising of a vast circus tent by the hauling of a thousand willing hands, the court rose majestically again.

Good news for many is usually bad news for some, and so it was at Whitehall. Royal palaces, indeed all the palatial residences of the greater nobility, were then vast, rambling, ill-organized structures of large numbers of rooms, together with a warren of stables, bakehouses, washhouses, breweries, slaughterhouses, barns, tackrooms and stabling. In the absence of their owners, sometimes even in their presence, these tended to become refuges for a rich variety of people whose common characteristic was indigence combined with insecurity of tenure. Squatters are not only a late twentieth-century phenomenon. In Greenwich House there were squatters who had to be dislodged, but the worst and most prolonged problem lay within the Whitehall mews. Whitehall Palace was not so much a building as a small township of many buildings, containing roughly 2,000 rooms, sprawled over 23 acres, and divided by the public road from Charing Cross to Westminster which not even Henry VIII had succeeded in enclosing. Among its numerous stables and outhouses a number of former menial members of the old royal household, or their relics or offspring, had clung on in holes and corners ever since 1642, living the discreet lives of mice in a world ruled by cats. Now the need to provide for the Protector's horses, his life guard and their horses, and his grooms, ostlers and other menial servants and their families, meant that these forgotten survivors must lose their refuge. The Council ordered a clean sweep of them in March 1654 – but the mice were tenacious, for some were still a problem in November 1655. Some petitioned the Protector on the grounds that they or relatives had fought for the parliamentary cause during the Great Civil War, others more humbly that at least they had not fought for the king. It took nearly two years to remove these relics, among them a Mother Goose, although not without financial compensation or alternative arrangements for at least some of them. An order made in 1654 that royal debts to former royal servants should be paid would have helped many of them. Mercifully the occupation of the remainder of the palace brought less human dislocation, although some more august squatters had to locate elsewhere: the Admiralty Commissioners and the Committee for the Approbation of Public Preachers had to shift from their Whitehall offices to Derby House to provide apartments for Richard Cromwell, Oliver's eldest son.

The household with which the Protector was provided was modelled closely on that of Charles I, although not as large. The noblemen who had presided over its operations under the monarchy were replaced by men who found careers open to talent during the Interregnum, men of the 'middling sort', blessed by ability rather than birth.[13] The Court was divided into three discrete departments: the household above stairs, the household below stairs and the stables. The household below stairs was largely a catering organization charged with wining and dining the household and controlled by two household stewards. That this was a considerable undertaking may be deduced from the fact that the great kitchen was responsible for cooking for the household in general but not for the Protector and his lady in particular, who were fed from a privy kitchen supervised by the Protector's own chef (Mr Hamor). The records of the stewards have not survived but the scale of their operation is suggested by the consumption of French and Spanish wine, which the Protector enjoyed duty-free, which amounted to tens of thousands of gallons a year (more than 17,000 gallons in 1657 alone). The household staff must have been very large (although the number is not recorded), but smaller than the army which served in the royal household. In addition to such obvious tasks as cleaning and laundering there would have been large numbers of specialist servants such as cooks, bakers and brewers (all the household would have been entitled to a ration of beer daily), and the sub-departments therefore included 'the kitchen', 'great beer cellar', 'wine cellar', 'spicery', a slaughterhouse and a laundry. When the Protectorate became more monarchical during 1657 the household became more hierarchical and elaborate and many of the Protector's servants became entitled to servants of their own 'on the establishment'. The Comptroller of the Household (a post revived in 1657 which replaced the stewards and which was held by Councillor Philip Jones) had his own waiters, butler and kitchen staff. During the first years the household's cost appears to have amounted to between £60,000 and £70,000 annually, which shows that it was run remarkably economically by court standards of that age and that the scale of graft and peculation customary in great households, especially royal households, must have been modest.[14]

The stables represented a department which expanded rather than revived, for throughout the Commonwealth horses and coaches had been maintained to transport foreign ambassadors and their entourages to official, ceremonial and more social occasions. The Protectoral stables, now under the new Master of the Horse (Cromwell's son-in-law John Claypole), performed the same function but in addition transported the Protector and his family, and furnished him with horses for riding about and for hunting and hawking. Moreover, Cromwell, possessed of the concerns characteristic of the country gentleman, was interested in horse-breeding, particularly with the Arab strain, and he imported horses from Turkey and elsewhere. His Gentleman of the Horse, second in the stable hierarchy to Claypole, was sent to Rotterdam in 1657 to bring back an Arab stallion. Cromwell was also sent gifts of horses by the Prince of East Friesland and the Count of Oldenberg. Certainly the stables, with its complement of avenor, who was responsible for horse-feed, coachman, postilion, grooms and footmen in handsome livery (a velvet-collared coat of grey cloth welted with velvet, silver and black silk lace), clerks, equerries and pages, would all have contributed to the public image of the Protector as a ruler with a court and its traditional appurtenances. Not all the royal household was revived, however. There was no Lord Chamberlain, although a chamberlain did appear after the Protectorate later took on more of the trappings of monarchy. He was not a great nobleman like Charles I's Earl of Pembroke who was replaced in 1641 as a sop to the Puritans by the Earl of Essex, but rather a country gentleman. He was Sir Gilbert Pickering, a baronet of Nova Scotia, MP for Northamptonshire in the Short, Long and Nominated Parliaments, and member of the Protectorate Council of State. An opponent dismissed him as 'being so finical, spruce and like an old courtier', but the description reveals him as admirably qualified for the job of running the Protector's household 'above stairs'. He was not appointed until 1655, however, and even then his post may have been in abeyance until the following year. Before the household became more royally elaborate the Protector's household above stairs was probably as unostentatious and practical as that of a wealthy nobleman of high rank. He had a secretary, perhaps as many as thirty young men, gentlemen-in-waiting, pages, etc., who conducted visitors to his presence, ran his errands and generally acted like a modern politician's 'minders', and an array of domestic servants to wait upon himself, the Protectress Elizabeth and their immediate family.

This simplicity did not mean that he did not receive official deputations, especially foreign emissaries and resident ambassadors, with elaborate and imposing ceremonial. Foreign deputations were officially received in the Whitehall Banqueting Hall – the splendid room which Charles I had passed through to the scaffold (an irony not lost on spectators). The organization of such ceremonies, in which any unwitting slight or breach of protocol could cause deep offence to a foreign government with whom the Protector wished to be on excellent terms, was discharged with skill and a keen eye for the proprieties by Sir Oliver Fleming, the court's Master of Ceremonies. Under his watchful eye foreign ambassadors or special emissaries for particular occasions would advance towards the Protector as he sat on a throne, under a canopy of state, at the head of the Banqueting Hall, supported by a cloud of senior officers, councillors and courtiers. On three occasions their reverential progress would be punctuated by pauses to make low bows to His Highness. 'Good God, what damned arse-lickers were here', exclaimed one despairing Royalist in a letter which found its way unerringly on to the desk of Cromwell's master of Intelligence, John Thurloe. The Venetian ambassador watched the Protector sitting amid deep cushions on a throne which stood on Turkey carpets while bareheaded men pressed forward to do him homage 'in the obsequious and respectful form observed to the late kings'.

However, English republicans of the more austere stamp, who feared monarchy was now certain as pomp turned Oliver's head, need not have worried. The Republic was not to be overthrown while he was alive and these monarchical ostentatious ceremonies were designed to impress on foreigners that the Protector was as much a ruler in Britain as their royal masters were in their own states. Cromwell himself, the least ostentatious of men, bore it all with dignified reserve. The outward show was a mask. He was much more neatly dressed now that gentlemen-of-the-bedchamber daily got this notoriously careless dresser into his clothes, but the head of the man within remained unturned. He was still the same man who had ridden through cheering crowds towards Scotland in 1650 with General Lambert at his side, and who, when Lambert remarked on the enthusiasm of the spectators, cynically retorted: 'They would cheer as loudly if we were going to be hanged.' Such a man is not to be demoralized by the bowings and scrapings of courtiers and ambassadors.

These were in any event the formal side of his public life. The Protectorate court's other function of dispensing hospitality and maintaining and winning friendship took place in a much more relaxed atmosphere. Here the ageing soldier-politician was at his best. He was naturally affable and had a capacity for putting strangers at ease which certainly exceeded that of his royal victim although not of his royal successor. (Of Charles II an observer noted that 'he was not only easy in himself but the cause that others were easy about him' – for 'easy' read 'at ease' – and the Protector shared at least some of that ability.) He frequently held lavish dinners at Whitehall for councillors, leading citizens, ambassadors and other foreign visitors, and more informal dinners for army officers once a week (at which we are informed he eschewed foreign 'kickshaws' in favour of good English fare). Ordinarily he dined in modest state with seven tables to seat his family and household: one for the Protector, one for the Protectress, one for chaplains and strangers, one for the household steward and gentlemen servants, one for coachmen, grooms and other domestics, and at the foot of the ladder of status, a table for 'Inferiors or sub-servants' (that is, the servants of servants). This was no more than would have been encountered in the residence of a post-Restoration high officer of state, such as Lord Chancellor Guildford or a wealthy nobleman.

While it has been claimed that Cromwell lacked the visual appreciation of the arts for which Charles I was rightly famed, he had a keen ear for music. Visitors to his court were likely to be entertained by the best vocalists and instrumentalists of the period and to be invited to hear choirs and organ music. The quality of some of the leading virtuosi can be measured from the fact that only one was not subsequently rehired for the court of Charles II. The old legend that the Puritan era was barren of artistic expression has long been buried under an avalanche of evidence to the contrary, and the Protectorate court played its part in the musical revival of the Interregnum. Sir William Davenant, who is said to have aspired to be Cromwell's Master of the Revels, although there is no evidence that he succeeded, introduced opera to England by placing dramas in an elaborate musical setting in order to circumvent the bans on the theatre.[15] Music and dancing and revelling, with fifty trumpets and forty-eight violins – an instrument which achieved popularity under the Protectorate – accompanied the marriage of Cromwell's daughter Frances to Robert Rich, the grandson of the Earl of Warwick. (The latter, a strong supporter of Cromwell, re-emerged into public life during the Protectorate after his forced retirement from the Admiralty in 1649.) The marriage of Cromwell's daughter Mary to Lord Fauconberg, although more sedate, seems have been accompanied by something resembling a masque (by Andrew Marvell) in which the Protector is said to have taken part, a curious echo of the court of Charles I. While the evidence for the details of day-to-day life at the Protector's court is very scanty, accounts which have survived, even accounts by unfriendly witnesses, all suggest that it was well able to carry out the functions for which it had been designed: to promote the image of a strong and powerful government capable of inspiring respect as well as alarm among the European courts. However, if the establishment of the Protectorate brought a degree of stability to the British Isles and certainly put an end to fears of anarchy, the Protector and his Council soon found that however skilfully constitutions are drawn and however stable a government is made, the old problems can remain as intractable as ever.

CHAPTER TEN

The Protectorate and Its Problems

Cromwell proceeds with strange dexterity towards the reconciling all kinds of persons and chooses out those of all parties whose abilities are most eminent.

Edward Hyde, 4 March 1654[1]

Hyde's remark was inspired by the policies of Cromwell and the Council during the Protectorate's first nine months. They sought to heal old wounds, reconcile old enemies and give the country a sense of security which it had not enjoyed since 1642. Indeed England had a more powerful and effective central government than it had ever had before. The members of the Council, the majority of them army officers and the rest sympathetic to their views, worked hard during those nine months of 'conciliar' government to effect a number of long-sought reforms.[2] The methods chosen were novel, indeed irregular, in terms of legal precedent. Eighty-two laws were made by proclamation in defiance of Chief Justice Coke's forty-year-old legal decision that proclamations could do no such thing. Of course, the Councillors expected that the Protectorate Parliament would confirm these laws when it met in September and clothe them with constitutional decency. Parliament disappointed this expectation but this could not be foreseen as the Council issued ordinance after ordinance through the spring and summer of 1654.

As might be expected of a body whose membership had been chosen partly because of their opposition to the headlong radicalism within the Nominated Parliament, many of the reform measures were minimal or at best cautious. Access to Chancery was made simpler and cheaper, which offended the legal interest, but this fell far short of the abolition demanded by the radicals. This government was powerful enough to have carried out a root-and-branch reform of the legal system but contented itself with a few useful reforms which left the structure of the Common Law untouched. On the most important issue on the Protectorate's agenda, the church, the radicals were again frustrated, especially over tithes which again displayed their capacity to survive in a hostile environment (although Cromwell subsequently claimed he had wished to abolish them but had been outvoted). Toleration of the sects had been settled by the *Instrument*. The

Nominated Parliament's radicals had wanted simultaneously to abolish patronage and tithes by a system under which congregations would both select and fund their ministers. Those who devised the *Instrument of Government* would have none of this assault on property. Nevertheless, the Protectorate government had to determine how ministers should be appointed and dismissed, how far the state should restrict their nonconformist doctrines and how they should be paid. In fact the Council issued no ordinance on maintenance until September 1654 and this simply sought to increase inadequate stipends and to provide lectureships from funds derived from former ecclesiastical property.

In general the Protectorate's religious settlement offered nothing very novel, being based on the proposals which Cromwell's former chaplain, John Owen, and a group of Independent ministers had submitted to the Purged Parliament in 1652 and which others had made in the Nominated Parliament since.[3] These had proposed a centrally located commission which could eject unsatisfactory ministers and locally organized 'triers' who would determine who were suitable for appointment and who were unfit for their ministry. This proposal was now reversed, with the 'triers' in London and the 'ejectors' in the provinces. A general commission was set up in London in March 1654 (the 'triers') with the power to confirm appointments, but the rights of lay patrons were retained, and it was with their blessing that candidates came before the commission. The 'triers' consisted of twenty-three Independent, Presbyterian or Anabaptist ministers and ten laymen. Most of them supported the concept of both a national church and independent congregations. Candidates who lived remote from London could be examined by local ministers who reported on their religious and moral suitability. In August 1654 a second ordinance established county commissions (the 'ejectors') of between twenty-five and thirty laymen assisted by eight to ten ministers. These acted as assessors, with the authority to expel both ministers and schoolmasters who were 'scandalous in their lives or conversations', or who were guilty of blasphemy or atheism as proscribed by the 1651 Blasphemy Act, or who were guilty of conduct unsuitable in a minister (or schoolmaster). Unsuitable conduct was certainly wide ranging. It included besides such obvious failings as Papistry, neglect, non-residence, drunkenness, adultery, gambling, perjury, swearing, and scoffing at the Godly, using the Book of Common Prayer, but also favouring maypoles, stage-plays, morris dancing, wakes and church-ales, or opposing the government in print, from the pulpit or in school. Any found guilty of such offences could be expelled by the 'ejectors' and replaced by a candidate who had been approved by the 'triers'. This system placed considerable power in the hands of local congregations who could rid themselves of unwanted ministers by testifying against them. However, the Protectorate government prescribed no doctrine or form of worship, preferring to preside benevolently over a situation in which, as Owen and his associates had wanted, there was both a national church and independent congregations whose worship was unsupervised.

This tolerant attitude meant that although individual ministers might fall foul of 'ejectors' the Anglican service, prayer book and all, survived in barely clandestine ways at the parish level by conspiratorial cooperation between clergyman, congregation and local patron. In the roughly 9,500 parishes across the country many Anglican ministers must have survived because only about 3,000 ministers were expelled or resigned under the Act of Uniformity of 1662, and surely not all the other 6,000 were religious weathercocks, mere 'Vicars of Bray'.[4] Other congregations contentedly enjoyed the ministry of professed Presbyterians. Many clergymen who had long been a disgrace to their cloth were ejected, as congregations who had too long endured ministers whose only qualification was access to patronage now found devoted ministers and inspiring preachers. For many congregations the Protectorate was a golden age which ended in bitterness, disappointment and frustration when bishops and patrons resumed their old incontestable authority after the Restoration. The melancholy truth is that in practical religious policy the rule of the Swordsmen was more tolerant of Anglicans than the government of Charles II would be of Sectarians. The Protector even allowed his old friend Archbishop Ussher, now chiefly remembered for his misguidedly precise dating of the Creation, to be buried in Westminster Abbey according to the rites of the Book of Common Prayer. Indeed the use of the prayer book discreetly survived in at least one London church close to Whitehall Palace, as well as in numberless provincial parishes. Toleration was extended in practice even to recusants so long as they forbore Royalist activities, for they found Cromwell's avowedly hostile regime less burdensome than that of Archbishop Laud who had zealously persecuted Catholics to counter the accusation that his Arminianism was Papistical. Cromwell considered that he had shown greater tolerance towards recusants than the Commonwealth, assuring Cardinal Mazarin that he had 'as Jude speaks, plucked many out of . . . the raging fire of persecution, which did tyrannize over their consciences and encroach by arbitrariness of power over their estates'.[5] Indeed his toleration extended to non-Christians, for Cromwell insisted on readmitting the Jews to England in 1656, although he had a terrible struggle with some of his councillors about the decision.

The Quakers, who were a rapidly expanding sect, had a mixed experience of toleration and persecution under the Protectorate – but then the early Friends were decidedly mixed in their behaviour. They were at risk from the Blasphemy Act while their interruptions of services, refusal to doff their hats in church and regular inveighing against all ministers of religion inevitably led to prosecutions. George Fox tried to curb his more extreme followers, and had frequent meetings with Cromwell, who always treated him with courtesy, although he sometimes teased that solemn figure. One of Elizabeth Cromwell's maids may have been a Quaker and this may explain the Protector's willingness to rescue persecuted Quakers occasionally.[6] Hugh Peter, former army chaplain and inveterate revolutionary, once remarked that 'The Protector sleeps upon no easy pillow. If 'twas such a matter for King Charles to be Defender of the Faith, the Protector has a thousand faiths to protect.'[7] No easy pillow indeed, where Cromwell was beset by those who deplored the lack of a firm doctrine and practice universally enforced, and others condemned the religious settlement as not nearly loose enough. Of course, the policy of toleration was personal to him and could wax and wane according to temporary needs and dangers. Both Anglicans and Catholics at various times felt the heavy hand of persecution. Nevertheless, there was more toleration under this government than under any earlier or for decades after. Even his unsparing critic the Presbyterian Richard Baxter admitted that 'it was his design to do good in the main, and promote the gospel and the interest of godliness, more than any had done before him'.[8]

The Council tackled energetically a number of social, economic and administrative problems. Duelling was forbidden because private warfare undermined the law. Lord Macauley declared that the Puritans banned bear-baiting not for the pain it gave the bear but for the pleasure it gave the spectators. This is witty but a travesty. The Protector was no enemy of pleasure, as anyone who observed him out hawking or following his buck-hounds or listening to music could have attested. Cock-fighting and horse-racing were proscribed because they involved gambling which could lead to social disruption and affrays, and because Royalists and other conspirators could take cover among large gatherings of people. Stage plays were banned more for the behaviour of the audience – the 'pit' was notoriously a place to pick up prostitutes – than for the dramas presented. Other ordinances dealt with the governance of Ireland and Scotland which must be considered later. Suffice to say that Scotland was united with England in 'one free State and Commonwealth' while the *Instrument of Government* had already decreed that, like Ireland, it should elect thirty members of the Protectorate Parliament. Still others concerned the regime's finances, with decrees continuing the monthly assessments and the unpopular excise. However, in general the administration of the Protectorate much resembled that of the Commonwealth, and if it differed, it rather suggested a harking back to still earlier days than to novel experiments.[9]

All regimes take steps to protect themselves from recalcitrants. Here the Protectorate had a mixed record, ranging from a statesmanlike mildness which sought reconciliation to unnecessarily violent reactions to 'rebellions' which were no more than ill-organized exercises in futility, exposing the feebleness of the regime's opponents rather than threatening to overthrow it. Two judges, Chief Baron Wilde and John Puleston, Chief Justice of the Common Pleas, both notorious for their harshness towards Royalists, were dismissed. Matthew Hale, the courageous counsel of Archbishop Laud, replaced Puleston, a markedly conciliatory appointment.[10] From the beginning the Protectorate had internal enemies, as close as the Council of Officers. Such recalcitrants were brought before the Council and warned to mend their ways. If they remained obdurate they were imprisoned in remote fortresses. A change of heart usually brought release. None were tried let alone executed under the Treason ordinance, although all were vulnerable to its provisions. This was merciful policy but it meant the Swordsmen were denying their own colleagues the processes and protections of the criminal law. Two received special treatment because of their eminence and influence: Major-General Harrison, the Fifth Monarchist, and Lieutenant-General Edmund Ludlow, the obdurate republican. Harrison was too wedded to his vision of the reign of King Jesus to accept the reign of 'King' Oliver. He was exiled to his father's Staffordshire home, although later allowed to return for a time to London. It was Harrison's fate to be one of the 'usual suspects' who were routinely rounded up whenever there was a plot against the government, but since he was never involved he was invariably released. Unlike Harrison Edmund Ludlow was destined to survive the Restoration and during a long exile wrote his memoirs – an advantage for his posthumous reputation denied to other revolutionaries. After an adventurous Civil War, Ludlow had been one of the leading destroyers of the monarchy and architects of the Republic. Ludlow planned Pride's Purge with Ireton while Cromwell was still in the north. The failings of the Purged Parliament had never moved him from his loyalty to it and he never forgave Cromwell or even Harrison for the coup of 1653. He welcomed the attempts at reform by the Nominated Parliament and blamed Cromwell for its extinction. His devotion to republicanism prevented him from ever accepting the Protectorate. He had served under Ireton in Ireland, succeeding him both as commander-in-chief and Lord Deputy until Fleetwood's appointment, and was still there in 1653. Beside his military command he was also a commissioner charged with civilian responsibilities. He refused to sign the proclamation of the Protectorate and resigned his civilian appointments. However, he remained a lieutenant-general because, as he later wrote, he hoped to lead his troops against Cromwell later. (His enemies claimed he simply wanted the salary.) In January 1655 Fleetwood discovered that Ludlow was encouraging the distribution of anti-Protectorate pamphlets and dismissed him from the army. Not allowed to return to England until October 1655 he was arrested as soon as he landed and interrogated before Cromwell and the Council but then released. All the government wanted was his promise to support the

Protectorate but as he told Walter Strickland, who had been sent to persuade him, he would never submit to the rule of the sword. Strickland reminded Ludlow that he had held Wardour Castle 'by the sword', but Ludlow replied that there was a difference between 'a sword in the hands of a Parliament to restore the people to their ancient rights and a sword in the hands of a tyrant to rob and despoil them thereof'. Either because of his eminence or his past services Ludlow escaped imprisonment, living quietly in Essex, but he was not allowed to return to his native Wiltshire. No such mercy was shown to a third eminent opponent of the new regime. John Lilburne had been exiled under the Purged Parliament but returned after the *putsch* arguing that Parliament's extinction also extinguished his banishment. He was arrested and brought to trial where as usual he was acquitted. However, the Council refused to release him and the advent of the Protectorate saw him imprisoned in Mount Orgueil Castle on Jersey where the writ of *habeas corpus* did not run. He was transferred to Dover Castle in October 1655. Here he became interested in the Quaker sect and his last pamphlet proclaimed his conversion. Gradually the government relaxed his imprisonment, permitting visits to Quaker meetings around Kent. In the summer of 1657, now aged forty-two, while visiting his pregnant wife he caught a fever and died. By then, however, that perturbing spirit had long been silenced.

A parliament must now meet, not simply to fulfil the terms of the new constitution, or to sanctify the Council's legislative ordinances, but because of the desperate need for revenue. The Commonwealth had spent a million a year more than it had received in taxation and other earnings, and had lived for years on that wasting capital asset, confiscated property of the Crown, the Church and the Royalists. The Dutch War which the Commonwealth had too lightly entered had proved ruinously expensive, and the Nominated Parliament's refusal to end the war had further increased the national debt. English commerce had survived its losses to Dutch privateers and there was no danger of grass growing through the London or Bristol cobbles, but the scale of government indebtedness discouraged merchants from advancing it money. The Protector made peace with the Dutch, as we shall see, but his government still spent £350,000 more than it received in revenue during 1654. The Protector had also cut the monthly assessment which however politically desirable had only made things worse fiscally.

The day chosen for the meeting of the first Protectorate Parliament was 3 September, a day of great significance to all the Swordsmen, for it was the anniversary of Dunbar and Worcester. Unfortunately it was also a Sunday, and so a decidedly scandalous choice to all civilian Sabbatarians. This first parliament of the Protectorate demonstrated that while Cromwell was a very effective politician among soldiers he was a less effective politician among parliamentarians. Like many of his background he held an idealized view of Parliament, seeing it as a body of country gentlemen much as he had been before unexpected military glory hoisted him to greatness. These gentlemen were assembled to debate public affairs, legislate for local concerns, pass national legislation framed by himself in Council, and above all to vote taxes to sustain his government and its giant army and navy.[11] Although he had witnessed the parliamentary management of Pym, Hesilrige and Hampden during the 1640s as a member of Pym's junta he behaved as though he did not believe the Commons should be managed. His Puritan countrymen would know what to do without direction. Certainly he would not intervene himself, leaving what leadership was required to councillor-members such as Lambert, Disbrowe and Thurloe. He saw his role as remaining detached from Parliament, much as the early United States presidents honoured their constitutional separation from Congress. For the Protector to seek to steer parliamentary legislation smacked of the methods of Charles I in the 1620s.

The Council itself had done little to organize a government party prior to the opening of Parliament. The *Instrument of Government* had reduced the executive's ability to plant loyal Cromwellians in Parliament by reducing the number of borough members and increasing the number of county members. (A remarkable example was Cornwall, whose two county members and forty-two borough members were reduced to four borough and eight county members respectively.) Nevertheless there were enough enfranchised boroughs left in which to plant suitable members, while the government had the advantage of the sixty seats from Scotland and Ireland which would be filled by their conquerors rather than elected by the conquered. Unfortunately there was a tendency to have men elected because their eminence and loyalty deserved recognition, but who, like General Monck, could not take their seats because they could not be spared from their duties. Certainly there were a substantial number of 'government members' in the House, and these members were to resist strongly the hostile initiatives of the Republican opposition, but they failed to win control of important committees. These stalwarts included such councillors as Lambert, Disbrowe, and Lawrence, while Sir Anthony Ashley Cooper tried to mediate between the two until despair drove him into opposition.[12]

The election was fought along traditional lines, except that active Royalists were supposedly excluded both from voting and candidature. This discrimination was often honoured in the breach since local sheriffs could not be relied on to exclude voters who were their kinsmen, patrons or men to whom they owed deference. Otherwise local issues and rivalries usually predominated in those constituencies where there was a contest (always a minority since local gentlemen traditionally strove to avoid them). For a government devoted to unity, consensus, reconciliation, it must have seemed an ill omen that the most divisive national issue was the body of reforming ordinances (especially those relating to religion) which the government expected Parliament to ratify. Significantly the voters tended to prefer the sort of member that Pride's Purge had been designed to remove from the Long Parliament: 'Presbyterians' who had supported Parliament during the Civil War, sought an accommodation with the king after it and totally opposed the Regicide. Only four of the radical wing of the Nominated Parliament got in, although several of the moderates were successful, including Francis Rous and Ashley Cooper. More than a hundred members had sat in the Long Parliament, most of whom had been purged by Colonel Pride. Others had survived the Purge until Cromwell's coup sent them packing, the fiercest of whom was Sir Arthur Hesilrige who had nursed his wrath ever since, and the Regicides Thomas Scot and John Bradshaw. A few Levellers or Leveller-sympathizers crept in along with Lord Grey of Groby, who would be arrested as a Fifth Monarchist-Leveller conspirator the following year.[13]

In the seventeenth-century fashion the Parliament was slow to assemble, but some three hundred were in the Painted Chamber on 3 September to hear an address from the Protector in which he described the dangers and difficulties which the nation had recently faced, rehearsed the measures already taken to protect its peace and unity, and called upon the new assembly to assist him with the task of 'healing and settling' the body politic. He did not invite them to express any opinion on the new constitution which he expected them to work within. Of course, if the *Instrument of Government* had not existed neither would Parliament, so Cromwell's position had the advantage of logic but not political foresight. Meanwhile he asked them to confirm the legislation already proclaimed and to vote him taxes with which to maintain his army and navy and to reduce the heavy burden of debt which his government had inherited. The members could certainly see where the main burden of expense lay. Soldiers crowded the precincts of Westminster, including the Protector's life guards and musketeers, and an array of brilliantly uniformed senior officers swarmed about the Protector as he entered the Painted Chamber. This overwhelming military presence during a parliamentary occasion in a country at peace must have been provoking to the crypto-monarchist Presbyterians, Republicans and over-taxed country gentlemen who together chiefly composed the first Protectorate Parliament.

The first strike came from the Hesilrige Republicans who quickly seized control of the principal committees and when the government supporters managed to elect the Speaker swiftly won a division to form a 'committee of the whole House' (during which the Speaker steps down) so as to bypass him. Their expertise and experience, combined with their public reputations, made them men who could sway the opinions of others merely by confiding their own, and enabled them to establish their leadership over the inexperienced majority. Not averse to questioning the legality of the *Instrument of Government* (although technically this was treason) their prime objective was to revise it so as to increase the power of the legislative at the expense of the Protector and Council. The troubles began when Hesilrige suggested that Parliament should establish one good form of religion and outlaw many of the sects, which, he suggested, would establish religious and political peace. The suggestion certainly did not bestow religious and political peace on the House, as no doubt he had foreseen. The Presbyterian Hesilrige envisaged a Presbyterian system which would have been supported by those members who were not there as supporters of the Protectorate and who were not members of a particular sect. However, this was not a proposal which either Cromwell or the New Model Army would have accepted for a moment. At this point one of the councillor-members rather oddly suggested that the House should devote the next day to discussing the *Instrument of Government.* Secure in the knowledge that ultimate power lay with the Swordsmen, and that no contest could be lost by the Protectorate, the proposer may have hoped to get the acceptance of the *Instrument* and the Protectorate out of the way early, before opposition could organize. If so the scheme backfired. Even without debating the right of the officers to devise the *Instrument* and by what right they had appointed Oliver Protector, the Republicans felt they had a perfect right to debate and to settle such fundamental questions as the relationship between Parliament and Protector and whether Parliament or Protector was to be the supreme governing authority. As one member stoutly observed, the Protector's authority was simply 'the length of his own sword'. The Protectorate was the product of force even though the people had peacefully accepted it. Cromwell's coup had ended the Purged Parliament. Fraud and force had brushed away the Nominated Parliament. It was a government with no constitutional validity but, as usurpers will, it aspired to legitimacy and looked to the Protectorate Parliament to provide it. This gave those MPs who believed the Swordsmen had betrayed the 'good old cause' their opportunity in the great debate which opened on 6 September, during which the government members rallied to defend the Protectorate. Sir Arthur Hesilrige moved that the House was free to debate the government despite the treason ordinance, but this was lost because the majority accepted that even to assert the right of the House to debate anything might weaken its authority by implication. This was clearly an assembly which the Swordsmen were going to find difficult to manage.

It was the following day that the members agreed by a vote of 141 to 136 (with barely two-thirds of the House yet attending) to turn the House into a 'committee of the whole', which shows how narrow was the division between the Parliamentarians and the government supporters. The fierce debate which now ensued stirred the memories of many MPs because it revisited disputes as old as the first days of the Long Parliament. One side asserted that the House was the People of England in miniature, and therefore the fundamental authority and so superior to any executive, be he protector or king; the government's supporters countered that the House had been summoned by the Protector under an *Instrument* which the House had no constitutional right to change. The Protector was necessary to prevent Parliament exceeding its authority, turning itself into an executive or perpetuating its existence indefinitely. This was not a dispute which argument could settle, but everyone knew the sword could end it. Moderate men like Matthew Hale and Ashley Cooper sought to mediate by devising a middle way in which Parliament would serve as a brake on the powers of both the Protector and his Council, by electing the Council every three years while the Protector, who would bear the executive responsibility, would be a brake on Parliament. However, the division between the government's supporters and Parliamentarians was by now unbridgeable. John Bradshaw, who had sentenced Charles I to death, was heard to say that if he must have a master he would prefer Charles to Oliver, revealing the depth of bitterness and disillusionment among those who had resisted absolutism since 1642.

At this point the members were reminded of the realities of their situation: the Swordsmen were in power and Parliament was there to ratify that situation, not dispute it. On 12 September the members were summoned to the Painted Chamber, passing through armed soldiers thronging the courts and corridors of Westminster Palace, and during a reproachful speech the Protector informed them that they must all sign a document (called the Recognition), agreeing to be faithful to him and not to seek any alteration in government as settled in one person and a parliament. A majority (according to one contemporary account 240) did sign during the next few days, and a week later the House declared that only those who had signed could take their seats.[14] In their bitterness Hesilrige and about a hundred recalcitrants refused to sign and so perforce gave up their advantage, although the Recognition only applied to the first clause of the *Instrument of Government*, not the *Instrument* as a whole. The House was now confined to the government's supporters and a still larger number who were either too uncommitted to leave or too aware of the possibilities of changing the *Instrument* by a series of nibbling amendments to wish to do so. Parliament quickly resolved that legislative authority was vested in Protector and Parliament and that Cromwell was Protector for life. Parliaments would meet triennially for six months. The House also settled the question of the militia by declaring the Protector to be commander of all forces by land and sea for life. Cromwell was now effectively more powerful than his Stuart predecessors and much more powerful than any British monarch would be in the future.

Nevertheless Cromwell had not achieved that fully cooperative parliament which he needed, for the diminished House soon divided once again into government supporters and those determined to increase Parliament's power at the executive's expense. The strength of the dissidents was demonstrated when Lambert's proposal that the office of Protector should be made hereditary in Cromwell's family was overwhelmingly defeated, 200 to 65. The Protectorate succession was much on men's minds of late because they had been sensationally reminded that the current government was only a heartbeat away from destruction. On 29 September after a Hyde Park picnic Cromwell decided to demonstrate his skill with horses by driving his coach and six Friesland greys himself. Despite the protests of his entourage the ageing general mounted the box with Thurloe at his side, the lively horses got out of control, pulling the Protector from his perch as his foot became caught in the reins. He was dragged a short way before his guards could rescue him and a pistol he carried in his pocket accidentally discharged. Thurloe was also thrown off but escaped with a sprained ankle. Cromwell took a bad tumble and was confined to bed for three weeks recovering from his bruises.

Cromwell was determined to have the Parliament survive for the minimum five months laid down in the *Instrument*, but his patience was sorely tried over the succeeding weeks. He needed taxation and he needed his ordinances confirmed. He was prepared, therefore, to concede that the House could modify some details of the *Instrument* and so had the mortification of seeing the constitution debated clause by clause and modified so as to enhance Parliament's powers at the expense of his own. Councillors, originally appointed for life, must face re-election by the House every three years, which would reduce their independence. The next Protector would also be chosen by the House if sitting when the Protector died. While debate raged in Parliament the public became increasingly disturbed. Leveller pamphleteering once more became a problem, as did preaching hostile to the government. The navy showed symptoms of disaffection which only speedy measures to meet arrears of pay could extinguish.[15] The junior officers of the army, who were not consulted when the Grandees established the Protectorate, had no solid commitment to it and would have preferred to tread a more radical path. Meanwhile, instead of passing at least some of Cromwell's legislation and desperately needed money bills, Parliament continued its interminable debate. Finally with an irony which may have been lost on the Protector, executive and legislative fell out on the two issues which destroyed the regime of Charles I: religion and control of the militia. The religious debates threatened all Independent congregations with persecution because a majority of the House wanted religious liberty curtailed and the national church to have a Presbyterian doctrine. As for the militia, the members agreed to vote a new assessment only if the army was reduced by a third, its duties gradually devolving on to local militia which the Protector and Council would command only with Parliament's consent. The New Model Army, the protector of the sects, would wane as the power of the institution longing to impose religious uniformity would wax. Since this was totally unacceptable to the Swordsmen the infuriated Protector arrived to pour down another impassioned speech on the members' heads and dismiss them. The Swordsmen's attempt to share power with a civilian parliament had failed.

Autocracies tend to distrust their citizens' thoughts and to fear their possible actions. Military autocracies are as prone to such anxieties but are better able to take drastic action in their own defence. It was doubly unfortunate for Cromwell's policy of reconciliation and unity that the constitutional failure was shortly followed by a Royalist rising. Royalists had long dreamed of a successful rebellion, but the wiser heads knew that this could only succeed if the New Model Army's leaders split and a substantial number persuaded their soldiers to declare for the king. The Royalists in England and Scotland were badly split between those who grimly accepted this reality and the impatient thrusters who decried the cowardice of the wise. Thurloe's spies were omnipresent in Royalist circles at home and abroad, so the outbreak of Penruddock's rebellion in the West Country surprised many Royalists but not the government. 'Rebellion' is merely a courtesy title for a very minor, very damp squib in the depths of Wiltshire by a few country gentlemen, their servants and tenants, called out in a semi-feudal spirit, and its failure was abject. The local militia even helped General Disbrowe's Ironsides to suppress it. The irresponsible landowners and their hapless tenantry were treated with the contempt for the rule of law too often found when the Sword rules. They were promised a jury trial and of thirty-three found guilty only twelve were executed, but not only were the remainder transported to the West Indies, so also were those who had been acquitted and others still awaiting trial. Instead of belittling the outbreak the government exaggerated the danger to emphasize the Protectorate's value as a shield against another civil war. Meanwhile soldiers were busy knocking on doors, especially in London, rounding up the 'usual suspects'. Anabaptist preachers, Fifth Monarchists (including Harrison of course), Levellers and others too obsessively clinging to the hopes of 1649 found themselves placed where they could only proselytize each other. The Royalists, whether innocent or guilty, now faced a grimmer time than they had experienced for some years. Still bereft of money bills the government must seek involuntary financial help elsewhere. All who had been supporters of Royalism since 1642 were under suspicion, and the wealthier were ordered to pay a 'decimation tax' upon their property to pay for local militia whose prime duty would be to keep them harmless. This was serious overkill. The Royalists were no threat to the regime. Even when the Protectorate had fallen and the Restoration was imminent five years later they were helpless to shape events. How much less now with the Protector alive and commanding an army of 57,000 experienced soldiers! Most Royalists were desperate for tranquillity, lower taxes and the sort of economic progress that would allow them to mend their broken fortunes on their depleted estates. They would have quietly supported the Protector's policy of peaceful reconciliation had he persisted in it because they needed it most.

In place of these harmonious courses the Protectorate government resumed laws by proclamation, only this time without the excuse that a parliament would soon transform them into legally respectable statutes. More dramatically it interfered in local government to a degree and in ways which would have staggered the Earl of Strafford and aroused the envy of Charles I. One of the Protector's proclamations restricted the eligibility of men to sit on municipal corporations to 'godly men' – thereby eroding jealously prized local liberties. 'Godliness' was not defined but it became clear that its distinguishing characteristic was unswerving loyalty to the Protectorate. More dramatic, and affecting all folk urban or rural, was the division of England and Wales into ten (subsequently eleven) military districts over which were placed major-generals with extraordinary powers and a range of functions defined in very detailed instructions. The appointments ranged from such famous soldiers as Lambert, Disbrowe and Fleetwood to more obscure officers, some of them, to much local annoyance, of undistinguished social origins. They commanded the soldiers and militia within their district and were to participate in the civil government. They did not supersede the existing organs of local government, ranging down from the County Committees (a product of the Revolution) through the mayors and aldermen, common councillors, justices-of-the-peace, churchwardens, down to the lowly parish constable, but they would reinforce them, supervise them, invigorate and command them. The generals could disarm all they judged enemies of the state (and had considerable discretion in deciding who they might be), keep them under surveillance and report on their activities. They were to suppress all immoral activities likely to serve as a cloak to plotters or the disaffected, cock-fighting mains, horse-races, stage-plays and other licentious gatherings, unlicensed alehouses, as well as riots and unlawful gatherings of people whatever their political allegiances. They would enforce laws on such vexed topics as enclosures, fen-drainage, depopulation, the poor law, engrossing, and against 'sturdy beggars' and such sinful behaviour as adultery, fornication, assault, poaching, wood-stealing, profaning the Sabbath, swearing, drunkenness and a range of other ways of having a good time of which Puritans disapproved.

Later they would claim that they had faithfully governed the people, and so they had, but with an unflinching, inflexible efficiency to which the governed were unaccustomed. Provincial Englishmen had always tended to regard proclamations, regulations and commands from the centre as interesting suggestions rather than orders which must be precisely obeyed. They applied those which seemed relevant, sensible, practical or unavoidable and ignored those which did not. Now the central authority had come among them with inquisitorial eye and the power to rebuke, chivvy into line and enforce in every detail a whole range of policies and regulations the local people wished to ignore. Moreover, these super-constables had regiments of infantry and troops of cavalry to enforce their authority, and unlike village constables they would not hold office only for a year nor be constrained by the need to conciliate their neighbours among whom they must live afterwards. These Swordsmen-equivalents of the French Intendants had only to please their government and were answerable only to the Protector who had installed them. Their only weakness was that the central government tended to ignore their reports even when it bothered to read them. No doubt John Thurloe squirrelled away the information they contained but Oliver was a lazy administrator. They could not even obtain replies to specific requests for guidance or information.[16] Beggars indeed disappeared. Royalists lay very low, hardly daring to ride their local lanes alone, certainly not in the company of others. The generals were efficient, able – and loathed. The sense of spies everywhere and police (in the form of soldiers) ever at hand to act on often self-interested tattle aroused fear and resentment. After the political drama of the English Revolution, after the devastation of the Civil War, after the horrifying melodrama of the Regicide and all that had followed, the country had come full circle. It had reverted to the personal rule of Charles I with his interference in local liberties and his oppressive illegal taxation, but now magnified a thousand times. Worse, it was undiluted by the passive resistance which had been possible in the 1630s, for Charles had possessed neither army nor police to enforce his edicts. Now there was a huge army with nothing else to do. The Swordsmen were everywhere for, quite apart from the major-generals, other officers served as sheriffs, sat on the Commissions of the Peace, and on the Commissions of Assessment (which meant that tax evasion was far more difficult, indeed dangerous) and by their varied role in local government filled the gaps left either by the exclusion of local gentlemen or by their reluctance to serve the regime. Even more galling, many of these officers were men of more lowly origins than the office-holders of pre-revolutionary times. It was this experience of military authority in civil concerns far more than the high cost of the New Model Army which left a profound detestation of standing armies which would endure for two centuries. It also left local government with a suspicious resentment of central interference which would play its part in the Glorious Revolution thirty years later.

With the country quiescent, with a regular army of nearly sixty thousand and with close to two hundred men-of-war afloat the Protector could consider himself the most powerful ruler in Europe, and his thrusting foreign policy (considered in the following chapters) would not leave these powerful instruments idle. The problem was they were costly to maintain and even costlier to employ. The financial difficulties faced by Charles I returned to haunt his successor, but increased a hundredfold because the Stuart administration during the eleven-year personal rule was comparatively inexpensive. Charles's navy had been growing but was a pigmy compared to the New Model Navy, there was no army at all and England was at peace with her neighbours. The first Protectorate Parliament had called for a massive reduction in the army and a reduced burden of taxation. The Protector had angrily dismissed it but reductions there must be, even though the Protector's foreign policy would bring war with Spain. What Parliament had not been allowed to do by bill the Protector now did by proclamation: the assessment was cut by £60,000 per month; the army was reduced from 57,000 (in the British Isles) to 40,000; and the soldiers' pay was reduced. (The last may appear a courageous decision but it brought no mutinies because bumper harvests had reduced food prices to half the levels of 1649.) Taxes might be cut but resistance to taxes was repressed. In June 1655 a wine-merchant named Coney, an old comrade and long-time supporter of Cromwell, tested the legality of Protectorate taxes by refusing to pay them. He gave up the fight when his three lawyers were imprisoned for taking his case. Perhaps unwittingly he was questioning the whole basis of the Protectorate, including the *Instrument of Government*, and the Council would employ any means to crush such dangerously subversive activity. Coney was fortunate not to be arraigned for treason. Of course, reducing expense was not enough, particularly if it was accompanied by a reduced assessment, because of the immense debt the Protectorate had inherited and to which it was adding. Despite all its efforts the Protectorate was never to solve its financial problems, although it certainly raised larger sums in taxes than the English had ever been compelled to pay before. Its problems would finally come home to roost in Charles II's hard-pressed Treasury.

The Protector, despite his tendency to indolence when confronted by boring administrative detail, had never allowed his eye to stray long from Scotland or Ireland. After the military conquests in Ireland and Scotland between 1649 and 1651, for which nobody was more responsible than Cromwell himself, opportunities were lost in Ireland which might have led to a more permanent settlement for that unhappy country. In Scotland mistakes of policy and too weak an army of occupation had led to an outbreak of rebellion in the Highlands combined with widespread disaffection from the English regime in the Lowlands.[17] In Ireland, as we have seen, the war of 1649 had been succeeded by a ruinous guerrilla campaign and a vengeful land settlement which only encouraged the Irish to prolong it. Things improved after 1652 under the Deputyship of General Fleetwood with the Irish resistance dwindling to occasional raids by a *banditti* called 'Tories', who occasionally raided Protestant settlers for their horses and cattle. Fleetwood, who favoured the extreme sectarians, had hoped to convert the Irish to Protestantism by installing preachers and opening schools. However, he lacked the financial resources to make this policy work, for the cost of the army swallowed all. In July 1655 Henry Cromwell arrived to take command of the army in Ireland. His strong personality, gifts as an administrator, his jaundiced attitude to the sects, all combined with his position as the Protector's son, soon rendered the sectarian Fleetwood uneasy, but the latter was recalled to London in 1655. Thereafter Fleetwood was Deputy *in absentia* while Henry Cromwell exercised a deputy's authority on the ground although he did not officially replace Fleetwood until 1658. Aged only twenty-six Henry was too young to have fought in the Civil War or to have experienced the outpouring of fear, wrath and religious idealism which had driven the revolutionaries after 1640. He did not share the commitment to 'enthusiastic religion' of those who had endured those trials. He was able, conscientious, clear-headed and inflexibly honest. He had earlier commanded a cavalry regiment in Ireland for two years. However, he was over-sensitive to criticism and had an uneasy relationship with his father, feeling that he never fully enjoyed his trust or support. He often contemplated resigning but was urged to persevere by Thurloe, among others, who advised him to develop his father's thick-skinned imperturbability in the face of hostile criticism. In time Cromwell came so to admire his son's performance in Ireland that he spoke of it to his closest advisers with tears of pride.

Henry wished to reduce the influence of the sectaries in and out of the army and pursue a policy of consensus and reconciliation among his more conservative officers and members of his Council, and among the Protestant Irish. His father's close friend Lord Broghill became an adviser and supporter, drawing in the Old Protestant families of the south-west whom the Protector and his Council had pardoned in droves in 1654, a belated reward for their abandoning Ormonde in 1649. Those who had not were still liable to heavy fines for their 'malignancy', but Henry deliberately neglected to collect them. The sectarians received no encouragement and witnessed with horror his determined efforts to rebuild the Church of Ireland. By 1655 there were about 150 English ministers scattered over the four provinces, most of them encouraged to migrate there by the

Protector's guarantee of financial support.[18] These men included most shades of religious commitment but many were extreme sectaries, loosely termed 'Anabaptists'. They were opposed to Henry's conciliatory policies. Nor were these ministers isolated in their recalcitrance, for it was claimed twelve governors of cities, ten colonels and a number of other officers and officials shared their religious ideology.[19] Moreover, thanks to the Protector's invariable habit of appointing men of opposed opinions, either to reconcile different factions or to 'divide and rule', Henry's Council included 'fanatics'. These dissidents troubled Henry Cromwell's government during its first two years. Henry, like his father, was also much troubled by Quakers, but these he tended to arrest and expel while officers sympathetic to their views were rebuked and sometimes dismissed. Henry was determined to check religious extremism by installing as many moderate Presbyterians and conservative-minded Independents as possible in the Irish ministry. The difficulty was to find appropriate recruits in England and guarantee them an income without further inflating the charge on the Treasury. In April 1658 Henry persuaded a gathering of ministers at Dublin to agree to the restoration of the tithes system while supplementing poorly endowed ministers with state salaries, a pragmatic solution which further outraged the 'Anabaptists'. The survival of the Scots Presbyterian church in Ulster presented another sectarian problem. The Irish Presbyterians had fought against the Commonwealth on behalf of Charles II. Once the Ironsides had reconquered Ulster most Presbyterian ministers had been exiled, and in 1653 the Council of State had seriously considered forcibly transplanting Scots settlers from Antrim and Down to Kilkenny, Tipperary and Waterford. This policy was abandoned under the Protectorate and many Presbyterian ministers returned to Ulster during the next four years. This caused anxiety in London and Dublin, for the Scots could have no affection for the regime of their conqueror. As Henry Cromwell wrote in November 1655: 'Our Scots in the north are a pack of knaves but we shall have an eye on them.'[20] In 1656 he even revived the old concept of transplanting Ulster Scots, forbade further Scots migration to Ulster and ordered that all vacant livings in Ulster should be filled by Englishmen. All these orders came to nothing and indeed proved unnecessary, for during the coming months as the Scots lived peaceably they and the government became grudgingly reconciled. The Scottish ministers, the local Ironside commander informed Henry in 1657, 'may with more ease be led than driven; the tenderness your lordship shows them is the likeliest way to gain them.'[21] Henry did not need the hint for by then it encapsulated his policy.

The much more numerous Catholic Irish gave Henry less trouble. They were too involved with surviving in circumstances which would have defeated a less resourceful people to be a political, much less a military, problem. On the other hand Henry Cromwell's government was incapable of realizing the Puritan dream of converting the Irish from benighted Papistry to enlightened Protestantism. Catholic priests who slipped furtively but unstoppably into Ireland during Henry's rule were astonished by the failure to make any resolute attempt to convert the Irish to Protestantism. There were many reasons for this failure, one being the Protestant divisions; another was Henry's lack of clergy, schools or money for so vast an undertaking. Schools were vital because language was itself an obstacle to conversion. It may also be doubted how sincere was the desire of Protestants to see Irishmen converted from the faith which, it was alleged, justified the seizure of their lands. Some Catholic Irish, particularly among the gentry with estates to protect or recover, were converted, but for the rest Catholicism was intertwined with patriotism. It was not just a faith, it was a cause. All in all, during his service in Ireland Henry Cromwell achieved much. He protected the Catholics from the worst excesses of the bigotry of the Protectorate Parliament. He strengthened the Protestant Irish Church at the expense of the sects while maintaining peaceful coexistence with the Scots Presbyterians. Agriculture and trade revived during his rule despite the administrative shortcomings of the Protectorate government. He failed to attract large numbers of English settlers to take up forfeited Irish land, and the ex-soldiers who were granted land usually sold it in disgust and returned to England. As a result the Protestant ascendancy which he did so much to encourage in association with conservative Parliamentarians and former Royalists was not matched by the English demographic ascendancy which the Commonwealth and Protectorate governments had intended. Rather the Catholic population drifted back on to their old lands as tenants of new or old owners, and into the largely deserted towns. Henry was bedevilled by the fact that the government repeatedly cut taxes but it was not safe to cut the army's size proportionately, although it was markedly reduced when the guerrilla war ended. The second Protectorate Parliament made everything worse by reducing the Irish assessment to £9,000 a month, while the near-bankruptcy of the Protectorate after that Parliament's dismissal meant the subsidy to Ireland (which had at one time been £22,000 a month) could be no more than £8,000. The army's pay fell nine months in arrears in 1658, a dangerous situation, and the Irish deficit stood at nearly £100,000.[22]

In Scotland matters went more easily at least after Cromwell sent Monck back to his old command in April 1654. Under the Commonwealth matters had got out of control, largely because the government made the compounding errors of depriving Scotland of Monck by launching him on his naval career, reducing the size of the army there and interfering with the Highlanders who would only tolerate the new government if it left them alone. The consequence was the Glencairn Rebellion, named for the

Lowland nobleman, William Cunningham, 9th Earl of Glencairn, whom Charles II had appointed to lead his Scottish forces. He was later replaced by a professional soldier, John Middleton. The rebellion was withstood for many weary months by General Robert Lilburne, the Leveller's brother but a loyal servant of both Commonwealth and Protectorate. The Highlanders were not strong enough to defeat Lilburne, even if their hereditary leaders could have been persuaded to stop feuding long enough to confront the Ironside regiments unitedly. On the other hand Lilburne's forces were not strong enough to subdue the Highlands, and suffered from the fact that occupying armies are always atomized by garrison duties. Fortunately for Lilburne and his Lowland allies Glencairn was no Montrose and the most he achieved was expensive raids across the country, reaching as far south as the Borders. Nevertheless the rebellion was a drain on resources, made the Commonwealth seem vulnerable and encouraged unrest among those Scots who had accepted that further resistance would be pointless.

General Monck arrived in April when the ending of the Dutch War freed him from sea duty. He soon saw how desperately Lilburne had needed men and money, but unlike Lilburne he had the ear of the Protector. Soon 3,000 badly needed reinforcements arrived in Scotland and a war chest of £50,000 was scraped together. A master of effectively employing limited resources, Monck formed his army into columns capable of cutting themselves off from their bases by carrying their basic provisions on their backs or on strings of packhorses. For three summer months his columns ranged the Highlands, burning crops, destroying houses, and driving off the cattle and sheep so vital to the Highland economy. His subordinate Colonel Morgan trapped and dispersed Middleton's army at Dalnaspidal. The rebellion collapsed, although Middleton did not fly abroad until the following spring, and Glencairn and other leaders were captured. So total was the defeat that Cromwell felt able to offer the leaders mercy (although Monck would have executed the lot). Thereafter Monck moved to hold Scotland in a grip of steel even though his forces were reduced. (In December 1654 his army stood at 18,000 men. By July 1655 there were thirteen regiments and one company of infantry, seven regiments of cavalry, and four companies of dragoons, i.e. 14,000 including officers. This was further reduced in December to about 10,500 with two cavalry regiments sent south.)[23] He built formidable citadels at Ayr, Leith, Inverness and Perth, all of which were impressive examples of fortress architecture and an attraction for sightseers for decades. He also built a strong fort at Inverlochy to guard the Highlands and lesser strongholds in other places.

Meanwhile the work of reorganizing and absorbing the old kingdom proceeded with new energy. Cromwell wished Scotland to be a peaceable, cooperating member of the Protectorate, not simply a conquered province, so he sought to demonstrate the benefits of such membership. Ordinances were proclaimed uniting Scotland to England, reforming the system of justice and providing relief to debtors.[24] Attempts to bring the Scottish legal system into conformity with the English common law failed, but there was some success in making justice speedier and cheaper, heritable courts were replaced by courts baron in every county with power to determine all suits of less than forty shillings value, and Latin was replaced by English in all courts. Efforts were made to involve Scots in the administration of the country. Highland chieftains and Lowland landowners policed their own regions and many Scottish gentlemen were appointed JPs, although their inveterate Royalism kept out the larger landowners. As early as May 1655 Cromwell and the Council of State transferred executive power from Monck to a nine-member Council for Scotland, chaired by Lord Broghill, which contained two Scots (Sir William Lockhart of Lee and John Swinton) as well as Monck, four other officers and one English civilian, Samuel Disbrowe.[25] It was directed to settle Scotland's finances, which it did by collecting the assessment more efficiently and stabilizing the revenue at £8,500 a month, and to reform the Kirk. In the latter it was less successful, for its attempt to apply the 'trier' system to church appointments failed because both the Kirk's bitterly divided factions rejected it. Moreover, as Broghill reported to his master, the two factions were composed of those who loathed the Protectorate and adhered to Charles Stuart and those who loathed both with equal virulence. If the Protectorate gave power to one over the other it would acknowledge the Protectorate but never 'cordially support it'. On Broghill's advice Cromwell sought always to win the support of the moderates in both parties and urged them to 'agree to differ'. Broghill, who achieved remarkable popularity, managed to persuade the great majority of Scottish ministers to refrain from public prayers for Charles, a symptom of the fact, as the moderates assured him, that he had won the support of 750 of the 900 Scottish ministers. The Protectorate government also sought to encourage the settling of godly ministers in the benighted Highlands and furthered its Scottish religious policy by liberality to the universities. An ordinance of August 1654 settled on Glasgow University the lands of the former bishopric of Galloway and on Aberdeen University those of the bishopric of Aberdeen, together with grants to both from local customs revenue. However, no benefits the Protector could bestow could balance the aspect of his government which the Kirk found most odious: religious toleration. Although the Protector's early encouragement of separatist sects in Scotland did not persist, probably because of his eagerness to win Presbyterian support, religious toleration applied to Scotland as to England and his soldiers unofficially found there rich opportunities both for supporting Independency and offending the Kirk. It was some consolation to outraged Presbyterians that Monck deported Quakers in droves.

In the meantime the Protectorate never forgot that it was an imperial government. The *Instrument of Government* had decreed that Scotland should have thirty members (compared with the five who had sat in the Nominated Parliament). In fact only twenty-one members attended the 1654 Parliament, of whom twelve were English officers or officials and nine were Scots. Of the thirty who would sit in the second Protectorate Parliament of 1656 (described below) twenty-one were of the first category and again nine were 'honest and peaceable Scotsmen', as Monck described them to Thurloe 'and all right for my Lord Protector'. Conversely, the English officers and officials seem to have been vigorous advocates of Scottish interests in both parliaments. The record of the Upper House which the second Protectorate Parliament established would have been less positive if that Parliament had survived, for although it included three Scottish members out of four, Sir William Lockhart was in Paris, Archibald Johnston of Warriston declined to attend on plea of ill-health and the Earl of Cassilis refused the summons. (The fourth, of course, was Monck who could not be spared to attend it.) The franchise continued to be very restrictive, despite attempts by Monck to persuade the Protectorate government to broaden it. Too rigid an exclusion of old enemies, he argued, would simply keep men loyal to Charles Stuart. However, the government was not prepared to allow the vote to impenitent Royalists in Scotland any more than in England. The problem was that while in England this disenfranchised less than half the electorate, in Scotland it disenfranchised the great majority. Although Monck omitted to collect fines on Royalists, like Henry Cromwell in Ireland, in January 1657 he wrote to Broghill that although all things were quiet the Scots were as Royalist as ever. Several thousand Scots would be present to hear the Proclamation of the refashioned Protectorate in July 1657, but they would do so in stony silence. Nevertheless, if resentful the Scots were resigned. During the last two years of Cromwell's life the Council would not sit and government would remain in the capable hands of General Monck. Although the second Protectorate Parliament would reduce the Scottish monthly assessment, which would leave the income of his government slightly less than the cost of his army, his deficit by 1658 would be small compared with Ireland, and trivial compared with England. Of course, the financial situation in England, which shaped the final twenty months of the Protectorate, had been made far worse by the Protectorate's assuming the role of a great European power.

CHAPTER ELEVEN

Western Designs and Protestant Crusades

> ... we think God has not brought us hither where we are but to consider the work that we may do in the world as well as at home.
>
> *The Protector to his Council, 1654*

The Protector's foreign policy has encountered severe criticism which began a few years after the fall of the Protectorate and has continued to our own day, although recently some historians have found in it strengths as well as errors.[1] When the Protector and his Council first turned their attention to continental Europe their army was powerful and their navy had won a string of victories over the Dutch navy. Nevertheless, the problems the new regime faced appeared formidable. England was isolated and seemed (although this was illusory) to be in danger of having to face a European coalition. The list of her enemies was long. The claims of Charles II were nominally supported by his cousin, the boy-king Louis XIV. The undeclared maritime war with Mazarin's France persisted still. Denmark, hardly a great power, felt able to close the Baltic to English trade and imprison many English ships. Portugal, that ancient ally, was at war with England. The corsairs of Tunis and Algiers continued to prey on English merchantmen and enslave their crews. Despite her naval victories England was still at war with the Dutch who rose, phoenix-like, from the flames of naval defeat with new squadrons to menace English trade routes. Although it was true that England had captured more than 1,500 Dutch ships, including 120 men-of-war, which far outweighed English losses to the Dutch, and while it was true that England had put to sea a fleet of more than 150 warships, comprising a naval fire-power for which history provided no precedent, the Treasury was staggering under the financial burden all this imposed.

The Protectorate government addressed these problems cautiously but confidently. Cromwell had never liked the war against the nation he regarded as England's natural Protestant ally, but he could not just make peace on any terms or the regime would seem feebler than its predecessor or in thrall to the Dutch.[2] Many of the visionaries who preached to large and enthusiastic London congregations believed that England was destined to conquer Holland on land and then use this as a springboard for a triumphant march on Rome, overthrowing Catholicism along the way as the instrument of Divine Providence. While Cromwell as an experienced soldier did not share these dotty illusions he had to tread carefully because many influential preachers and pamphleteers regarded them as a divine command. As the Protector considered his options foreign observers became increasingly confused, one ambassador reporting that Cromwell needed the war with the Dutch to maintain his regime, while another reported that he needed peace to bolster his popularity. Cardinal Mazarin was eager for England to make peace, especially if his government was involved in the peace treaty. Cromwell delayed his decision, hoping to exploit a favourable opportunity. However much he might dislike the Dutch War he would not even appear to betray England's interests simply to end it. Meanwhile all efforts by the French to lure the Protector into an alliance came to nothing as the first year of the Protectorate advanced, and the French ambassador's early optimism sagged.

Sure enough the Protectorate negotiated a peace treaty with the Dutch without reference to the French. Ignoring those who clamoured that just a few more months campaigning would compel the Dutch to accept the Commonwealth's original demands, Cromwell intervened decisively in the negotiations. The call for a union of the two republics was abandoned along with his own desire for an offensive alliance to advance the Protestant cause. The practical Dutch negotiators would only discuss a defensive alliance, and even that proved impossible to achieve. However, when Cromwell made it clear that he would not make peace at any price the Dutch finally conceded his minimum terms. By the treaty of 5 April 1654 they agreed to acknowledge the flag in British waters, reluctantly accepted the Navigation Act of 1651, and promised compensation for the loss of English merchants in the East. Each state agreed to expel the enemies of the other from its borders, which meant that Charles II and his starveling court must seek new quarters. By a separate agreement the province of Holland agreed to exclude the Prince of Orange from command by land or sea. Since this grandson of Charles I was a toddler the agreement had no immediate significance. The fact that the infant William would one day not only hold the very commands which the English were seeking to deny him, but would also occupy the English throne, was mercifully unforeseeable by Cromwell's busy envoys. English commerce was now safe from Dutch privateers, and the Navigation Act protected English shipping from Dutch competition within the Empire. The fear of Dutch help for a descent on England by Charles in combination with a Royalist rebellion was put to rest. The Dutch ambassadors were entertained at a banquet in Whitehall Palace at which they solemnly joined with their host in singing the 123rd Psalm ('Behold how good and how pleasant it is for brethren to dwell together in unity').

Good news soon followed this treaty. The Protectorate Council's attention never strayed far from the Baltic, a vital English commercial highway blocked since the Dutch War by Denmark.[3] The great northern power was Sweden, and like the Commonwealth before them the Protectorate councillors were eager to be on good terms with Queen Christina. On 11 April 1654 Bulstrode Whitelocke, the new envoy to Sweden, signed a commercial treaty with the Swedish government. Sweden was much admired in England because of the exploits of King Gustavus Adolphus during the Thirty Years War. Cromwell, still dreaming of a Protestant league capable of imposing its will on Catholic Europe despite the Netherlanders' lack of enthusiasm, had been as eager for a treaty with Sweden as for peace with the Netherlands. Apart from Cromwell's Protestant dream, they had interests in common and he offered to assist the Swedes to assert the freedom of the Sound by sending a fleet. Queen Christina admired Cromwell, comparing him to her ancestor Gustavus Vasa, and declaring to Whitelocke that 'your general hath done the greatest things of any man in the world'. However, the Swedes were fearful of being drawn into a war with the Dutch, and perhaps with France, and therefore declined an alliance in favour of a commercial treaty, although promising not to assist Charles Stuart. Fortunately the end of the Dutch War ended the Danish blockade, and a treaty with Denmark in September ensured that English vessels could pass the Sound on the same terms as the Dutch. Moreover, English merchants would be compensated by the Danes for the long detention of their ships.

This fruitful series of diplomatic initiatives also included in July a treaty with Portugal by which English merchants received compensation for their losses, were guaranteed freedom from the interference of the Inquisition in carrying on their Protestant services, and were given liberty to trade with the Portuguese colonial empire in both the East and the West Indies. This treaty is the more interesting because some of the conditions insisted on by the English were akin to those refused by the Spanish ambassador when a treaty with Spain was under discussion in London that same summer. The King of Portugal himself did not like the terms but it was as well he accepted them, for in the long term the heretic Protectorate would help save Portuguese independence. The king was slow to ratify, however, and only did so in 1656 when the dreaded shadow of Admiral Blake and his fleet fell over the mouth of the Tagus.[4] After nine months in supreme power Cromwell had told his first Protectorate Parliament that: 'There is not a nation in Europe but is willing to ask a good understanding with you.' This was true but within limits: the Protestant powers would not join a Cromwellian Protestant League, and Spain was not prepared to purchase a treaty at the price the Protectorate demanded. Nevertheless Cromwell's boast had substance. Rumours of coalitions to restore Charles II had been succeeded by a spectacle which must have caused Royalist despair: the kings of France and Spain bidding for an English alliance. Spain wished England to land an army in southern France to support the rebellion of the Prince of Condé, promising in return to assist England to recover Calais, lost a century earlier and, despite the Spanish government's normal financial difficulties, offering substantial subsidies to cover the expenses of the English regiments. In turn Mazarin offered to abandon the cause of Charles II and to assist England to capture Dunkirk, which would remove the worst nest of privateers and give England both a commercial and military bridgehead on the continent. The Protector preferred to keep his options open for the present and ally with neither, sending Blake with a strong fleet to the Mediterranean where he would be poised to operate against French or Spanish targets if either became necessary, and with orders to seek the release of English captives from the Deys of Tunis and Algiers. Meanwhile Secretary Thurloe continued to negotiate with the Spanish ambassador for better terms while Cromwell deliberated which way to throw his support.

The key elements in the Protectorate foreign policy were, first, to maintain, perhaps to push further, the boundaries of Protestantism; second, to maintain and advance English commerce and third, to guard against any threat of a Royalist restoration with foreign aid. The last peril seems of little consequence to our eyes because we know with hindsight that such a restoration was never a serious possibility. However, it was taken very seriously by the Protectorate government, as it had been by the Commonwealth, and it is impossible to evaluate Cromwell's foreign policy without considering the impact of this anxiety on it. When Cromwell finally made his much-criticized choice of war with Spain rather than war with France in alliance with Spain, one element in the equation was his realization that Spain was less able to mount an expedition to restore Charles II than was France. However, to conclude that Thurloe's negotiations with Cardenas during 1654 were nothing but a blind, that Oliver had resolved on war, is to claim to know more about Cromwell's intentions than Cromwell knew himself. The evidence suggests first that Cromwell seriously considered negotiating a treaty with Spain if acceptable terms could be agreed, and, second, that he believed he could have a war in the West Indies without this necessarily involving an Anglo-Spanish war in Europe. The first he was denied more by Spanish intransigence than by his own reluctance to treat with the old enemy. The second proved illusory but was not as foolish as it might seem today. The notion of 'no peace beyond the line' was an old one, and equally entertained by both Spanish and English. When the Spaniards had made peace with James I's government nearly half a century earlier they never conceded the English had a right to establish Virginia and were determined to destroy the colony at a more convenient time. The fact that the Spanish plenipotentiaries could solemnly sign the Treaty of London while planning to massacre or enslave the Virginia colonists seemed as reasonable to them as Cromwell's mistaken assumption of 1654 did to him. (The Spanish attitude towards English colonial expansion was to be vividly displayed in 1656. When Charles II came secretly to Brussels to negotiate for modest military help to restore him to his throne – a mere 4,000 soldiers who would not be handed over until the English Royalists had captured a port – not only had he to promise to surrender the colonies of Antigua, Montserrat and Jamaica, he had to undertake that his subjects would never establish another colony across the Atlantic.) Cromwell had hankered after a war with Spain from soon after the end of the Dutch War, wanting to keep his splendid fleet at sea and hoping (of course, vainly) that a war with Spain would meet the cost of keeping it there. Nevertheless he wished to see what more peaceful courses could achieve. The Protector made two significant demands which the Spanish ambassador Cardenas rejected with the famous words that this would be asking his master 'to give up his two eyes'. This seems a curious over-reaction. Cromwell had not deliberately sought concessions he knew would never be agreed. Indeed he sought less than the Portuguese government had already conceded. He wished Spain to allow peaceful access to English colonies in the West Indies rather than attacking all English ships on sight as interlopers. He did not, however, insist on freedom to trade with the Spanish colonies – a valuable concession made by the King of Portugal for his colonies.

He also sought religious toleration for English merchants domiciled in mainland Spain, again a Portuguese concession. This was neither unreasonable nor new. It simply sought a modification of the nineteenth clause of Charles I's Anglo-Spanish treaty of 1630 which had agreed that such worship had to be 'discreet' and that the Inquisition would decide what 'discreet' meant and whether the English had been 'discreet'. The Spanish insisted on retaining the clause while Cromwell wanted 'discreet' struck out. Cromwell's request was reasonable because although there was no incentive for the merchants to behave 'scandalously' there was a financial incentive for the Inquisition to claim that they had. Nor was Cromwell demanding something of no concern to the merchants themselves, as has been alleged. The Merchant Venturers had made complete freedom of worship a condition of their residence in Bruges in September 1649. Nor was his demand new to Cardenas for the Commonwealth had complained in March 1651 about the Inquisition's ill-treatment of English merchants at Malaga, and had sought to extend the existing toleration when it offered Cardenas a draft commercial treaty in 1652. Perhaps Cardenas believed that as Spain had been the first country to recognize the Republic, and as England's commercial links with Spain must be too valuable to risk, England and Spain could remain at peace without the need for concessions, but if he did he miscalculated. The Protector was determined to do something in the West to demonstrate the English were there to stay and to seek reparation for past losses.

This was soon translated into a project for an ambitious assault on the Spanish Empire. As he wrote to Colonel Venables before he set forth in command of this expedition, either there was peace in the West Indies or there was not. If there was peace then the Spanish had violated it by their attacks on English shipping and to seek reparation was just. If there was no peace then there was nothing 'acted against articles with Spain'. This sounds logical but is not exhaustive. Never has a British government embarked on a more ambitious imperial project, nor one with less competent preparation. Cromwell dreamed of seizing the gold convoys' route through the Isthmus of Panama. Even more absurdly he believed he could hang on to this territory despite the immensely long lines of communication involved and the fact that the garrisons would be established in a region infested with Spanish settlements from which they could be raided. His optimistic assessment is the more startling because it was based on no precedent. Drake and the other Elizabethan freebooters had done remarkable things at sea but on land had only temporarily occupied and sacked a few ports. Perhaps the exploits of the New Model Army in Scotland and Ireland had misled him, particularly since most of them had been achieved under his command. No doubt the exploits of his fleet against what had been considered the greatest maritime power in Europe had persuaded him that it could do anything. His tendency to see all his victories as signs of God's approval of the regime in general and his own aspirations in particular was most misleading of all.

Certainly the Protectorate government received villainously bad advice from 'old West India hands'. Among them was Thomas Gage, a lapsed Catholic who had been sent to South America by the Dominicans before the Civil War, but who had returned in 1641, converted to Protestantism and Parliamentarianism and joined the clergy. He confirms Malcolm Muggeridge's aphorism that 'travel narrows the mind and as we grow older our judgment becomes less sure'. How else can we explain his assurances that the Spanish colonies would be easy to conquer, being thinly populated, the few white inhabitants lightly armed and unwarlike? Hispaniola could be quickly taken and even colonies on mainland South America could not hold out long. Such imbecilities may explain the insouciance with which the Protectorate embarked on West Indian conquest, but it can hardly excuse it. Nothing can excuse the inadequate military preparation which preceded it. Amphibious expeditions have a long history of divided and unsatisfactory commands. Cromwell was convinced that he could not put either a general or an admiral in overall command, which seems odd in an age of 'generals-at-sea', and so decided to put a committee of five commissioners who would act as a council of war in this role. Penn and Venables were members, along with three civilians: first, Edward Winslow, a former Pilgrim Father and three times governor of Plymouth colony, who had extensive knowledge of colonial affairs; second, the Governor of Barbados, an able, experienced man, but who would remain at his post once the expedition left his shores; and third a man called Butler, the most charitable explanation for whose appointment was that the Protectorate Council had confused him with somebody else of the same name. As one of the senior officers later observed he was 'the unfittest man for a commissioner I ever saw employed'. Thus they had appointed one man who might have been useful if he had been there and another who was useless anywhere. It was a bad beginning but worse was to come. Meanwhile Penn's extraordinarily brief instructions gave him no opportunity to comment on the grand design because only Venables knew what it was, and he was only to reveal it after they were at sea. This snub to Penn did not promote a harmonious relationship between the commanders.

In fact Venables was bound to no precise plan although the fantasists who drew up his instructions were fertile in alternatives. He might seize Hispaniola or Puerto Rico – or both. He might before resting on his laurels then seize Havana, the port at which the homeward-bound treasure fleet rendezvoused before it tackled the Bahama Channel. The possibility of a landing on the Spanish Main was referred to with the understanding that the long-term objective should be the capture of Cartagena. A third proposal saw a capture of San Domingo or Puerto Rico, followed by an attack on Cartagena rather than Havana. Those on the spot, that is Venables, Penn and the civilian commissioners, would decide the target. Cromwell's objective was to deny the King of Spain the wealth of the West Indies by blocking the path of the Plate Fleet in the short term and to deprive him of his West Indies settlements altogether in the slightly longer term. Castles in New Spain indeed. Empires are not to be won by such irresponsible vapourings, nor are military campaigns. Venables was himself confused. Like his soldiers he believed he was off to found a new colony, and even took along his new wife, a mature widow, subsequently justifying this extraordinary decision by observing that 'his Highness did only intend a plantation where women would be necessary'.

The army sent was disastrously composed and reflects very badly on a government which was dominated by a general of remarkable abilities aided by subordinates of whom many were able and experienced officers. Venables, despite his protests, was given no complete regiments, nor even companies, but rather drafts from regiments scattered all over Britain, the men to be chosen by their commanding officers. This inevitably led to an assemblage of misfits and ne'er-do-wells, selected so as to be rid of them. They were supplemented by sweeping the London streets of the worst of its riff-raff. Everything was done in haste because Cromwell had been warned that the campaign must be launched before the rainy season began in May 1655. Despite his protests Venables was not even permitted to muster and inspect his Falstaffian companies at Portsmouth before embarkation. He might have sailed with a carefully selected part of the best army in Europe. Instead he sailed with 2,500 rejects, only 1,000 of whom were veterans. At Barbados he was 'reinforced' by a very much worse rabble of 4,300 islanders who had enlisted in the hope of plunder. These warriors, according to Venables later, and more disinterested witnesses then, were too rowdy to be disciplined and too cowardly to fight. This increasingly amateur army was further diluted by 1,200 colonists picked up at Montserrat, Nevis and St Kitts. All these, with a much superior naval regiment under Vice-Admiral Goodson, brought the force above 9,000 divided into eight companies.

The consequences of this poor preparation, made worse by the non-arrival of the store ships, were much as one would expect. Venables and his council of war chose to attack San Domingo on Hispaniola, with the general ordering the troops not to pillage but to take six weeks pay in lieu. This was logical since Venables wished to colonize San Domingo, not ruin it. His raggle-taggle army determined to disobey the order at the first opportunity but this scarcely mattered since they never came close to capturing San Domingo, the approaches to which were defended resolutely by the inhabitants, who poisoned wells, ambushed English formations, killed stragglers, and produced panic among the ill-assorted companies whenever they attacked. Dysentery felled many including Venables but he at least was nursed back to health by his wife. The routed army was rescued by Admiral Penn, his command being just as efficient as any other formation of the New Model Navy. In an attempt to justify the expedition it sailed for Jamaica and easily took it, but Jamaica's feeble defences reflected the small value placed on it by the Spanish government. This colony was to be the sole acquisition of the Cromwellian Western Design. Although valuable in the long term it would prove costly to retain and slow to yield a profit. Moreover, it was ill-placed to serve as a base for assaults on the Plate Fleet.

Meanwhile the commanders sailed separately for England, having quarrelled comprehensively. Penn sensibly brought home the major warships which consumed stores too quickly while the frigates could defend Jamaica and cruise for prizes. He arrived first and was not welcomed. The Hispaniola fiasco was not his fault, for Venables had refused his repeated offers to bombard the San Domingo forts and had refused to cooperate with him in a direct assault on the town. He had acted with great resolution at Jamaica, leading the assault close to the beach from the 12-gun *Martin* while his larger men-of-war bombarded the forts. However, all this was overshadowed by the fact that during the voyage home he had learned that the Plate Fleet had arrived at Havana and had not turned back to assault it. Penn had considered such a course, but his captains urged against it, pointing out that they would have to beat slowly back against the prevailing wind and then confront the Havana forts and their formidable artillery with a depleted force. Blake would not have been so easily overborne. Penn was not forgiven and quickly found himself lodged in the Tower where Venables soon joined him. The latter had sailed home because he was weakened by dysentery and was so disillusioned with his command that he could scarcely bring himself to look at his soldiers. He was never to have an opportunity to do so again for half of them died of disease within six months of their arrival in Jamaica. Both commanders were brought separately before the Council to explain their leaving their commands. When Cromwell asked Venables if there was any precedent for a commander to leave his forces without being ordered home, he hesitated long and then bethought him of the Earl of Essex in Elizabeth's reign. 'A sad example', Cromwell sombrely replied. In October 1655 they were released after fulsome acknowledgement of their faults and formally surrendering their commissions. The Protector never again gave Penn employment but must have known that the expedition's failure was due to the errors of greater men, himself included.

During the months that the Western Expedition was away Cromwell had continued to ruminate on the advantages and disadvantages of an alliance with either France and Spain, as if he had not forfeited his Spanish option once the ill-fated expedition had left England. Both were Catholic powers so the Protestant cause was irrelevant except in so far as it could be argued that the Huguenots in France, still sporadically persecuted despite the Edict of Nantes, could be helped more easily by a French alliance than by a French war. More cogent was the fact that France was a more dangerous enemy than Spain, and thus a more valuable ally. An alliance with France was slow to mature, however. Although the expulsion of Charles Stuart and his adherents was settled in principle and it was agreed that the losses of English merchants should be sent to arbitration, the cause of the Huguenots remained an intractable problem. France steadfastly, and quite naturally, refused to consider the Protector's demand that he should be allowed to intervene on their behalf if the terms of the Edict of Nantes were infringed. For his part the Protector, as Thurloe explained to an English agent, had embraced the cause of Protestantism for it was 'dearer to him that his life'. The result, unsurprisingly, was no treaty with France at the time that Penn and Venables sailed west in December 1654, and when Admiral Blake sailed for the Mediterranean in October he had a mandate to attack French vessels in reprisal as well as to protect English trade and pursue gunboat diplomacy with the Tunisian and Algerian corsairs.

Cromwell was mistaken in assuming that a campaign in the West Indies need not involve war with Spain, but he was certainly a master of misdirection. In the August of 1654, not many weeks before Penn and Venables were due to sail west (although their departure was to be delayed until December) the Protector informed the King of Spain that Blake would shortly sail for the Mediterranean and asked him to receive the admiral in his ports as the representative of a friendly power. Commerce raiding against France still continued and the king could expect that this would continue with the two powers acting cooperatively. Good news is always welcome and therefore the more readily believed. Blake's presence would be very welcome to the Spanish government because during that summer the Duc de Guise was fitting out a fleet at Toulon to carry an expedition for the conquest of Naples. In December, two months after Blake's departure, Cardenas reported to Madrid as a fact well known in London that Blake had been ordered to attack and destroy the duke's invasion fleet. Mazarin had received the same intelligence with less enthusiasm the same month. Blake's orders have not survived but there is no reason to doubt that Guise was on Blake's agenda.[5] However, although Blake should have sailed in August bad weather held him in Plymouth until October. By the time he arrived off Cadiz the Spanish had heard rumours about Penn's destination while Blake's orders were still unknown. Polite but wary the Spanish were relieved that news of a French flotilla heading for the Straits, presumably en route to join Guise, sent Blake hurrying to Gibraltar. He was not destined to meet the French commander, the Duc de Nieuchese and his seven-ship flotilla, but four strayed English warships encountered them near Cadiz. A fight ensued in which the fourth rate, *Princess Marie* (34 guns), took a French fire-ship and the French captured the *Dolphin* victualler, a fifth rate of 16 guns. However, when the *Dolphin*'s master told his captors that Blake was at sea with a fleet of nearly thirty warships, the duke released his ship with fulsome apologies and fled to Lisbon. Blake was never to encounter the Duc de Guise either, for his search for de Nieuchese delayed his arrival at Naples until 11 December. Guise had sailed from Toulon on 26 September only to encounter storms which temporarily dispersed his fleet. Although he began an attack on Naples he soon abandoned it, partly because of his anxiety about Blake's fleet which was the focus of concern in European chancelleries. On 7 December de Guise abandoned the campaign and sailed for Toulon – and just in time, for Blake arrived four days later to be greeted with wild enthusiasm.

Hearing from Thurloe's indefatigable agent, Longland, that seven French ships were in Leghorn, Blake sailed north only to find the birds had flown for Toulon. Leghorn greeted the fleet almost as enthusiastically as the

Neapolitans but from fear rather than relief. The pro-Dutch Grand Duke of Tuscany had badly treated Captain Badiley when he had been worsted by a Dutch flotilla there. It was feared that Blake had been sent to punish and the fact that he refused to come ashore to take any part in diplomatic conviviality did little to dispel the grand duke's anxieties. In fact Blake had held aloof in his cabin at all the ports at which his fleet had called. The Venetian envoy at Naples reported that Admiral 'Blach (*sic*) was a deep sombre man of few words. Owing to his advanced age [he was 57] he never showed himself even on his own ship except when the sun shines.' The Spanish, he wrote, were beginning to doubt Blake's intentions. His Florentine colleague reported that at Leghorn the grand duke was trying to keep the admiral friendly because 'he seems to be a very touchy and particular old man'. This aloof behaviour, however, kept the various parties guessing, and allowed Blake to mask his intentions completely.

Meanwhile off Leghorn Blake, who had never regained his health after his wounding in the Dutch War, was gloomy at his lost opportunity against Guise. His master, better informed, was well pleased. Guise had lost 5,000 men of his forces to disease, battle and privations, and the presence of Blake at Gibraltar had prevented the two French forces from combining. Although Guise begged for another attempt Mazarin would not permit a second expedition while Blake's fleet remained at large. The Neapolitan venture was doomed. Once satisfied that the French had abandoned their Neapolitan campaign Blake moved against those other enemies of English commerce, the Deys of Tunis and Algiers. Blake had heard rumours that the Corsair states of North Africa intended to gather a fleet to help the Turks who, while besieging the Venetian city of Candia on Crete, had themselves been cut off by the Venetian navy. Candia (now Iraklion) was besieged for years, only surrendering in 1669. Cromwell's help had been sought by Venice but the Protector was too aware of the interests of the Levant Company and London's Aleppo and Smyrna merchants to become involved in a war with Turkey. However, frustrating a corsair reinforcement while rebuking these old enemies was another matter. On 8 February the fleet was off Tunis at La Goletta engaged in hard bargaining for the return of English captives. Blake reminded the Dey of Tunis that by a treaty of 1646 each country had agreed to respect the ships of the other and not make captives of each other's nationals. Blake accused the Dey of breaking this treaty and demanded the return of a ship, the *Princess*, compensation for other losses and the return of all captives. In rejoinder the Dey reminded Blake that in 1651 the captain of an English ship hired to carry Turkish soldiers to Smyrna had treacherously sold his passengers to the Knights of Malta as galley slaves. Without an army Blake could not attack La Goletta, and it was clear that the rumour of a concentration of ships for the relief of the Turks

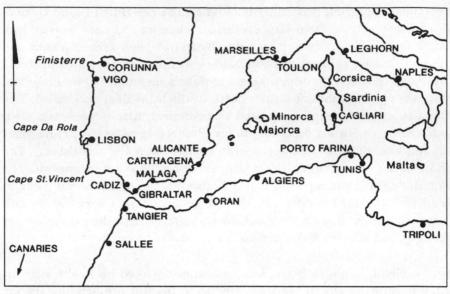

Area of Blake's Southern Campaigns

was false. However, learning that some warships were moored at Porto Farina to the north, Blake sortied to attack them. On 22 February Blake's fleet arrived while the Dey appeared at the head of an army on shore, and men could be seen busily erecting extended fortifications and batteries to protect the ships and the harbour. Eight Turkish men-of-war were in the bay, as was the English prize. The council of war was worried that an attack on Turkish ships was beyond their brief, particularly since the Turks had been trying to persuade the Dey to come to terms. Moreover, some captains could see no way to turn their ships in the narrow harbour. For the time being Blake chose to leave six warships on blockade while the fleet sailed for Cagliari for much-needed provisions. Since Cagliari was insufficient to supply the fleet's insatiable need for bread and other foodstuffs, ships were sent to the Balearic Islands and eastern Spain, while two others sought more in Leghorn and Genoa. On 20 March the fleet returned to Tunis, where, the Dey being still intransigent, a resolute attack was launched against Porto Farina on 4 April 1655.

At four o'clock in the morning the fourth- and fifth-rate ships came ghosting in on the sea breeze, led by Nathaniel Cobham's *Newcastle*, and lined up opposite the Turkish men-of-war, while Blake in the *Andrew* led the second and third rates, *Plymouth*, *George*, *Worcester*, *Unicorn* and *Bridgwater*, to bombard the castle and other fortifications. As the light improved the

Tunisian gunners must have marvelled to see such vulnerable-looking vessels anchoring within a musket shot of their cannon. Then came the first English broadsides, devastating in their effect: splinters of stone flying like case shot, the inadequate Tunisian cannon dismounted, their crews cut down or fled. Turkish sailors on their warships took to their boats or leapt into the sea as they saw boarding parties swarming down the sides of the English ships into their longboats. Some even began to destroy the outworks before taking refuge behind the more formidable walls of the castle. A great wall of acrid gun-smoke was now borne from the ships into the faces of the Tunisian soldiers, concealing their targets from those gun-crews who were still maintaining a desultory fire. Blake took no prizes. Getting his own ships out of a situation which many would have considered a dangerous trap, against a now adverse wind, and with scant room for manoeuvre, was going to take skilled and disciplined seamanship without the burden of quarter-manned prizes. Even the English prize, the *Princess*, was burned to the water-line. The Council of War had decided the only way of escape was to warp out. As they sailed into harbour they had all dropped anchor but continued to pay out their cables until they reached their designated positions. Once the withdrawal was signalled they hauled up to their anchors, Cobham's division retiring first once the Turkish ships were well alight, and then slowly and painfully the larger ships followed. From first to last the whole operation took only seven hours, the fleet losing only twenty-five killed and eighty wounded.

This action was a remarkable feat. On very few occasions have ships taken on shore batteries successfully, and never in such confined waters can they have escaped unscathed. Certainly Blake's already formidable reputation was further enhanced by this exploit. However, the action had little significance. The Dey of Tunis was humiliated by his incapacity to protect ships sheltering under his own forts, but, as he pointed out after the battle, they were not his ships. He remained adamant in his refusal to negotiate. Blake himself had expected no better. His action was intended to be punitive rather than persuasive, for as he wrote afterwards: 'We judged it necessary for the honour of our fleet, our nation and religion, seeing they would not deal with us as friends, to make them feel us as enemies.' It is possible but not very likely that the exploit made the Dey of Algiers more amenable to a treaty than he already was. An envoy had negotiated a treaty before the fleet arrived to be warmly welcomed and reprovisioned. This was gratifying to many of the ships' crews, some of which were down to their last biscuit. All English and Irish slaves were freed and carried away although trouble arose when Dutch slaves seized their opportunity and swam to freedom. They were not covered by the treaty but the Dey accepted compensation in lieu of getting them back when the English sailors voted to surrender their pay to buy the freedom of their fellow mariners. The objects of the expedition had now largely been achieved. The hopes of Guise had been frustrated, French commerce raiders had been sunk or harried to their home ports, a new treaty had been signed with Algiers, and the Dey of Tunis had been punished for his intransigence. It was not clear what this fleet would do now but, although cool but 'correct' relations with the Spanish were still maintained there were hints of a change in the wind for those sailors who were alert to signs and portents. A French ship off Tunis withdrew into the harbour of La Goletta until it received despatches from home at which it promptly and mysteriously moved to a mooring within the ranks of the English ships. Ships returning from cruises against French commerce raiders were not sent back on patrol. The long-running maritime war against France was over. The naval war against Spain was about to begin.

First, however, Cromwell was to strike a blow for the Protestant cause where his navy could not help him. In 1655 came the news of the massacres of the Vaudois (or Waldensian) peasants by the troops of the Regent of Savoy within whose borders they lived. In January 1655 the duke (or the regent in his name) ordered all those living outside the Vaudois mountain valleys, where their religion was grudgingly tolerated by an edict of 1651, to return to the mountains, with only three days to move or suffer death. In April they were attacked and large numbers massacred. The English sects were outraged at this progenitor of 'ethnic cleansing', and the regiments of the New Model Army urged the Protector to act. He needed no prompting. First he launched an appeal for funds to succour the surviving victims, contributing £2,000 from his own purse, and declared 30 May as a day of 'national humiliation'. He informed the French ambassador, Bordeaux, that there could be no treaty with France until the wrongs of the Vaudois were redressed. His secretary Milton drafted a stern letter to Louis XIV (besides composing his famous sonnet of protest, 'Avenge, O Lord, thy slaughtered saints!'). Cromwell summoned all Protestant powers to intervene, and considered ordering Blake to bombard Nice or Villafranca. Diplomatic argument proved sufficient. Mazarin was eager to enlist English regiments for the campaign against the Spanish Netherlands and dreaded the implications for French maritime interests of Blake's Mediterranean expedition. Samuel Morland, a son of the parsonage who had been summoned from a Cambridge fellowship to serve on Whitelocke's Swedish mission, bore the Protector's letter to Paris where he only had to wait three days before receiving a satisfactory reply, and then set off for the court of Savoy at Turin. Morland's reception there was remarkably warm considering that he told the young duke about the massacres in gory detail, although carefully adding that 'no man can say [this] was done by the will of Your Highness', and that the duke's mother, the regent, who replied on his behalf, was the sister of Henrietta Maria. She displayed remarkable sang-froid at this confrontation with the representative of the ruler she must have perceived as the murderer of her brother-in-law. Having expressed her sympathy with the Lord Protector's concern, and denounced the malice with which a just chastisement of rebels had been misrepresented to him, she promised on her son's behalf to pardon the Vaudois and bestow on them the privilege Cromwell was seeking for them: the free exercise of their religion. The Treaty of Pignerol, which made these undertakings official, left some contentious matters unresolved, to Cromwell's discontent, but the massacres ceased and the Vaudois were left to rebuild their lives around their Protestant churches. Certainly in Protestant eyes both in Britain and on the continent Cromwell was perceived as the saviour of the Vaudois. It inspired Waller to write:

> Hither the oppressed shall henceforth resort
> Justice to crave, and succour at your court
> And then your highness, not for ours alone
> But for the World's Protector shall be known.

Unhappily it was at this time of glory and congratulation that the news of the disaster at Hispaniola arrived, news which caused Cromwell to shut himself in his room, sunk in melancholy. Spain's reaction was more positive: it withdrew its ambassador, laid an embargo on English shipping and declared war. This triggered the long-awaited signing of the French treaty, which in open form was no more than a commercial agreement, although there was a secret clause guaranteeing the expulsion from France of the Stuarts and their supporters, and the Protector was given a private promise from the King of France that the rights of the Huguenots should be respected. It was clear that more than a commercial alliance would follow, even though the Protector still delayed making a continental military commitment.

Meanwhile, he had been urged to send troops to the continent by another monarch. Christina of Sweden had abdicated in favour of Charles Augustus Vasa, now Charles X. In June 1655 the young warrior monarch invaded Poland and sent an ambassador to London to seek aid in men, ships and money. Cromwell gave the envoy, Christer Bonde, an almost royal welcome, not only wining and dining him in great splendour, but carrying him off to the hunting field and the less strenuous pleasures of the bowling green. However, the problem he faced in reaching an agreement with Charles X illustrates the logical absurdity of Cromwell's dream of a Protestant League: the wrong countries were Protestant. England and the Netherlands were the logical pillars of such a league but were bitter commercial and maritime rivals. The Dutch regarded the Swedes with hostility as rivals in their northern trade. Sweden was not a commercial rival to the English and could be a useful check on Danish hostility, but much as Cromwell approved of Sweden, and much as he might voice approval of capturing Poland and taking it out of the Catholic camp ('Wresting a horn from the head of the beast' was his characteristically colourful description), he was not blind to the realities of European power politics. It was not in England's interest to have the Baltic transformed into a Swedish lake. Nor was it in the interests of the Danes and the Dutch and for that matter the Brandenburgers, who were just as Protestant as the Swedes. Reinforcing the King of Sweden with English regiments and a naval flotilla would arouse enmity where Cromwell sought only friendship. Despite the lavish hospitality for his Swedish guest Secretary Thurloe and Christer Bonde negotiated only a commercial treaty. Cromwell's dream of a Protestant League of England, Sweden, the Netherlands, Brandenburg and Denmark against Catholic Austria could never happen. Charles X had no intention of fighting a religious war against Austria which would be expensive and probably fruitless while England fought a naval war against Spain which might involve the profitable capture of the Plate Fleet. Charles was not a Protestant crusader. He marched to a different drum. As Cromwell represented the past, so he represented a brutal and rapacious future.

Events during the last year of Cromwell's life demonstrated how remote was Cromwell's dream of a Protestant alliance. Although Lockhart in Paris made heroic and successful efforts during 1657 to mediate between the Dutch and the French to prevent war breaking out between the two powers, the Dutch were still hostile to the Protectorate. They had not forgotten the humiliation of defeat in the naval war and the treaty which followed it. Moreover the Anglo-French alliance was perceived as inimical to any close association with England. The war between England and Spain also presented an insuperable problem: the Dutch had no intention of suspending their trade with Spain which was so essential to their prosperity. In the north although the King of Sweden might have won Cromwell's admiration by his conquest of Poland, his rapacious policies soon turned against him a combination of his Protestant neighbours. He had appealed to Cromwell for help in the spring of 1657 but the Protector demanded a concession which Gustavus would not make: the temporary occupation of Bremen by English troops. (Bremen would have served as a military base from which Cromwell could put pressure on the Danes.) Cromwell sought to mediate between Denmark and Sweden, but in May 1657 the Danes declared war and forced Gustavus to withdraw from much of Poland. Brandenburg, the Netherlands and Austria combined against the Swedes. The sight of a combination of Protestant states in alliance with Catholic Austria, a state which, like many Englishmen, Cromwell feared and detested, appalled the Protector. He had refused to join Gustavus in his plans to divide Denmark, but he had no intention of being a party to a division of the Swedish empire by Gustavus's Protestant enemies allied with Austria. The destruction of Sweden might bring to pass that old Protestant nightmare: the extension of the Hapsburg Empire to the Baltic. His speech to Parliament in January 1658 was full of gloom, declaring the Protestant interest was 'quite trodden under foot'. Gustavus was 'a poor prince, and yet . . . as gallant and as good as any that these late ages have brought forth'. He had 'adventured his all' in conquering Poland for the Protestant religion but now was 'reduced into a corner', and it was Protestants who had forgotten his deeds and sought his ruin. Moreover, the combination against Sweden was potentially a threat to England's prosperity, indeed her very existence. The allied powers might shut English ships out of the Baltic, as the Danes had done during the Dutch War, and then where would be England's trade? Where would be the vital materials to preserve English shipping? Cromwell urged that since English naval might depended on Baltic supplies of naval stores they must turn their merchant shipping into 'troops of horse and companies of foot and fight to defend' themselves 'on terra firma'. Happily for the Protectorate's beleaguered Treasury the crisis passed, and after Gustavus made a winter march across the ice to besiege Copenhagen, Denmark was compelled to comply. In February 1658 the Protectorate ambassador, Philip Meadowes, mediated a peace between the contending powers at Roskilde. It did not last. Not a month before Cromwell's death the war resumed and once more the Dutch and the Brandenburgers came to Denmark's aid. A Northern Protestant league, with or without the Dutch, was a hopeless project.[6] The Danes and the Swedes were ancient rivals, while Brandenburg was only interested in establishing itself as an autonomous power. As for the Dutch, once their independence was achieved, they saw Spain as a valuable market rather than a traditional foe, for, like English merchants and tradesmen, they simply wished to trade peacefully with all the world, Protestant or Catholic.

CHAPTER TWELVE

A Spanish War and
a French Alliance

I dare say that there is not a nation in Europe but they are very willing to
ask a good understanding with you.

Oliver Cromwell, September 1654[1]

If in the wake of the commercial treaty of 1655 the French government
fretted at the lack of a full English alliance and a commitment of regiments
for their northern campaign, they could not complain of a lack of English
activity at sea. The naval war with Spain had broken out at last. Blake must
have foreseen this when he sailed for the Mediterranean. However, he
exploited as long as possible the Spanish desire for peace by victualling his
ships from Spanish ports. However, the news from Hispaniola had outraged
Madrid. Cardenas was withdrawn, there was a prompt embargo on English
shipping in Spanish ports and a declaration of war. There would be none of
the large sea-battles which had characterized the Dutch War. The King of
Spain lacked the resources to challenge the New Model Navy. He preferred
the less expensive but effective weapons of privateering from such ports as
Dunkirk and embargoes on English trade to Spanish and Flemish ports.
During the second half of 1655 the English fleet was restricted to
blockading the Atlantic ports of Spain and dreaming of capturing the
annual Plate Fleet.

Admiral Blake early sought to bring this dream to fruition. In June 1655
he had two ships engaged in salvaging and loading the cannon from
Rupert's wrecked ships at Cartagena, which required the cooperation of the
Spanish authorities, and the fleet was still using Spanish ports. Nevertheless
he spread his ships in an arc between Cape St Mary and Cape Spartel to
watch hungrily for the Plate Fleet. 'They of Cadiz are very mistrustful of us',
he reported to Cromwell. The watchful Spaniards had noted that Blake
went to great trouble to victual from store ships outside Cadiz harbour
rather than doing it more conveniently within. The King of Spain took the
hint and had prayers said in the churches for the safety of the Plate Fleet. In
July Cromwell authorized Blake to attack Spanish vessels despatched to

counter English commerce raiders in the West Indies. In fact Blake's blockade prevented Spanish forces being sent to recapture Jamaica or to attack English colonies, as well as protecting English merchant ships sailing for the Mediterranean. Unfortunately the order contained an unintended ambiguity, implying that only warships westward bound should be attacked. This cost Blake his only chance to bring the Spanish fleet to battle. On 15 August Blake sighted a Spanish fleet of thirty-one sail near the Bay of Lagos north of Cadiz. From its course the English captains correctly deduced that it was not heading for the West Indies but was charged with escorting the Plate Fleet, whose arrival was imminent. At one time Blake found himself on a parallel course with the Spaniards and ordered an attack, only to be told the lowest tier of guns could not be run out because of the heavy swell. Grimly Blake stormed below to check that this was true. The Blake of the early months of the Dutch War would have attacked regardless and might well have triumphed, but he had never forgotten the result of his rashness at Dungeness. The opportunity was lost, the following day offered scarcely a breeze, while Blake's council of war resolved that their orders gave them no licence to attack the Spaniards if they were not bound west. The following night the Spaniards altered course and slipped through his fleet to safety at Cadiz.

Blake could not pursue further. His fleet was almost out of provisions and his victuallers had been delayed by storms. He had no choice but to leave the unguarded Spanish coast open to the Plate Fleet and return home. War is the art of the possible. In blockading that storm-beaten Atlantic coastline Blake and his captains were trying to do something which had never successfully been done before and would only be perfected by Admiral Lord Collingwood's fleet a century and a half later – and Collingwood had several bases, including both Lisbon and Gibraltar. Blake only had Lisbon and the uncertain resource of supply ships. A letter from Cromwell met Blake off the Lizard, empowering him to fight the Spanish fleet wherever he came upon it but observing that he could not from distant Whitehall give him precise orders. Blake 'must handle the reins' as he should find his 'opportunity and the ability of the fleet to be'. Arriving in the Downs in October he was welcomed by the Protector who knew that Blake had done his best on a long and difficult expedition, and there were no reproaches for his failure to destroy the Spanish fleet, although Cromwell mourned the lost opportunity.

Problems ashore soon replaced problems afloat, notably the dire circumstance that Blake's men had not been paid in twenty months' service at sea, nor had their wives and families received a penny of the £120,000 in wages owed. This lamentable situation of a powerful fleet, well commanded and manned, serving a government too financially beset to pay for it was the more dangerous because there was disaffection among senior naval officers.

Vice-Admiral John Lawson, who was in the crucial post of commander of the Channel Fleet, had involved himself in a treasonable conspiracy with Levellers and Royalists which in turn also involved the Spanish court. Under his guidance his fleet had submitted a petition to the Protector asking that arrears be paid, impressment be abolished and that seamen should be permitted to decide whether they would serve outside home waters. The petition was subversive in intent and tantamount to mutiny. No navy could function where the sailors could choose the length of their voyage and no English navy could function without impressment. Cromwell borrowed £16,000 from a London merchant and paid off the arrears of Lawson's men. This quelled the mutiny but dangerously increased Lawson's popularity in the Channel Fleet. The Royalist-Leveller conspiracy collapsed when several army officers and civilian Levellers were arrested, and when funds expected from Spain with which Lawson had hoped to suborn the fleet, were paid to Secretary Thurloe instead. Thurloe's spies were busy wherever Royalists abounded, and the conspirator entrusted with carrying the funds was a double agent. When Lawson found he was to be exiled to the Spanish coast as Blake's second-in-command he resigned.

He was replaced by Edward Montagu (or Mountagu), who appeared an odd choice even then. He had no maritime experience. He served as a soldier in the Civil War, distinguishing himself at Naseby and the siege of Bristol, and since 1645 had spent a life of political inactivity because he had never approved of the Revolution. The Protector, having recently plucked him from obscurity and made him a member of the Protectorate Council, included Montagu among those whom he trusted because they were his protégés. By contrast Blake was a self-made man who owed little to the Protector beyond continuing professional employment which was the due of the hero of the Dutch War. Blake's 'independence' has led to speculation that Cromwell did not trust him and sent Montagu to keep an eye on him, and that Blake resented the appointment as a mark of no confidence in him. In fact the Protector seems always to have trusted his greatest seadog, held him in the highest esteem and felt bereaved at his death. Far from resenting the appointment, Blake had particularly requested a deputy, fearing he might die at sea leaving his fleet without a designated successor of sufficient eminence. Montagu, who was the last 'general-at-sea' appointed, proved an aggressive admiral, a good foil to the level-headed, resolute Blake. His career displayed an opportunistic eye, for it would survive the collapse of the Republic. Untainted by Regicide he would one day bring Charles II back to England, be ennobled as first Earl of Sandwich, and later escort Queen Catherine of Braganza to her nuptials. Montagu's future role would hardly have astonished Blake, for he must have been aware that Montagu was no Republican. (He would be prominent among those urging Cromwell to take the Crown.) However, Montagu won over

Blake the steadfast Republican because, as emerges from Samuel Pepys's diary, he was a man of great charm, an adept courtier. (Pepys's rise to eminence began with his appointment as Montagu's secretary in 1660.) Moreover, like Blake and Monck before him, Montagu was determined to master the technicalities of his new profession and Blake found him an apt pupil. Moreover, with a deputy as close to the Protector as Montagu Blake no longer needed to worry about politically significant decisions for which Montagu could take responsibility while his commander concentrated on purely naval matters.

The fleet which sailed back to its blockade in the spring of 1656 contained thirty-seven men-of-war and a fire-ship divided into three squadrons, led by Blake's flagship *Naseby* (74 guns), with Montagu also aboard. Admiral Badiley, who had replaced Lawson as commander of the second squadron, hoisted his pennant in the 84-gun *Resolution* and although the third squadron, commanded by Rear-Admiral Nehemiah Bourne in the 56-gun *Swiftsure* lacked ships as large as these, it contained four ships of more than 50 guns. The first and second squadrons contained respectively five and six ships of more than 50 guns, and only two of the thirty-seven had fewer than 30. It was a most formidable force, for if the ships were fewer than the large fleets which fought at the Gabbard and Scheveningen the fire-power was still immense. Most of the ships were the larger 'frigates' built since 1649.[2]

The belated 1655 Plate Fleet, depleted by shipwrecks to only two galleons and four lesser vessels, reached safety during Blake's absence, much to his fleet's chagrin. Once on station he quickly learned that thirty-one ships had sailed west to escort the 1656 Plate Fleet home, while twenty more were in the yards awaiting rigging from Flemish ports. Blake at once sent a flotilla of frigates to try to intercept the Flemings. His frustrated captains agreed reluctantly that their orders did not permit them to pursue the Spanish escort westward and that Cadiz, recently re-fortified, was too strong to assault. Cromwell had suggested an attack on Gibraltar. He cogently argued that it would furnish a base from which frigates could cruise on blockade while the capital ships, so costly to maintain and supply, could return home. However, although Montagu reconnoitred and sketched the seaward approaches to Gibraltar even his combative spirit recognized that it could only be taken and held by regular Ironside regiments. Meanwhile gunboat diplomacy was needed at Lisbon. They learned from Edward Meadows in Lisbon that the King of Portugal was baulking at signing the treaty negotiated in 1654 and was procrastinating until the Brazilian Plate Fleet reached safety, at which he would probably refuse to sign at all.[3] Two clauses troubled him: guaranteeing the return of deserted sailors who claimed to be Roman Catholics and the liberty for English merchants to practise their religion in their own houses. He disingenuously suggested that these might be matters for the Pope, much to Cromwell's wrath since accepting papal mediation implied a recognition of the Pope's spiritual authority. Then an assassination attempt on Meadows frightened the king who feared naval reprisals and sent the royal doctors to Meadows to consult on his wounds. However, the indomitable ambassador continued to press for the royal assent and when Meadows made it clear that Blake would soon arrive in the Tagus to carry him away, with the implication that the Plate Fleet would then be attacked, the king's nerve broke. Soon Meadows climbed aboard the *Naseby* triumphantly brandishing the treaty. Although Montagu felt the ambassador should have demanded more in view of his wounds, which could be construed as an unpardonable assault on the Protectorate, Blake with more political sense simply congratulated the ambassador. He knew how much his master wanted the treaty and how much he himself needed the Lisbon base to prosecute the Spanish war.

The blockade persisted during 1656. There was no hope of the Spanish fleet putting to sea. Blake had to assail the enemy where he could in small actions of limited value. On 12 June Captain Edward Blagg was sent with an eight-ship flotilla, led by the *Fairfax* (56 guns) to raid the Galician and Biscayan ports. Early on 24 June the *Fairfax*, the *Centurion*, and the fire-ship *Beaver* were towed by their boats into Vigo harbour during a flat calm which had given the Spaniards a false sense of security. Too late two large Ostend privateers and their English prize tried to seek safety in the shallows up-river. The English gunfire blew up both privateers and the prize was burned. A second flotilla bombarded Malaga and burned five ships in the roadstead. The bombardment was so severe that the Spanish gun-crews fled their fort and boats-crews got ashore and spiked their guns. In September Blake and the fleet retired to Lisbon to pick up mail from home and water the ships. In view of the fact that Spain had eighteen galleons and twelve other vessels which would be ready to sortie within a matter of weeks it was decided to retain the great ships despite the impending autumn gales. Meanwhile Blake had left Captain Richard Stayner to watch Cadiz with eight ships. On 8 September Stayner was forced off station by a gale and that evening his lookouts spied eight Spanish ships five or six leagues west of Cadiz. They were part of the Plate Fleet en route from Havana who had risked dashing home unescorted. There were two huge galleons, two armed store-ships, three merchantmen and a Portuguese prize. The master of the Portuguese ship had mendaciously assured the Spanish commodore that a Spanish fleet had driven Blake from Cadiz a month before. This perhaps explains why the commodore strangely misidentified Stayner's flotilla, which included second rates, as simply large fishing vessels.[4] During the night Stayner lurked close to his prey, a feat made easier by the guileless Spaniards hanging out lights and regularly firing signal guns so that they could keep station. Feeling the loom of the land they considered themselves safely home. In the morning, with the coast well in sight, came disillusionment. Stayner's big ships bore down to the attack. One onlooker ashore thought the English warships appeared puny compared to the towering galleons but appearances were deceptive. Stayner in the *Speaker* delivered a broadside into the 'vice-admiral', and then, leaving her to the *Bridgwater*, pressed on to attack the 'rear-admiral' which he captured after a hard fight. Meanwhile the vice-admiral's ship fought for six hours until her crew fired her and took to the boats. Aboard her when she sank were the Governor of Peru and his wife and daughter. The governor chose to perish with them for they were unconscious and helpless but his younger children, including his heir the Marquis of Baydex, were rescued – although penniless, for all the governor's wealth perished with him. The *Plymouth* engaged a large transport and would have taken her but unhappily she accidentally caught fire and sank with a loss of 600,000 pieces of eight. The *Tredagh* snapped up a straggling transport with a rich cargo. So at the close of several hours of manoeuvring and cannonading, two ships were captured, three were sunk or burned and three escaped into Cadiz, one of which was the Portuguese prize. Stayner took his prizes into Lagos where he discovered that the 'rear-admiral' contained forty-five tons of silver, 700 chests of indigo, and 700 chests of sugar. The Spanish government was deprived of £2 million, sunk and captured, but the latter would have been more helpful to the Protectorate's beleaguered Treasury if it had not been thoroughly plundered by the English sailors before its residue reached safety in the Tower.[5]

Stayner took his booty to Lisbon, bearing with him the sixteen-year-old Marquis of Baydex. Questioned by the admirals, Montagu reported him 'a most ingenious and intelligent youth'. He should have added ingenuous for Baydex innocently confided the invaluable intelligence that the rest of the Plate Fleet, ten galleons carrying several millions in specie, were then in Havana intending to sail via the Canaries in December. Meanwhile the admirals received from Thurloe the unwelcome news that Lawson in retirement had not retired from plotting. A dangerous combination of Fifth Monarchy men and Levellers had planned to 'put us into blood', and Lawson and others had been arrested. Lawson had made renewed efforts to suborn elements of the Channel Fleet, and the mail which Blake's fleet had met at Lisbon had contained letters to similar purpose which had been quietly confiscated. There had also been an alarm of an outbreak of war with the Dutch. For some reason a flotilla of fifty Dutch merchantmen and their escorts had got into a fight with English men-of-war at Torbay. All this persuaded Cromwell that the Channel Fleet must be strengthened and commanded by a man he could completely trust. He therefore ordered Montagu home with the *Naseby*, *Andrew*, *Resolution* and *Rainbow*, together with seven ships badly in need of repair, and Stayner's prizes. Montagu carried Badiley with him who was replaced by Nehemiah Bourne, promoted to vice-admiral, while the victorious Stayner replaced Bourne as rear-admiral. Blake moved his pennant to the *Swiftsure*.

Considering Blake's poor health it might have seemed more sensible to recall Blake and leave Montagu in command. However, Blake was to have one last victory to crown his career. It came after a hard winter, blockading Cadiz and occasionally sailing into the Mediterranean to confirm that the Dey of Algiers was honouring his treaty. For Blake it was a miserable time, his thigh wound troublesome, and his painful, gravel-infested kidneys restricting his diet to broths and jellies. The fleet was running low on victuals when on 19 February 1657 there arrived an English merchantman commanded by a former naval officer named Young who had lost a hand in the Dutch War. Young brought momentous news. He had found himself one morning in the midst of the Plate Fleet, a dozen large galleons. He had followed them far enough to determine that they were steering for Tenerife. Then on passage from Barbados to Genoa he had immediately altered course to seek Blake off Cadiz.

Blake considered Young's hypothesis that the Plate Fleet had gone to Santa Cruz de Tenerife was probably correct. He had long foreseen the Plate Fleet's commodore might shelter in Santa Cruz, one of the best harbours in the North Atlantic, to await an escort from Cadiz or for news of Blake's withdrawal home. The problem was what to do about it. Admirals Bourne and Stayner, with prize money dancing before their eyes, wanted to equip eight of Blake's fittest frigates with six months' victuals obtained by stripping the remainder of the fleet, and send them west after the Plate Fleet. This advice the sombre Blake decisively rejected. He would not divide his fleet when the Dons might sortie against the remainder of his under-victualled ships. Moreover, he had learned that de Ruijter had recently sailed on an unknown mission with a powerful squadron. De Ruijter had caused alarm in London when he sortied with nine of the Netherlands' largest warships, arriving in Cadiz in January 1657 with a convoy of 80 merchantmen. There the Spanish strenuously sought to persuade him that Spain and Holland were now allies and that he should aid his hosts against Blake. De Ruijter was not deceived and headed for the Mediterranean where his mission was to negotiate treaties with the Barbary States and to protect Dutch commerce. Nevertheless even Thurloe had believed that his mission was to escort the Plate Fleet to safety.[6] Blake reasoned that, even without the de Ruijter alarm, if the Plate Fleet was at sea the frigates could easily miss them. If they were in Santa Cruz they would not be strong enough to assault them under the shore batteries. Apart from a fruitless sweep by frigates down to the North African coast the main fleet maintained the blockade.

For eight weary weeks the frustrated sailors peered mournfully and hungrily westward while their implacable admiral held his station. On 26 March a victualling convoy of twenty sail arrived and the fleet replenished its depleted stores. On 12 April an English privateersman, William Saddleton, confirmed that the Plate Fleet was still lying in the roadstead of Santa Cruz and Blake finally relented. De Ruijter had turned up in Cadiz with a strong fleet so that Blake could not divide his command but if he waited longer he might lose the prize altogether. On 14 April he sailed for the Canaries with twenty-three men-of-war, leaving only the *Rainbow* and *Yarmouth* on watch, and was off Santa Cruz on Saturday the 20th. After a Sabbath of rumination Blake, who had recently moved his pennant to the *George*, told his captains that the initial assault would be with twelve ships, four from each division, and agreed that Stayner should command them. Stayner's force consisted of *Speaker, Lyme, Lambert, Nebular, Bridgwater, Plymouth, Worcester, Centurion, Winceby, Newcastle, Foresight* and *Maidstone.*

The Spaniards had espied Blake's topsails on the Saturday but had no apprehensions. An English prisoner there, taken at Hispaniola, later reported that they 'laughed our intentions to scorn and were for Spaniards very jolly'. A Flemish sea captain eyed those topsails with more foreboding than jollity, having served against Blake in the Dutch War, and decided to put to sea. 'Be gone if you will', contemptuously replied Don Diego Diagues, the Spanish admiral, 'and let Blake come in if he dares.' His confidence was not without foundation. Blake might not be confronted by a confined harbour with a shallow entrance, as at Porto Farina, for the town faced a gentle curving shore to which the roadstead ran parallel with the only projection a stubby artificial mole, but the Spaniards had prepared their defences well. A line of seven forts ran northwards from the town along the coast, all connected by a triple line of breastworks, and these formidable defences were linked to the forty-gun St Philip's Castle which lowered over the town's northern quarter. Nine of the smaller galleons lay in a line parallel with the shore but with their hulls at right angles to it, bow out, stern in. They were covered by the forts on one side and by seven great galleons of between 1,000 and 1,200 tons, anchored in line ahead further out, just within the five fathom line, their broadsides facing the sea. All treasure had been unloaded and stored safely ashore. The admiral felt his position was so strong that he was more likely to destroy the English fleet than suffer harm by it.

He was to be given his chance. Blake's plan had the virtue of simplicity. The twelve ships commanded by Stayner would take on the galleons by entering the road and anchoring opposite their quarry ship by ship. Blake would remain in reserve with the other eleven ships and intervene according to need. Monday's unfavourable wind disappeared overnight and with a sea breeze the next morning the English moved steadily to the assault. Stayner had ordered that all ships should hold their station and that none should open fire until they were anchored. In fact two latecomers which had missed the council of war, the *Plymouth* and the *Nantwich*, somewhat spoiled the disciplined symmetry of the attack by steering to the sound of the guns, the *Plymouth* opening fire too early and the *Nantwich* forcing her way into the line and breaking the formation. Stayner, commanding from the forecastle of the *Speaker*, led his squadron down the outside of the Spanish line, writing years later that he could have sunk the towering 'admiral' and 'vice-admiral' of the fleet at the very beginning but their bulk was useful in providing 'my barricades for the castle'. This appears to give the lie to Michael Baumber's reconstruction which has Stayner steering his ships between the small and the large galleons. Stayner had given orders that his ships should leave themselves sea-room so that they could come about and warp themselves off (after the manner of Porto Farina) once the attack was over. This again appears to preclude a course

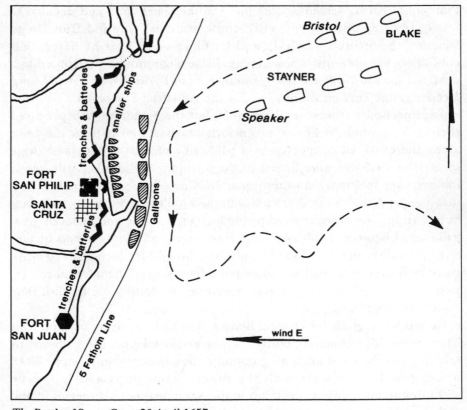

The Battle of Santa Cruz, 20 April 1657

inshore of the galleons.[7] All reconstructions must be partly conjectural because the diagram with which Stayner accompanied his report to Charles II, written sometime between 1660 and Stayner's death in 1663, has not survived.[8] Once opened the cannonade seems to have been as ferocious as anything in the Dutch War and the carnage on the galleons must have been appalling. The Spanish gunners ashore could neither engage the English warships effectively on their approach because of the smaller Spanish ships which lay close before them, having indeed to fire through their yards; nor could they see their enemy once they were in position beyond the galleons because they disappeared in vast clouds of smoke which the sea breeze wafted ashore.

The inshore wind gave Blake a better view of the battle and about noon he closed in to engage the shore batteries and finish off the smaller vessels. He feared that the disappearance of the Spanish ships, for many had sunk or were burning to the water-line, would unmask the Spanish batteries to the squadron's peril. Stayner reports firing several broadsides into the 'admiral' and 'vice-admiral' which promptly caught fire and blew up, and then clawing his way to sea by heaving up on his forepeak anchor under a galling fire from the forts. However, an account by Thomas Lurting, boatswain of the *Bristol*, describes the deaths of these galleons differently. His ship came late to the fight with Blake's reserve squadron which had been sent in to destroy any surviving Spanish vessels and to cover the withdrawal. Either Stayner or Blake ordered the *Bristol*'s master to squeeze in wherever he could find room, and her crew found themselves only 'half a cable-length' (fifty fathoms or about 300 feet) from the Spanish 'vice-admiral' and as far again from the 'admiral'. His captain ordered Lurting to steer nearer the 'vice-admiral' with a view to boarding, but the Spaniard in turn veered away having apparently slipped her stern anchor. The *Bristol* then moored with a spring on her cable to hold her steady on the stream as she fired into the 'vice-admiral' from across her bow. Running out her twenty-eight starboard guns the *Bristol* fired only two broadsides before a shot 'fell into her magazine and she blew up, not a man escaping'. The third broadside from the *Bristol* may have set the 'admiral' on fire for her crew leapt overboard and a few moments later she also exploded. All that could be seen of the ship moments later was her elaborately gilded stern floating disconsolately towards the shore. This was at two o'clock. From then on the English sought to withdraw from the fight with as little damage as possible, although four of Stayner's command, *Plymouth*, *Worcester*, *Maidstone* and *Swiftsure*, each made desperate efforts to haul off a prize until peremptory orders from Blake compelled them to burn their captives.

With only two of the galleons showing even their masts above water the order to withdraw was given between three and four o'clock. Blake was right to insist on burning the prizes his hungry men were trying to tow to sea.

Getting away from the shore batteries with no enemy ships to mask them and in the face of an onshore wind was a formidable enough task. Few sailing-ship navies, then or later, could have accomplished it. As it was one frigate went temporarily aground, some were disabled, and were with difficulty towed off by their companions. The English broadsides had driven the Spaniards from their guns both in the forts and the castle in the early afternoon, but these guns reopened fire with renewed fury once the English withdrew. The experience of the *Speaker* is revealing. Seeing Stayner struggling to get clear under a heavy fire Blake ordered *Swiftsure* to give *Speaker* a tow. However, the shot flew so thick that the *Swiftsure* cut loose and the *Speaker* hauled herself to safety, her guns still defiantly booming shoreward and to such good effect that a massive explosion was seen on St Philip's Castle, whose guns at once fell silent. Nevertheless the damage she had sustained was staggering and her crew despaired of her. She was barely at sea before her masts came crashing over the side one after the other. She had holes between wind and water 4 feet long and 3 feet deep over which hides were nailed, while empty water butts were fastened to her sides to help her stay afloat. The *Plymouth* took her under tow and Blake sent extra carpenters and seamen to assist in repairs and the frantic pumping. By seven o'clock every ship was 'by the good hand of God' once more at sea, battered and bloody, their crews amazed to be alive, deafened and exhausted, but triumphant. Amazingly, as Blake reported to Cromwell, they had lost 'only fifty slain and 120 wounded . . . to God be all the glory'.

So extraordinary was their achievement in getting the ships off in the face of fierce bombardment and an adverse, onshore wind that a legend grew up that God sent a miraculous offshore wind which blew Blake's fleet to safety. In reality the wind did not change until two busy days had been spent trying to cobble the ten worst damaged ships together for the voyage back to the mainland. Then came a wind from the south-west which blew the fleet back to its station near Cape St Mary, where it arrived safely on 2 May. Blake had already sent his victorious despatch home with the *Hampshire* and on 28 May Thurloe read it to a stunned Parliament, for no hint of the possibility of such a battle had preceded it. As Thurloe commented: 'Though we received no benefit from it' (all the silver being ashore) 'yet certainly the enemy never had a greater loss.' A Day of Thanksgiving was proclaimed, Blake was voted a jewel worth £500, and Cromwell would knight Stayner on his return. (The jewel, a portrait of Cromwell set in crystal and gold, surrounded with forty-six diamonds, was sent out to the victorious admiral with remarkable promptness.)[9] Meanwhile Cromwell had heard that Blake was dangerously ill, and a letter accompanied the jewel ordering him home with some of the fleet. Captain John Stoakes was to cruise off Cadiz with fourteen ships, and a squadron of five frigates was to be despatched to the Mediterranean to protect commerce and strike at the enemy. Before the letter could reach him Blake had recovered from the stress of battle and had sailed for the Mediterranean himself, where the mere appearance off Sallee of this dreaded warrior sufficed to induce the Moors to resume the broken off negotiations of 1656. All English prisoners were released and a treaty of peace signed. It was Blake's last service to his countrymen. By 26 June he was back before Cadiz. In his absence three Dutch ships had tried to run the gauntlet with part of the silver locked up uselessly at Santa Cruz. Two of the ships got into St Lucar, while the *Flying Fame* of Amsterdam was driven ashore. Only part of her silver was got off before the English arrived to tow her off and make prisoners of 300 of her passengers, while the seamen looted the remaining silver. The imprisonment of the bulk of the treasure in the Canaries devastated the Spanish capacity to wage war. In May their troops had invaded Portugal and the conquest of the country seemed certain. By July the King of Spain could neither pay nor feed his soldiers who deserted in thousands, and Portugal was secure. Blake's presence also prevented the Spanish from seizing Lisbon from the sea – a triumph which would certainly have ended Portugal's independence.

Meanwhile the author of these Spanish frustrations was quitting the scene. On 9 July Blake sailed north in the *George*, leading nine major vessels and the ketch *Nonsuch*. On 11 July he dropped anchor in the Tagus where Maynard, Edward Meadow's successor, was alarmed at his condition, reporting that he was 'very weak'. Off the Lizard his failing sight could barely discern the loom of the land he had served so faithfully. In no doubt that death was close, and anxious to get ashore to settle his estate, he commanded his captain to steer for Plymouth, leaving the remainder of the fleet to continue up Channel. He promoted six lads to midshipmen, including two of his servants, and he wrote to the Commissioners charging them to take care of the needy ships he had left on station under Stoakes. As the *George* moved up the Sound at 10 o'clock in the morning of 7 August Blake died in the great cabin in her stern. His body was carried to lie in state at Greenwich in the Great Hall of the Queen's House. On 4 September it was carried in state in a procession of barges up the Thames, Blake's armour, crested helmet and sword on the coffin, trumpeters summoning crowds to the river bank to see the great admiral make his final journey. Mournful and silent Londoners thronged the streets as his coffin wended its way to burial in Henry VII's Chapel in Westminster Abbey with every regiment in London firing volleys in salute. He was England's greatest admiral before Nelson and none has surpassed him since.

The focus of the war with Spain now moved from sea to land. Mazarin had decided during 1656 that reinforcing the French army in the Low Countries with regiments of the New Model Army was worth a high price. He was prepared to concede a Flemish port, probably Dunkirk, if only the Protector would send him troops to assist in taking it, and would even pay a subsidy to cover their expenses. It took months of frustrating effort to persuade the Protector to embrace the offer. Cromwell might see Spain as a natural enemy of the English Republic but he did not see France as a natural ally. If he intervened would his men be paid? If paid, would the French honour their promise to help them take Dunkirk? If they took it would they honour their promise to surrender it to the English regiments which had besieged it? However, these fears and suspicions ebbed. There was a logic to a full French alliance. The Spaniards had adopted the cause of Charles II as early as April 1656, promising him a pension, and financing a regiment in Flanders made up of Irish and English Royalists. They even undertook to furnish ships to carry the regiment to England to support a rising there, and 4,000 Spanish soldiers to help on the work. Spanish money financed Leveller plots to assassinate the Protector. The Protectorate government, warned by Thurloe whose spies were active in several European capitals but especially in Madrid and the Spanish Netherlands, took these threats seriously. They were even concerned at the threat of a Spanish-backed Royalist invasion although there could hardly be a project more likely to fail; or less likely to be attempted considering the New Model Navy's capacity to sink it on the way over and the New Model Army's capacity to knock any survivors on the head as they crawled ashore. Nevertheless the war with Spain must be fought more vigorously. The hopes of waging war at a profit had proved delusory. The Spanish government must be forced to the peace table.

On 23 March 1657 Cromwell finally committed himself to an offensive alliance with Louis XIV by which he undertook to furnish 6,000 infantry supported by a fleet. They would campaign in Flanders and would receive Mardyke and Dunkirk as their share of the fruits of victory. Seizing Dunkirk would pluck a thorn from the side of English commerce by expelling the privateers. It would be a secure base on the continent from which France could be kept honest and from which the King of Spain could be menaced. As Thurloe pithily observed: 'It would be a bridle to the Dutch and a door into the continent.' Once he had made his mind up the Protector moved quickly. Only six weeks after signing the treaty Sir John Reynolds landed with 6,000 men at Boulogne and marched off to serve under Marshal Turenne in Flanders. At first events seemed to confirm the Protector's suspicions of French perfidy. The English campaigned north-eastwards with Turenne's 20,000 French, never approaching the Flemish ports to which Turenne appeared to assign a low priority. Even without Cromwell's prodding this did not escape the vigilant eye of that truculent Scot, Sir William Lockhart of Lee, Cromwell's ambassador in Paris. Once a captain in the French army, then a lieutenant-colonel in the Scottish army, knighted by Charles I after his surrender to the Scots in 1646, he had served in the army of the 'Engagement' in 1647 and had fought valiantly to protect the rear of the army after the battle of Preston. In 1650 he had been appointed general of horse in a new Scottish army but quarrelled with Argyle and retired to his estates. Charles II had foolishly snubbed him when Lockhart offered his services prior to the ill-fated invasion of England so that he had happily missed the disaster at Worcester. Ever a realist Lockhart later offered his services to the Protectorate and was welcomed by Cromwell, who appointed him a Justice Commissioner for Scotland. He represented Lanark in the Protectorate Parliaments. As his second wife he married Cromwell's niece-by-marriage. Arriving in Paris in April 1656 Lockhart shared his master's suspicion that Mazarin, that master of duplicity, wished to exploit the valour of the English regiments but not to see the English gain a continental foothold. Observing that Turenne had not even turned north against Gravelines, which the treaty allocated to the French, he bluntly protested to Mazarin. In this he faithfully obeyed his master who indignantly dismissed all French excuses as 'mere parcels of words for children' and ordered Lockhart to 'take boldness and freedom to yourself in your dealings with the French on these accounts'. The command could hardly have come to a man more willing or able to carry it out. Thanks to his eloquence orders were sent to Turenne which in September turned the army north against Mardyke, which was soon taken and handed over to the English.

Despite Lockhart's protests Turenne had postponed the siege of Dunkirk until June 1658. When at last it began the English in Mardyke marched west to join the besiegers, where Lockhart soon joined them. The pugnacious ambassador was itching to resume his former profession of arms, even if only for a few weeks. The English commander, Reynolds, had recently perished in a small vessel which was cast away on the Goodwin Sands and Lockhart seized the chance to take his place. There can have been few occasions when a serving ambassador took command of an army of several thousand men. The Spanish, although they had massively entrenched Dunkirk, had failed to reinforce the place and the outworks were too large for the Marquis de Leyde to hope to defend for long with a garrison of only 1,000 foot and 800 horse. There was no hope from the sea, where the sails of a large English squadron loomed on the horizon. Nevertheless, although Leyde's case appeared desperate he had no intention of tamely surrendering, for he knew an army would soon be marching to his relief. This Spanish force of about 15,000 men, commanded by Don John of Austria, and containing among its officers the Prince de Condé, the Prince de Ligny, Marshal d'Hocquincourt and the young Duke of York, advanced along the coast and encamped among the sandhills to await a favourable opportunity to assault the besiegers. It was not as strong an army as the French, being ill-composed for the task before it as more than half its strength was cavalry, and while the Spanish infantry was traditionally perceived as the best in Europe only four of its regiments were Spanish. The remainder were recruited from several nations including Charles II's little army of one English, one Scottish, and three Irish regiments, commanded by the Duke of York, but organized into three battalions, together with some Walloon and German regiments and Condé's infantry, some of whom were French.

For the Spanish army the battle had an unfortunate prelude for Marshal d'Hocquincourt was killed on the evening before in a foolish skirmish which endangered many of the generals including the Duke of York himself. The Spanish army then drew up in a long line of infantry with their right and centre on the dunes above the beach and the left, with some of the horse, on a road and meadows which lay in a narrow strip between the dunes and the Furnes canal which ran parallel to the coast. Most of their cavalry was either to the rear or out foraging. Don John's army lacked entrenching tools and the artillery and ammunition train had not yet caught up with the main body. Marshal Turenne, warned of their approach, could at first hardly believe that the main body of the army was prepared to encamp so close to his own forces, but when prisoners confirmed it he at once decided that he would advance to the attack the next morning. He also urgently summoned the English regiments from the siege of Dunkirk. Lockhart was seriously unwell and had to accompany his soldiers in a coach with Major-General Morgan in immediate command.

Meanwhile the Spanish army was behaving as if no enemy was near at hand, sending the horse out to forage and making no defensive dispositions against a sudden assault. The Duke of York, an old head on young shoulders, found this lack of preparation disquieting and that night warned the Marquis de Caracena, among other senior officers, that he believed the French would attack in the night or the next morning.[10] Caracena and the others dismissed his fears, merely jesting that this was what they most desired, to which the duke replied grimly that he was well acquainted with Marshal Turenne and they could be assured their wishes would be gratified. So it proved, for the next morning Turenne's army could be seen moving out of its lines and the Duke of York was interested to see the English infantry, easily distinguished by their red coats, advancing steadily forward to attack the extreme right of the Spanish line among the dunes. Again he found it difficult to persuade his hosts that a full-scale battle impended, Don John of Austria being the sceptic on this occasion, but the duke's report was soon confirmed by a weightier source, the Prince de Condé. The generals then dispersed to their positions to await the onslaught, Don John having no intention of surrendering the advantage of the ground by advancing from his lines.

The Spanish regiments were on the right and were strongly posted on a great sand ridge, about 150 feet high, which turned in at right angles to the beach. Any assault here must be made uphill in loose sand. The French and English army advanced in two lines of infantry with the Ironsides on the left of the line among the dunes and therefore destined to strike the enemy at his strongest point. As if in anxiety for their fellow-countrymen several of the smaller English warships weighed anchor and moved in on the flood-tide closer to the beach, hoping to train their guns on the Spanish regiments, one of which was posted on the seaward-facing crest of the big dune to guard against a flank attack. Still further to Turenne's left some divisions of horse commanded by the Marquis de Castelneau advanced along the beach. Turenne was advancing cautiously for that experienced commander wanted to reconnoitre the Spanish lines before selecting the points at which to lunge. Lockhart's seven battalions, each one a regiment and in all amounting to between 4,000 and 5,000 men, were full of fight and advanced too far. Unlike the French formations to their right which had halted earlier, they were now in musket range of the enemy but they refused to retire. The Duke of York, who had been sent with a few Royalist soldiers to reinforce the Spaniards on the great dune, believed an opportunity was lost when the Ironsides outmarched the French on either side and that better-organized cavalry might have taken them in the flank.

After a pause for breath and to redress their lines, which were by now under fire, Major-General Morgan, their immediate commander, ordered the attack and the regiments advanced resolutely up the dune, led by Colonel Fenwick. They were compelled by the yielding surface to scramble on hands and knees dragging their heavy pikes while their skirmishers kept up a sporadic fire at the Spaniards on the crest. Fenwick was shot down but the regiments maintained the assault and their breathless exertions drove the Spanish from the crest at push of pike. Seven of eleven Spanish officers were left dead on the crest, along with two of the Duke of York's English officers. After a rest and a cheer the Ironsides now advanced down the dune only to be assaulted by the Duke of York's regiment and a regiment of Don John's guards, but these they repulsed with heavy losses, the duke only being saved by the quality of his armour. The duke managed to rally some remnants of his horse after this disaster and with some infantry once more attacked the Ironsides who suffered some casualties, but it was all for nothing. The overthrow of the Spanish infantry, the most feared in Europe from its position on the strongest part of the line, disheartened Don John's army and the rest of the line was quickly routed, despite a disciplined charge by the Prince of Condé in the centre. In general the Spanish infantry fought well but were defeated and it was not necessary to defeat the cavalry who ran like rabbits although they scarcely sighted their enemy. The Ironsides suffered about a hundred casualties from the several thousand engaged and nine officers killed, including Colonel Fenwick.

By the standards of the Thirty Years War this was not a battle of major dimensions, but the English regiments' defeat of the Spanish infantry, long regarded as invincible, astonished European governments and impressed two eminent observers who were on the spot: Cardinal Mazarin and the youthful Louis XIV. This victory decided the long war between France and Spain and ten days later Dunkirk surrendered. It also marked the end of Charles II's hopes of invading and conquering Cromwellian England. The Protectorate navy had captured his ships and the Battle of the Dunes had destroyed or dispersed half of his little army. Lockhart took charge of Dunkirk and was promptly made its governor by his grateful master. England now had that continental gateway which she had desired ever since the loss of Calais a century before and had also rid herself of the most dangerous of all nests of privateers. It was the final achievement of Cromwell's foreign wars and indeed of his foreign policy.

How are we to assess the Protector's record in foreign affairs? Foreign policy is always a difficult arena and not one for which a minor Huntingdonshire gentleman, albeit a retired cavalry general and former member of parliament, could be well qualified or in which he would be likely to excel. Not surprisingly, therefore, ever since his death in September 1658 he has been subjected to a barrage of criticism, but while some of this criticism is cogent, much is overstated and some is perverse to the point of absurdity. To characterize his policy even prior to the Western Design as 'indulging in a game of international smash and grab rather like the regimes controlling Germany and Italy during the late 1930s' appears too exaggerated and anachronistic to be illuminating.[11] In the past even authors with some sympathy for Cromwell's objectives like Sir Charles Firth and S.R. Gardiner were dismayed by Cromwell's choice of Spain as an enemy and the France of the young Louis XIV as an ally. Rather than allying himself with the burgeoning power of France and going to war with the declining power of Spain he should have sought, it is argued, to weaken France and sustain Spain so that a balance of power might have been maintained in Europe. Even though a few seventeenth-century critics and commentators could speak of the English ruler, whether king or Protector, 'balancing' the kings of France and Spain by throwing his weight one way or the other, criticism of Cromwell for failing to seek a 'balance of power' appears anachronistic. The viewpoint is coloured by eighteenth- and nineteenth-century perspectives and experiences, and would have sounded odd in the Council chamber of the Protectorate. In the seventeenth century *realpolitik* was less subtle and more brutal: you allied with the strong because he was strong, and you waged war on the weaker because he was weaker and seized your share of the spoils. France could be a dangerous enemy and a valuable ally. In the long term Spain could be neither. It is true that Cromwell was criticized even in his own era for pursuing a policy which was 'Elizabethan' in outlook. As early as 1668 Slingsby Bethel, an apostate republican who was doubtless eager to ingratiate himself with the restored monarchy, published an attack on the Protectorate in a pamphlet whose title ostentatiously displayed its author's prejudices, *The World's Mistake in Oliver Cromwell*. Bethel charged the Protector with being obsessed with Spain as the traditional enemy, and this had misled him into allying with France. In general he accused Cromwell of seeing Europe and its states in religious terms, taking no account of England's real (that is, commercial) interests, and seeking to build a Protestant League against the Hapsburgs in Europe as well as in the West Indies.

The bare facts can, of course, be mobilized to support this. He did go to war with Spain. He did pursue the unrealizable objective of a Protestant League with the Dutch and the Baltic states. He did tend to admire Charles X of Sweden just because that unlovable king appeared from a safe upwind distance to be a reincarnation of Gustavus Adolphus, and if Cromwell had ever sought a role model, an improbable eventuality, it would have been that Protestant hero of the Thirty Years War. As for Dunkirk, Cromwell made its capture an object of English policy and he did so over the protests not merely of posterity, including historians, but of his own Council, some of whom thought it a needlessly expensive acquisition. However, Cromwell was an ardent Protestant, and, as deeply religious people all too often will, he believed that God shared his religious preferences.[12] He did not, like more cynical contemporaries, compartmentalize his views so that in one box he put England's commercial interests and in another carefully isolated box the cause of 'true religion'. He did not support the religious cause with suitable rhetoric while supporting the material advantage of his country with all the forces at his command with no regard for religious propriety. He never saw these pious and material objectives as incompatible, but rather complementary. He was not a cynical opportunist when he formed an alliance with Catholic France in order to gain a foothold on the continent and shut down a nest of privateers. He believed that advantages might be won for French Protestants by negotiation just because Mazarin was so anxious to obtain his help in France's war with Spain in Flanders, but that no such advantages would be won by war with France. In this his judgement was sound. He certainly had no intention of repeating the criminal lunacy of the Duke of Buckingham thirty years earlier by involving England in war with both Catholic powers at once. The Commonwealth had long been involved in an undeclared maritime war against French commerce. This the Protector ended when he knew that war with Spain was certain, but he did not rush into an alliance with France. It may have pleased his vanity to be courted so desperately by both the great powers before the Spanish War. He would not have been human if it had not. Vanity did not cause him to rush into an alliance with France, however, even when the ill-conceived and worse-executed West Indian expedition brought a European war with Spain. He agonized over important and impatiently awaited decisions not least because of his deep suspicions of Mazarin's reliability, suspicions which were shared by every European statesmen who had dealings with that cynical opportunist.

Nevertheless his policies had an inner logic. If England was prosperous it was because God had decreed it and that decree was due to the wonderful spirit of reform and cleansing which had swept through England since 1642. To Cromwell, his own career quite clearly demonstrated this wonder-working Providence. Had he not risen from the ranks of a back-bench MP of modest significance before the first Civil War, and from a second rank cavalry general during it, to the height of Lord Protector, an uncrowned monarch not merely of England and Wales but of Scotland and Ireland also, countries which he had conquered? In the Protector's eyes pursuing policies with no regard to the supposed will of God, leaving such matters to the prayers of priests, made no sense at all. It defied the lessons of recent experience and was simultaneously perilous, blasphemous and silly. Our understanding of the Protectorate government's actions and policies will not be noticeably improved if we simply condemn Cromwell for being bereft not merely of the skills but also of the mentality of a Talleyrand or a Bismarck or even a Castlereagh or Disraeli. Cromwell was never blind to England's commercial interests. It would have been remarkable if he had been. London, his seat of government, was also the commercial and financial capital of his country. Its streets were thronged with merchants, shipowners and goldsmiths, whose eloquent and informed representatives could always gain the ear of his Council or of the Protector himself, who was a much more accessible ruler than his continental counterparts. While still ruminating on the foreign policy options which confronted his new government he had sent Blake with a powerful fleet to the Mediterranean to chastise commerce raiders both French and Moorish, and to pursue gunboat diplomacy with the North African rulers with the same objective of protecting English commerce. He had declined, however reluctantly, the Venetian appeal to use his fleet to raise the siege of Candia on Crete because of the impact of war with Turkey on English commercial interests in the Levant. This, among other evidence, must undermine the case of those who have criticized Cromwell's foreign policy for its lack of concern for England's commercial interests.[13]

So also in the Baltic where the options were more complicated than in the Mediterranean. Here the Protector was deeply concerned and not simply because of some idle dream of a Protestant League against Austria. The naval supplies of the Baltic states were just as vital to England's security then as they were in the eighteenth and early nineteenth centuries. While the threat of the Hapsburg empire encroaching northwards inspired the

Protector's most virulent anti-Catholic rhetoric, he could not ignore the fact that his Protestant 'white knight', Charles X of Sweden, was seeking hegemony over the Baltic. Making the Baltic a Swedish lake was not in England's interest while it aroused the violent enmity of Denmark, Brandenburg and the Hanseatic League. Sensibly Cromwell did not permit his heart to rule his head, preferring to mediate between the Protestant powers rather than ally himself with the Swedish king he so much admired. Neither Denmark nor Sweden must be permitted to close the Baltic to English shipping in the future as Denmark had done recently. For either to control both sides of the Sound would threaten such a closure in the future. In September 1657 he sent Philip Meadows to Denmark to mediate between them, and although the Treaty of Roskilde, which Meadows brokered, only kept the peace for three months it proved a long term success from the English point of view, for its territorial provisions have endured to our own time. Sweden obtained the north bank of the Sound, the Danes remained masters of the south bank, and the uninterrupted passage of English commerce has ensued almost continuously for three centuries.

He is most vulnerable to criticism for making war on Spain but not because he failed to grasp the principles of that balance of power so dear to Lord Beaconsfield or the Marquis of Salisbury. His belief that a war with Spain could pay for itself, including maintaining a navy of at least 160 men-of-war which by his own count cost £120,000 a month to keep at sea, reveals an ignorance of financial realities which would reduce any modern economist to helpless merriment. However, when Englishmen of his generation thought of Spain they thought of gold. The Plate Fleet mesmerized them. Invulnerable to pirates because of the size of the galleons and their large crews, the Plate Fleets were hopelessly vulnerable to the heavily armed English warships. Surely the capture of one fleet could well pay for the war? So indeed it might but this naive concept of war finance, which savours of selling the lion's skin before he has been hunted let alone slain, also failed to take into account the enormous cost of searching for and entrapping the Plate Fleet and, worst of all, that this entrapment might never occur – for luck was needed as well as strategy and seamanship. Nor did it take into account the possibility that the King of Spain might simply forbid its sailing or order it to take refuge at some intermediate port like Havana or Santa Cruz. Such a decision would (and indeed did) cause the king intense financial embarrassment and restrict his capacity to wage war. Nevertheless, the result would be the same: the cost of the war would fall on the English state unrelieved by Spanish silver.

Modern critics of Cromwell's war with Spain have asserted that while some Englishmen saw Spain as a source of plunder their own merchants and cloth manufacturers did not. They would have wished the Plate Fleet a safe arrival at Cadiz for their debtors throughout western Europe would find it difficult to make their remittances if the Spanish government defaulted on its debts. Spain was a market of great value to English manufacturers, merchants and shipowners. War with Spain meant greatly increased dangers from Flemish privateers when they were at sea and an increasing likelihood that English vessels would rot in harbour for lack of consignments as Spain closed its Iberian and Flemish ports. To all this there could be no effective retaliation because the Spanish merchant fleet was inconsiderable and blockading it would do little harm to the Spanish economy. The Dutch would provide neutral bottoms to carry Spanish goods (and indeed to carry English goods if permitted to do so, to the detriment of the English shipping industry). During the Dutch War, expensive though it undoubtedly was both in revenue and in ships lost to Dutch privateers, at least the government could point to hundreds of Dutch prizes carried into English ports. No such benefits could flow from war with Spain. Rather the gains were reversed. We shall never know how many English merchantmen and fishing vessels were lost to Spanish and Flemish privateers but all contemporary estimates (admittedly all from hostile or partial commentators) claim losses well in excess of a thousand. These losses must have held many other vessels idle in port and forced up the insurance rates of those which ventured to sea.

The critics point out that English merchants and manufacturers had other concerns. A complete embargo on English goods vigorously enforced by the Spanish authorities in Spain and the Low Countries would devastate a number of their trades. They would be unable to sell English cloth in the Spanish market and they would be unable to import the fine merino wool they needed for the best cloths, and red cochineal used in dyeing. However, the picture was not as completely adverse as all this suggests. The Protectorate government, well aware of the merchants' interests, gave them six months notice to recover their investments before the likely outbreak of war, and was prepared to waive the prohibitions of the Navigation Act to permit Dutch ships to move English goods to Spain (especially fish) and import vitally needed goods from Spain and the Low Countries. Many Spanish officials in effect cooperated with the Protectorate's efforts and ignored their royal master's orders. Antwerp refused to apply the embargo until at least March 1658. Some English bottoms carried cargoes to Spain under a Tuscan flag of convenience, all of which led Secretary Thurloe to retort to three mercantile protesters that 'you export as much commodity, and import as much from Spain as ever you did'. Moreover, exports were partly kept up because by making peace with Portugal the Protector had provided an alternative market of considerable value. Thurloe complacently observed that 'it is said that a full trade with Portugal (which we can have as we will) will be near as good as the other'.[14] Moreover trade to the Mediterranean became safer and more profitable once peace with France had ended the depredations of French commerce raiders there, and Blake's menacing presence had 'persuaded' the Tunisian and Algerian corsairs to abandon their attacks on English shipping.

So Cromwell fought on and had he lived might have made a better peace than could his sorely divided successors. It is a commonplace to say that the war gained England nothing and lost it much. As we have seen the commercial losses were not as great as has often been alleged and there were positive gains. The objectives of the war, apart from Oliver's premature dreams of seizing large parts of the Spanish empire, were largely achieved. France deserted the Stuart cause, as had the Dutch after the Dutch War. This was a significant benefit because only the Dutch or the French had the capacity, at least on paper, to launch a successful Royalist invasion. Now the Stuarts could only lean on Spain and it proved, as Cromwell had calculated, a feeble crutch. Of less importance to Cromwell but of great significance nevertheless, was the preservation of Portugal's independence – a country whose perilous position made it possible to extract valuable concessions which the King of Spain would always reject. There were other benefits. French piracy in the Mediterranean ceased and Flemish privateering was greatly curtailed by the acquisition of Dunkirk. This became in the short term an insurance against France seeking a separate peace and in the long term could have served as a gateway through which England could intervene on the continent in the event of a future war. This long-term benefit evaporated because Charles II later sold it, but that was his decision and it was greatly regretted in the last decade of the century and during the reign of Queen Anne when the depredations of its privateers reached plague proportions. It cost about £70,000 a year to maintain, which is why an impecunious Charles II parted with it, but some expenses need to be endured. The losses in ships, in ransoming their crews and above all in cargo, sustained by the merchant marine to Dunkirkers later in the century and in the first decade of the next might have come to less than the £3,700,000 it might have cost to maintain Dunkirk from the Restoration to the end of Marlborough's War but, even without including inflated insurance premiums, it might well have come to more. This is apart from the strategic value the port would have had during King William's War and later or the lives lost in Dunkirker attacks. England had acquired another colony, Jamaica, an important base in the West Indies which she was to retain to her long-term advantage. The reverse side to these achievements was the disastrous impact of the war on the Protectorate Treasury since, like all wars, and despite the facile optimism of the Protector and his Council at its beginning, there was not the faintest possibility of its paying for itself.

CHAPTER THIRTEEN

The Failure of a Settlement

> . . . my design is to make what haste I can to be gone.
>
> *Cromwell on his deathbed, August 1658*

Pressing financial difficulties, rendered still more pressing by the expensive war with Spain, brought about the summoning of the second Protectorate Parliament. The decimation tax had proved inadequate to pay the militia and neither Protector nor Council would accept the Major-Generals' suggestion that the tax threshold should be lowered to apply to less affluent Royalists. By the winter of 1655/6 annual income was falling short of annual expenditure by almost £250,000. Something had to be done. The Council naturally shrank from the option of raising taxes by applying the decimation tax to non-Royalists and the Major-Generals were encouraging them to embrace the other option: summoning a parliament. They promised that, thanks to their considerable local power and influence, loyal government supporters would be elected, a promise they would largely fail to keep. The electoral arrangements prescribed by the *Instrument of Government* were better able to exclude enemies of the government than to ensure the election of men who could be guaranteed to support it. The Major-Generals managed to get themselves elected along with a number of councillors, and other loyal government supporters and dependents, because they had 'remodelled' some of the boroughs to make them controllable – but the old problem remained. The *Instrument* which had reduced the number of boroughs, made them single member constituencies and swept away most of the rotten boroughs altogether, had made it impossible for the government to pack the House. In Nottingham the corporation would choose where the redoubtable Major-General Whalley gave his nod but in the county he even failed to prevent a Royalist from being elected; an embarrassment felt all the more keenly because he was a kinsman, Pennington Whalley. Elsewhere Sir Henry Vane was active urging the electors not to vote for 'swordsmen, Major-Generals and Decimators'. Similarly Sussex electors marched under the slogan 'no soldier, decimator or man that hath salary'.[1] As a result the second Protectorate Parliament's membership closely resembled that of the first except that the Independents elected by many counties were even more opposed to the Protectorate than in 1654 because of the heavy hand of the Major-Generals in local affairs. Cromwell knew who to blame for this embarrassment, reminding the Major-Generals grimly that although he had voted against it they had been impatient for a parliament because 'you were confident of your own strength and interest to get men chosen to your heart's desire. How you have failed therein, and how much the country is disobliged, is well known.'[2] However, the truth is that Cromwell in 1656 was in the same position as Charles I in 1640. Financial necessity dictated the calling of a parliament, however little he relished the thought of meeting it. Unlike Charles the Protector and his Council had the power to cull it of its more obvious enemies so the House lost more than a hundred members, the egregious Hesilrige, Bradshaw and Scot prominent among them. However, for many this exclusion proved impermanent. Although a Council-supplied 'ticket' was required to get past the watchful soldiers this check was only applied early. Later some of the excluded such as Sir Anthony Ashley Cooper (a notable Cromwell-monarchist) applied for leave to sit and were granted it, and some others would furtively sidle in unhindered.

The survivors naturally included a strong bloc of friends of the regime, among them about a hundred officers of all ranks including Generals Lambert, Disbrowe, Skippon and Goffe, such officials ('salary-men') as John Thurloe, Sir Gilbert Pickering, the Protector's Court Chamberlain, and such firm friends of the Protector as Lord Broghill, and Council members including President Henry Lawrence. In addition there were the sixty reliable supporters from Ireland and Scotland. General Goffe's remark that it was not as good as they could have wished nor as bad as the regime's enemies would have hoped was not unreasonable. Many members possessed parliamentary experience, for two hundred and thirty had sat in the first Protectorate Parliament and eight in the Nominated Parliament. One hundred and eighty had never sat before.[3] The bulk of the House consisted of the same type of conservative-minded gentlemen as had sat in 1654. In that Parliament the chief struggles had been between government supporters and 'Independents' (chiefly either crypto-monarchist Presbyterians or Commonwealth's-men of the Hesilrige-Scot stamp who had never accepted the Protectorate). In the 1656 Parliament the government forces were stronger but harmony would not prevail because the struggles would be between two increasingly divided factions of the Protectorate's supporters, with the back-benchers aligning themselves with one or the other. Charles I once declared that parliaments were of the nature of cats, 'they grow ever more curs't with age'. It was a remark Cromwell would learn to appreciate.

The new Parliament showed its truculence early by trying to condemn the exclusions (an illegality 'as gross as a mountain, open, palpable', as one member indignantly described it) but was persuaded to abandon the issue. Thurloe thought this 'a great Providence of God' but it was really the government bloc demonstrating its managerial muscle. Nevertheless about fifty members indignantly withdrew, although many of them gradually filtered back. The history of this Parliament was neither altogether unhappy nor altogether unproductive, even before it embarked on its constitutional phase. It was preceded by one of the Protector's long, rambling and ill-prepared speeches in which he justified the system of Major-Generals, 'a little inspection upon the people', because Royalists had foully sought to plunge the country once more into the horrors of civil war. However, although this necessity was 'much regretted' it had at least done more 'towards the discountenancing of vice and settling religion than anything done these fifty years'. Notwithstanding the 'envy and slander of foolish men' the Protector declared he would 'abide by it'. This was ill news for the many members who saw ridding the state of these over-mighty meddlers as the principal reason for their journey to Westminster but comforted the Major-Generals, who already feared for their positions. Meanwhile, although much progress had been made towards reform of religion, of manners, of the law and of finance, much more needed to be done by this Parliament, and especially, he might have added, regarding revenue. Under the *Instrument of Government* no parliament need be summoned before 1658, so this was an emergency parliament called for the purpose of raising taxes for the Spanish War. At first things went moderately well. Some law reform, mainly designed to decentralize the administration of justice by carrying it into the shires, was carried out. That favourite obsession of our seventeenth-century forefathers, extravagance of dress, received legislative condem-nation. Meanwhile the members engaged in such traditional activities as getting bills passed which were of interest to their particular constituents. In November the Protector congratulated the members on the number of good laws they had already passed. Harmony could not endure long, however, not least because many members were merely awaiting a favourable opportunity to rid the country of the Major-Generals.

Three issues disturbed the peaceful progress, and the first was religion. A majority was uneasy about the Protectorate religious settlement because even those who were themselves members of Independent congregations were coming to believe that toleration had gone too far. No sect had done more to encourage this attitude than the Quakers, who had not yet become the pious quietists of later years. Then they were fierce proselytizers, ready for an outrageous confrontation with the authorities or with members of other congregations. In December 1657 a Quaker leader, James Naylor, was brought before Parliament for staging at Bristol a re-enactment of the entry of Christ into Jerusalem with himself in the principal role. His action was considered so outrageously blasphemous that only Parliament could deal with it. Refusing to acknowledge that the Protectorate Parliaments were not courts of law and had no authority in the matter the members vented their unease and outrage in a violent denunciation of Naylor and his sect, and sentenced him to be branded, whipped and imprisoned. Cromwell was disturbed by the case, demanding to know by what authority Parliament had acted in the matter. He had been cautious and ambivalent in his treatment of the Quakers according to his principle that 'witness suppressed might mean light extinguished'. He probably feared that the other sects would see Parliament's trial of Naylor as the forerunner of an attack on them which might cause social unrest and strain the loyalty of the army. Still more alarming, the debate over Naylor had split the government's supporters.

Shortly after this sensation General Disbrowe moved in the House that the Decimation Tax should be renewed to sustain the militia. If he had hoped to give a legal foundation to decimation as well as to sustain the Major-Generals by a short act quickly passed he was to be disappointed. It became a major issue, repeatedly attacked as divisive and unjust, and was rejected on 27 January by thirty-six votes, thereby disbanding the militia and the Major-Generals whose prime role had been to command it. The latter realized that the Protector had turned against them. He remained silent, itself unhelpful, but his attitude was clear from the actions of his friends and kinsmen. Cromwell's son-in-law, John Claypole, moved that the bill be rejected. A nephew, Colonel Henry Cromwell, accused the Major-Generals of acting 'unjustly and against law' while a prominent Cromwellian squire, Sir John Trevor, described the bill as 'the usher to arbitrary power'.[4] The Major-Generals concluded that they had been sacrificed in return for substantial subsidies when on the following day the House voted £400,000 for the Spanish War. Certainly the rule of the Major-Generals in local government was at an end and the decimation tax was lifted from Royalist estates.[5] This was the second bitterly divisive issue for the government members.

The third issue would be the most heated of all. Some members had a daring and ambitious objective: they wished to make Cromwell king. This proposal had been talked of, sometimes furtively, sometimes openly, since at least 1653. Now the talk became more purposeful. In October the proposal of an Irish member, Colonel William Jephson, that the office of Protector should be made hereditary had been 'talked out'. (According to Ludlow Cromwell clapped Jephson on the shoulder and jovially exclaimed 'Get thee gone for a mad fellow!', but this highly partial source also alleges that his initiative was rewarded with a regiment and an ambassadorship to Sweden. In fact Jephson, who had commanded a regiment under Inchiquin as early as 1646, was well qualified for both appointments.)[6] In November another officer-member, Colonel Bridges, argued that Cromwell should be empowered to nominate his successor to avoid the perils of a disputed

succession. Although a few senior officers might grudgingly accept
'nomination', their real feelings were exposed at a meeting at Wallingford
House of thirty senior officers which voted against all constitutional change
– opposing monarchy and hereditary or nominated succession. They had
been alarmed at something in the wind, which was also scented by the
Venetian ambassador who prematurely reported that Cromwell's
assumption of the crown was 'expected at any moment'.[7] At last on Monday
23 February Sir Christopher Packe, formerly the Lord Mayor of London,
introduced the proposals of the 'kingmakers' to the House. These asked
Cromwell to consider the problem of what would happen in the event of his
death and urged him to accept a crown. However, they went much further
than a mere change of title or ordering the succession. They were devising a
civilian constitution to replace the one created by the Swordsmen. It would
include an Upper House of seventy members, parliaments would be
triennial and while Royalists were barred from membership elected MPs
could only be rejected by a committee of the House joined with the Council
of State. Cromwell would be empowered to nominate his successor which
temporarily shelved the question of an hereditary office. Taxes could not be
levied without parliamentary consent. In general the power of Parliament
would increase and that of the Council wane.

Once again the government's forces divided into warring factions. Lord
Broghill and Sir Anthony Ashley Cooper were prime movers, supported by
civilian officials like Thurloe and Pickering, the judges, various other
lawyers and a majority of the country gentlemen. The proposal also had the
support of the Irish members apart from three army officers. All the senior
officers opposed it, even Cromwell's relatives Fleetwood and Disbrowe,
while Lambert was its bitterest opponent despite his former leaning towards
a Cromwellian monarchy. Either he feared he would lose his unofficial
status of Cromwell's heir-apparent or, like the other Grandees, he feared
the civilians intended to remove government from the Swordsmen's
control. As one soldier wrote percipiently: 'Sword dominion is too sweet to
be parted with, and the truth is . . . that the single issue, the main dread, is
that the civil power shall swallow up the military.'[8] The Protector offered no
comfort, for when Lambert and other officers visited Cromwell he simply
waved the issue aside, remarking that it was their parliament – for had they
not admitted whom they pleased and kept out whom they pleased, 'and now
do you complain to me?'[9]

Significantly when debate resumed next day the officers abandoned the
argument that Cromwell would not 'endure' such a proposal, instead
claiming that it was a monstrous suggestion which would ruin the
Protectorate. For the next month debate raged clause by clause over what
would become known as the *Humble Petition and Advice*, a document which
despite its quaint name was a constitution, and one, unlike the *Instrument of*

Government, which had been devised by an elected parliament. The rearguard action of the Swordsmen in the House, despite the support of a plethora of pamphlets from Fifth Monarchists, Levellers, and committed Republicans, was swamped by numbers. The fears of the army were finally exacerbated beyond endurance when the House added a clause which foreshadowed imposing a doctrine on the national church. Lambert promptly led a deputation of senior officers to Whitehall Palace. Cromwell had let them down over the Major-Generals. He was not to be allowed to betray them again. They had forgotten that the day-to-day indolence of their leader masked a formidable temper. They encountered a furious tirade of accusation and reproach for their failure to settle the country since 1653. Now a permanent and peaceful settlement was in sight which their intransigence might very well shipwreck. If the proposed Upper Chamber, he reminded them, had existed in December it could have saved Naylor from martyrdom at the hands of Presbyterians and worse among the members. Cowed if not convinced, the generals allowed the debate to continue which it did with increasing fury both inside and outside the House. Cromwell was assailed by the lobbying not simply of the army officers and the committed Republicans but also by delegations and letters from the Independent congregations who feared that if the civilians achieved monarchy they would also achieve their aim of a universal doctrine for the church. Toleration might survive under King Oliver but who would succeed him? Once England became a monarchy again the death of Cromwell might soon be followed by the accession of Charles II and where would toleration for the sects be found then? On the other hand, he was lobbied with even greater assiduity and to greater effect by the civilian members of his Council and by delegates from a Parliament overwhelmingly in favour of the proposal.

On 6 May Cromwell appears to have bowed to the pressure and informally consented to be crowned. This moved the Grandees to a final effort. Lambert, Disbrowe and Cromwell's son-in-law Fleetwood deliberately encountered the Protector as he walked in St James's Park, something he was wont to do when ruminating on a difficult problem. There they told their master they would resign if he accepted a crown. This conversation may have been the final straw in persuading Cromwell to change his mind, but his decision to reject must have been reinforced by the news that Colonel Pride had gathered signatures for a petition against monarchy among the regiments quartered near London to present to Parliament. The petition had been drafted by the man Oliver had made vice-chancellor of Oxford University, his former chaplain John Owen. For Cromwell, who had become ruler from the camp not the court, by the sword not hereditary or constitutional right, these must have been salutary reminders. He had the power because the Swordsmen were in power. Without them on whom could he rely? Haunted by the past, determined to protect his country from future civil strife while he lived, desperate that peace should continue after his death, Cromwell reluctantly yielded. A loyal army could guarantee these things. An alienated army, split into contending factions, meant political chaos. Although he knew he would seem to be turning his back on the best hope for a long term civilian constitutional settlement, he officially rejected the crown.

However, since the army had won its great point they must give way on the others. The disappointed, disillusioned civilians must be conciliated, not least because many of them had no particular loyalty to Cromwell. If he would not be their king there was somebody waiting across the Channel who would be only too happy to oblige. To win the crown in 1649 Charles had even agreed to embrace Scots Presbyterianism and the Covenant. Seven hungry years later Charles would have swallowed the *Humble Petition* without a gulp. The outcome was, therefore, not a total victory for the Swordsmen but a compromise in which the monarchical conservatives appeared to get the substance and the Swordsmen appeared to get the shadow. The country would have the *Humble Petition and Advice* as its constitution. The status of Protector would be raised to king in all but title, with Oliver enthroned on state occasions with royal robes and sceptre and his household made larger and more elaborate. He was invested with the power to choose his own successor. There would be an Upper Chamber of sixty-three members nominated by the Protector. Cromwell agreed that an assembly of divines should devise a doctrine for the national church. He accepted a harsh law which made possible the confiscation of two-thirds of all Catholic estates. However, the civilians' substance proved less substantial than it appeared and the Swordsmen's gain proved less shadowy than they feared. Cromwell never summoned the assembly of divines and he ensured that nobody enforced the law against Catholics. Moreover he vetoed a bill which required anyone failing to attend the services of the national church to produce a certificate from the minister of an independent congregation. (The veto was perhaps a cuff over the ear for Naylor's parliamentary persecutors, for the act was chiefly aimed at the Quakers.) However, Lambert was devastated by the eclipse of his constitution, the *Instrument of Government*, and his ambitious soul could not forgive the fact that he had lost his privileged status as Cromwell's heir-apparent. He refused to cooperate, was deprived of his offices and military commission and retired to Henrietta Maria's delightful house and estate at Wimbledon with his wife and ten children. There he painted flower pictures, gardened, gloomily licked his wounds and awaited future opportunities.[10]

The Council now consisted of Cromwell's close supporters and clients and his position was stronger than ever. However, if the Protector thought that the Protectorate would move steadily forward under a more traditional type of ruler assisted by a more traditional form of parliament he was to be quickly undeceived. Even while it was busy trying to make him king, for which purpose it had not been summoned, it had failed to achieve the prime objective for which it had been summoned: supply. Certainly it had voted a revenue of £1,900,000 a year, a sum Charles I would have found unbelievable, with an addition of £400,000 a year for the duration of the Spanish War. However, this brought the Exchequer no comfort because first, Parliament did not agree on how this income was to be raised, and second, not even sums as large as these were enough. The armed forces were currently costing £2.5 million a year without considering all other expenses of government.[11] Moreover the Parliamentarians had courted popularity among their constituents by reducing the monthly assessment to £35,000. Nor would the 'reformed' Parliament with its new Upper House solve the government's financial problems, for it was to go into a long recess until January 1658 and once it reassembled it was destined to be abruptly cut short in the old Cromwellian way. First, however, Oliver had to be enthroned as Protector under the new constitution, which occurred with much greater solemnity and magnificence than the induction of 1653 for, as one member had told the House, they were making 'His Highness a great prince, a king indeed' and in such cases 'ceremonies signify much of the substance . . . as a shell preserves the kernel, or a casket a jewel'. To underline the monarchical character of the office the coronation throne was dragged from Westminster Abbey into Westminster Hall (the sole occasion of its removal). Genoese velvet decorated the dais, a table bore a gilt-bound Bible, a Sword of State and an elaborately sculpted gold sceptre, while the Protector wore a purple velvet robe lined with ermine identical in form to those traditional to royal coronations. Sir Oliver Fleming summoned the foreign ambassadors who eagerly flocked to the spectacle, which was also attended by the City aldermen, the Parliamentarians who had made all this necessary, and a bevy of senior officers who doubtless attended more in resignation than enthusiasm. Oliver was preceded into the hall by his gentlemen-in-waiting, pages, an array of heralds, the Earl of Warwick carrying the sword and the Lord Mayor carrying the sword of the city. There he was clothed in his robe, was bound with the Sword of State and took the Protectorial oath.[12] The following day he entered London in pomp and was proclaimed again at Chancery Lane, in Cheapside and finally at the Royal Exchange. Parliament now adjourned and Protector and Council resumed normal business.

For the second half of 1657 the Protector could hope that the new constitution, as a parliamentary creation, would work successfully and fulfil his dream of achieving a permanent political settlement. In the absence of Parliament, in recess until the following January, domestic affairs were dominated by establishing the two new branches of government: the new

Council of State and the Upper House. The first was a good deal easier than the second. The previous Council of State had consisted of fifteen members, of whom seven would form a quorum. The new Council was to have twenty-one, but again only seven would form a quorum. All must be approved by Parliament and none could be removed without its consent, an indication of the shift to parliamentary power embodied in the *Humble Petition*. The councillors, unlike their predecessors, must take an oath of loyalty to the Protector, and to maintain the Protestant religion and of secrecy. This novelty had caused much controversy in the Parliament even among the current councillors. All the old members were appointed to the new body, even Lambert initially although he refused to attend. To the old councillors were added Thurloe and, in December, Richard Cromwell, a clear hint about Cromwell's intentions concerning the succession. The other additional places were left unfilled.

Filling the Upper House proved much more difficult. The responsibility was entirely the Protector's, for, after much fierce debate, it had been decided that appointments to it should not be subject to parliamentary approval. Critical parliamentary scrutiny would discourage candidates, and as many MPs would be aspirants parliamentary participation in selection would involve conflicts of interest. The Protector laboured for months to perfect a list of sixty-three nominees. Even then only forty-two accepted. Weakening the prestige of the new body was the absence of members of the old peerage, for although Cromwell nominated seven only two accepted: Thomas Bellasis, Lord Fauconberg, the Protector's new son-in-law and the impoverished Yorkshire peer, Lord Eure.[13] Fauconberg's uncle, the Earl of Warwick, although by now a close friend of Cromwell and supporter of the regime, declined, as did Manchester who had consistently refused to take part in any government after the Regicide. Mulgrave's refusal was probably due to age and infirmity. Philip Lord Wharton was inclined to accept but was finally persuaded to decline by Lord Saye. Saye had two sons in the new Upper House, Nathaniel and John Fiennes, but was himself firmly committed to the restoration of the Stuarts. Lord Broghill accepted appointment as an Irish member but Lord Cassilis bluntly rejected his appointment for Scotland. Some nominees would accept but would never attend because their duties kept them abroad: Henry Cromwell in Ireland, Montagu at sea, Monck in Scotland and Lockhart at the Paris embassy. Some nominees were surprising choices. The ageing William Lenthall, the former Speaker in the Long Parliament, was a late addition to the list and in his joy urged Sir Arthur Hesilrige to accept also. Hesilrige, the most prominent of the excluded members of 1656 and no friend to the Protectorate, was presumably included in the faint hope of buying his support. He firmly declined, and this might have warned Cromwell of trouble to come. Many of the members who had taken part in the debates on the *Humble Petition and Advice* had opposed the creation of a 'Lords' House', finding a Protector easier to swallow than this echo of ancient privilege. However, its supporters felt that a constitutional review of parliamentary legislation was needed, not least because during the sitting a huge body of legislation (mainly confirming Protectorate ordinances) had been passed in such haste that many bills could not have been read by members who voted for them. However, the Protector and his advisers should have reflected that the creation of the Upper House would have removed about thirty supporters of the new constitution from the Commons when it resumed. Meanwhile the defeated opposers would be reinforced by a much larger number of the 'excluded', who were now returning, led by ardent Republicans like Hesilrige and Thomas Scot. The new constitution was certain to come under rigorous scrutiny, particularly the Upper House.

Parliament resumed on 22 January although, as usual, many members turned up late and the Upper House was never to achieve an attendance of more than thirty or so. Cromwell greeted them with an amiable speech, briefer and more general than in the past, leaving the foreshadowing of parliamentary business to others. The pattern of events was soon clear. The Republicans seemed determined to wreck the constitution by making the Parliament unworkable, endlessly debating the issue of the Upper House rather than settling the desperate finances of the Protectorate. Although they had not the wit to grasp it, they were undermining not just the Protectorate which they loathed but the Republic to which they were devoted, and increasing the probability of a Stuart restoration in the long run. They had forgotten nothing, forgiven nothing and learned nothing. Hesilrige would narrowly escape the hideous death which overtook other Regicides after 1660 but he deserved to share their fate if only because of his reckless, destructive opposition to the one regime which might have brought the Republic long-term stability. Cromwell made a final attempt to turn the tide by a forceful and pertinent speech to both Houses, reminding them of the desperate financial needs of his government, but the opposition resumed their baneful blethering. Finally, his patience at an end, he resolved to send them packing and with an impulsive haste reminiscent of his dismissal of the Rump in 1653, rushed to Westminster with a few life guards at his side. Fleetwood begged him to reconsider but the Protector called him 'a milksop' and declared that 'as the Lord liveth I will dissolve the House'. Having summoned them to the Upper House from a session in which they had resumed their endless debate on what the Upper House should be called he delivered a blistering speech in which he pointed out that during the sixteen days they had sat they had caused more disquiet and disaffection in the country than had occurred during months of parliamentary recess. The Upper House they claimed to dislike had been created not by him but by Parliament in the *Petition* and not on a basis of 'lordship' or titles but as its nominees valued a Christian and an 'English interest', men of their own rank and quality, who would be true to the old parliamentary cause. The Parliament's endless bickering had cloaked attempts to subvert the army and to bring in a 'commonwealth' again, by which some 'tribunes of the people' should 'rule all' (a scarcely veiled reference to Hesilrige and Scot). If this was their aim it was high time to end their sitting and he declared the Parliament dissolved. 'And let God be judge between you and me.'

Cromwell's accusation that the Parliament had sowed disaffection abroad had some basis. A petition had been circulating in London, supported by Fifth Monarchists, sectaries and disaffected officers and soldiers, which called for the abolition of the Protectorate and the restoration of a single chamber parliament (really only a restoration of the Purged Parliament) with complete sovereignty and no written constitution with its tedious checks and balances. To guard against the Presbyterianism of men like Sir Arthur Hesilrige, who were bound to loom large in such an assembly, complete freedom of conscience must be guaranteed. Its promoters claimed that thousands signed it but they must have formed a coalition which would have fallen apart once in power, for although united in the things they opposed they were disunited in their objectives. Its promoters intended to present it to the Commons on 4 February. The night of the 3rd was disturbed by rumours of plots and risings. This would not have disturbed the Protector's sleep normally because although risings were rare plots were endemic. However, the progress of the petition brought a genuine crisis which moved the Protector to sweep away the institution which the petition addressed. The Republicans believed that the dissolution was a triumph for them, demonstrating that Cromwell ruled only through the power of the sword. In a sense they were right, but they were much to blame that this should be so, for they had cast away a genuine opportunity to establish a parliamentary republic under a hereditary head of state, rather like the Dutch Stadtholder. Moreover they had not weakened the power of the sword, for the disappearance of Parliament did not cause the Protectorate to totter. They had forgotten that however hateful they found the power of the sword it was a real power. Far from rising against the most successful soldier England had ever known the army closed ranks behind him, and agitation among the soldiers for a return to a Commonwealth faded away as the defiant or disconsolate Parliamentarians left London. It was soon clear that the Republicans had no more to hope for than the Royalists so long as Oliver Cromwell lived. The Protectorate's real weakness was that the old general's life was now on the ebb.

All through its final months Oliver's Protectorate, despite the final accomplishments of Cromwell's foreign policy, the Peace of Roskilde which by bringing peace to the Baltic favoured English trade, the acquisition of

Dunkirk, the powerlessness of Spain to restore Charles Stuart by force of arms, the close alliance with France, a darker thread poisoned the Protector's happiness. The failure to achieve a stable constitutional settlement based on a parliament which could and would vote a sufficient revenue for the government meant that the fatal paradox of rule by the sword remained. The Protector could not rule without the support of the army, could not collect the monthly assessments which kept the state going without its help, could not hold Ireland and Scotland without its massive presence there, could not personally survive the plots and conspiracies and Royalist hopes of a restoration without its pikes and muskets. Yet the longer it survived the deeper in debt the regime became and the harder it became to borrow from the City. The Protectorate's taxes came in surely and efficiently but they were set too low and came in too slowly, and loans were vital to bridge the gap between expenditure and receipt. By the summer of 1658 the Protectorate was £2 million in debt and the clerks of the Exchequer's gloom deepened when they found that Dunkirk was going to cost the government a further £70,000 a year to maintain. Not even peace with Spain would solve the problem nor a massive reduction in the armed forces, for these would only halt the increase of the debt. Further Herculean efforts would be needed to reduce the debt itself. Although the able men in the government laboured on during those final months, their leader seems to have drifted. Only news of his regiments in France could stir him from his lethargy, for their welfare and achievements meant much to him. Otherwise he drifted towards death, although this is more obvious to posterity than it was to contemporaries. Perhaps a contributing factor was personal bereavement. Through that hot July his much loved daughter, Betty Claypole, endured a prolonged and painful death by cancer which ended early in August. This so prostrated her father that neither he nor Elizabeth Cromwell nor his daughter Mary Fauconberg could even attend the funeral.[14] He never fully recovered. George Fox saw him riding with his life guards in the park at Hampton Court on 20 August but he wrote, 'I saw and felt a great waft of death go forth against him and when I came to him he looked like a dead man'. He was sick again the next day with a fever, almost certainly malarial (diagnosed then as 'a bastard tertian ague') complicated by a severe attack of the stone. He was removed to Whitehall to be closer to his doctors. It was soon clear that his case was desperate, for a severe septicaemia from a stone-caused infection in the kidneys and bladder had combined with debilitating fever. On 28 August 1658 England was struck by the greatest storm she had endured during the past hundred years, tearing down groves of trees, demolishing church steeples, sinking ships. By 3 September, the portentous anniversary of Dunbar and Worcester, it had blown away easterly and his astounded subjects discovered that the Protector's life had departed with it.

CHAPTER FOURTEEN

The Fall of the Swordsmen

Obedience is my great principle and I have always and ever shall reverence
the Parliament's resolutions in civil things as infallible and sacred.

General George Monck

He is a black Monck and I cannot see through him.

Lord Mordaunt to Charles II[1]

Richard Cromwell, the Protector's eldest son, now succeeded to this
increasingly bankrupt regime. Thanks to Cromwell's capacity for
procrastination and reticence it has been disputed whether he actually
named Richard Cromwell his successor, but the balance of evidence strongly
favours it.[2] Never given an army command or a significant civilian post,
Richard had been living obscurely as a Hampshire squire. Oliver had
tended to disparage him as lazy, although since he gave Richard no
opportunity to be busy he gave him no opportunity to shine. In fact during
his brief Protectorate he revealed that he was more politically able than is
suggested by his nickname, 'Tumbledown Dick', and showed more
awareness of the country's needs than the experienced men who bickered,
postured and intrigued about him. Richard even demonstrated that if the
army had let him he might have made the Protectorate work as it had been
designed to work: as a tripartite government with responsibilities shared
between Protector, Council and Parliament, something his father had never
achieved. He made tactical errors but he was undone by lesser men of
blinkered vision who persisted in self-indulgent ambition, greed or in
clinging to ideological positions which had lost touch with reality. Within a
year and a half many of them would pay dearly and some would suffer
horribly for their failure to free themselves from these fetters.

Meanwhile the junior officers of the New Model Army regarded Richard
with surly suspicion as an unreliable outsider. Even a soldier like Henry
Cromwell had proved a friend to Presbyterian Irish landowners but no
friend to the sects. What hope was there from his civilian brother?[3] As for
the soldiers, although many were individually devoted to one or other of
the sects, their prime obsession was their pay, as it always had been. As one

observer cynically noted, 'the Good Old Cause was now money'. Pay was months in arrears and even if more regularly paid it would have been inadequate because bad harvests had recently driven up food prices to levels not seen for almost a decade. The soldiers had loved Oliver for his victories and for his sake had accepted the Protectorate, had forgiven unpopular policies and even, despite much grumbling, endured their increasing arrears. Nevertheless those rankers and junior officers, even some of the colonels, who were most politicized and most committed to various sects, had deeply disliked the monarchical flavour of the Protectorate and had resented those officers most identified with the Protector. These politically active regiments, unfortunately concentrated around London, even before Cromwell's death had been indulging in subversive politics at camp meetings. The most reliable commanders and the most disciplined regiments were distant in Scotland and Ireland. These politicized soldiers were soon agitating for redress of grievances while their officers were demanding that Richard should surrender command of the army to one of the Grandees. The most significant Grandees were now his brother-in-law Fleetwood and his uncle by marriage Disbrowe, of whom at least Disbrowe resented Richard's sudden eminence. From head to foot the Army in England was becoming unreliable because it felt alienated from a regime, which in the form established by the *Humble Petition and Advice* had been forced on it by a civilian Parliament.

To the surprise of many Richard immediately displayed his mettle, making sensible concessions yet retaining all the Protector's real power. He appointed his brother Henry Lord Lieutenant of Ireland thereby making Henry's military authority more complete. Richard could never match his father's calculated blend of terrifying outbursts of anger and old soldier joviality but he won over his senior officers with charm and tact. He appointed Fleetwood army commander and promoted him to lieutenant-general but retained the supreme command himself. This included the power to grant commissions and to dismiss the disloyal. However, in granting commissions he promised to take the Grandees' advice. He won the personal loyalty of such major-generals as Goffe and Whalley and maintained his father's close relationship with Monck in Scotland and Montagu at sea. To smother the embers of discord among the ranks he increased pay rates and organized a small reduction of the year-old arrears.

These successes were overshadowed by the government's desperate need for revenue. Only a parliament could reform the Protectorate's finances, as Oliver had always known, although he had never managed to persuade one to do so. Richard must now make the attempt. Although the Upper House was unchanged the Parliament which assembled on 27 January 1659 was not elected under the terms of the *Instrument of Government*. For reasons now unknown the government reverted to the old constituencies, which meant that a majority of the House was borough members. Since the Commons still contained the Irish and Scottish members it had an unprecedentedly large membership of 549. Inevitably many members, perhaps a third, lacked parliamentary experience. The government's clients and supporters largely got in but once again the government's best debaters were in the Upper House. Meanwhile the government's bitterest enemies won election, including Hesilrige and Scot and several other Republicans from the Purged Parliament, all experienced in seizing control of debate. An unexpected supporter of Richard's Protectorate proved to be Lambert, elected for Pontefract.

The government members in the House had learned something from Oliver's Parliaments and tried to steer the debate in useful directions. They found it hard going because the Republicans were trying to frustrate them and the bulk of the members, conservative country gentlemen much like the members of the two previous Parliaments, had no relish for being led. The tactic of the government leaders should have been to enlist their support for government business in return for guaranteeing them support for their private bills on local issues, but such parliamentary sophistication was beyond them. Nevertheless the government had some early success and the 'monarchy without a king' constitution began to work. The Commons accepted the Upper House and, grudgingly, the presence of the Scottish and Irish members. The Protector's command of the armed forces was confirmed, and a committee was established to discover the true horrors of the financial situation so that it could be remedied. Richard could congratulate himself on two months of modest success in the House. It proved only the calm before the storm. The Protector was trying to drive the coach of state with two unruly horses, Parliament and the army, who disliked sharing the same shafts. The squirearchy was ready to accept the political situation under Richard which it had never accepted under Oliver, but the qualities which made Richard acceptable to the Presbyterian country gentlemen – above all that he was not a Swordsman – made him unacceptable to the army. Richard had temporarily won the cooperation of the Grandees, even of the Council of Officers, but he had little hope of winning the politicized junior officers and he could not win the soldiers without money to pay their arrears. The Republican MPs had been undermining the soldiers' loyalty by spreading propaganda accusing Richard of hostility to the sects, of aspiring to monarchy and of planning to disband the army. To undermine the radical officers and soldiers Richard needed to pay his soldiers' arrears. Parliament must agree to levy a greater tax burden, and here the parliamentary horse jumped the traces. When the House discovered that the revenue had an annual shortfall of £330,000, that the accumulated debt stood at £2.5 million and was steadily rising, and that the soldiers' arrears amounted to £890,000, it preferred disputing the figures to remedying them.

As days drifted by and Parliament continued to procrastinate Richard knew that the army's patience was becoming exhausted. His error was to attempt to defuse the army rather than to establish the government's grip on the Commons. He soon persuaded the House to vote that the Council of Officers should only meet with Parliament's permission and that all officers had to sign a declaration against coercing the Parliament. Richard then told the Council that it must disperse and its members rejoin their regiments. Fleetwood and Disbrowe would not permit Richard to emasculate the army politically by dispersing its officers. They called for the dissolution of Parliament and assembled all soldiers quartered around London to be ready to advance on Westminster. Richard responded by summoning troops to his own rendezvous, expecting that at least the regiments commanded by colonels loyal to him would rally to his call. The colonels remained loyal but the soldiers simply marched off to join their comrades. They had all been infected by the propaganda of the Republicans against Richard and were as disenchanted with the third Protectorate Parliament as the Grandees. They dreaded power passing into the hands of a civilian government for fear of disbandment before their arrears had been met, and feared a persecution of the sects. They still dreaded being left to wander home without an act of indemnity to protect them from vengeful prosecutions or lawsuits.[4] Power now shifted from the Protector to the Council of Officers, and Richard, furious but impotent, had to grant a dissolution of Parliament while the Council rid itself of officers who were Richard's warm supporters while restoring officers cashiered by his father.

Dissolving Parliament simply slew the one instrumentality capable of solving the financial problem without replacing it with another which might prove more effective. Like Cromwell in 1653 Fleetwood and Disbrowe had ended a government without first deciding what should take its place. The difference was that the Republic's finances were in a worse case and there was no man-of-destiny to put the applecart back on its wheels. Nor did the Grandees have much leisure for calm deliberation, for although Fleetwood and other conservative officers would have kept the Protectorate, they were beset by radical officers, backed by their hungry companies, who demanded the restoration of the Purged Parliament. Hesilrige and other Commonwealthsmen had been making this improbable solution enticing to junior officers and soldiers. They with silver tongues, so apt with promises, so poor at fulfilling them, assured the soldiers that the restored Parliament would perform prodigies: pay the soldiers, protect religious liberty, maintain the army, and pass an act of indemnity. Their eloquence and the soldiers' gullibility doomed Richard. The Council of Officers agreed that the Protectorate and Upper House would be abolished and the Purged Parliament reinstated if the Republicans agreed to establish a senate in which Swordsmen would be well represented, and Richard was enabled to retire honourably with a palace and a pension. Richard's hopes for rescue by either Henry Cromwell's Army of Ireland or Monck's Army of Scotland proved vain. Henry's soldiers were fifteen months in arrears and their only hope of payment lay in London, not in a dubious civil war. Monck's soldiers were better paid but many of his junior officers sympathized with the aspirations of their comrades, so Monck hastened to assure Parliament of his loyalty. Over the coming months he would work to strengthen his regiments' loyalty to him still further, but this process was at first threatened by Parliament ordering him, despite his protests, to purge his army of 'Cromwellian' officers and replace them with sectarian radicals from the south. He could do no more than keep the sacked officers in Scotland and hope their replacements would be slow to arrive. If the qualifications of a man-of-destiny include knowing how to wait then George Monck was well qualified indeed. After three months Richard Cromwell, furious but helpless, retired into private life, as did his brother Henry. When Montagu returned from the Baltic, where he had taken a squadron to show the flag, he also chose to retire. Montagu and even Henry would have served most governments which could guarantee stability and solvency but they drew the line at that discredited old pantaloon, the 'Rump' – an opprobrious term which was to be increasingly applied to the Purged Parliament.

The exact size of the now assembling Purged Parliament is disputed but a leading authority on the fall of the Republic observes that of the old Purged Parliament dismissed by Cromwell in 1653 only ninety-one MPs were still available, of whom only seventy-eight were willing to resume their seats and only sixty-five of these turned up.[5] Certainly the revived Purged Parliament was very small, much smaller even than the Nominated Parliament, and therefore could organize itself much more easily than one of more than five hundred. During its first weeks Parliament acted speedily and effectively. However, its very effectiveness in matters which interested it naturally caused the army radicals to expect it to accomplish the things which interested them. In fact although the parliamentary leaders made gestures towards the sects – freeing Quakers from prison, for example – they did little to satisfy radical wishes. Moreover, they offended the Grandees by ignoring their demand for a senate or for a pension for Richard. Parliament resurrected the old Council of State, and packed it with its own members but included several senior officers. The Speaker replaced Fleetwood as the bestower and withdrawer of army commissions, and several Cromwellian officers were sacked. They were replaced by Republicans or at least men the Council of State believed it could trust, among them Admiral John Lawson, the Protectorate's old enemy, who was given command of the fleet. The Speaker was William Lenthall, who now bemusedly found himself replaying an earlier role from his long career. (Speaker of the Long Parliament between 1640 and 1647, and in 1653, he had knelt at the feet of Charles I when he arrived to arrest the five members in 1642.) This smaller Purged Parliament was even more dominated by Presbyterian-Republicans led by Hesilrige and Scot. It also included John Lambert, soon to be restored to his commission, a man with no respect for the Purged Parliament and who would have had no objection to seeing the Protectorate restored, so long as he was installed as the Protector. Present also was Sir Anthony Ashley Cooper. The future Earl of Shaftesbury, still serving an invaluable apprenticeship in politics, attended the House despite a long-disputed election and was appointed to the Council.

Good relations between Parliament and army would not survive long. Hesilrige and his associates had forgotten no past injury and remembered few of their own errors. The Commonwealthsmen were determined to be the sole power in the land, with the army as no more than a tolerated subordinate whose loyalty was demanded but not earned. Parliament's chief objective should have been to raise revenue, no matter how harsh the tax bill, so as to pay the soldiers' arrears. Then companies could have been disbanded quickly and past debts and annual expense reduced together as the army diminished. This Parliament failed even to attempt. The explanation that the members could not face the unpopularity which such a heavy tax burden would bring seems unpersuasive. Nothing could have made this miserable vestige of the Long Parliament more unpopular than it already was. Electors resented the fact that Parliament frustrated all attempts of purged MPs to resume their seats, using the despised soldiers to keep them out. No by-elections were called for seats vacated by death since 1653 because the Republican leaders knew that only their enemies would win election. Further unpopularity was due to a mistaken belief that this Parliament was intensely radical and would bring all manner of Anabaptist horrors on the country while undermining such pillars of property and the social order as the Common Law and a national church. These fears were due to the propaganda disseminated among the soldiers when the Republican leaders were enticing them during Richard's Protectorate. Still, despised though it was, the Purged Parliament was the only civilian government the country possessed and therefore preferable to the universally detested army. Indeed the unpopularity of the army may have disguised from Hesilrige and Scot their own vulnerability, believing that since the Parliament was the Swordsmen's only civilian friend the Swordsmen must stick with it. It should have occurred to them that this cut two ways: since the Swordsmen were *their* only friends it behoved them to stick fast to the army.

The warning signs for the army appeared early. The Parliament's response to the soldiers' perennial concern about indemnity produced an act which had too many loopholes to satisfy them. Lambert complained of this to Sir Arthur Hesilrige who complacently declared: 'You are only at the mercy of the Parliament.' To this Lambert pertinently rejoined: 'I know not why they [Parliament] should not be at our mercy.'[6] Pertinent indeed, for Lambert knew and Hesilrige should have remembered that the Parliament could not dissolve a single company without the Swordsmen's consent, whereas it would take no more than a squad of musketeers to sweep away the despised 'Rump'. Even in June Parliament's demise was being confidently predicted. The army was then briefly distracted by a minor crisis from the other side of politics. Some Royalists could not reconcile themselves to government by this Regicide-infested parliamentary remnant and felt impelled to action by its very unpopularity. The result was a series of minor plots across England which failed to coalesce in a general rising. However, Sir George Booth, a Cheshire landowner, put an army in the field which seized Chester and temporarily controlled Cheshire and southern Lancashire, until Lambert by a rapid lunge north reminiscent of 1651 dispersed the Royalists at Winnington Bridge on 19 August. Fleetwood was believed to have despatched Lambert because he dared not go himself leaving Lambert politicking in his rear. To such depths of division had the Swordsmen sunk only a year after the death of their great commander.

The rivalries among the Grandees combined with the ignominious defeat of Royalism may have led Parliament's leaders to believe that it could crush the Swordsmen's unacceptable pretensions to an equal share of power. Certainly it reacted with extraordinary tactlessness to the soldiers' belief that the settlement of their arrears should be their reward for defeating the Royalists and that it was high time Parliament delivered the reforms for which they had called so long. Instead the members had confirmed the Protectorate religious settlement, favoured clergy who supported a national church (although with tolerance for Independent congregations) and worst of all, Parliament had enforced the payment of tithes. It was time to remind the members who had brought them to Westminster. The result was the so-called Derby Petition which was drawn up and signed by the soldiers of Lambert's regiments. The petition called as usual for pay but also demanded a number of reforms and the creation of a senate to limit the power of the Commons. Parliament angrily debated not the demands but whether to punish their initiators (which it wrongly assumed to be the Grandees), although finally it confined itself to an official rebuke. Lambert, Disbrowe and some other senior officers protested at Parliament's response and, mistakenly fearing that this signified a resolution to move on Westminster, Parliament panicked. In defiance of common sense and past experience the members stripped Lambert, Disbrowe and seven other of the more political generals of their commissions, expelled Lambert from Parliament and ordered his arrest. Fleetwood's post of commander-in-chief was put into commission and while the seven commissioners included

Fleetwood they also included his enemy Hesilrige. Parliament also hastened through a bill invalidating all ordinances or patents issued or legislation passed or grants made since the coup of 1653 unless formally and specifically approved by them, and declared that it was treason to levy taxes without parliamentary consent. While the bill was certain to be unacceptable to the army the declaration was supposed to ensure Parliament's survival since without it there would be no hope of raising taxes to fill the pay-chests. Lenthall then called on supposedly loyal regiments to defend Parliament from the wrath of the Grandees, with the same result which Richard had so recently experienced. A few bewildered officers turned up at Parliament's summons but their soldiers voted with their feet in favour of Lambert. The following day the Grandees dispersed the members and took government back into the hands of the Council of Officers, a body even more inadequate for the responsibility than was Parliament.

This was the most politically meaningless, the most self-indulgent, the most irresponsible military *putsch* of the Interregnum. In that of 1653 Cromwell may have acted under a misapprehension about what the Purged Parliament was trying to do but at least his action had a public cause to drive it. In 1659 the army acted for no loftier reason than to save the careers of some of the senior officers, although the move was supported by their juniors and soldiers because of their anger against Parliament for its procrastination and for disappointing their hopes. This patently self-interested act dismayed and divided the civilian radicals who had been the army's sole supporters. When the Council of Officers set up a Committee of Safety to run the country it was composed of the Grandees and a majority of civilians, few of whom were genuine radicals. Sir Henry Vane was one, but most of the others were akin to that conservative weathercock, Bulstrode Whitelocke. There were also two London aldermen, a wholly ineffective gesture towards reconciling the City. The junior officers at once reiterated their old demands for the abolition of tithes and Chancery but the Committee would do nothing so drastic in the absence of some form of parliament. Parliament had only just begun to tackle the deficit before its dismissal, so the financial situation continued to deteriorate. No money could be raised in the City until a legislature had voted taxes as security for the loans. Spanish privateering continued to deplete English commerce so that Customs revenue decreased while the navy, with no funds to keep it at sea, lay helplessly at its moorings. England needed both peace and a parliament. The Committee of Safety could provide neither.

A further element made the crisis far worse, indeed disastrous for all Republicans, civilian or military, could they but see it. The army, for so many years that constant in a divided polity, was now showing signs of breaking up with several garrisons protesting against Parliament's dissolution and demanding its recall. However, these local symptoms of disaffection paled into insignificance when weary riders on lathered horses arrived with despatches from Scotland. On 20 October General Monck had issued a public proclamation which called for the restoration of the Purged Parliament. Throughout the summer the thoughts of men from all sides of politics had repeatedly turned to George Monck. As early as July Charles II had written to him that should he decide to declare for the monarchy Charles would leave it entirely to Monck to determine the best time to do so. This letter was carried by Monck's kinsman Grenville, but characteristically Monck would not permit Grenville to deliver it until he considered it opportune to receive it. Although Monck was one of the few unreservedly Cromwellian senior officers still in command he was named a commissioner when Parliament put the post of Commander-in-Chief into commission. When the Grandees retaliated by dismissing Parliament Fleetwood had felt it necessary to write to his subordinate a disingenuous explanation of the coup. When he heard of Monck's demand for the Purged Parliament's recall Lambert also thought it politic to write justifying the Grandees' actions. (He also sent agents to Scotland to try to undermine Monck's authority but they were promptly arrested or otherwise frustrated.) It soon became clear that the Grandees faced the fearsome prospect of an army of several thousand well equipped veterans, led by one of the best soldiers in Europe, marching south to restore their enemies.

The disparity in size between Monck's army and the army in England gave little comfort. Discipline and loyalty had sadly deteriorated in the latter which seldom saw its officers because they were politicking in London, while the Grandees had become as remote as monarchs. Poor pay irregularly paid, long arrears and unkept promises, officers more interested in power than in the day-to-day welfare of their men, produced an army which was deteriorating into an armed rabble, bad-tempered, fearful, scenting betrayal from those who had neglected it. Such an army becomes alienated from the civilians among whom it must live, for the soldiers know the civilians hate their exactions, their unpaid requisitions, their billeting backed by no authority but the sword. Morale worsens and the downward slide becomes more difficult to reverse. Lambert, for all his ambitions, was a professional to his fingertips once he was in the field, but he had been sulking in his Wimbledon manor since early 1658 and his regiments had deteriorated in his absence. Monck also had an advantage which far outweighed numbers: the ordinary, unpolitical soldiers were united in wanting their condition bettered, their arrears paid and their status elevated above that of beggars and brigands. Only a parliament bringing stability and increased taxes could provide this, and Monck had declared for the restoration of Parliament. Thus far his stated objective and their need marched in step.

In Monck's army the regiments marched where their commander's finger pointed so long as it was not in a Royalist direction or in one which meant fighting their own comrades. In Scotland Monck was almost a Protector, but this did not prevent him from acting like the best type of regimental officer. He had scarcely spent a day away from his soldiers since his arrival in Scotland and they trusted and respected him. He had always been able to feed his troops, pay them regularly, house them in military garrisons and pay their Scots suppliers. Scottish taxation, the rates heavier than in England, had been regularly collected, and the government had sent a substantial addition to his war-chest when it feared that Booth's rebellion might trigger a Scottish Royalist rising. The soldiers knew they were better off than the rest of their comrades and knew who to thank for it. There were about a hundred radical officers who were not prepared to follow his lead, but Monck toured his regimental headquarters with a force of picked men to arrest them. Some fled south, others he cashiered. As Monck purged his regiments of dissidents he filled their places by reappointing officers Parliament had earlier ordered dismissed but who were still in Scotland. He filled the rest by internal promotions and issuing field commissions.

The irony of the situation was that the political crisis would now be shaped and indeed largely resolved by an officer who had never been a politician. George Monck had been a professional soldier for about thirty-four of his fifty-one years. His military education was largely acquired serving the Dutch Republic from 1629 to 1637 where, as he had told Speaker Lenthall the previous June, 'soldiers received and observed commands but gave none'. He believed that a soldier's duty was to obey and that this applied to lieutenant-generals as much as to common soldiers. He believed that the civilian government should be the master and abhorred the notion of a government of Swordsmen, especially radical sectarian swordsmen. He had supported the Protectorate not only out of loyalty to Cromwell but because he believed that it represented the likeliest way to achieve a predominantly civilian government, and had supported the *Humble Petition* because of its monarchical tendencies not in spite of them. In September 1658 Lord Colepeper, then in exile with Charles II, had remarked that the best chance for his master's restoration lay with Monck. He spoke more than he could then know because Monck would have done nothing for Charles if the Grandees and the third Protectorate Parliament had permitted Richard's Protectorate to flourish. There is some dubious evidence that Monck may have contemplated joining Booth, but it is difficult to believe that Monck would delude himself that his army would follow him in a Royalist rising.[7] After Booth's defeat Monck had briefly offered his resignation to the Purged Parliament but as abruptly withdrew it. Now the Protectorate was gone, the Parliament was locked out and

Monck had had enough. A conservative in both religion and social policies, as might be expected of one who was both a senior officer and a landowner, he seems to have dreaded the radical changes in religion and the menaces to the safeguards of property which might follow Parliament's extinction. On the other hand he must have distrusted Parliament because of the propaganda with which it had showered the regiments on behalf of radical reform and sectarian religion and because of the officers it was determined to force upon him.

Monck rowed towards his objectives on muffled oars. Few politicians since have matched his capacity for silence, for secrecy, for opacity. Lord Mordaunt's reaction that he was 'a black Monck' and he could not 'see through him' reflected a common experience. Historians, who at least know what transpired, are unable to agree what his ultimate objectives were when he declared for the Purged Parliament – so the confusion among his contemporaries is hardly surprising.[8] His friends, relations and his chaplain-biographer would later claim that his intention from the first was to restore Charles II, but as by then Charles was comfortably restored this is unsurprising. However, it does not follow that the claim is untrue. One expert doubts the claim because in October 1659 too many things had still to happen over which Monck had no control before even he could bring about the king's restoration.[9] Certainly Monck was a practical, pragmatic, professional soldier. That does not mean that he had never considered matters relating to statecraft. If he had never taken part in politics that does not mean that he had not closely observed the turbulent politics of the era through which he had lived. Significantly, while a prisoner in the Tower in 1645, he had written a manual for officers, *Observations on Military and Political Affairs* (although it was not published until after his death) which combined general reflections on war and politics with more technical instruction on infantry tactics and siegecraft. The former were written with lucid brevity and a flavour of Machiavelli.[10] Although he was never more cool, even phlegmatic, than when he was in physical danger, storming a town or commanding a naval battle, he knew enough to approach the morass of politics warily. No man was less likely to commit himself to a political leap in the dark. However, his steadfast reserve and refusal to reveal his hand ensured that he made no commitment at all save for the Purged Parliament's restoration and the ending of the rule of the Swordsmen.

His lack of open commitment, however, does not mean he had no options in mind. He later claimed to have risked everything to save the country from the 'fanatical party' who 'blasphemed against Christ'. The reference is partly political, partly religious. By the blasphemers he primarily meant the Quakers, who had been as troublesome in Scotland that summer as they had been in England. Attempts have been made to argue that the 'Purged

Parliament had become a bulwark against the religious radicals, and this explains Monck's support for it. The problem here is that it was this very body which had made him sack officers of his own political, and indeed religious, inclinations and replace them with the sectarian radical officers he detested. Parliament might be to the 'right' of the sectarian General Fleetwood but it was to the 'left' of General Monck. It seems reasonable to suppose that Monck had rather larger long-term objectives in mind when he declared for the Purged Parliament. That declaration, as we shall see, led to a series of events by which the Swordsmen fell and Parliament was restored – and all while Monck was still north of the Tweed. If that was his sole objective why march his army to London? In view of what happened later it seems reasonable to suppose that Monck hoped all along not simply to restore the Purged Parliament, but the Long Parliament itself by making it possible for the secluded members to take their seats. If the victims of Pride's Purge once regained the Commons chamber a 'free' general election would shortly follow and in view of the mood of the country such a free election meant a royal restoration. In this sense at least it can be argued that Monck envisaged a process which would probably end in the king's return, although this is far from claiming that he was sure it could be carried through successfully. The problem, of course, was the army, and not just the regiments commanded by Lambert, Fleetwood or Disbrowe but the regiments commanded by Monck himself. The doubts about Monck's objectives are due to his need not simply to deceive his opponents in England but also his own soldiers in Scotland and later on the march south. However, if Monck did not intend to betray the Purged Parliament by bringing about the admission of the excluded it is reasonable to ask why he came south at all, as we shall see.

He was, however, not yet ready to march south. Once again he demonstrated his capacity for waiting, watching and meticulous preparation. Lambert had gathered an army together by reducing the number of regiments around London and hastened north, but winter had descended on the Border and even Lambert shrank from a campaign in that inhospitable climate. He preferred to station himself first at York and then at Newcastle to see what negotiations might achieve. Monck was happy to send agents to London to negotiate with Fleetwood and the Committee of Safety, for this would win time for Lambert's idle regiments to suffer a further loss of morale. Monck was still purging dissidents and negotiating with a convention of the Scottish estates that there would be no rising in Scotland behind him when he marched south. Such a rising would unite the wavering army of England and he would be overwhelmed by superior force. Meanwhile he wrote pacificatory letters to England, assuring London's Lord Mayor and aldermen that he simply intended to restore the authority of Parliament to whom he would leave the governance of the country. Letters, of course, came across the Border to him, asking questions, making overtures, but all sank into the bottomless well of his reserve. His refusal to commit himself beyond the recall of the Parliament inflamed resentments and rivalries among his opponents, for none could be sure that another was not secretly intriguing with him. Increasingly the common soldiers were saying they wished they were with General Monck for then they should be paid and have some hope of their arrears, whereas in England they were called no better than 'rogues and traitors' – a clear symptom of low morale in the face of civilian detestation. Nevertheless at first Lambert believed that he was winning the waiting game for some of Monck's soldiers deserted to him, probably from fear of finding themselves on what they assumed would be the weaker side. They found it a poor choice whether for food, pay or quarters. Gradually this flow of deserters was reversed, and Lambert found his army melting as some soldiers slipped away north and others to their homes, particularly after Monck advanced to Coldstream in December.

Monck instructed his envoys to negotiate for the recall of the Purged Parliament with security for it to sit until 6 May 1660 and for a guarantee that no extra-Parliamentary taxes would be levied. The Council of Officers must approve Monck's purging of officers and they must agree that its future decisions could not be binding without the consent of the officers of the Scottish and Irish armies. Monck must have known that these demands would never be conceded, but their very unacceptability gained time. Monck's wrath was great when he learned that his commissioners had lost the plot by signing an agreement on 15 November. They withdrew the demand for Parliament's immediate recall and agreed that a Council of the Army be summoned with delegates from every region, including Ireland and Scotland, to draw up a new constitution. They had even agreed that a joint commission of seven officers should investigate all recent dismissals including Monck's purge of dissidents. The gullible commissioners had been assured by the Grandees that Monck's army was disintegrating and that whole squadrons of cavalry were deserting south to join Lambert. Monck repudiated the agreement on 24 November, the day following Lambert's arrival in Newcastle.

Meanwhile the Council of Officers and its creature, the Committee of Safety, found themselves in shoaling waters. The process which Monck had launched was unfolding. On 3 December officers of the Portsmouth garrison, inspired by Monck's declaration, declared for Parliament and took control of the port. Companies sent to suppress this mutiny defected to their comrades on 20 December. This blow was reinforced by the defection of the Channel Fleet which sailed for the Thames where its commander, Admiral Lawson, announced it would impose a blockade until Parliament was recalled. Meanwhile in various parts of the country the Swordsmen's authority was challenged by civilians demanding the recall of Parliament, the readmission of the excluded members of 1648 or even the holding of a free election, which was virtually a call for Charles's restoration. The City of London now once more demonstrated its political weight. In the City attachment to the Republic appears to have been in proportion to the degree of wealth. The Lord Mayor was a weathercock who would always lean to the strongest but the aldermen were heavily involved financially with the Republican regime either as creditors or investors in former Church or Crown lands. By contrast the less affluent members of the Common Council, elected in December, opposed paying taxes to the military usurpers, called for a free parliament and hoped that Monck could bring this about. The young men of London, especially the apprentices, whose predecessors two decades earlier had been the storm-troopers of revolution, were now the army's open enemies. On 5 December they rioted, drove out isolated groups of soldiers and closed the gates of the city. When Colonel Hewson broke down the Temple Gate and forced his way in with a company of infantry the soldiers were bombarded with brickbats and chunks of ice and opened fire, killing two apprentices and wounding others. Hewson soon found himself indicted for murder. As for the Grandees, they knew that although they might temporarily cow the City with their soldiers its hostility and determination to withhold taxes until the Swordsmen yielded to the civil power meant that they were doomed. Bulstrode Whitelocke actually besought Fleetwood to accept the inevitable and try to bring back the king on terms and so save himself. Fleetwood wavered but after an interview with Disbrowe and the others came out wringing his hands and crying that he could do nothing because they had promised Lambert to come to no important decision without his agreement.

Lambert had more to worry about than broken promises. Recalled south with his army to stabilize the situation around London he found himself with no army to lead, for it melted before his eyes until he had little more than a company of the 12,000 men he had led north. Fairfax had emerged from retirement, after secret negotiations with Monck, and had raised Yorkshire against the army and in favour of Parliament (although he had tactfully excluded from his forces members of notoriously Royalist families). Lambert found his best regiments had fled to join their old commander. Only with difficulty did he succeed in escaping down the London road with a few of his staff. In London the so-called Council of the Army had met and tried to resolve the constitutional situation. At first they rejected the suggestions of the Council of Officers and tried to go their own way (which moved Fleetwood to send some of them back to their regiments). They then took up the Council's notion of a senate along with a full parliament, although how its members were to be chosen or vetted was never explained.

This parliament actually got as far as having its writs drawn up but they were no sooner issued than recalled. This constitution-mongering was an empty show, for the Grandees quickly recognized that the situation was beyond their control. On 23 December the Council of Officers met for the last time, wasting this historic moment on a futile ratification of the paper constitution. The Grandees would soon be leaving London or under virtual house arrest, desperate, disillusioned and powerless. On 24 December the Speaker received back the key to the Parliament House as regiments around London declared for the Purged Parliament. A minority of MPs assembled furtively and hastily that night to thwart the intentions of some secluded members to assert their right to take their seats at Parliament's reopening. The lack of dignity, the determination to keep out the secluded members, the indifference to the people's desire for a free parliament, all boded ill for the future of the Parliament. (By the end of January declarations or petitions for either a free parliament or the readmission of all excluded members had been drawn up in ten counties and the Exeter apprentices had rioted in sympathy with the London apprentices and for the same cause.)[11] Significantly it was during Parliament's last days that the insulting nickname, Rump, which it has never since lost, was most widely used.

The crisis appeared to be at an end with the radicals having the army where they had always wanted it: under civilian control. Sir Arthur Hesilrige with several supporters dashed up from Portsmouth, appearing to acclamation in the House still in riding habit. It was probably his greatest moment but it was not destined to be prolonged, and his own inability to learn from past errors would be partly to blame. Meanwhile he and his supporters employed their unexpected restoration, which they owed largely to Monck, to emasculating the army. Hesilrige sought to protect the Grandees from the members' vengeance, but they were ordered out of London and remained under threat of arrest. Sir Henry Vane was expelled from the House over Hesilrige's objections along with a few others who had cooperated with the military government. While Monck sacked radical officers in Lambert's regiments the Parliament dealt with southern regiments itself. All this strengthened the hand of those members who were hostile or indifferent to reform and weakened those who were committed to it, for the officers who had clamoured for reform earlier in the year now found themselves impotent civilians. No less than three-eighths of the officer corps, including half the field officers and two-thirds of the captains, disappeared into civilian life.[12] Many survivors were transferred to other regiments or garrison duties and most soldiers found themselves commanded by strangers, especially in the regiments about London.

If Hesilrige's party noticed that the effect of the purges was to make the greater part of the army weaker and the smaller part commanded by Monck correspondingly stronger they maintained a brave face. It was a consideration which might have crossed their minds because, with the crisis over and the Parliament installed, General Monck had at last crossed the Tweed. Without Monck's declaration for the Purged Parliament it would not have been restored, not least because his threat to come south had drawn Lambert and 12,000 men north, fatally weakening the Grandees. Moreover, it had encouraged Lord Fairfax, a man whose name was a legend to the veterans among the soldiers, to declare himself for Parliament and seize York. The northern capital from now on would be in the hands of those who desired a free parliament. Monck's declaration had also encouraged Lawson to lead the fleet to a blockade of London and had encouraged the very damaging mutiny on the Purged Parliament's behalf at Portsmouth, where the governor was a friend of Monck. The Parliament had good reason to be grateful to George Monck, but they no longer needed him in London. Hutton states that Parliament ordered him to London.[13] However, when Lenthall wrote to Monck informing him of the Parliament's restoration he said nothing of Monck's coming south, an extraordinary omission if they wished him at the capital. Acting on his own initiative Monck ordered his leading regiments across the Tweed on 1 January. He received an order to come south only when he was already 150 miles on his journey. That order looks more like a desperate effort to assert authority by ordering the general to do what he was already doing. Reflecting its anxiety the House sent Thomas Scot and Luke Robinson to Monck's headquarters to try to learn what he was up to and to ensure he made hostile responses to the petitions for a free parliament which he received on the march. Monck's replies to the petitions with which he was bombarded were more equivocal than hostile and may have been inspired more by the prejudices of his own officers than by the presence of his 'minders'. Londoners to whom he wrote privately were left in no doubt of his views on religion and while he expressed hostility to a Royalist solution he would hardly commit to paper any other opinion before he could judge the situation in London for himself. He publicly declared that to readmit the excluded members of 1648 would be unacceptable to the army and cause dangerous divisions in the nation. However, his qualifying remark that Parliament would become free 'naturally' by filling the gaps through free elections (that is, by-elections) was unlikely to reassure Hesilrige's faction if they weighed its implications. It revealed that Monck believed the Purged Parliament in its present form, a beggarly fifty-five members, should not continue long. Worst of all when Scot and Robinson offered him the oath against Charles Stuart and government 'in a single person', which the radicals were then trying to impose on their fellow MPs, he refused to consider it before he reached London.

The journey between York and London took three weeks of hard uncomfortable marching on snowy roads. As the regiments drew nearer

Hesilrige must have felt apprehensive, for all his confident assertions that Monck was 'our man'. Monck is sometimes depicted as simply an opportunist with neither plan nor precise objective. However, it should be noted that when he had to make a crucial decision he invariably made the right one. He *de facto* surrendered the Scottish civil administration to Scots under his old Royalist opponent Glencairn, on condition that Scotland would remain peaceful (although he sent back two regiments from York once he was sure all danger from Lambert was passed). He only advanced into England when he knew Lambert's army was collapsing to avoid fighting between different formations of the army. Learning that the Parliament was peacefully restored and that the navy had intervened under Lawson, which suggested that his work was done, he made the remarkable decision to cross the Tweed and march on London. With tens of thousands speculating about what he would do when he got there, including his own officers, he continued to conceal his intentions under an affable mask of loyalty to Parliament, devotion to a national church and, more vaguely, the eventual election of a proper parliament. When he reached the environs of London he demanded that the regiments quartered there should be sent into the provinces, broken up and widely dispersed. This would not only leave his 5,800 men in military control of London, Parliament would be unable to recall the regiments it had sent out for they would no longer be whole formations. (For example, the six troops of Hesilrige's own cavalry regiment were divided between Oxford (two) and Reading, Worcester, Gloucester and Hereford.)[14] This was acceded to although some units mutinied on behalf of their Good Old Cause – pay – and had to be bought off before they would march out. On 2 February Monck's regiments reached Whitehall, watched by a largely silent populace, although some shouted for a free parliament. The disciplined efficiency of these legionaries compared to the disillusioned rabble that they were replacing must have given both the members of the Parliament and the Parliament's enemies among the citizens pause for thought. As that normally unostentatious man rode on a well-mettled horse at the head of his life guards, attended by trumpeters, footmen and grooms in red livery decked with silver lace, and followed by about a hundred men of quality mounted or in coaches, many onlookers must have wondered if a new Protector had arrived.

CHAPTER FIFTEEN

The Last Act

> I am engaged in conscience and honour to see my Country freed . . . from
> that intolerable slavery of a sword government, and I know England cannot,
> nay will not endure it.
>
> *General George Monck*[1]

Monck's first priorities were to maintain the trust of both City and
Parliament while gaining an accurate assessment of the situation he faced.
In the month since the Rump Parliament had been restored it had
succeeded in alienating many who had called for its restoration and, despite
its small size, had divided into factions. The two factions can be described,
although they would not have so described themselves, as the followers of
Sir Arthur Hesilrige and the friends of George Monck. The first were the
supporters of diehard Republicanism, the second were the moderates like
Sir Anthony Ashley Cooper who could happily contemplate the admission
of the excluded members or the calling of a free election. Although
Hesilrige's voice appears dominant his will did not automatically prevail in
the House. He had not been able to save Sir Henry Vane from expulsion
(for joining the Committee of Safety) and he and his faction were
infuriated to discover that their opponents could baffle their efforts to
impose the oath renouncing Charles Stuart or government by a single
person or with an 'upper house'. They had first tried to impose it on the
new Council of State but although twelve took it, nineteen, including Ashley
Cooper, refused, while the bill to impose it on the House failed to pass. The
House had, however, united to declare on 3 January that the conservative-
minded had misrepresented them. Tithes would remain, 'fanatical
principles' would not be encouraged, they did not mean to perpetuate
themselves or to govern by force. Rather the Commonwealth was to be re-
established with a representative parliament, while the army, much reduced,
would be under civilian control. All this was very well. The problem was how
to achieve a political settlement by restoring Parliament to its old
dimensions without holding a free election which would almost certainly
doom the Commonwealth. It was simple to resolve that vacancies in the
Purged Parliament due to the deaths of members since 1653 should be
filled, or to resolve that all the seats of the members purged in 1649 and not

since readmitted should be declared vacant and draw up writs for by-elections. It was another matter to determine the qualifications of parliamentary candidates and voters. It was 3 February before the House managed to resolve that the House should be 'filled up to 400 members, with seats distributed as in 1653', and even then it had to be left to a committee to decide how they should be filled, the very crux of the matter. With this dilatory progress the House would take months to expand much beyond its current numbers. It was soon manifest that neither the country in general nor the City of London in particular was prepared to wait. The provinces were less threatening because distant and geographically divided. London, however, was at the door. In February 1660, though, Parliament had George Monck's regiments to guard it – so long, of course, as he had not decided that the City's objectives coincided with his own.

The Hesilrige faction now demonstrated that they had learned nothing from the fate of their military opponents. When the City's government showed that it had no control, indeed sought no control, over those within who called for a free Parliament, it ordered Monck to march on the city, to pull down its chains, to wedge the portcullises and to destroy its gates, a terrible humiliation. Even worse, he was ordered to arrest the leaders of the Common Council. (The lack of opposition to these reckless courses from the moderates in the House strongly suggests that they wished their opponents to have every opportunity to destroy themselves.)[2] The City hoped that Monck would protect them and disobey his orders. However, Monck knew that he must go no faster than his officers and men would follow. Indeed it would be better if he seemed to move so slowly and reluctantly in the direction at which he aimed that his officers would find themselves urging him on rather than holding him back. He therefore carried out part of his instructions, pulling down the gates at the Temple, removing the chains (his officers acting with increasing reluctance when they witnessed the fury and distress of the citizens) and then halted the work, informing the Speaker that he felt it was not necessary to go further at that time. Hesilrige, who had greeted his obedience with the cry 'All is our own, he is honest', was infuriated at this manifestation of military independence and demanded the order be carried out and that even the portcullises be destroyed. In his protest to the Speaker Monck had also called for the admission of the excluded members, echoing the demand of the Common Council. Hesilrige now leapt into a pit he had dug for himself. He declared the Common Council dissolved, although the only power capable of dissolving it was Monck's soldiers.

All the while Monck was holding lengthy meetings with his officers, making them aware of the Rump Parliament's intransigence and arrogance, their disdain for the liberties of the subject, until they were as angry against the Rump as the citizens who thronged to watch the soldiers' every move.

Monck, of course, was besieged by advisers from all sides. They included his senior officers, his brother-in-law Dr Clarges, his chaplains, his wife and leading members of the Common Council, crypto-Royalists and excluded members of parliament, several of whom had gathered in London in the hope of recovering their seats. He listened patiently but largely in silence to all they had to say. He continued to give his officers the impression that they were urging him forward rather than that he was dragging them in his wake. As for his soldiers, their enthusiasm for the Rump Parliament had ebbed swiftly since they arrived in London. The Parliamentarians who gave them their orders they saw as tyrants; the Londoners they were meant to cow into submission they saw as an embattled citizenry contending for their liberties. Incredibly Hesilrige decided that this pregnant moment was a favourable time to rush through a bill depriving Monck of his post of commander-in-chief and put it into commission. (The Rump had appointed Monck acting commander-in-chief in November.) Only a man who had lost touch with reality would have so gratuitously offended the commander of the only force which could preserve the Rump from the fury of the populace. Monck knew that now he could act. Having received advice from Colonel Morley, the governor of the Tower, that the soldiers he and Colonel Fagg commanded would support whatever course he chose, Monck resolved to move his regiments back into the City the next day and called a meeting of fourteen of his most trusted officers at six in the morning of 11 February. Gathering in the frosty darkness at his house he set before them the heads of a letter he proposed to send to the Speaker. This was the crucial moment in his relations with his regimental officers. He had gently steered them down the path he wished them to follow while concealing their ultimate destination. Would they baulk at this crisis? In fact they made no demur and all signed the letter. Two colonels carried his bombshell to Westminster and Monck sent word to the Guildhall that he and his army would quarter that night in the city.

Monck's momentous letter was both a protest and an ultimatum. It protested against the use of force against the City; against the presence in the House of men impeached of treason (a reference to Ludlow and three companions who had been accused of treason in Ireland after a conservative coup there by Monck's ally, Sir Charles Coote) and against leaving Vane and Lambert at liberty; and that Parliament had countenanced the recent venomous petition from Praise-God Barebone which proposed the forcing of a quite unacceptable oath on all who served the state. The ultimatum came at the end. Monck gave the Rump six days to issue the writs for the promised election with the implication that they would be dismissed if they disobeyed. Even if the writs went out, the letter made clear, the Rump must not sit long for 'the time hastens wherein you have declared your intended dissolution'. The people must have assurance 'that they shall have a succession of parliaments of their own election'. Meanwhile he intended to quarter his forces in 'that great city, formerly renowned for their resolute adhering to Parliamentary authority'.[3]

Although the Rump Parliament continued to sit that day all men knew it was doomed. As Hesilrige, beside himself with rage, left the house after the reading of Monck's letter his arm was seized by a Quaker printer, Billing, who cried contemptuously: 'Thou man, will thy beast carry thee no longer? Thou must fall!' The 'beast' was now London's darling and would soon be a national hero. Barebone's windows were smashed yet again, the magnificent peals of bells of the City's churches rang out, and bonfires burned triumphantly. Pepys saw thirty-one from just one vantage point. The loathing of the Rump was given vivid expression as rumps were roasted more for display than consumption, 'tied upon sticks and carried up and down' as Pepys reported, and 'the butchers at the May Pole in the Strand rang a peal with their knives when they were going to sacrifice their rump'. He saw the soldiers everywhere given drinks and the people cried out 'God bless you!' as they walked in the streets. Indeed Ludgate Hill was 'a whole lane of fire' from bonfires and roasting rumps; there were fourteen fires between St Dunstan's and Temple Bar.[4] Monck was greeted with loud cheers whenever he appeared. It was all very different from the situation of Fleetwood's regiments in the previous October when soldiers dare not venture into back-alleys for fear of being murdered and when, the crowning humiliation, the Swordsmen dare not wear their swords in the streets. All this adulation and relief might seem surprising because to all appearance the Rump still ruled. Certainly writs were prepared for elections to vacant seats, but, as the Speaker mildly pointed out, this process had been going on prior to Monck's letter. Lambert's arrest was ordered but he was in hiding. Vane was again ordered to leave London. Otherwise little might seem to have changed. Hesilrige and Scot even persisted with their bill to put Monck's position in commission with a quorum of which Monck need not be one. However, the bonfires and feasting were not ill judged. Hesilrige and Scot with their bill were busily rearranging seating at the captain's table as their ship slowly sank beneath them. The populace knew that the force which had been the Rump's instrument of tyranny over the Londoners was now London's shield against the Rump, and that the Rump was simply like the corpse which twitches spasmodically even though life has departed.

Although for some days Monck deceptively persisted in issuing disclaimers against admitting the excluded members, he had been secretly conferring with excluded members who were rapidly gathering in London. He finally came out in the open and arranged a meeting between Purged and Rumpers which Hesilrige furiously declined to attend although the moderates were happy to cooperate. Finally Monck informed the City authorities that he intended to seek the return of the excluded members and the winding-up of the Long Parliament, to be followed by that free election which vast numbers of his fellow countrymen continued to demand. Excitement once more became intense in the streets, coffee houses and taverns of the City. The writs for the elections to vacancies which the Rump had finally decided on were supposed to go down to the country on 20 April but Speaker Lenthall, normally a timid man, stubbornly refused to send them on the transparently disingenuous excuse that the excluded members might sue him for filling their seats. Professor Woolrych persuasively suggests that he was acting on instructions from Monck who knew the excluded members would carry out their coup the next day. On 21 February, just ten days after Monck's garrisoning of the City, more than seventy of the two hundred or more secluded members still extant entered the House unhindered by the guards and took the radicals by surprise. The game was over. Even without moderate support, which was instantly forthcoming, they had the numbers to outvote the Rump's members. Since these men had all been purged because they had wished to preserve the monarchy of Charles I, albeit under constitutional constraints unknown to the Crown before the Great Rebellion, there could be no doubt that England was marching towards the king's restoration. Monck had agreed to their return, indeed had master-minded it, but on his conditions: first he must be confirmed as commander-in-chief (which was instantly done), the Long Parliament must be wound up and writs issued for an election no later than 21 April, and the election would be free (except that former Royalist officers and their sons were supposed to be disqualified from candidature). He told them he believed that the temper of the nation was opposed to a restoration of the bishops and would prefer a religious settlement along moderate Presbyterian lines. In this he appears to have been continuing his unswerving policy of refusing to move forward faster than the people, certainly his officers and men, could be expected to follow. The Convention Parliament, once elected, he declared, should arrange to confirm all sales of land, both Crown and ecclesiastical, and organize the paying of all soldiers' arrears while providing for an army capable of maintaining order. The unspoken implication was that at this point the king might return on suitable terms. In the meantime he opposed the restoration of the House of Lords. It would have alarmed too many of the soldiers and worse, its reappearance might have tempted the Long Parliament dangerously to prolong its existence. Monck would be on tenterhooks until the election to which he had long aspired was held, for once a freely elected Parliament was in Westminster his long sojourn behind a shield of stealth, secrecy and dissimulation would be at an end. He could at last rest from the stress of pulling off the near-impossible: pursuing a path down which not even his soldiers would have followed him had they realized early enough where they were being led, and achieving a civilian political solution in a state dominated by the suspicious, hostile army.

The Long Parliament, at last reconstituted, although still only a fraction of the size it had possessed in the days of its glory, quickly set up a new Council of State served by two secretaries, one of whom was John Thurloe. The lack of devotion to republicanism of the Council's members may be deduced from the fact that six of them would soon be raised to the peerage by a grateful Charles II. While many of the diehard Republicans refused to attend the House several faces from the past resumed their prominence, among them Lord Fairfax, Sir Harbottle Grimstone, Sir William Waller and that irrepressible Royalist pamphleteer, William Prynne, whose outrage at being excluded time had never mellowed. While they adjusted to the reins of power after their decade in the wilderness Monck was steadily working to ensure that the soldiers would accept whatever settlement the Parliamentarians devised. Regiments were dismembered, resolutely Republican officers were retired. A group of officers waited on him seeking a guarantee that the monarchy would not be restored, Colonel Okey speaking at length about the dangers facing their religious and political liberties and that the army must intervene if there was any such attempt. Monck would have none of it, pointing out the disaster that would befall the country if the Long Parliament was interrupted by the Swordsmen yet again. If they thought he would take over the government of the country as Protector they deceived themselves. They must no longer meet in military councils 'to interpose in civil things'.[5] He ordered them back to their regiments and in the first week of April all officers found themselves compelled to sign an engagement binding both them and their soldiers to obey their superiors unquestioningly, to hold no political meetings and submit to whatever settlement the incoming Parliament should devise.

Monck's control of the army was soon put to the test. On 10 April Lambert escaped from the Tower and summoned loyally Republican regiments to meet him at a rendezvous heavy with symbolism, the battlefield of Edgehill. However, Monck sent Colonel Ingoldsby (who had a Regicide past to redeem and little enough time in which to do it) with trustworthy regiments in pursuit. Too few of the 'true believers' turned up even to make a skirmish, let alone a battle, although the defiant Okey was among them. Lambert was soon ridden down and having been sentenced to stand beneath the Tyburn gallows as a humiliation for himself and a warning to others, he was returned to the Tower. The Long Parliament also tamed the militia, sweeping aside the Republican Commissioners the Rump had appointed. In their place appeared men who had served Parliament in the first Civil War but who had never sought the Revolution of 1649. They even included that recent rebel Sir George Booth. The Commissioners cheerfully signed a declaration which asserted that the war waged against Charles I had been 'a just and lawful war' but no loyalty to the Republic could be expected from them. To the horror of good Commonwealthsmen Parliament voted to affirm the right of the House of Lords to constitute a part of future parliaments. Meanwhile the Long Parliament had tried to establish a moderate Presbyterian religious settlement by ordering the adoption of the Westminster Confession and replacing the 'Triers' with central commissioners on Presbyterian lines. This was presumably an attempt to confront the coming parliament with a *fait accompli* but it was ill-judged, arousing the resentment and suspicion of the large majority of English folk who were either still wedded to Anglicanism and the Cranmer prayer book or to the congregationalism of the sects. On 16 March, three weeks after its coming together and twenty years after its first assembling, the Long Parliament finally dissolved itself. No one was more relieved to see it depart than Monck himself. His extraordinary achievement in winning a settlement to which the majority of the Swordsmen were opposed was nearly complete.

With the army under control the time had come for Monck to negotiate with another old soldier. He at last allowed his kinsman Grenville to deliver Charles II's letter which he had been carrying about for several months. In general it promised him great rewards but allowed him a free hand. On 16 or 17 March Monck finally told Grenville that he had committed himself to the king's restoration, although it took a further ten days, the time Grenville spent making his stealthy way to Brussels, before the king joyfully received the news. Monck had characteristically put nothing in writing, and so it was through Grenville that he begged the king to forgive his past military career and assured him that, although he had been unable to do him any useful service until now, he had always been faithful to him in his heart. This assurance must have entertained His Sardonic Majesty – although he would forgive any man anything who would restore him to his throne, and he would have found it particularly easy to forgive Monck's military exploits since they were chiefly against Scots Presbyterians. However much historians may argue about what Monck's long-term objectives were after the fall of Richard Cromwell or even after his declaration for the Rump, the king never displayed any doubts about who was chiefly responsible for his unexpected restoration. It was to Monck that the king felt the deepest gratitude and it was Monck who would be the most richly rewarded.

The events of the winter of 1659/60 had stunned the gloomy little court at Brussels like a thunderclap. A brief surge of optimism after Cromwell's death had been damped by Richard's painless succession, only to be revived by Richard's fall and the summer of plotting culminating in Booth's rebellion. The fact that the army, despite its internal divisions and declining discipline, could still brush aside the best efforts of the Royalists with contemptuous ease had extinguished all hope. It was painfully clear that the Royalists could never restore the king. Now it seemed there was a real possibility that a New Model Army general might pull it off by exploiting his control over the very instrument which had destroyed Charles's father and which had driven Charles himself from his kingdom nine years earlier. At first it had seemed doubtful that the enigmatic Monck wanted to do this, and even less likely that he could do it even if he wanted to. However, as the weeks passed, Royalist spies sent report after report of strange accidents and frustrations and disasters which successively befell the king's enemies, all in some way connected to the obscure proceedings of General Monck. At the little court conflicting fears and hopes reached an unbearable intensity. Now Monck had thrown off the mask, at least in the privacy of the king's quarters. He was also tendering cogent advice. The king should leave Brussels, a city notable for being Spanish and Catholic and repair to Breda, a tactfully Protestant haven in Holland. From there he should offer a general pardon and indemnity, a substantial degree of religious toleration, and promise to accept a land settlement devised by Parliament. This would ensure that men who had invested in Crown or ecclesiastical estates would not be terrified at the prospect of a restoration. The king acted promptly on this advice and in Breda Edward Hyde, the king's chancellor and closest adviser, began to draft the document which became known as the Declaration of Breda and which embodied Monck's suggestions. However, these proceedings were kept a close secret from all the court save for Hyde, Sir Edward Nicholas, the king's surviving Secretary of State, and the Marquess of Ormonde.

England now found itself undergoing a free general election for the first time for twenty years. Of course, even in this momentous election there were many constituencies in which there was no contest because the gentry established beforehand who should represent them. Nevertheless in some constituencies, usually in the boroughs, there were fierce contests and while sometimes these reflected local rivalries, in others they undoubtedly involved Royalists, Presbyterians and Commonwealth's-men. Although supposed to be debarred from candidature some sixty men who were either former Royalist soldiers or their sons were elected. The local sheriffs and electors simply ignored the regulations. The fights between Independents and Presbyterians on borough hustings helped the cause of Anglicans who openly called for the king's restoration. In many seats the election crowds bellowed 'no swordsmen, no swordsmen' and indeed former Swordsmen who hoped to pursue political careers found thin pickings. In Middlesex the crowds shouted 'no Rumpers, no Presbyterians that will put bad conditions on the king', a slogan to chill the hearts of all Puritans, Presbyterian or Independent.[6] No Rumper or prominent Independent won a county seat, while of the Rumpers of 1659 only sixteen were successful in boroughs, and these were chiefly moderates who had supported Monck like Sir Anthony Ashley Cooper. Moderates who were too conspicuously anti-monarchist like Chief Justice St John were defeated. Regicides, men associated with military rule, men prominent for their republicanism, and prominent sectaries, felt the cold wind of rejection. Ludlow, Scot and Luke Robinson were elected by towns in which they were still influential but the results were challenged by their opponents who confidently expected Parliament to reverse the result. Lambert stood from prison but was defeated. Hesilrige and Vane did not even stand. Presbyterians were elected in substantial numbers, but those who had hoped to impose a Presbyterian religious settlement on Charles II largely met defeat. There was not a vestige of party organization, not even as much as had been mustered on behalf of the government in the three Protectorate Parliaments. In spite of this, or perhaps because of this, the Convention Parliament was probably remarkably representative of the wishes of the country's citizens for an era in which the majority were not enfranchised.

It was clear when the Parliament assembled on 25 April that it was determined to restore the king. Those diehards who had hoped to vote out any Royalist interlopers were quickly disillusioned. It was the few Regicides and sectarian radicals who found themselves bundled out. Moreover the House of Lords also assembled, at first only former 'Parliamentarian' peers because Monck politely but firmly held back for a few days the 'young lords', the heirs of Royalist peers. However, once he decided it was safe for them to be admitted they were quickly joined by the older Royalist peers until all were present save those still sharing the king's exile in Breda. Otherwise only the bishops were missing for they could not enter the Lords until the Bishops' Exclusion Act of 1642 was repealed (which it finally was on 30 July). It was beginning to dawn on the Presbyterian Parliamentarians that Monck's objective was to restore the king on easy conditions rather than with the constitutional shackles which they still wished to impose on him. When they protested Monck pointed out that time was of the essence and that he could not guarantee to hold the army back for ever. They slowly realized that although conservative Presbyterians were probably a majority of the Commons they were becoming as powerless to control events as the arch-Republicans had been before them. The latter were indeed in the toils. Ludlow had briefly hoped to raise the country for the Good Old Cause and had appealed to Hesilrige to join him, but he found Sir Arthur utterly crushed, sitting with his head in his hands and crying 'we are undone, we are undone!' Ludlow soon realized the Commonwealth's cause was hopeless and retired to the country. Hesilrige threw himself on Monck's mercy, who jested that if he gave him tuppence he would save his life so long as Hesilrige retired quietly to his country house, which that broken man gratefully did.[7]

On 1 May Sir John Grenville, the king's emissary to Monck, appeared before the Lords with letters from the king to the speakers of both Houses and a copy of the Declaration of Breda. It contained the four conditions which Monck had recommended: a free and general pardon for all save those which Parliament should except; religious liberty for those of tender consciences; Parliament to determine the thorny issue of title to confiscated estates; and payment of the army's arrears. The Declaration of Breda was a well drafted document which exhibits the political skills of Monck, on whose advice it was based, and Edward Hyde, Nicholas, and Charles himself, who all cooperated in its composition. The king knew that its terms gave him room for manoeuvre, particularly on religious matters, and that the reference to 'parliament' so far as the land settlement was concerned need not necessarily mean the Convention Parliament.[8] Moreover, by appearing to place all matters in the hands of Parliament, the anxious would be reassured that the Great Rebellion had not all been for nothing and that this second Charles was a constitutional-minded king. It also ensured that the king would gain the credit for any clemency shown, while Parliament would be blamed by all those who were dissatisfied with what happened later, and they were certain to be legion.[9] Undaunted, both Houses welcomed the Declaration and on the following day voted 'that, according to the ancient and fundamental laws of this kingdom, the Government is, and ought to be, by King, Lords and Commons'. That May Day was celebrated by the Londoners with bonfires burning, bells pealing, wine and ale flowing in rivers. A week later the celebrations broke out again as the king was proclaimed with the old pageantry. On 10 May the Presbyterian leadership made one last effort to revive the constitutional conditions they had sought to impose on Charles I in 1648, but once again Monck intervened. Opposing any such delay he moved that commissioners be sent to Holland immediately to bring the king home. The House responded with vociferous cheering. General Monck's long march was over. The Republic was at an end.

Epilogue: The King Returns

> ... the King ... was received by Generall Monck with all imaginable love
> and respect at his entrance upon the land at Dover.
>
> *Samuel Pepys, 25 May 1660*

> I went out to Charing Cross to see Major-Generall Harrison hanged, drawn
> and quartered – which was done there – he looking as cheerfully as any man
> could do in that condition.
>
> *Samuel Pepys, 13 October 1661*[1]

The king landed at Dover on 25 May, a bright, sunny morning, with breeze
enough to set waving bravely the many flags, banners and bunting on ship
and shore. He was met by Monck and other dignitaries, including the Mayor
of Dover, and was accompanied by the Duke of York and Edward Montagu,
the last general-at-sea to be appointed, who, with the old Anabaptist
Lawson, had taken the fleet to Scheveningen to bring his master home.
King and admiral travelled on the *Naseby*, which had been renamed the
Charles at the instance of the king and the Duke of York. After dinner on the
23rd the brothers had sat at the quarterdeck table and bestowed more
suitable names on several ships. Parliamentary victories or personalities
were transformed into relatives, courtiers or other Restoration symbols, so
that the *Richard* became the *James*, the *Speaker* became the *Mary*, the *Dunbar*
(although not in the flotilla) the *Henry*, the *Winceby* the *Happy Return*, the
Wakefield the *Richmond*, the *Lamport* the *Henrietta*, and the *Cheriton* became
the *Speedwell*. There would be time enough to take down the elaborately
carved arms of the Commonwealth or of the Protector from the sterns and
replace them with the royal coat of arms.[2]

This quick renaming of the ships the king saw about him, indeed the fate
of the great Cromwellian fleet as a whole, seems symbolic of how the
Restoration would go as England transformed itself back into a monarchy
again. The king was coming home not as result of some successful Royalist
rebellion or conspiracy nor, most fortunately, as a result of an invasion by a
Spanish army (although he had long dreamed of such possibilities). He had
been restored to his throne by one wing of the New Model Army and he was
brought home by the New Model Navy. That navy's ships would meet a
variety of fates, some renamed, some retained, some laid up, some hastily

scrapped – just as would the leading figures of the Republican era now slipping away into the long night of history. Some Regicides like Ludlow would replace the king and his court in exile in Europe. Three found refuge in Massachusetts, John Dixwell, Edmund Whalley and William Goffe, where any requests for their arrest and deportation fell on deaf ears. In Hadley, Massachusetts, there is a strong legend that during an Indian attack years later the now venerable Goffe emerged from a cave in the hills and employed all the skills of a New Model colonel to lead the town's militia to victory. As Parson Weems said of George Washington and the cherry tree, it is a story 'too true to be doubted'. Thomas Scot fled to Brussels, an improbable refuge for a Puritan Regicide, but surrendered there to the English ambassador and returned home to face his prosecutors. 'I bless His name that He hath engaged me in a cause not to be repented of', he asserted as he composed himself for the same hideous death as General Harrison. Hugh Peter had not signed the warrant but he had rejoiced at the Regicide, preached often against the king, and shared Scot's fate. Death had already removed Cromwell, Ireton and Bradshaw, so vengeful Royalists dug up their tombs in Westminster Abbey and exhibited their remains like common criminals, and so less forgivably they treated the remains of Admiral Blake. In general the most resolutely Puritan in religion and ideologically consistent in politics were most at risk. The most unscrupulous – or politically realistic – tended to survive. The king left it to Parliament to decide who should be spared, who should suffer death, no doubt cynically amused by the indecent enthusiasm with which the time-servers denounced their former colleagues as they sought to ensure their survival.

Only nine Regicides suffered the severest penalty for treason, General Harrison and Sir Henry Vane being the most prominent; others were hanged, some were imprisoned like Henry Marten, who lived out his years in Chepstow Castle. A remarkable number were forgiven, among them Hesilrige, and Colonel Ingoldsby who hunted Lambert down at the last. Ingoldsby's explanation that he had signed the king's warrant under duress with Cromwell holding down his hand was graciously believed despite the bold flowing signature which silently testified against him. Lambert's uninvolvement in the king's trial and execution, thanks to resolute Royalist resistance at Pontefract Castle, saved his life, although he was initially condemned for treason. He spent much of his life immured with his wife on Drake's Island in Plymouth Sound where in 1683 the king and the Duke of York chatted affably with him for more than an hour. All these were the scrapped and the laid up among the prominent architects of the Republic. Others fared better. Admiral Lawson, the former Anabaptist plotter, was knighted. Montagu became Earl of Sandwich, and several members of the Council of State gratefully took their seats in the House of Lords. For George Monck, principal architect of the Restoration, there were greater honours. The minor Devon squire, the professional soldier whose realism made him turn his coat at the war's end, the general whose ferocious assault on Dundee brought horrors long remembered, became Duke of Albemarle. For the rest of his life the grateful king addressed him with familiar affection as 'uncle'. The king had cause to be grateful. Although restored by some of his 'enemies' Monck had ensured that the terms were very mild. As a result men would look back on the period between 1642 and 1660 and be unable to discern any benefits gained from all the slaughter, destruction and social upheaval. There were constitutional gains but these had been achieved by 1641. The only justification for the Civil War was to defend those constitutional gains and to preserve the lives and property of the junta of politicians who had achieved them. The Republic need not have been a mere aberration, no more than a fascinating interlude in the history of England and its monarchical form of government, but the manner of the Restoration ensured that it could be little more in the immediate future. Fortunately, the tradition of religious and political nonconformity survived. So also survived the tradition of resistance to the pretensions of centralized autocracy, whether monarchical or oligarchical. That tradition was to prove dynamically salutary in the American colonies a century later, but less dramatically it would inspire much social and political reform from the late eighteenth century to the present day. The limited achievements of the Commonwealth and Protectorate were largely swept away but the subversive ideas which had inspired those governments at their best proved more resistant. Some slept, most went underground, but none perished.

Notes

PROLOGUE: THE REGICIDE
(between pages 1 and 2)

1. For a detailed account of the king's last days see C.V. Wedgwood, *The Trial of Charles I* (1964).
2. Sir Thomas Herbert's main claim to distinction prior to 1649 was that in 1628 he had visited Persia with Sir Robert Shirley and Sir Dodmore Cotton; *DNB*.
3. Princess Elizabeth, aged thirteen, and the eight-year-old Duke of Gloucester, both of whom were in the care of the Earl of Northumberland.
4. Phillip Henry, *Diaries and Letters 1631–96*, ed. M.H. Lee (1882), 12.

CHAPTER 1: THE SWORDSMEN EMERGE (between pages 3 and 24)

1. Rushworth's *Historical Collections* (1703–8), vol. vi.
2. For the origins of the Civil War and Revolution see the guide to Sources and Further Reading.
3. The 'political nation' here includes all capable of participating in parliamentary elections and in county or urban government.
4. For the Scottish Revolution see the guide to Sources and Further Reading.
5. Edward M. Furgol, 'Scotland Turned Sweden: the Scottish Covenanters and the Military Revolution 1638–1651', in John Morrill (ed.), *The Scottish National Covenant in its British Context* (Edinburgh, 1990).
6. For the Civil War see the guide to Sources and Further Reading.
7. For an excellent brief analysis, Austin Woolrych, 'Cromwell as a

Soldier', in John Morrill (ed.), *Oliver Cromwell and the English Revolution* (London, 1990).
8. W.C. Abbott (ed.) *Writings and Speeches of Oliver Cromwell* (Oxford, 1939, 1974) (hereafter Abbott, *W. & S. O. C.*), ii, 310.
9. Ian Gentles, *The New Model Army* (Oxford, 1992) (hereafter Gentles, *New Model Army*).
10. Sir Thomas Fairfax (1612–71) was the son of Ferdinando, second Baron Fairfax of Cameron, a Scottish peer. Ferdinando was himself a parliamentary general and commanded the infantry at Marston Moor. Sir Thomas succeeded as third Baron Fairfax in 1648; *DNB*.
11. For the naval mutiny see Chapter 3.
12. Gentles, *New Model Army*, 286 ff., where a much more detailed analysis may be found.
13. For masterly analyses of the Purged Parliament see David Underdown, *Pride's Purge* (Oxford, 1971) and Blair Worden, *The Rump Parliament* (Cambridge, 1974). See also Chapter 7.
14. The other five serving officers were Major-General Skippon, Sir Arthur Hesilrige, Colonels Valentine Walton, Sir William Constable, and John Jones. The six included Henry Marten, Colonel Hutchinson and Edmund Ludlow. Gentles, *New Model Army*, 313.
15. The peers were Pembroke, Salisbury, Denbigh, Mulgrave and Grey of Wark; Abbott, *W. & S. O. C.*, ii, 14.

CHAPTER 2: THE REPUBLIC AND ITS ENEMIES (between pages 25 and 38)

1. Addressing the Council, 28 March 1649; Abbott, *W. & S. O. C.*, ii, 41–2.
2. John Morrill, 'The Scottish

National Covenant in its British Context', *Nature of the English Revolution* (London, 1993) 117.

3. Its charming full title was *The Hunting of the Foxes from New-Market and Triploe Heaths to Whitehall by Five Small Beagles, Late of the Army*; Gentles, *New Model Army*, 318–19.

4. S.R. Gardiner, *History of the Commonwealth and Protectorate 1649–1656* (London, 1901) (hereafter, Gardiner, *C. & P.*), i, 39.

5. Other Digger communes across ten counties shared a similar fate during 1650. Christopher Hill's *The World Turned Upside Down* (1972), a study of the radical movements of the period, discusses the Diggers sympathetically.

CHAPTER 3: THE NAVY NEW MODELLED (between pages 39 and 56)

1. Michael Baumber, *General-at-Sea: Robert Blake and the Seventeenth Century Revolution in Naval Warfare* (1989) (hereafter Baumber, *General-at-Sea*); Revd J.R. Powell, *Robert Blake: General-at-Sea* (1972) (hereafter Powell, *Blake*) and 'The Siege of Lyme Regis', *Mariners' Mirror*, xx, 1934.

2. Bernard Capp, *Cromwell's Navy: the Fleet and the English Revolution 1648–1660* (Oxford, 1989), 47. My account is much indebted to this definitive study.

3. Appointment as a 'general-at-sea' did not preclude an officer from resuming his military career on land. Blake declined Cromwell's invitation to command the foot in Ireland but Deane commanded the artillery at Wexford, and in 1650 commanded the army in Scotland; Capp, *Cromwell's Navy*, 54.

4. Moulton, who flew his flag in the *Leopard*, had with him the *Bonaventure*, *Elizabeth* and *Adventure*.

5. Rupert's flotilla included the *Ark*, *James*, *George*, *Culpepper*, *Roebuck*, *Blackmoor Lady*, *Ambrose* and *Charles*.

6. R.C. Anderson's two articles, 'The Royalists at Sea in 1649' and 'The Royalists at Sea in 1650', in *Mariners' Mirror*, xiv, 1928 and xvii, 1931 respectively.

7. Revd J.R. Powell, 'Blake's Reduction of the Scilly Islands', *Mariners' Mirror*, xvii, 1931.

8. Revd J.R. Powell, 'Blake's Reduction of Jersey in 1651', *Mariners' Mirror*, xviii, 1932.

9. The others were *Phoenix* (38 guns), *Elizabeth* (36 guns), *Laurel* (36 guns), *Paragon* (34 guns), *John* (28 guns), *Nightingale* (24 guns), *Pearl* (24 guns), *Tresco* (24 guns), *Hunter* (22 guns), *Tenth Whelp* (16 guns), *Eagle* (14 guns). There was also a battery ship.

CHAPTER 4: THE CONQUEST OF IRELAND (between pages 57 and 79)

1. *W. & S.O.C.*, ii, 38.

2. For background and more detailed reading for this chapter see the guide to Sources and Further Reading.

3. W.E.H. Lecky's dispassionate analysis of the claims and counter-claims in his *History of Ireland in the Eighteenth Century*, 5 vols (1892), suggests that at least 4,000 Protestants were murdered and perhaps a further 8,000 died of their privations after being driven from their homes. Of the Protestant revenge, Lecky grimly observed that it was 'difficult to decide where the balance of cruelty rests'. Quoted by P.J. Cornish, *Early Modern Ireland*, 290, 291.

4. James Butler succeeded his grandfather as 12th Earl of Ormonde 1633; created Marquess 1642; created Duke of Ormonde in the Irish peerage 1661, and in the English peerage 1682; *DNB*.

5. Inchiquin, a Royalist, had turned Parliamentarian in 1644 because since Parliament controlled the sea lanes, only they could help the Munster Protestants. Parliament appointed him President of Munster and he gradually

became master of the south of Ireland. He reverted to Royalism in 1648, and fled to France in 1650; *DNB*.

6. For Monck, of whom more later, see Ashley, *Monck*.

7. Armstrong's cavalry, former Parliamentarians who had defected after the Regicide, lost several men as prisoners in a skirmish outside Dublin the previous day, among them Jones's nephew. The implacable general promptly hanged him as a deserter. In London Jones was admiringly compared to Brutus; Gardiner, *C. & P.*, i, 113.

8. After a remarkable career under the Commonwealth and Protectorate this agile survivor would be created 1st Earl of Orrery by Charles II in 1660; *DNB*.

9. Abbott, *W. & S. O. C.*, ii, 142.

10. These Irish numbers were achieved despite heavy emigration. As Professor Gentles points out: 'many of the 34,000 Irish soldiers who would enlist in continental armies during the early 1650s had already departed.' *New Model Army*, 381.

CHAPTER 5: SCOTLAND: THE PRE-EMPTIVE STRIKE (between pages 80 and 95)

1. Archibald Campbell, the Covenanter Earl of Argyle, had been created Marquess by Charles I in 1641; *DNB*. For Jaffray see *Diary of Alexander Jaffray*, 3rd edn, ed. John Barclay (Aberdeen, 1856), 55.

2. For the texts, Abbott, *W. & S. O. C.*, ii, 283 ff., 290–1.

3. Gentles, *New Model Army*, 388.

4. Gentles, *New Model Army*, 387.

5. Sir Charles Firth, 'The Battle of Dunbar', *Trans. Royal Historical Society*, ns., xiv, 36.

6. It is based chiefly on Firth's 'Dunbar', and on the contemporary pictorial plan which illustrates it. See also Gentles, *New Model Army*, Ashley, *Monck*,

and W.S. Douglas, *Cromwell's Scotch Campaigns 1650–1* (Edinburgh, 1898), among other accounts.

7. See Ashley, *Monck*, 81.

8. Abbott, *W. & S. O. C.*, ii, 324.

9. Colonel Strachan, an extreme Covenanter, in a letter to Cromwell a few weeks later; Abbott, *W. & S. O. C.*, ii, 333 n.

CHAPTER 6: THE LAST CAMPAIGN: WORCESTER (between pages 96 and 106)

1. Written in Worcester on 3 September 1651 at 10 o'clock at night immediately following the battle; Abbott, *W.&.S.O.C.*, ii, 461.

2. Gardiner, *C. & P.*, i, 439–40.

3. John Buchan, *Oliver Cromwell* (1941) (hereafter Buchan, *Cromwell*), 334.

4. The march is described in detail in Abbott, *W. & S. O. C.*, ii, 447–54.

5. He escaped to France, but later joined in the Highland rising which was dispersed by Monck in 1654 (see Chapter 10); was created Earl of Middleton 1656; died Governor of Tangier 1674; *DNB*.

CHAPTER 7: WAR WITH THE DUTCH (between pages 107 and 136)

1. For the sources for this chapter see the guide to Sources and Further Reading.

2. Sir George Ayscue (obit. 1671) reappears commanding the Swedish navy in 1658. In 1660 Charles II appointed him a navy commissioner and he was successively rear-admiral and admiral in the Second Dutch War until taken prisoner; *DNB*.

3. I have here largely followed Michael Baumber's reconstruction in *General-at-Sea*, 171–8.

4. A graduate of Oxford and Leyden,

currently the Linacre Reader in Medicine at Oxford, Whistler was successively Registrar and President of the Royal College of Physicians; *DNB*.

5. For the political drama see Chapter 8.

6. *The First Dutch War*, iv, 263.

7. *The First Dutch War*, v, 367.

8. *The First Dutch War*, v, 372.

CHAPTER 8: THE SWORDSMEN TAKE POWER (between pages 137 and 153)

1. Quoted in David Underdown, *Pride's Purge* (Oxford, 1971) (hereafter Underdown, *Purge*), 266.

2. Gentles, *New Model Army*, 413.

3. William Cole, *A Rod for Lawyers* (1659), quoted by E.W. Ives, 'Social Change and the Law', in Ives (ed.) *The English Revolution 1600–1660* (London, 1968).

4. Quoted in Christopher Hill, *Intellectual Origins of the English Revolution* (Oxford, 1965), 264.

5. Hale had been counsel to Archbishop Laud (1643), and had defended Hamilton at his trial for treason (1649). A judge in 1654, MP for Gloucestershire in the first Protectorate Parliament, and for Oxford University in the Convention Parliament of 1660, he was knighted at the Restoration and appointed Chief Justice in 1671; *DNB*.

6. Gardiner, *C. & P.*, ii, chapters 24, 25.

7. Blair Worden, *The Rump Parliament* (Cambridge, 1974) (hereafter Worden, *Rump*), chapters 13–17.

8. Austin Woolrych, *Commonwealth to Protectorate* (Oxford, 1982) (hereafter Woolrych, *Commonwealth*), 67 ff.

9. Gardiner, *C. & P.*, 205.

10. This is based on Edmund Ludlow's account. Ludlow was then in Ireland but received reports from Harrison and others who were present. I can find no evidence that Cromwell used the words

so often quoted (or misquoted) as in Leo Amery's famous denunciation of the Chamberlain government in 1940: 'You have sat here too long for any good you have been doing; in the name of God, go!' Edmund Ludlow, *Memoirs* (ed. Firth) i, 351–5, quoted *in extenso*, in Abbott, *W. & S. O. C.*, ii, 642–3.

11. Quoted in Worden, *Rump*, 380.

12. The conversation with Whitelocke is reprinted in Abbott, *W.&.S.O.C.*, ii, 587–92. For Calamy's tale see Gentles, *New Model Army*, 436.

13. Professor Woolrych finds this story at least credible, but if it happened nothing came of it because the men declined to carry the message. Woolrych, *Commonwealth*, 107–8.

14. Woolrych, *Commonwealth*, chapter 4 *passim*.

15. Woolrych, *Commonwealth*, 153.

16. Quoted in Woolrych, *Commonwealth*, 165.

17. Woolrych, *Commonwealth*, 151–2 and chapter 4 *passim*.

18. For a particularly lively version see H.R. Trevor-Roper, 'Oliver Cromwell and his Parliaments' in his *Religion, the Reformation and Social Change* (1956/1972) (hereafter Trevor-Roper, 'Cromwell's Parliaments').

19. Woolrych, *Commonwealth*, 231.

20. Hale's proposed law relieving indigent prisoners for debt and reforming the system did inspire a very inadequate measure but it emerged from the Prisons and Prisoners Committee; Woolrych, *Commonwealth*, 268.

21. Gardiner, *C. & P.*, ii, 279. Wolseley, a Staffordshire baronet, was also a member of the Council of State. Only twenty-two or three he would be a member of the Protectorate Council under both Oliver and his son, MP for Staffordshire in Cromwell's parliaments, a Cromwellian peer, and a member of the Convention Parliament of 1660. Pardoned at the Restoration he lived to see the Hanoverian succession in 1714; *DNB*.

22. For the end of the Nominated Parliament see Gardiner, *C. & P.*, 278–81, and John Buchan, *Cromwell*, 371. Carew, although a Cornishman, had represented Antony in Devon in the Long Parliament after the Civil War. A Regicide and a member of the Purged Parliament, he was to endure imprisonment under the Protectorate and a much worse fate at Charing Cross after the Restoration; *DNB* and Woolrych, *Commonwealth*, 210–11.

CHAPTER 9: THE PROTECTOR
(between pages 154 and 169)

1. To the first Protectorate Parliament, Abbott, *W. & S. O. C.*, iii, 455.

2. Abbott, *W. & S. O. C.*, iv, 418. Cromwell related this in February 1657.

3. Woolrych, *Commonwealth*, 358.

4. Abbott, *W. & S. O. C.*, iii, 587–8. For the *Instrument of Government* see J.P. Kenyon (ed.) *The Stuart Constitution* (Cambridge, 1966), 342.

5. Woolrych, *Commonwealth*, 379–80.

6. Woolrych, *Commonwealth*, 384–5.

7. Or so a Royalist reported in a letter abroad which was intercepted by Cromwell's Secretary of State, John Thurloe; D.L. Hobman, *Cromwell's Master Spy* (London, 1961), 13.

8. The French ambassador is hereafter referred to as Bordeaux.

9. Ronald Hutton, *The British Republic 1649–1660* (London, 1990) (hereafter Hutton, *Republic*), 59.

10. Roy Sherwood, *The Court of Oliver Cromwell* (London, 1977) (hereafter Sherwood, *Court*); see also Antonia Fraser, *Cromwell: Our Chief of Men* (London, 1973) (hereafter, Fraser, *Cromwell*) chapter 17.

11. The latter was one of the royal estates which had just been sold and so had to be expensively repurchased; Sherwood, *Court*, 17–18. St James's Fields, part of the grounds of Windsor Castle and of Greenwich House,

together with Greenwich House itself, also had to be recovered from purchasers or lessees.

12. Fraser, *Cromwell*, 458, 460. Sherwood, *Court*, 31.

13. For a detailed survey see Sherwood, *Court*, chapters 2, 3 and 4.

14. See Maurice Ashley's introduction to Sherwood, *Court*.

15. Charles II appointed Davenant one of his two Masters of the Revels in 1660 to the indignation of his father's and grandfather's master, Sir Henry Herbert, who considered that he had a patent to the post. He accused Davenant not only of being a fervent supporter of the Protector but of being his Master of the Revels. In fact Davenant was probably merely a theatrical entrepreneur who cultivated powerful patrons. In 1652 he had been released from a two year imprisonment for Royalism; Sherwood, *Court*, 145–6.

CHAPTER 10: THE
PROTECTORATE AND ITS
PROBLEMS (between pages 170 and 190)

1. The exiled Hyde, who kept a close watch on English affairs for his royal master despite the frequent interception and copying of his mail by John Thurloe, the Protector's master of intelligence, was writing to the Earl of Rochester; Abbott, *W. & S. O. C.*, iii, 208.

2. Gardiner, *C. & P.*, ii, chap. XXIX; Roots, *Rebellion*, chapter 19 *passim*.

3. Owen, a Presbyterian turned Independent, had served Cromwell as his chaplain in Ireland and in Scotland and was Vice-Chancellor of Oxford University 1652–8 and Dean of Christ Church until his expulsion at the Restoration; *DNB*.

4. Roots, *Rebellion*, 179.

5. Letter to Mazarin dated 26 December 1656; Abbott, *W. & S. O. C.*, iv, 368.

6. For a much fuller account of Cromwell's relations with the Quakers see Fraser, *Cromwell*, 571–3.

7. Fraser, *Cromwell*, 574.

8. Buchan, *Cromwell*, 375.

9. 'The Protectorate was not notable for financial or administrative innovation at the centre.' Roots, *Rebellion*, 176.

10. See Chapter 8 n 7.

11. Trevor-Roper, 'Cromwell's Parliaments.'

12. Trevor-Roper, 'Cromwell's Parliaments' and Roots, *Rebellion*, chapter 20 *passim*.

13. Thomas, Baron Grey of Groby (1623?–57), a Regicide, son of the first Earl of Stamford, a Civil War soldier; active in Pride's Purge and served as a judge at the king's trial; a member of the successive Councils of State between 1649 and 1654; *DNB*.

14. Abbott, *W. & S. O. C.*, iii, 464, 467.

15. See Chapter 12.

16. Hutton, *Republic*, 69.

17. For Ireland and Scotland see Hutton, *Republic*, chapter 2, part iii, *passim*, which makes Henry Cromwell's problems seem easier than he found them. Compare C.H. Firth, *The Last Years of the Protectorate* (1909) (hereafter Firth, *Last Years*), ii, chapters xiii and xiv.

18. The total sum paid to Irish ministers during the two years to 1 November 1657 was £34,141; Firth, *Last Years*, ii, 152.

19. Firth, *Last Years*, ii, 126.

20. Firth, *Last Years*, ii, 151.

21. Firth, *Last Years*, ii, 152.

22. Hutton, *Republic*, 103.

23. Firth, *Last Years*, 87.

24. Firth, *Last Years*, 85.

25. Samuel Disbrowe (1619–90), an experienced bureaucrat, was the brother of General Disbrowe. Appointed keeper of the Great Seal of Scotland in 1657, he was MP for Midlothian in 1656 and Edinburgh in 1658–9. In 1641 he had been one of the founding settlers of Guildford, Connecticut; *DNB*. Lockhart was to be Cromwell's redoubtable ambassador to France, see Chapter 12.

CHAPTER 11: WESTERN DESIGNS AND PROTESTANT CRUSADES (between pages 191 and 207)

1. The first seventeenth-century critic was Slingsby Bethel, *The World's Mistake in Oliver Cromwell* (1668) although the date of publication is significant.

2. For the ending of the Dutch War see Charles P. Korr, *Cromwell and the New Model Foreign Policy* (Berkeley, 1975).

3. For Cromwell and the northern powers see Michael Bradley, 'Cromwell and the Baltic', *English Historical Review*, 76 (1961), 102 ff.

4. See Chapter 12.

5. For Blake's voyage see Baumber, *General-at-Sea*, chapter 15 *passim*, together with Powell, *Blake*.

6. However, Roskilde had more lasting benefits than the resumption of war suggests. See the critical review of Cromwell's foreign policy at the close of Chapter 12.

CHAPTER 12: A SPANISH WAR AND A FRENCH ALLIANCE (between pages 208 and 229)

1. Addressing the first Protectorate Parliament; Abbott, *W. & S. O. C.*, iii, 441.

2. J.R. Powell, 'The Expedition of Blake and Mountagu in 1655', *Mariners' Mirror*, 52 (1966), 341–69.

3. Prior to his ambassadorship Meadowes had been Latin secretary to the Council with Milton, and would later mediate the Treaty of Roskilde as ambassador to Denmark. Cromwell knighted him in 1658; *DNB*.

4. The squadron included the *Speaker* (56 guns), *Plymouth* (50 guns), *Bridgwater* (52 guns), and *Tredagh* (50 guns). Powell, 'Expedition', 364–5.

5. Powell, *Blake*, 290: 'all except a quarter or a third had been embezzled by its captors'; Baumber, *General-at-Sea*,

224, claims the treasure which reached the Tower was only worth about £200,000.

6. Baumber, *General-at-Sea*, 227; Powell, *Blake*, 294–5.

7. Baumber, *General-at-Sea*, 231. Powell, who quotes Stayner's account more fully, describes a seaward course, *Blake*, 301. However, Powell shows the galleons as moored south of the mole with the first galleon south of the last of the smaller craft. Baumber shows the galleons as completely overlapping the smaller craft which is much more likely (see battle-plan, p. 216).

8. 'A Narrative of the Battle of Santa Cruz . . . by Sir Richard Stayner, Rear-Admiral', Navy Records Society, *The Naval Miscellany* II (1912), 125 ff.

9. Baumber, *General-at-Sea*, 306.

10. *The Memoirs of James II*, trans. A Lytton Sells (1962), 254 ff.

11. Hutton, *Republic*, 110, an odd lapse in a masterly compression.

12. I am indebted for much that follows to the interesting analysis in Roger Crabtree's 'The Idea of a Protestant Foreign Policy', in Ivan Roots (ed.), *Cromwell: a Profile*.

13. See particularly Menna Prestwich, 'Diplomacy and Trade in the Protectorate', *Journal of Modern History*, 24 June 1950, 103 ff.

14. Quoted in Crabtree, 'Protestant Foreign Policy', 174. Crabtree points out that the populations of the two countries were less disparate in that era and that the market for cloth was 'almost identical'.

CHAPTER 13: THE FAILURE OF A SETTLEMENT (between pages 230 and 241)

1. Roots, *Rebellion*, 197 and n. 291.

2. *Parliamentary Diary of Thomas Burton 1656–1659* (ed.) J.T. Rutt (1828), vol. i, 384, quoted Trevor-Roper, 'Cromwell's Parliaments', 380.

3. Roots, *Rebellion*, 198–9.

4. Roots, *Rebellion*, 202.

5. Hutton, *Republic*, 71–2.

6. Abbott, *W. & S. O. C.*, iv, 316; for Bridges, 334–5.

7. Francisco Giavarina to the Doge, 21 November 1656, Abbott, *W. & S. O. C.*, iv, 334.

8. *Clarke Papers*, vol. iii, 105, and quoted in Roots, *Rebellion*, 293.

9. Abbott, *W. & S. O. C.*, 414.

10. Having lost salaries of £6,000 a year he was sustained by a pension of £2,000 a year which Cromwell paid him from his own pocket; Fraser, *Cromwell*, 615.

11. Hutton, *Republic*, 74. For a detailed study of Cromwellian finances see Maurice Ashley, *Financial and Commercial Policy under the Cromwellian Protectorate* (3rd edn, 1972).

12. For the ceremonies see the detailed description in Fraser, *Cromwell*, 615–17.

13. Eure had been a member of the Nominated and both Protectorate Parliaments. Surprisingly neither the Earl of Salisbury nor the Earl of Pembroke was chosen, although both had served the Commonwealth in the old Council of State and in the Purged Parliament; Firth, *Last Years*, ii, 14.

14. Her corpse alone of Cromwell's family escaped the vengeful disinterments of the Restoration and she still lies in Henry VII's chapel after a brief rediscovery in 1725; Fraser, *Cromwell*, 665.

CHAPTER 14: THE FALL OF THE SWORDSMEN (between pages 242 and 258)

1. Monck to Speaker Lenthall and Lord Mordaunt's comment both quoted in Austin Woolrych, 'Historical Introduction 1659–1660' to *The Complete Prose Works of John Milton*, vii (New Haven, 1980) (hereafter Woolrych, *Milton*), 134, 160.

2. Woolrych, *Milton*, 4.

3. Hutton, *Republic*, 114–15.

4. See Gentles, *New Model Army*, Chapter 5 *passim*.

5. Ronald Hutton, *The Restoration: A Political and Religious History of England and Wales 1658–1667* (Oxford, 1985) (hereafter Hutton, *Restoration*), 305.

6. Quoted by Roots, *Rebellion*, 243. The source, Ludlow's *Memoirs*, is suspect in detail but the exchange defines the reality of the situation between the army and the Rump.

7. Hutton, *Restoration*, 69. However, Woolrych believes this should be treated with scepticism; Woolrych, *Milton*, 134.

8. Ashley's *Monck*, although containing much interesting detail, is no more successful in penetrating the obscurity.

9. Hutton, *Restoration*, 70.

10. Ashley, *Monck*, chapter 4; Jasper Ridley, *The Roundheads* (1977), 222–3.

11. Hutton, *Republic*, 127.

12. Hutton, *Republic*, 126; Hutton, *Restoration*, 85.

13. 'To ensure security . . . the MPs ordered Monck to bring his loyal troops to London.' Hutton, *Restoration*, 85.

14. Godfrey Davies, *The Restoration of Charles II 1658–1660* (1955) (hereafter Davies, *Restoration*), 273.

CHAPTER 15: THE LAST ACT
(between pages 259 and 268)

1. In a letter to the Revd John Owen, 29 November 1659, *Clarke Papers*, iv, 153.

2. Davies, *Restoration*, 278.

3. Woolrych, *Milton*, 171.

4. *The Diary of Samuel Pepys*, ed. Robert Latham and William Matthews (1970) (hereafter Pepys, *Diary*), i, 532.

5. Woolrych, *Milton*, 193.

6. Roots, *Rebellion*, 255.

7. Woolrych, *Milton*, 196.

8. Roots, *Rebellion*, 254.

9. Woolrych, *Milton*, 220.

EPILOGUE: THE KING RETURNS
(between pages 269 and 271)

1. Pepys, *Diary*, i, 158, 265.

2. Pepys, *Diary*, i, 154.

Sources and Further Reading

Place of publication London unless otherwise stated.

The scholarly literature and printed primary sources for this period are vast. This guide is not intended to be comprehensive but simply to assist newcomers to the period to pursue further study of it. For the seventeenth century as a whole G.M. Trevelyan's *England Under the Stuarts*, originally published in 1904 but never long out of print since, is beautifully written and a lucid if rather dated introduction; see also Christopher Hill, *The Century of Revolution 1603–1714* (Norton edn, New York, 1961); see also Keith Wrightson, *English Society 1580–1680* (1984). For an unsurpassed narrative of the events preceding the Republic see C.V. Wedgwood's *The Great Rebellion*: i, *The King's Peace*, ii, *The King's War* (1955–8). However inadequately, this account seeks to carry her narrative forward to 1660. See also Samuel Rawson Gardiner, *History of England . . . 1603–1642*, 10 volumes (1883–4) and *History of the Great Civil War 1642–49*, 3 volumes (1886–91); Ivan Roots, *The Great Rebellion 1642–1660* (1966); Conrad Russell's *The Fall of the British Monarchies* (Oxford, 1991); John Morrill, *The Nature of the English Revolution* (1993); Robert Ashton, *The English Civil War: Conservatism and Revolution 1603–1649* (1978); Brian Manning, *The English People and the English Revolution 1640–9* (1976). For the Scottish Revolution see the excellent accounts and analyses in David Stevenson, *The Scottish Revolution 1637–1644* (Newton Abbot, 1973). For the Civil War see additionally Austin Woolrych, *Battles of the English Civil War* (1966); C. Hibbert, *Cavaliers and Roundheads* (London, 1994); Mark Kishlansky, *The Rise of the New Model Army* (Cambridge and New York, 1979) and Ian Gentles, *The New Model Army in England, Ireland and Scotland 1645–1653* (Oxford, 1992). For a healthily unromantic view of the war see Charles Carlton's *Going to the Wars: The Experience of the British Civil Wars 1638–1651* (London and New York, 1992). The king's trial and execution is well described in C.V. Wedgwood's *The Trial of Charles I* (1964). For excellent analyses of Pride's Purge and the history of the Purged Parliament ('the Rump') see David Underdown, *Pride's Purge* (Oxford, 1971) and Blair Worden, *The Rump Parliament* (Cambridge, 1974). An invaluable collection of essays on the Republican period is G.E. Aylmer (ed.) *The Interregnum: the Quest for Settlement 1646–1660* (1972).

For entertaining gossip about many of the participants in this dramatic period see John Aubrey, *Brief Lives*, and for useful short biographies Jasper Ridley's *The Roundheads* (1976). For modern biographies of leading players see: Christopher Hill, *God's Englishman: Oliver Cromwell and the English Revolution* (1970); see also Antonia Fraser, *Cromwell: Our Chief of Men* (1973), John Buchan, *Oliver Cromwell* (Readers Union, 1941) and see Abbott below; Robert W. Ramsey, *Henry Ireton* (1949); for Lambert, W.H. Dawson, *Cromwell's Understudy* (1938); John Wilson, *Fairfax* (1985); Maurice Ashley, *General Monck* (1977); Ronald Hutton, *Charles II* (Oxford, 1989); for Lilburne P. Gregg, *Free-born John* (1961); Philip Aubrey, *Mr Secretary Thurloe* (1990); for Montagu, Richard Ollard, *Cromwell's Earl* (1994). Among contemporary memoirs of the period see particularly Clarendon's *History of the Rebellion and Civil Wars in England*, ed. W.D. Macray, 6 volumes (Oxford, 1888) and the condensation

Clarendon, introduction by H.R. Trevor-Roper (Oxford, 1978); Lucy Hutchinson's *Memoirs of the Life of Colonel Hutchinson* (Everyman edn, 1968), and Edmund Ludlow, *Memoirs* (ed. C.H. Firth) (Oxford, 1894). For a vivid account of the impact of the war, revolution and radical religion on an English community (Dorchester), David Underdown, *Fire From Heaven* (1992).

An invaluable resource for the whole period but especially for its leading figure is Wilbur Cortez Abbott (ed.) *Writings and Speeches of Oliver Cromwell* (Oxford, 1939/88), 4 volumes; in general S.R. Gardiner, *History of the Commonwealth and Protectorate 1649–1656* (1901) is invaluable for the period to 1656 when it is succeeded by C.H. Firth, *The Last Years of the Protectorate* (1909); more recently Ivan Roots, *The Great Rebellion* (1966); Ronald Hutton, *The British Republic 1649–1660* (1990); Blair Worden, *The Rump Parliament* (Cambridge, 1974); for the Levellers, H.N. Brailsford, *The Levellers and the English Revolution*, ed. Christopher Hill (Stanford, 1961). For radical religion among soldiers and civilians see J.F. McGregor and B. Reay (eds) *Radical Religion in the English Revolution* (Oxford, 1984); Murray Tolmie, *Triumph of the Saints* (Cambridge, 1977); William M. Lamont, *Godly Rule: Politics and Religion 1603–1660* (1969). For Levellers, Quakers and others who combined radical politics with radical religion Christopher Hill, *The World Turned Upside Down* (1972), and Barry Reay, *The Quakers and the English Revolution* (1985). For the impact of lay ownership of tithes and advowsons before the Civil War, Christopher Hill, *Economic Problems of the English Church from Archbishop Whitgift to the Long Parliament* (Oxford, 1956); for an exploration of the workings of lay presentment see D.R. Hainsworth, *Stewards, Lords and People: the Estate Steward and his World in Later Stuart England* (Cambridge, 1992), Chapter 9, 'Filling the Pulpit'.

For naval matters Bernard Capp, *Cromwell's Navy: the Fleet and the English Revolution 1648–1660* (Oxford, 1989), Michael Baumber, *General-at-Sea: Robert Blake and the Seventeenth Century Revolution in Naval Warfare* (1989); Revd J.R. Powell, *Robert Blake: General-at-Sea* (1972). For the Dutch War the principal printed sources are *Letters and Papers Relating to the First Dutch War 1652–1654* (eds) S.R. Gardiner and C.T. Atkinson, *Navy Record Society*, 13, 17, 30, 37, 41 and 66 (1899–1930) and *The Letters of Robert Blake* (ed.) J.R. Powell, *NRS*, 76 (1937); Charles Wilson, *Profit and Power: a Study of England and the Dutch Wars* (1957). For the development of Anglo-Dutch commercial rivalry see Jonathan Israel, 'Competing Cousins: Anglo-Dutch Trade Rivalry', *History Today*, July 1988, 17–22, and his general history *The Dutch Republic: Its Rise, Greatness and Fall 1477–1806* (Oxford, 1995); also C.R. Boxer, *The Dutch Seaborne Empire 1600–1800* (1977).

For Ireland see the detailed analysis of this period in *A New History of Ireland*, iii, *Early Modern Ireland 1534–1691*, eds Moody, Martin and Byrne, (Oxford, 1976); Richard Bagwell's *Ireland Under the Stuarts*, ii: *1642–1660* (1909) and T.C. Barnard, *Cromwellian Ireland 1649–60* (1975). For Scotland, F.D. Dow, *Cromwellian Scotland* (Edinburgh, 1979); Gentles, *New Model Army*, chapter 12 *passim*; old-fashioned even in 1898 but rich in detail is W.S. Douglas, *Cromwell's Scotch Campaigns 1650–1* (Edinburgh, 1898); see also Richard Ollard, *The Escape of Charles II after the Battle of Worcester* (1966).

For the Nominated Parliament and the *Instrument of Government* see Austin Woolrych's magisterial *Commonwealth to Protectorate* (Oxford, 1982). For the Protectorate court, Roy Sherwood, *The Court of Oliver Cromwell* (1977). For Cromwell's foreign policy, Menna Prestwich, 'Diplomacy and Trade under the Protectorate', *Journal of Modern History* (1950) with its cogent corrective: R. Crabtree, 'The Idea of a Protestant Foreign Policy', in I. Roots (ed.) *Cromwell* (1973); Michael Bradley, 'Cromwell and the Baltic', *English Historical Review*, 76 (1961) and Charles P.

Korr, *Cromwell and the New Model Foreign Policy: England's Policy Towards France 1649–1658* (Berkeley, 1975).

For the fall of the Swordsmen and the coming of the Restoration, Godfrey Davies, *The Restoration of Charles II 1658–1660* (1955), now largely superseded by the livelier Ronald Hutton, *The Restoration: A Political and Religious History of England and Wales 1658–1667* (Oxford, 1985); and remarkable for detail, cogency of analysis and compression, Austin Woolrych, 'Historical Introduction 1659–1660', to *The Complete Prose Works of John Milton*, vii (New Haven, 1980). For a sharp-eyed Londoner's view of the last weeks of the Rump and the bringing home of Charles II, *The Diary of Samuel Pepys*, ed. Robert Latham and William Matthews (1970).

Index